Fodor's 97
Costa Rica

" "When it comes to information on regional history, what to see and do, and shopping, these guides are exhaustive."
—*USAir Magazine*

"Usable, sophisticated restaurant coverage, with an emphasis on good value."
—Andy Birsh, *Gourmet Magazine* columnist

"Valuable because of their comprehensiveness."
—*Minneapolis Star-Tribune*

"Fodor's always delivers high quality...thoughtfully presented...thorough."
—*Houston Post*

"An excellent choice for those who want everything under one cover."
—*Washington Post* "

D0423534

Fodor's Travel Publications, Inc.
New York • Toronto • London • Sydney • Auckland
http://www.fodors.com/

Fodor's Costa Rica '97

Editor: Jason Oliver Nixon

Editorial Contributors: Steven Amsterdam, Robert Andrews, Robert Blake, David Brown, David Dudenhoefer, Audra Epstein, Justin Henderson, Laura M. Kidder, Mary Ellen Schultz, M.T. Schwartzman (Gold Guide editor), Dinah Spritzer

Creative Director: Fabrizio La Rocca

Cartographer: David Lindroth

Cover Photograph: Bob Krist

Design: Between the Covers

Copyright

Special Sales

Fodor's Travel Publications are available at special discounts for bulk purchases for sales promotions or premiums. Special editions, including personalized covers, excerpts of existing guides, and corporate imprints, can be created in large quantities for special needs. For more information, contact your local bookseller or write to Special Markets, Fodor's Travel Publications, 201 East 50th Street, New York, NY 10022. Inquiries from Canada should be directed to your local Canadian bookseller or sent to Random House of Canada, Ltd., Marketing Department, 1265 Aerowood Drive, Mississauga, Ontario L4W 1B9. Inquiries from the United Kingdom should be sent to Fodor's Travel Publications, 20 Vauxhall Bridge Road, London SW1V 2SA.

PRINTED IN THE UNITED STATES OF AMERICA

10 9 8 7 6 5 4 3 2 1

CONTENTS

Maps and Charts

ON THE ROAD WITH FODOR'S

WER'RE ALWAYS THRILLED to get letters from readers, especially one like this:

It took us an hour to decide what book to buy and we now know we picked the best one. Your book was wonderful, easy to follow, very accurate, and good on pointing out eating places, informal as well as formal. When we saw other people using your book, we would look at each other and smile.

Our editors and writers are deeply committed to making every Fodor's guide "the best one"—not only accurate but always charming, brimming with sound recommendations and solid ideas, right on the mark in describing restaurants and hotels, and full of fascinating facts that make you view what you've traveled to see in a rich new light.

About Our Writers

Our success in achieving our goals—and in helping to make your trip the best of all possible vacations—is a credit to the hard work of our extraordinary writers and editors.

David Dudenhoefer is a freelance hack who has spent the better part of the past decade in Central America. Based in San José, he travels regularly within the isthmus, writing about everything from surfing to presidential summits. During the past 10 years his articles have appeared in about two dozen publications in North, Central, and South America. He is a regular Fodor's contributor and is the author of *The Panama Traveler.* When not chained to his computer, he can usually be found wandering through the woods, playing in the waves, or propping up the bar at one of San José's seedier nightspots.

The affinity **Justin Henderson** has for the beaches of Guanacaste comes easy, since he's a native of southern California who grew up surfing the waves of Malibu and Santa Monica. In his delirious youth he bailed on L.A. for New York City, searching for a writing career more meaningful than the work for TV that his father did.

He spent 10 years writing for magazines—work that was no more meaningful and far less lucrative. After 14 years, it was off to Seattle, where he now lives with his wife, the photographer Donna Day. The two would like to move to the beach in Costa Rica, but the web connections there are tenuous, and buying Costa Rican land smacks of economic imperialism.

Editor **Jason Oliver Nixon** learned to speak Spanish when he headed off to Salamanca, Spain, during his junior year abroad. These multilingual skills came in handy when he neurotically called every hotel and restaurant in this book to ensure that all the listings were up-to-the-minute. Before coming to Fodor's, Jason was an associate editor at *Condé Nast Traveler* magazine, where he played with travel products and then wrote about them. After visiting Costa Rica this past summer, he plans to take cooking classes, religiously study the techniques of Martha Stewart, then open a bed-and-breakfast on the Nicoya Peninsula.

New this Year

This year we've reformatted our guides to make them easier to use. Each chapter of *Fodor's Costa Rica '97* begins with brand-new recommended itineraries to help you decide what to see in the time you have; a section called When to Tour points out the optimal time of day, day of the week, and season for your journey. You may also notice our fresh graphics, new in 1996. More readable and more helpful than ever? We think so—and we hope you do, too.

We have added a new chapter on Excursions to Panama this year; dive amidst the spectacular reefs in the tourist-free Bocas del Toro Archipelago or explore the rugged terrain of Chiriquí Province.

Also check out Fodor's Web site (http://www.fodors.com/), where you'll find travel information on major destinations around the world and an ever-changing array of travel-savvy interactive features.

How to Use this Book

Organization

Up front is the **Gold Guide.** Its first section, **Important Contacts A to Z,** gives addresses and telephone numbers of organizations and companies that offer destination-related services and detailed information and publications. **Smart Travel Tips A to Z,** the Gold Guide's second section, gives specific information on how to accomplish what you need to in Costa Rica and Panama as well as tips on savvy traveling. Both sections are in alphabetical order by topic.

Icons and Symbols

★	Our special recommendations
✕	Restaurant
🏨	Lodging establishment
✕🏨	Lodging establishment whose restaurant warrants a detour
⊙	Rubber duckie (good for kids)
☞	Sends you to another section of the guide for more info
✉	Address
☎	Telephone number
FAX	Fax number
⊘	Opening and closing times
💷	Admission prices (those we give apply only to adults; substantially reduced fees are almost always available for children, students, and senior citizens)

Numbers in white and black circles— ㉑㊹㊿㉝ and ㉑㊹㊿㉝, for example— that appear on the maps, in the margins, and within the tours correspond to one another.

Addresses in Costa Rica and Panama

The most common street terms are *calle* (street) and *avenida* (avenue), and they are abbreviated C. and Avda., respectively. Street numbering does not enjoy the wide popularity in Costa Rica and Panama that it has achieved elsewhere. When giving directions, Costa Ricans will say that the site is "10 blocks north of thus-and-such park," or "50 feet east of the church." Sound confusing? It is. Mailing addresses for hotels and the like are usually *apartados* (post office boxes), abbreviated as Apdo. Sometimes, though, a hotel will have a mailing address in Miami—the mail is forwarded to Costa Rica in about half the time that the Costa Rican postal service by itself would take. In some rural areas, especially in the Atlantic Lowlands and the northwest, the name of the hotel followed by the town and province name serve as the mailing address.

Phone Numbers

The area code for Costa Rica is 506; for Panama it is 507. Chapters 3–7 deal with Costa Rica; in those chapters the 506 area code has been omitted. In the Gold Guide, Chapter 2, National Parks and Biological Reserves, and Chapter 8, Excursions to Panama, however, you'll find area codes before telephone numbers to clarify whether the particular listing is in Costa Rica or Panama.

Dining and Lodging

The restaurants and lodgings we list are the cream of the crop in each price range. Price categories are as follows:

For restaurants:

CATEGORY	COST
$$$$	over $20
$$$	$10–$20
$$	$5–$10
$	under $5

For hotels:

Lodging prices are for a double room, excluding service and 18.4% tax (in Costa Rica) or 10% tax (in Panama).

CATEGORY	COST
$$$$	over $90
$$$	$150–$90
$$	$25–$50
$	under $25

Hotel Facilities

We always list the facilities that are available—but we don't specify whether they cost extra: When pricing accommodations, always ask what's included.

Restaurant Reservations and Dress Codes

Reservations are always a good idea; we note only when they're essential or when they are not accepted. Book as far ahead as you can, and reconfirm when you get to town. Unless otherwise noted, the restaurants listed are open daily for lunch and dinner. We mention dress only when men are required to wear a jacket or a jacket and tie. Look for an overview of local habits under Dining in Smart Travel Tips A to Z and in the Pleasures and Pastimes section after each chapter introduction.

Credit Cards

The following abbreviations are used: **AE,** American Express; **DC,** Diners Club; **MC,** MasterCard; and **V,** Visa.

Don't Forget to Write

You can use this book in the confidence that all prices and opening times are based on information supplied to us at press time; Fodor's cannot accept responsibility for any errors. Time inevitably brings changes, so always confirm information when it matters—especially if you're making a detour to visit a specific place. In addition, when making reservations be sure to mention if you have a disability or are traveling with children, if you prefer a private bath or a certain type of bed, or if you have specific dietary needs or any other concerns.

Were the restaurants we recommended as described? Did our hotel picks exceed your expectations? Did you find a museum we recommended a waste of time? If you have complaints, we'll look into them and revise our entries when the facts warrant it. If you've discovered a special place that we haven't included, we'll pass the information along to our correspondents and have them check it out. So send your feedback, positive *and* negative, to the Costa Rica Editor at 201 East 50th Street, New York, New York 10022—and have a wonderful trip!

Karen Cure

Editorial Director

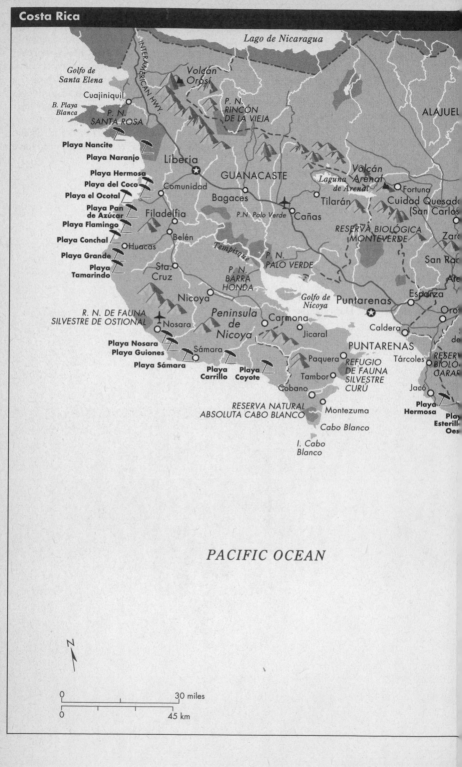

Lago de Nicaragua

Golfo de
Santa Elena

INTERAMERICAN HWY.

Volcán
Orosí

P. N.
RINCÓN
DE LA VIEJA

ALAJUEL

Cuajiniquil

B. Playa
Blanca

P. N.
SANTA ROSA

Playa Nancite

Playa Naranjo

Liberia

GUANACASTE

Volcán
Arenal

Laguna
de Arenal

Fortuna

Playa Hermosa

Playa del Coco

Comunidad

Playa el Ocotal

Bagaces

Tilarán

Cuidad Quesada
(San Carlos

Playa Pan
de Azúcar

Filadelfia

P.N. Palo Verde

Cañas

RESERVA BIOLÓGICA
MONTEVERDE

Playa Flamingo

Belén

Zarc

Playa Conchal

Huacas

Tempisque

P. N.
PALO VERDE

San Ra

Playa Grande

Sta.
Cruz

P. N.
BARRA
HONDA

Ate

Playa
Tamarindo

Nicoya

Golfo de
Nicoya

Puntarenas

Esparza

Oro

R. N. DE FAUNA
SILVESTRE DE OSTIONAL

Nosara

Península
de
Nicoya

Carmona

Caldera

de

Playa Nosara

Playa Guiones

Sámara

Jicaral

PUNTARENAS

Playa Sámara

Playa
Carrillo

Playa
Coyote

Paquera

REFUGIO
DE FAUNA
SILVESTRE
CURÚ

Tárcoles

RESERV
BIOLÓ
ÓARAR

Tambor

Jacó

Gobano

Playa
Hermosa

RESERVA NATURAL
ABSOLUTA CABO BLANCO

Montezuma

Playa
Esterill
Oes

Cabo Blanco

I. Cabo
Blanco

PACIFIC OCEAN

N

0   30 miles
0   45 km

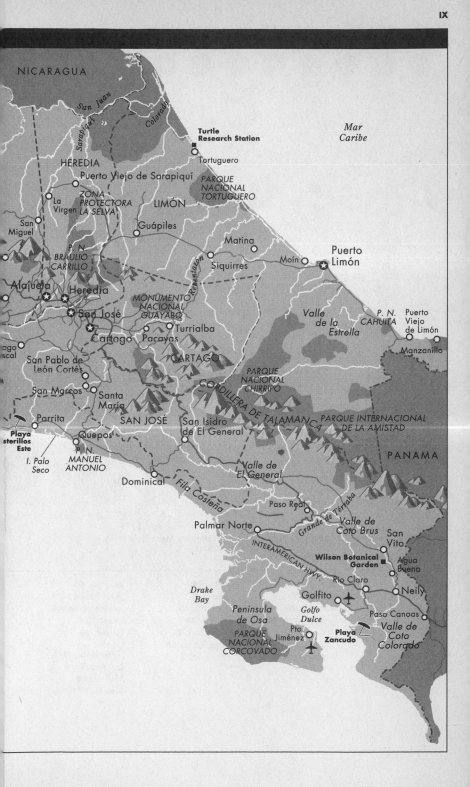

NICARAGUA

San Juan

Sarapiquí

Colorado

**Turtle
Research Station**

*Mar
Caribe*

Tortuguero

HEREDIA

Puerto Viejo de Sarapiquí

*PARQUE
NACIONAL
TORTUGUERO*

La
Virgen

*ZONA
PROTECTORA
LA SELVA*

LIMÓN

San
Miguel

Guápiles

Matina

P. N.
*BRAULIO
CARRILLO*

Moín

Puerto
Limón

Siquirres

Reventazón

Alajuela

Heredia

San José

*MONUMENTO
NACIONAL
GUAYABO*

Turrialba

Valle
de la
Estrella

P. N.
CAHUITA

Puerto
Viejo
de Limón

ago
scal

Cartago

Pacayas

CARTAGO

Manzanillo

San Pablo de
León Cortés

*PARQUE
NACIONAL
CHIRRIPÓ*

San Marcos

Santa
María

CORDILLERA DE TALAMANCA

*PARQUE INTERNACIONAL
DE LA AMISTAD*

Parrita

SAN JOSÉ

San Isidro
de El General

PANAMA

**Playa
sterillos
Este**

Quepos

P. N.
*MANUEL
ANTONIO*

*I. Palo
Seco*

*Valle de
El General*

Dominical

Fila Costeña

Paso Real

Grande de Térraba

*Valle de
Coto Brus*

San
Vito

Palmar Norte

INTERAMERICAN HWY.

**Wilson Botanical
Garden**

Agua
Buena

*Drake
Bay*

Río Claro

Neily

*Península
de Osa*

Golfito

*Golfo
Dulce*

Paso Canoas

*PARQUE
NACIONAL
CORCOVADO*

Pto.
Jiménez

**Playa
Zancudo**

*Valle de
Coto
Colorado*

World Time Zones

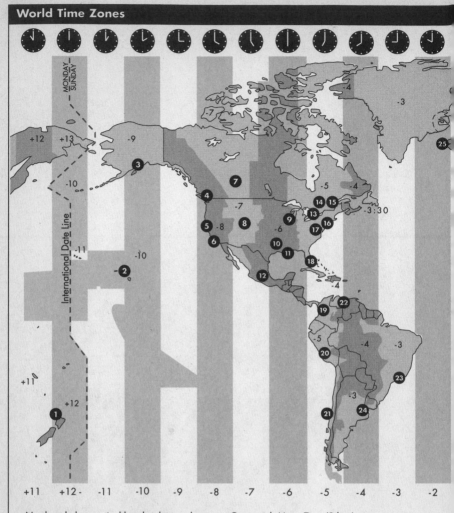

Numbers below vertical bands relate each zone to Greenwich Mean Time (0 hrs.).
Local times frequently differ from these general indications,
as indicated by light-face numbers on map.

Algiers, **29**	Berlin, **34**	Delhi, **48**	Istanbul, **40**
Anchorage, **3**	Bogotá, **19**	Denver, **8**	Jerusalem, **42**
Athens, **41**	Budapest, **37**	Djakarta, **53**	Johannesburg, **44**
Auckland, **1**	Buenos Aires, **24**	Dublin, **26**	Lima, **20**
Baghdad, **46**	Caracas, **22**	Edmonton, **7**	Lisbon, **28**
Bangkok, **50**	Chicago, **9**	Hong Kong, **56**	London
Beijing, **54**	Copenhagen, **33**	Honolulu, **2**	(Greenwich), **27**
	Dallas, **10**		Los Angeles, **6**
			Madrid, **38**
			Manila, **57**

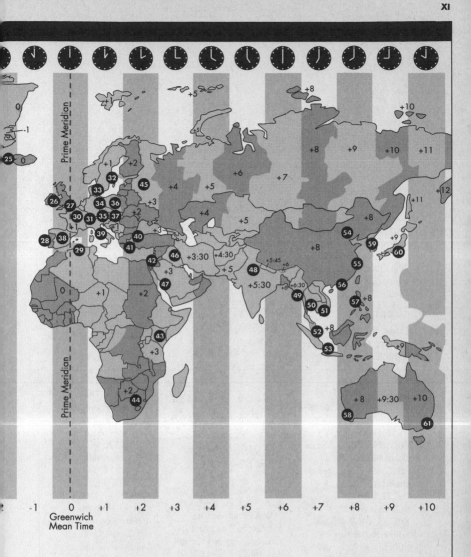

IMPORTANT CONTACTS A TO Z

An Alphabetical Listing of Publications, Organizations, & Companies that Will Help You Before, During, & After Your Trip

A

AIR TRAVEL

All flights arriving in Costa Rica from the United States and Canada pass through **Juan Santamaria International Airport** (☎ 011–506/443–2682), 16 kilometers (10 miles) south of downtown San José.

CARRIERS

From the United States, contact **Aero Costa Rica** (☎ 800/237–6274), **American** (☎ 800/433–7300), **Aviateca Guatemala** (☎ 800/327–1225), **Continental** (☎ 800/23–0856), **Delta** (☎ 800/221–1212), **Lacsa Costa Rican** (☎ 800/225–2272), **Mexicana** (☎ 800/531–7921), **Taca El Salvadoran** (☎ 800/535–8780), **Tan Sahsa Honduran** (☎ 800/327–1225), **United** (☎ 800/827–7777), and **USAir** (☎ 800/428–4322).

COMPLAINTS

To register complaints about charter and scheduled airlines, contact the U.S. Department of Transportation's **Aviation Consumer Protection Division** (✉ C-75, Washington, DC 20590, ☎ 202/366–2220). Complaints about lost baggage or ticketing problems and safety concerns may also be logged with the **Federal Aviation Administration (FAA) Consumer Hotline** (☎ 800/322–7873).

CONSOLIDATORS

For the names of reputable air-ticket consolidators, contact the **United States Air Consolidators Association** (✉ 925 L St., Suite 220, Sacramento, CA 95814, ☎ 916/441–4166, FAX 916/441–3520). For services that will help you find the lowest airfares, *see* Discounts, *below.*

DISCOUNT PASSES

See Discounts & Deals, *below.*

FLYING TIME

From New York, flights to San José are 5½ hours (via Miami); from Los Angeles, 8½ hours (via Mexico); from Houston, 4½ hours (via Guatemala); and from Miami, 2 hours (direct).

PUBLICATIONS

For general information about charter carriers, ask for the Department of Transportation's free brochure **"Plane Talk: Public Charter Flights"** (✉ Aviation Consumer Protection Division, C-75, Washington, DC 20590, ☎ 202/366–2220). The Department of Transportation also publishes a 58-page booklet, **"Fly Rights,"** available from the Consumer Information Center (✉ Supt. of Documents, Dept. 136C, Pueblo, CO 81009; $1.75).

For other tips and hints, consult the Consumers Union's monthly **"Consumer Reports Travel Letter"** (✉ Box 53629, Boulder, CO 80322, ☎ 800/234–1970; $39 1st year) and the newsletter **"Travel Smart"** (✉ 40 Beechdale Rd., Dobbs Ferry, NY 10522, ☎ 800/327–3633; $37 per year).

Some worthwhile publications on the subject are *The Official Frequent Flyer Guidebook,* by Randy Petersen (✉ Airpress, 4715-C Town Center Dr., Colorado Springs, CO 80916, ☎ 719/597–8899 or 800/487–8893; $14.99 plus $3 shipping); *Airfare Secrets Exposed,* by Sharon Tyler and Matthew Wunder (✉ Studio 4 Productions, Box 280400, Northridge, CA 91328, ☎ 818/700–2522 or 800/408–7369; $16.95 plus $2.50 shipping); *202 Tips Even the Best Business Travelers May Not Know,* by Christopher McGinnis (✉ Irwin Professional Publishing, 1333 Burr Ridge Pkwy., Burr Ridge, IL 60521, ☎ 800/634–3966; $11 plus $3.25 shipping); and *Travel Rights,* by Charles Leocha (✉ World Leisure Corporation, 177 Paris St., Boston, MA 02128, ☎ 800/444–2524; $7.95 plus $3.95 shipping).

For information on how to avoid jet lag, there are two publications: *Jet Lag, A Pocket Guide to Modern Treatment* by Peter Casano, MD (✉ MedEd Publications, Box 12415, Columbus, OH 43212, ☎ 614/488–9457; $5.95) and *How to Beat Jet Lag* (✉ Henry Holt, 115 W. 18th St., New York, NY 10011, ☎ 800/288–2131; $14.95).

Travelers who experience motion sickness or ear problems in flight should get the brochures **"Ears, Altitude, and Airplane Travel"** and **"What You Can Do for Dizziness & Motion Sickness"** from the American Academy of Otolaryngology (✉ 1 Prince St., Alexandria, VA 22314, ☎ 703/836–4444, FAX 703/683–5100, TTY 703/519–1585).

WITHIN COSTA RICA

Two domestic airlines serve Costa Rica. **Sansa** (✉ C. 24, between Avda. Central and Avda. 1, ☎ 506/233–5330, 506/233–3258, 506/233–0397, FAX 506/255–2176) flies out of Juan Santamaría International Airport near Alajuela. **Travelair** (☎ 506/220–3054, FAX 506/220–0413) uses Tobias Bolaños Airport in the San José suburb of Pavas.

Another addition to the air travel mix is **Alas Anfibias,** a seaplane service run by veteran Alaskan charter pilot Marty MacDonald. With a new turbo-prop jet floatplane in service as of mid 1996, in addition to its charter flights to almost any body of water large enough to land a plane, the company currently plans to set up regular flights to Drake's Bay on the Osa Peninsula (eliminating one of the longer treks in the country), and also to Isla de Coco, Playa Flamingo, and Lake Arenal. Alas Anfibias can be reached by phone/fax at 506/232–9567.

Perhaps the priciest way to get around Costa Rica is by helicopter. **Helisa** (☎ 506/222–9299 or 506/255–4138, FAX 506/222–3875) is authorized for international travel and is available for the not-inconsequential sum of $890 per hour. **Helicópteros de Costa Rica** (☎ 506/231–6564, FAX 506/232–5265) flies to several destinations within the country.

WITHIN PANAMA

Aeroperlas (☎ 507/269–4555, FAX 507/269–4564), Panama's main domestic airline, has several flights daily between David and Changuinola, and between those two towns and Panama City. At press time the Bocas del Toro airport was closed, but as soon as it opens, that town will be connected to Changuinola, David, and Panama City by daily flights. Aeroperlas also has flights from Panama City to Contadora and the Darien Gap. **Aerotaxi** (☎ 507/264–8844, FAX 507/269–7210) has daily flights to about a dozen airstrips in the San Blas region.

B

BETTER BUSINESS BUREAU

For local contacts in the hometown of a tour operator you may be considering, consult the **Council of Better Business Bureaus** (✉ 4200 Wilson Blvd., Suite 800, Arlington, VA 22203, ☎ 703/276–0100, FAX 703/525–8277).

BUS TRAVEL

There is bus service between Managua, Nicaragua, and San José; between several cities in Panama and San José; between Tegucigalpa, Honduras, and San José with an overnight stop in Managua; and between Guatemala City and San José with overnight stops in Managua and San Salvador. **Tica Bus** (✉ C. 9 and Avda. 4, ☎ 507/221–8954) buses leave Panama City daily at 11 AM and arrive at 4 AM the next morning, with buses leaving San José for Panama at 10 PM and arriving the following day at 4 PM. The round-trip fare was about $27.50 in mid 1996. A new daily luxury express service (14 hours instead of the usual 20) run by **Panaline** (☎ 506/255–1205) departs from the Hotel Cocorí (✉ C. 14 between Avdas. 5 and 7). The round-trip fare was about $34 at press time. **Tracopa** (✉ Avda. 18 and C. 4, ☎ 506/221–4214) buses leave San José daily at 7:30 AM, arriving at David, Panama, at 4 PM. From there, buses head on to Panama City seven hours away. The fare at press time was $11.70. **Bernardo Fumero** (☎ 506/556–1432) runs a daily bus from San José to Changuinola, in northeast Panama, at 10 AM. Leaving from the Hotel Cocorí, the eight-hour trip costs about $4 (each way). From Nicaragua, on Monday, Wednesday, Friday, and Sunday the Tica Bus (☞ *above*) buses leave Managua at 6 AM, arriving in San José 11 hours later. The buses leaving San José at 7 AM reach Managua at 6 PM. The round-trip fare was $12 at press time. Call Tica Bus for departure times and ticket prices to the other Central American capitals.

WITHIN COSTA RICA

Two new companies now offer hassle-free bus service to a number of popular tourist destinations. **Periferica Nacional de Turísmo** (☎ 506/221–5246, FAX 506/233–5503) provides one-day trips to Arenal, Monteverde, the Carara Biological Reserve, and elsewhere. Tickets run about $9, higher than regular buses, but the time-savings is worthwhile. And **Pura Natura** (☎ 506/233–9709, FAX 506/223–9209), run by Christian Muller and Robert Dresel, offers bus service—with

bilingual drivers—to a number of popular destinations. For specifics on bus prices and schedules consult Arriving and Departing and Getting Around within the relevant regional chapter.

C

CAR RENTAL

Costa Rica: Avis can be found at C. 42 and Avda. Las Américas (☎ 506/232–9922), and **Hertz** is at Paseo Colón and C. 38 (☎ 506/223–5959). For other listings look in the phone directory under "alquiler de automóviles."

Panama has fewer car-rental companies, which means prices aren't quite as competitive, but there are usually enough cars to go around. Familiar names include **Alamo** (☎ 507/260–0822), **Avis** (☎ 507/264–0722), **Budget** (☎ 507/263–8777), **Dollar** (☎ 507/225–3455), **Hertz** (☎ 507/226–7110), and **National** (☎ 507/264–8277). Budget, Dollar, and Hertz have offices in David.

The major car-rental companies represented in Costa Rica are **Avis** (☎ 800/331–1084; in Canada, 800/879–2847), and **Hertz** (☎ 800/654–3001; in Canada, 800/263–0600; in the U.K., 0345/555–888), and **National InterRent** (sometimes known as Europcar InterRent outside North America; ☎ 800/227–3876; in the U.K., 01345/222–525). Rates in Costa Rica and Panama begin

at $31 a day and $198 a week for an economy car with unlimited mileage. There is no tax on car rentals.

RENTAL WHOLESALERS

Contact **Auto Europe** (☎ 207/828–2525 or 800/223–5555).

CHILDREN & TRAVEL

FLYING

Look into **"Flying with Baby"** (✉ Third Street Press, Box 261250, Littleton, CO 80163, ☎ 303/595–5959; $4.95 includes shipping), cowritten by a flight attendant. **"Kids and Teens in Flight,"** free from the U.S. Department of Transportation's Aviation Consumer Protection Division (✉ C-75, Washington, DC 20590, ☎ 202/366–2220), offers tips on children flying alone. Every two years the February issue of **Family Travel Times** (☞ Know-How, *below*) details children's services on three dozen airlines. **"Flying Alone, Handy Advice for Kids Traveling Solo"** is available free from the American Automobile Association (AAA; send stamped, self-addressed, legal-size envelope: ✉ Flying Alone, Mail Stop 800, 1000 AAA Dr., Heathrow, FL 32746).

GAMES

Milton Bradley has games to help keep little (and not so little) children from fidgeting while in planes, trains, and automobiles. Try packing the Travel Battleship sea-battle game ($7); Travel

Connect Four, a vertical strategy game ($8); the Travel Yahtzee dice game ($6), the Travel Trouble dice and board game ($7), and the Travel Guess Who mystery game ($8). Parker Brothers has travel versions of Clue!, Sorry, and Monopoly.

KNOW-HOW

Family Travel Times, published quarterly by Travel with Your Children (⊠ TWYCH, 40 5th Ave., New York, NY 10011, ☎ 212/477–5524; $40 per year), covers destinations, types of vacations, and modes of travel.

The *Family Travel Guides* catalog (⊠ Carousel Press, Box 6061, Albany, CA 94706, ☎ 510/527–5849; $1 postage) lists about 200 books and articles on traveling with children. Also check *Take Your Baby and Go! A Guide for Traveling with Babies, Toddlers and Young Children,* by Sheri Andrews, Judy Bordeaux, and Vivian Vasquez (⊠ Bear Creek Publications, 2507 Minor Ave. E, Seattle, WA 98102, ☎ 206/322–7604 or 800/326–6566; $5.95 plus $1.50 shipping).

TOUR OPERATORS

Contact **Rascals in Paradise** (⊠ 650 5th St., Suite 505, San Francisco, CA 94107, ☎ 415/978–9800 or 800/872–7225).

If you're outdoorsy, look into family-oriented programs run by the **American Museum of Natural History** (⊠

79th St. and Central Park West, New York, NY 10024, ☎ 212/769–5700 or 800/462–8687) **Wildland Adventures** (⊠ 3516 N.E. 155th St., Seattle, WA 98155, ☎ 206/365–0686 or 800/345–4453).

CRUISES

Cruises are the most restful way of traveling. The U.S.–Panama/Costa Rica cruise season runs September–May with trips lasting from three days to a week. Luxury liners equipped with swimming pools and gymnasiums sail from Fort Lauderdale, Florida, to Limón, or through the Panama Canal to Caldera, south of Puntarenas. There are also some cruises that head out of Los Angeles to Caldera, continuing to the canal. Aboard the ship you can sign up for shore excursions and tours. Packages include the cost of flying to the appropriate port in the United States. Cruise lines operating these routes include **Carnival** (☎ 800/327–9501), **Crystal Cruises** (☎ 800/446–6645), **Cunard** (☎ 800/221–4770), **Holland America** (☎ 800/426–0327), **Ocean Cruise** (☎ 800/556–8850), **Royal Viking** (☎ 800/422–8000), **Seabourn** (☎ 800/351–9595), **Sitmar Cruise** (☎ 305/523–1219), and **Sunline** (☎ 800/872–6400). Your travel agent will be able to give you details of prices, which range from $1,000 to $5,000.

CUSTOMS

IN THE U.S.

The **U.S. Customs Service** (⊠ Box 7407, Washington, DC 20044, ☎ 202/927–6724) can answer questions on duty-free limits and publishes a helpful brochure, **"Know Before You Go."** For information on registering foreign-made articles, call 202/927–0540.

COMPLAINTS➤ Note the inspector's badge number and write to the commissioner's office (⊠ 1301 Constitution Ave. NW, Washington, DC 20229).

CANADIANS

Contact **Revenue Canada** (⊠ 2265 St. Laurent Blvd. S, Ottawa, Ontario K1G 4K3, ☎ 613/993–0534) for a copy of the free brochure **"I Declare/Je Déclare"** and for details on duty-free limits. For recorded information (within Canada only), call 800/461–9999.

U.K. CITIZENS

HM Customs and Excise (⊠ Dorset House, Stamford St., London SE1 9NG, ☎ 0171/202–4227) can answer questions about U.K. customs regulations and publishes a free pamphlet, **"A Guide for Travellers,"** detailing standard procedures and import rules.

D

DISABILITIES & ACCESSIBILITY

COMPLAINTS

To register complaints under the provisions of

THE GOLD GUIDE / IMPORTANT CONTACTS

the Americans with Disabilities Act, contact the U.S. Department of Justice's **Disability Rights Section** (✉ Box 66738, Washington, DC 20035, ☎ 202/514–0301 or 800/514–0301, FAX 202/307–1198, TTY 202/514–0383 or 800/514–0383). For airline-related problems, contact the U.S. Department of Transportation's **Aviation Consumer Protection Division** (☞ Air Travel, *above*). For complaints about surface transportation, contact the Department of Transportation's **Civil Rights Office** (☎ 202/366–4648).

LOCAL INFORMATION

For information on accessibility in Costa Rica, contact the Costa Rican Tourist Institute, known locally as the ICT (✉ C. 5, Avdas. Central y Segunda, San José, Costa Rica, ☎ 506/222–1090).

ORGANIZATIONS

TRAVELERS WITH HEARING IMPAIRMENTS➤ The **American Academy of Otolaryngology** (✉ 1 Prince St., Alexandria, VA 22314, ☎ 703/836–4444, FAX 703/683–5100, TTY 703/519–1585) publishes a brochure, **"Travel Tips for Hearing Impaired People."**

TRAVELERS WITH MOBILITY PROBLEMS➤ Contact the **Information Center for Individuals with Disabilities** (✉ Box 256, Boston, MA 02117, ☎ 617/450–9888; in MA, 800/462–5015; TTY 617/424–6855); **Mobil**-ity International USA** (✉ Box 10767, Eugene, OR 97440, ☎ and TTY 541/343–1284, FAX 541/343–6812), the U.S. branch of a Belgium-based organization (☞ *below*) with affiliates in 30 countries; **MossRehab Hospital Travel Information Service** (☎ 215/456–9600, TTY 215/456–9602), a telephone information resource for travelers with physical disabilities; the **Society for the Advancement of Travel for the Handicapped** (✉ 347 5th Ave., Suite 610, New York, NY 10016, ☎ 212/447–7284, FAX 212/725–8253; membership $45); and **Travelin' Talk** (✉ Box 3534, Clarksville, TN 37043, ☎ 615/552–6670, FAX 615/552–1182), which provides local contacts worldwide for travelers with disabilities.

TRAVELERS WITH VISION IMPAIRMENTS➤ Contact the **American Council of the Blind** (✉ 1155 15th St. NW, Suite 720, Washington, DC 20005, ☎ 202/467–5081, FAX 202/467–5085) for a list of travelers' resources or the **American Foundation for the Blind** (✉ 11 Penn Plaza, Suite 300, New York, NY 10001, ☎ 212/502–7600 or 800/232–5463, TTY 212/502–7662), which provides general advice and publishes **"Access to Art"** ($19.95), a directory of museums that accommodate travelers with vision impairments.

IN THE U.K.

Contact the **Royal** Association for Disability and Rehabilitation** (✉ RADAR, 12 City Forum, 250 City Rd., London EC1V 8AF, ☎ 0171/250–3222) or **Mobility International** (✉ rue de Manchester 25, B-1080 Brussels, Belgium, ☎ 00–322–410–6297, FAX 00–322–410–6874), an international travel-information clearinghouse for people with disabilities.

PUBLICATIONS

Several publications for travelers with disabilities are available from the **Consumer Information Center** (✉ Box 100, Pueblo, CO 81009, ☎ 719/948–3334). Call or write for its free catalog of current titles. The Society for the Advancement of Travel for the Handicapped (☞ Organizations, *above*) publishes the quarterly magazine **"Access to Travel"** ($13 for 1-year subscription).

The 500-page **Travelin' Talk Directory** (✉ Box 3534, Clarksville, TN 37043, ☎ 615/552–6670, FAX 615/552–1182; $35) lists people and organizations who help travelers with disabilities. For travel agents worldwide, consult the **Directory of Travel Agencies for the Disabled** (✉ Twin Peaks Press, Box 129, Vancouver, WA 98666, ☎ 360/694–2462 or 800/637–2256, FAX 360/696–3210; $19.95 plus $3 shipping).

TRAVEL AGENCIES & TOUR OPERATORS

The Americans with Disabilities Act requires that travel firms serve the needs of all travelers. That said, you should note that some agencies and operators specialize in making travel arrangements for individuals and groups with disabilities, among them **Access Adventures** (✉ 206 Chestnut Ridge Rd., Rochester, NY 14624, ☎ 716/889–9096), run by a former physical-rehab counselor.

TRAVELERS WITH MOBILITY PROBLEMS➤ Contact **Hinsdale Travel Service** (✉ 201 E. Ogden Ave., Suite 100, Hinsdale, IL 60521, ☎ 708/325–1335), a travel agency that benefits from the advice of wheelchair traveler Janice Perkins; and **Wheelchair Journeys** (✉ 16979 Redmond Way, Redmond, WA 98052, ☎ 206/885–2210 or 800/313–4751), which can handle arrangements worldwide.

TRAVELERS WITH DEVELOPMENTAL DISABILITIES➤ Contact the nonprofit **New Directions** (✉ 5276 Hollister Ave., Suite 207, Santa Barbara, CA 93111, ☎ 805/967–2841).

TRAVEL GEAR

The **Magellan's** catalog (☎ 800/962–4943, FAX 805/568–5406) includes a range of products designed for travelers with disabilities.

DISCOUNTS & DEALS

AIRFARES

For the lowest airfares to Costa Rica, call 800/FLY-4-LES.

CLUBS

Contact **Entertainment Travel Editions** (✉ Box 1068, Trumbull, CT 06611, ☎ 800/445–4137; $28–$53, depending on destination), **Great American Traveler** (✉ Box 27965, Salt Lake City, UT 84127, ☎ 800/548–2812; $49.95 per year), **Moment's Notice Discount Travel Club** (✉ 7301 New Utrecht Ave., Brooklyn, NY 11204, ☎ 718/234 6295; $25 per year, single or family), **Privilege Card** (✉ 3391 Peachtree Rd. NE, Suite 110, Atlanta, GA 30326, ☎ 404/262–0222 or 800/236–9732; $74.95 per year), **Travelers Advantage** (✉ CUC Travel Service, 49 Music Sq. W, Nashville, TN 37203, ☎ 800/548–1116 or 800/648–4037; $49 per year, single or family), or **Worldwide Discount Travel Club** (✉ 1674 Meridian Ave., Miami Beach, FL 33139, ☎ 305/534–2082; $50 per year for family, $40 single).

STUDENTS

Members of Hostelling International–American Youth Hostels (☞ Students, *below*) are eligible for discounts on car rentals, admissions to attractions, and other selected travel expenses.

PUBLICATIONS

Consult *The Frugal Globetrotter,* by Bruce Northam (✉ Fulcrum Publishing, 350 Indiana St., Suite 350, Golden, CO 80401, ☎ 800/992–2908; $15.95). For publications that tell how to

find the lowest prices on plane tickets, *see* Air Travel, *above.*

DRIVING

INSURANCE

Don't leave home without valid insurance: This may mean having to insure through a Mexican company such as **Sanborn's** (☎ 210/686–0711) in McAllen, Texas—talk to **"Mexico" Mike Nelson** who will write insurance for trips of any length south of the border.

GASOLINE

Gasoline costs around $1.50 per gallon.

E

ECOTOURISM

A partial listing of Costa Rican companies specializing in ecological and/or natural history tourism includes **Costa Rica Expeditions** (☎ 506/222—0333, FAX 506/257–1665), **Explore Costa Rica** (☎ 506/220–2121), **Geotur** (☎ 506/234–1867, FAX 506/253–6338), **Horizontes** (☎ 506/222–2022, FAX 506/255–4513), **Sun Tours** (☎ 506/255–2011), and **Tikal Tours** ☎ 506/223–2811). Also recommended are the three day natural history cruises along the Southern Pacific coast on board the 185-foot cruise ship, the *M/V Temptress Explorer* (☎ 506/220–1679 or, in the U.S., 800/336–8423).

There are numerous environmental organizations in Costa Rica and Panama, and most of them are heavily dependent on private donations and dedicated volunteers. To obtain a list of Costa Rican groups that might need a hand and/or donation, consult the **Directorio de Organizaciones, Instituciones y Consultores en El Sector de Recursos Naturales en Costa Rica,** published in Spanish by the Costa Rican Federation for the Preservation of the Environment (FECON). Look in local bookstores in Costa Rica, or call FECON for further information (☎ 506/224–0399). Also, for locally-generated advice about ecotourism, consult the **Sustainable Tourism Newsletter,** published by the **Eco-Institute of Costa Rica** (☎ 506/233–2200, FAX 506/221–2801).

The tour operator **Ecotours de Panama** (☎ 507/263–3076, FAX 507/263–3089) is one of that country's most experienced ecological and adventure outfitters, and their tours last one week or longer; all include a one-year membership in ANCON, Panama's leading conservation group. A newer company, **Rio Monte Ecological Tours** (☎ 507/720–1536, FAX 507/720–2055), in Boquete, belongs to the Collins family, which has been involved in ecotourism since long before the term was coined. **Turtle Divers** (☎ FAX 507/757–9594), in Bocas del Toro, is a member of the marine conservation group Pro Mar, and has supported an environmental education campaign in local schools.

G

GAY & LESBIAN TRAVEL

The **Costa Rica Human Rights Commission** in San José gives legal advice to gays and lesbians who feel their rights have been violated (☎ 506/226–2658 or 506/226–2081). The gay association known as **Abraxas** organizes activities every Sunday near Alajuela. Write to Apartado Postal 1619–4050, Alajuela, Costa Rica, for further information.

ORGANIZATIONS

The **International Gay Travel Association** (✉ Box 4974, Key West, FL 33041, ☎ 800/448–8550, FAX 305/296–6633), a consortium of more than 1,000 travel companies, can supply names of gay-friendly travel agents, tour operators, and accommodations.

PUBLICATIONS

Most local gay publications and several national magazines such as the **Advocate** include travel ads and listings in their pages, as well as run occasional travel-related news stories. Your best bet for complete coverage of the full range of travel opportunities for gay women and men is the 16-page monthly newsletter **"Out & About"** (☎ 212/645–6922 or 800/929–2268, FAX 800/929–2215; $49 for 10 issues, plus an 8-page quarterly calendar supplement listing cruises and tours). "Out & About" reports on hotels, guest houses, cruises lines, and airlines, and they pioneered a rating system to assess travel industry suppliers' policies and programs as they affect gay and lesbian travelers. The gay travel magazine, **Our World,** has fairly thorough coverage on many destinations (✉ 1104 N. Nova Rd., Suite 251, Daytona Beach, FL 32117, ☎ 904/441–5367, FAX 904/441–5604; $35 for 10 issues).

TOUR OPERATORS

Cruises and resort vacations for gays are handled by **R.S.V.P. Travel Productions** (✉ 2800 University Ave. SE, Minneapolis, MN 55414, ☎ 612/379–4697 or 800/328–7787). **Toto Tours** (✉ 1326 W. Albion Ave., Suite 3W, Chicago, IL 60626, ☎ 312/274–8686 or 800/565–1241, FAX 312/274–8695) offers group tours to worldwide destinations.

TRAVEL AGENCIES

The largest agencies serving gay travelers are **Advance Travel** (✉ 10700 Northwest Fwy., Suite 160, Houston, TX 77092, ☎ 713/682–2002 or 800/292–0500), **Islanders/Kennedy Travel** (✉ 183 W. 10th St., New York, NY 10014, ☎ 212/242–3222 or 800/988–1181), **Now Voyager** (✉ 4406 18th St., San Francisco, CA 94114, ☎ 415/626–1169 or 800/255–6951), and **Yellowbrick Road** (✉ 1500 W. Balmoral Ave.,

Chicago, IL 60640, ☎ 312/561–1800 or 800/642–2488). **Skylink Women's Travel** (✉ 2460 W. 3rd St., Suite 215, Santa Rosa, CA 95401, ☎ 707/570–0105 or 800/225–5759) serves lesbian travelers.

H
HEALTH ISSUES

FINDING A DOCTOR

For its members, the **International Association for Medical Assistance to Travellers** (IAMAT, membership free; ✉ 417 Center St., Lewiston, NY 14092, ☎ 716/754–4883; ✉ 40 Regal Rd., Guelph, Ontario N1K 1B5, ☎ 519/836–0102; ✉ 1287 St. Clair Ave., Toronto, Ontario M6E 1B8, ☎ 416/652–0137; ✉ 57 Voirets, 1212 Grand-Lancy, Geneva, Switzerland, no phone) publishes a worldwide directory of English-speaking physicians meeting IAMAT standards.

MEDICAL ASSISTANCE COMPANIES

The following companies are concerned primarily with emergency medical assistance, although they may provide some insurance as part of their coverage. For a list of full-service travel insurance companies, *see* Insurance, *below.*

Contact **International SOS Assistance** (✉ Box 11568, Philadelphia, PA 19116, ☎ 215/244–1500 or 800/523–8930; ✉ Box 466, Pl. Bonaventure, Montréal,

Québec H5A 1C1, ☎ 514/874–7674 or 800/363–0263; ✉ 7 Old Lodge Pl., St. Margarets, Twickenham TW1 1RQ, England, ☎ 0181/744–0033), **Medex Assistance Corporation** (✉ Box 5375, Timonium, MD, 21094-5375, ☎ 410/453–6300 or 800/573–2029), **Traveler's Emergency Network** (✉ 3100 Tower Blvd., Suite 3100A, Durham, NC 27702, ☎ 919/490–6065 or 800/275–4836, FAX 919/493–8262), **TravMed** (✉ Box 5375, Timonium, MD 21094, 410/453–6380 or 800/732–5309), or **Worldwide Assistance Services** (✉ 1133 15th St. NW, Suite 400, Washington, DC 20005, ☎ 202/331–1609 or 800/821–2828, FAX 202/828–5896).

PUBLICATIONS

The Safe Travel Book, by Peter Savage (✉ Jossey-Bass Publishers, Inc., 350 Sansome St., San Francisco, CA 94104, ☎ 800/956–7739, FAX 800/605–2665; $12.95 plus $5 shipping).

WARNINGS

The hot line of the **National Centers for Disease Control** (✉ CDC, National Center for Infectious Diseases, Division of Quarantine, Traveler's Health Section, 1600 Clifton Rd., M/S E-03, Atlanta, GA 30333, ☎ 404/332–4559, FAX 404/332–4565) provides information on health risks abroad and vaccination requirements and recommendations.

You can call for an automated menu of recorded information or use the fax-back service to request printed matter.

I
INSURANCE

IN THE U.S.

Travel insurance covering baggage, health, and trip cancellation or interruptions is available from **Access America** (✉ 6600 W. Broad St., Richmond, VA 23230, ☎ 804/285–3300 or 800/334–7525), **Carefree Travel Insurance** (✉ Box 9366, 100 Garden City Plaza, Garden City, NY 11530, ☎ 516/294–0220 or 800/323–3149), **Near Travel Services** (✉ Box 1339, Calumet City, IL 60409, ☎ 708/868–6700 or 800/654–6700), **Tele-Trip** (✉ Mutual of Omaha Plaza, Box 31716, Omaha, NE 68131, ☎ 800/228–9792), **Travel Guard International** (✉ 1145 Clark St., Stevens Point, WI 54481, ☎ 715/345–0505 or 800/826–1300), **Travel Insured International** (✉ Box 280568, East Hartford, CT 06128, ☎ 203/528–7663 or 800/243–3174), and **Wallach & Company** (✉ 107 W. Federal St., Box 480, Middleburg, VA 22117, ☎ 540/687–3166 or 800/237–6615).

IN CANADA

Contact **Mutual of Omaha** (✉ Travel Division, 500 University Ave., Toronto, Ontario M5G 1V8, ☎ 800/465–0267, in

Canada, or 416/598–4083).

IN THE U.K.

The **Association of British Insurers** (✉ 51 Gresham St., London EC2V 7HQ, ☎ 0171/600–3333) gives advice by phone and publishes the free pamphlet **"Holiday Insurance,"** which sets out typical policy provisions and costs.

L
LODGING

For information on hotel consolidators, *see* Discounts, *above.*

APARTMENT & VILLA RENTAL

Among the companies to contact are **Property Rentals International** (✉ 1008 Mansfield Crossing Rd., Richmond, VA 23236, ☎ 804/378–6054 or 800/220–3332, FAX 804/379–2073), **Rent-a-Home International** (✉ 7200 34th Ave. NW, Seattle, WA 98117, ☎ 206/789–9377 or 800/488–7368, FAX 206/789–9379, hmari-aaol.com), **Vacation Home Rentals Worldwide** (✉ 235 Kensington Ave., Norwood, NJ 07648, ☎ 201/767–9393 or 800/633–3284, FAX 201/767–5510), and **Villas International** (✉ 605 Market St., Suite 510, San Francisco, CA 94105, ☎ 415/281–0910 or 800/221–2260, FAX 415/281–0919).

HOME EXCHANGE

One of the principal clearinghouses is **Intervac International** (✉ Box 590504, San Fran-

cisco, CA 94159, ☎ 415/435–3497, FAX 415/435–7440; $65 per year), which publishes four annual directories.

M
MONEY MATTERS

ATMS

For specific foreign **Cirrus** locations, call 800/424–7787; for foreign **Plus** locations, consult the Plus directory at your local bank.

CURRENCY EXCHANGE

If your bank doesn't exchange currency, contact **Thomas Cook Currency Services** (☎ 800/287–7362 for locations). **Ruesch International** (☎ 800/424–2923 for locations) can also provide you with foreign banknotes before you leave home and publishes a number of useful brochures, including a "Foreign Currency Guide" and "Foreign Exchange Tips."

WIRING FUNDS

Funds can be wired via **MoneyGram**SM (for locations and information in the U.S. and Canada, ☎ 800/926–9400) or **Western Union** (for agent locations or to send money using MasterCard or Visa, ☎ 800/325–6000; in Canada, 800/321–2923; in the U.K., 0800/833833; or visit the Western Union office at the nearest major post office).

P
PACKING

For strategies on packing light, get a copy of

The Packing Book, by Judith Gilford (✉ Ten Speed Press, Box 7123, Berkeley, CA 94707, ☎ 510/559–1600 or 800/841–2665, FAX 510/524–4588; $7.95).

PASSPORTS & VISAS

IN THE U.S.

For fees, documentation requirements, and other information, call the State Department's **Office of Passport Services** information line (☎ 202/647–0518).

CANADIANS

For fees, documentation requirements, and other information, call the Ministry of Foreign Affairs and International Trade's **Passport Office** (☎ 819/994–3500 or 800/567–6868).

U.K. CITIZENS

For fees, documentation requirements, and to request an emergency passport, call the **London Passport Office** (☎ 0990/210410).

PHOTO HELP

The **Kodak Information Center** (☎ 800/242–2424) answers consumer questions about film and photography. The **Kodak Guide to Shooting Great Travel Pictures** (available in bookstores; or contact Fodor's Travel Publications, ☎ 800/533–6478; $16.50) explains how to take expert travel photographs.

S
SAFETY

"Trouble-Free Travel," from the AAA, is a booklet of tips for protecting yourself and your belongings when away from home. Send a stamped, self-addressed, legal-size envelope to Flying Alone (✉ Mail Stop 75, 1000 AAA Dr., Heathrow, FL 32746).

EDUCATIONAL TRAVEL

The nonprofit **Elderhostel** (✉ 75 Federal St., 3rd Floor, Boston, MA 02110, ☎ 617/426–7788), for people 60 and older, has offered inexpensive study programs since 1975. Courses cover everything from marine science to Greek mythology and cowboy poetry. Costs for two- to three-week international trips—including room, board, and transportation from the United States—range from $1,800 to $4,500.

For people 50 and over and their children and grandchildren, **Interhostel** (✉ University of New Hampshire, 6 Garrison Ave., Durham, NH 03824, ☎ 603/862–1147 or 800/733–9753) runs 10-day summer programs that feature lectures, field trips, and sightseeing. Most last two weeks and cost $2,125–$3,100, including airfare.

ORGANIZATIONS

Contact the **American Association of Retired Persons** (✉ AARP, 601 E St. NW, Washington, DC 20049, ☎ 202/434–2277; annual dues $8 per person or couple). Its Purchase Privilege Program secures discounts for members

on lodging, car rentals, and sightseeing.

Additional sources for discounts on lodgings, car rentals, and other travel expenses, as well as helpful magazines and newsletters, are the **National Council of Senior Citizens** (✉ 1331 F St. NW, Washington, DC 20004, ☎ 202/347–8800; annual membership $12) and Sears's **Mature Outlook** (✉ Box 10448, Des Moines, IA 50306, ☎ 800/336–6330; annual membership $9.95).

PUBLICATIONS

The 50+ Traveler's Guidebook: Where to Go, Where to Stay, What to Do, by Anita Williams and Merrimac Dillon (✉ St. Martin's Press, 175 5th Ave., New York, NY 10010, ☎ 212/674–5151 or 800/288–2131; $13.95), offers many useful tips. **"The Mature Traveler"** (✉ Box 50400, Reno, NV 89513, ☎ 702/786–7419; $29.95), a monthly newsletter, covers all sorts of travel deals.

TOURS

Two American companies specialize in tours for retirees who are considering moving to Costa Rica. They are: **Lifestyle Explorations** (✉ World Trade Center, 101 Federal Ave. Suite 1900, Boston, MA 02210, ☎ 508/371–4814, FAX 369–9192) and **Retirement Expedition Tours** (✉ Box 6487, Modesto, CA 95355, ☎ 209/577–4081).

BICYCLING

Although much of this region is mountainous, there are also many ideal-for-cycling flatlands in Costa Rica. Three Costa Rican companies currently offer mountain-biking tours out of San José: **Costaricabike** (☎ 506/224–0899), **Dos Montañas** (☎ 506/233–6455), and **Ecotreks** (☎ 506/289–8191). Tours range in length from a single day to a week. In La Fortuna de San Carlos, **Desafío** (☎ 506/479–9464) has mountain bikes for rent, and offers guided and unguided tours. You can also hire your own bicycles in most mountain and beach resorts.

BIRD-WATCHING

Many tour companies offer specialized bird-watching tours, including Costa Rica's **Horizontes** (☎ 506/222–2022) and **Costa Rica Expeditions** (☎ 506/222–0333), and Panama's **Ecotours de Panama** (☎ 507/263–3079) and **Pesántez Tours** (☎ 507/263–8771).

WATER SPORTS

The three big Costa Rican rafting outfitters are **Aventuras Naturales** (☎ 506/224–0899), **Costa Rica Expediciones** (☎ 506/222–0333), and **Ríos Tropicales** (☎ 506/233–6455). **Chiriquí River Rafting** (☎ 507/236–5217) runs two rivers, a class III and a class IV, in western Panama, while **Aventuras Panama** (☎ 507/260–0044) offers trips on the upper

Chagres, a mellow, class II river with one class IV rapid.

Two dive boats visit Isla Cocos on 10-day scuba safaris: the **Okeanos Aggressor** (☎ 506/232–6672) and the **Undersea Hunter** (☎ *506/224–2555*). In Panama, **Captain Morgan's** (☎ 507/250–4029), on Contadora, organizes dives around the Pearl Islands, and **Scuba Panama** (☎ 507/261–3841) can arrange scuba safaris off either coast in a 65-foot yacht. See Sports in regional sections for details.

One windsurfing specialist in Costa Rica is **Tilawa** (☎ 506/695–5050) on Lake Arenal.

STUDENTS

HOSTELING

In the United States, contact **Hostelling International–American Youth Hostels** (✉ 733 15th St. NW, Suite 840, Washington, DC 20005, ☎ 202/783–6161 or 800/444–6111 for reservations at selected hostels, FAX 202/783–6171); in Canada, **Hostelling International–Canada** (✉ 205 Catherine St., Suite 400, Ottawa, Ontario K2P 1C3, ☎ 613/237–7884); and in the United Kingdom, the **Youth Hostel Association of England and Wales** (✉ Trevelyan House, 8 St. Stephen's Hill, St. Albans, Hertfordshire AL1 2DY, ☎ 01727/855215 or 01727/845047). Membership (✉ in the U.S., $25; in Canada, C$26.75; in the U.K., £9) gives you access to

5,000 hostels in 77 countries that charge $5–$30 per person per night.

ID CARDS

To be eligible for discounts on transportation and admissions, get either the **International Student Identity Card,** if you're a bona fide student, or the **GO 25: International Youth Travel Card,** if you're not a student but under age 26. Each includes basic travel-accident and illness coverage, plus a toll-free travel hot line. In the United States, either card costs $18; apply through the Council on International Educational Exchange (☞ Organizations, *below*). In Canada, cards are available for $15 each ($16 by mail) from Travel Cuts (☞ Organizations, *below*), and in the United Kingdom for £5 each at student unions and student travel companies.

ORGANIZATIONS

A major contact is the **Council on International Educational Exchange** (✉ mail orders only: CIEE, 205 E. 42nd St., 16th Floor, New York, NY 10017, ☎ 212/822–2600, info @ ciee.org), with walk-in locations in Boston (✉ 729 Boylston St., 02116, ☎ 617/266–1926), Miami (✉ 9100 S. Dadeland Blvd., 33156, ☎ 305/670–9261), Los Angeles (✉ 10904 Lindbrook Dr., 90024, ☎ 310/208–3551), 43 other college towns in the U.S., and in the United Kingdom (✉ 28A Poland St., London W1V 3DB, ☎

0171/437–7767). Twice per year, it publishes *Student Travels* magazine. The CIEE's Council Travel Service is the exclusive U.S. agent for several student discount cards.

The **Educational Travel Centre** (✉ 438 N. Frances St., Madison, WI 53703, ☎ 608/256–5551 or 800/747–5551, FAX 608/256–2042) offers rail passes and low-cost airline tickets, mostly for flights that depart from Chicago.

In Canada, also contact **Travel Cuts** (✉ 187 College St., Toronto, Ontario M5T 1P7, ☎ 416/979–2406 or 800/667–2887).

PUBLICATIONS

Check out the **Berkeley Guide to Central America** (available in bookstores; or contact Fodor's Travel Publications, ☎ 800/533–6478; $16.50).

T

TELEPHONE MATTERS

The country code for Costa Rica is 506; for Panama, 507. All phone numbers listed without area codes in this book are prefaced with Costa Rica's 506 area code or Panama's 507 area code, which do not have to be dialed for calls originating within the country. For local access numbers abroad, contact **AT&T** USADirect (☎ 800/874–4000), **MCI** Call USA (☎ 800/444–4444), or **Sprint** Express (☎ 800/793–1153).

The best places to make

international calls and to send faxes, telexes, or telegrams in San José are the ICE office (✉ Avda. 2 between C. 1 and 3; ☉ Daily 7 AM–11 PM) and Radiográfica Costarricense (✉ Avda. 5 between C. 1 and 3; ☉ Daily 7 AM–10 PM); in Panama City, at the INTEL office (✉ C. Manuel María Icaza, 100 meters south of the Vía España, ☉ Daily 8 AM–10 PM).

TOUR OPERATORS

Among the companies that sell tours and packages to Costa Rica, the following are nationally known, have a proven reputation, and offer plenty of options.

GROUP TOURS

SUPER-DELUXE➤ **Abercrombie & Kent** (✉ 1520 Kensington Rd., Oak Brook, IL 60521-2141, ☎ 708/954–2944 or 800/323–7308, FAX 708/954–3324) and **Travcoa** (✉ Box 2630, 2350 S.E. Bristol St., Newport Beach, CA 92660, ☎ 714/476–2800 or 800/992–2003, FAX 714/476–2538).

DELUXE➤ **Globus** (✉ 5301 S. Federal Circle, Littleton, CO 80123–2980, ☎ 303/797–2800 or 800/221–0090, FAX 303/795–0962), **Maupintour** (✉ Box 807, 1515 St. Andrews Dr., Lawrence, KS 66047, ☎ 913/843–1211 or 800/255–4266, FAX 913/843–8351), and **Tauck Tours** (✉ Box 5027, 276 Post Rd. W, Westport, CT 06881, ☎ 203/226–6911 or 800/468–2825, FAX 203/221–6828).

FIRST CLASS➤ **Brendan Tours** (✉ 15137 Califa St., Van Nuys, CA 91411, ☎ 818/785–9696 or 800/421–8446, FAX 818/902–9876), **Caravan Tours** (✉ 401 N. Michigan Ave., Chicago, IL 60611, ☎ 312/321–9800 or 800/227–2826), **Collette Tours** (✉ 162 Middle St., Pawtucket, RI 02860, ☎ 401/728-3805 or 800/832–4656).

BUDGET➤ **Cosmos** (☞ Globus, *above*).

PACKAGES

Independent vacation packages are available from major tour operators and airlines. Contact **Adventure Vacations** (✉ 10612 Beaver Dam Rd., Hunt Valley, MD 21030–2205, ☎ 410/785–3500 or 800/638–9040, FAX 410/584–2771), **American Airlines Fly AAway Vacations** (☎ 800/321–2121), **Armadillo Tours International** (✉ 4301 Westbank Dr., #B360, Austin, TX 78746, ☎ 512/328–7800 or 800/284–5678), **Avanti Destinations** (✉ 851 S.W. 6th St., Portland, OR 97024, ☎ 503/295–1100 or 800/422–5053, FAX 503/295–2723 or 800/422–9505), **4th Dimension Tours** (✉ 7101 S.W. 99th Ave., #105, Miami, FL 33173, ☎ 305/279–0014 or 800/877–1525, FAX 305/273–9777, http://www.4thdimension.com), **Ladatco Tours** (✉ 2220 Coral Way, Miami, FL 33145, ☎ 305/854–8422 or 800/327–6162, FAX 305/285–0504), **M.I.L.A.** (✉ 100 S. Greenleaf Ave., Gurnee, IL 60031–3378, ☎ 847/249–2111 or 800/367–7378, FAX 847/249–2772, milalatinaol.com, http://www.a2z.com/mila), and **Sun Holidays** (✉ 26 6th St., #603, Stamford, CT 06905, ☎ 203/323–1166 or 800/243–2057).

Regional operators specialize in putting together packages for travelers from their local area. **Friendly Holidays** (✉ 1983 Marcus Ave., Lake Success, NY 11042, ☎ 800/344–5687).

THEME TRIPS

ADVENTURE➤ **Himalayan Travel** (✉ 112 Prospect St., Stamford, CT 06901, ☎ 203/359–3711 or 800/225–2380, FAX 203/359–3669) operates a range of adventure tours. **Mountain Travel-Sobek** (✉ 6420 Fairmount Ave., El Cerrito, CA 94530, ☎ 510/527–8100 or 800/227–2384, FAX 510/525–7710, infoMTSobek.com, http://www.MTSobek.com) operates hiking and rafting trips. Wildlife safaris are the focus of **Safaricentre** (✉ 3201 N. Sepulveda Blvd., Manhattan Beach, CA 90266, ☎ 310/546–4411 or 800/223–6046, FAX 310/546–3188).

BICYCLING➤ Mountain-biking enthusiasts can contact **Backroads** (✉ 1516 5th St., Berkeley, CA 94710–1740, ☎ 510/527–1555 or 800/462–2848, FAX

THE GOLD GUIDE / IMPORTANT CONTACTS

510/527–1444, goactiveBackroads.com).

FISHING➤ **Anglers Travel** (✉ 3100 Mill St., #206, Reno, NV 89502, ☎ 702/324–0580 or 800/624–8429, FAX 702/324–0583), **Cutting Loose Expeditions** (✉ Box 447, Winter Park, FL 32790–0447, ☎ 407/629–4700 or 800/533–4746), **Fishing International** (✉ Box 2132, Santa Rosa, CA 95405, ☎ 800/950–4242), and **Rod & Reel Adventures** (✉ 3507 Tully Rd., #B6, Modesto, CA 95356–1052, ☎ 209/524–7775 or 800/356–6982, FAX 209/524–1220).

HEALTH➤ Contact **Spa-Finders** (✉ 91 5th Ave., #301, New York, NY 10003–3039, ☎ 212/924–6800 or 800/255–7727).

HIKING➤ Adventurous hikers should try **Backroads** (☞ *above*).

HORTICULTURE➤ Amateur and professional gardeners alike should contact **Expo Garden Tours** (✉ 101 Sunrise Hill Rd., Norwalk, CT 06851, ☎ 203/840–1441 or 800/448–2685, FAX 203/840–1224) for a look at Costa Rica's gardens and rain forests.

LEARNING➤ **Earthwatch** (✉ Box 403, 680 Mount Auburn St., Watertown, MA 02272, ☎ 617/926–8200 or 800/776–0188, FAX 617/926–8532, infoearthwatch.org, http://www.earthwatch.org) recruits volunteers to serve in its Earth-Corps as short-term assistants to scientists on research expeditions. Try **National Audubon Society** (✉ 700 Broadway, New York, NY 10003, ☎ 212/979–3066, FAX 212/353–0190, travelaudubon.org), **Natural Habitat Adventures** (✉ 2945 Center Green Ct., Boulder, CO 80301, ☎ 303/449–3711 or 800/543–8917, FAX 303/449–3712), **Nature Expeditions International** (✉ Box 11496, Eugene, OR 97440, ☎ 503/484–6529 or 800/869–0639, FAX 503/484–6531, NaturExpaol.com), **Oceanic Society Expeditions** (✉ Fort Mason Center, Bldg. E, San Francisco, CA 94123–1394, ☎ 415/441–1106 or 800/326–7491, FAX 415/474–3395), **Questers** (✉ 381 Park Ave. S, New York, NY 10016, ☎ 212/251–0444 or 800/468–8668, FAX 212/251–0890), **Smithsonian Study Tours and Seminars** (✉ 1100 Jefferson Dr. SW, Room 3045, MRC 702, Washington, DC 20560, ☎ 202/357–4700, FAX 202/633–9250), and **Wilderness Travel** (✉ 801 Allston Way, Berkeley, CA 94710, ☎ 510/548–0420 or 800/368–2794, FAX 510/548–0347, infowildernesstravel.com).

NATURAL HISTORY➤ **Esplanade Tours** (✉ 581 Boylston St., Boston, MA 02116, ☎ 617/266–7465 or 800/426–5492, FAX 617/262–9829) books expedition cruises.

SCUBA DIVING➤ Contact **Go Diving** (✉ 5610 Rowland Rd., #100, Minnetonka, MN 55343, ☎ 612/931–9101 or 800/328–5285, FAX 612/931–0209), **Rothschild Dive Safaris** (✉ 900 West End Ave., #1B, New York, NY 10025–3525, ☎ 212/662–4858 or 800/359–0747, FAX 212/749–6172, rothdiveix.netcom.com, http://www.empg.com/rothschild), and **Tropical Adventures** (✉ 111 2nd Ave. N, Seattle, WA 98109, ☎ 206/441–3483 or 800/247–3483, FAX 206/441–5431).

VILLA RENTALS➤ Contact **Villas International** (✉ 605 Market St., San Francisco, CA 94105, ☎ 415/281–0910 or 800/221–2260, FAX 415/281–0919).

YACHT CHARTERS➤ **Ocean Voyages** (✉ 1709 Bridgeway, Sausalito, CA 94965, ☎ 415/332–4681, FAX 415/332–7460).

ORGANIZATIONS

The **National Tour Association** (✉ NTA, 546 E. Main St., Lexington, KY 40508, ☎ 606/226–4444 or 800/755–8687) and the **United States Tour Operators Association** (✉ USTOA, 211 E. 51st St., Suite 12B, New York, NY 10022, ☎ 212/750–7371) can provide lists of members and information on booking tours.

PUBLICATIONS

Contact the USTOA (☞ Organizations, *above*) for its **"Smart Traveler's Planning Kit."** Pamphlets in the kit include the "Worldwide Tour and Vacation Package Finder," "How to Select a Tour or Vacation Package," and information on the organization's consumer protection plan. Also get a copy of the Better Business Bureau's **"Tips on Travel Packages"** (✉ Publication 24-195, 4200 Wilson Blvd., Arlington, VA 22203; $2).

TRAVEL GEAR

For travel apparel, appliances, personal-care items, and other travel necessities, get a free catalog from **Magellan's** (☎ 800/962–4943, FAX 805/568–5406), **Orvis Travel** (☎ 800/541–3541, FAX 703/343–7053), or **TravelSmith** (☎ 800/950–1600, FAX 415/455–0554).

ELECTRICAL CONVERTERS

Send a self-addressed, stamped envelope to the **Franzus Company** (✉ Customer Service, Dept. B50, Murtha Industrial Park, Box 142, Beacon Falls, CT 06403, ☎ 203/723–6664) for a copy of the free brochure "Foreign Electricity Is No Deep, Dark Secret."

TRAVEL AGENCIES

For names of reputable agencies in your area, contact the **American Society of Travel Agents** (✉ ASTA, 1101 King St., Suite 200, Alexandria, VA 22314, ☎ 703/739–2782), the **Association of Canadian Travel Agents** (✉ Suite 201, 1729 Bank St., Ottawa, Ontario K1V 7Z5, ☎ 613/521–0474, FAX 613/521–0805), or the

Association of British Travel Agents (✉ 55-57 Newman St., London W1P 4AH, ☎ 0171/637–2444, FAX 0171/637–0713).

U

U.S. GOVERNMENT TRAVEL BRIEFINGS

The U.S. Department of State's American Citizens Services office (✉ Room 4811, Washington, DC 20520; enclose SASE) issues **Consular Information Sheets** on all foreign countries. These cover issues such as crime, security, political climate, and health risks as well as listing embassy locations, entry requirements, currency regulations, and providing other useful information. For the latest information, stop in at any U.S. passport office, consulate, or embassy; call the interactive hot line (☎ 202/647–5225, FAX 202/647–3000); or, with your PC's modem, tap into the department's computer bulletin board (☎ 202/647–9225).

V

VISITOR INFORMATION

Contact the **Costa Rican Embassy** (✉ 1825 Connecticut Ave., NW, Suite 211, Washington, DC 20009, ☎ 202/234–2945). There are also consulates in Chicago (✉ 8 S. Michigan Ave., Suite 1312,

60603, ☎ 312/263–2772), Houston (✉ 2901 Wilcrest, Suite 347, 77042, ☎ 713/266–0484), Miami (✉ 1660 N.W. Le Jeune Rd., 3rd Floor, 33126, ☎ 305/871–7485), Los Angeles (✉ 3450 Wilshire Blvd., Suite 404, 90010, ☎ 213/380–6031), and New York (✉ 80 Wall St., 10005, ☎ 212/425–2620).

In Canada, the **Costa Rican Embassy** (✉ 150 Argyle Ave., Suite 115, Ottawa, Ontario, K2P 1 B7, ☎ 613/562–2855).

From the U.S., you can also call the **Costa Rican Tourism Institute (ICT)** direct at 800/343–6332.

W

WEATHER

For current conditions and forecasts, plus the local time and helpful travel tips, call the **Weather Channel Connection** (☎ 900/932–8437; 95¢ per minute) from a Touch-Tone phone.

The *International Traveler's Weather Guide* (✉ Weather Press, Box 660606, Sacramento, CA 95866, ☎ 916/974–0201 or 800/972–0201; $10.95 includes shipping), written by two meteorologists, provides month-by-month information on temperature, humidity, and precipitation in more than 175 cities worldwide.

SMART TRAVEL TIPS A TO Z

*Basic Information on Traveling in Costa Rica &
Savvy Tips to Make Your Trip a Breeze*

The more you travel, the more you know about how to make trips run like clock-work. To help make your travels hassle-free, Fodor's editors have rounded up dozens of tips from our contributors and from travel experts all over the world, as well as basic information on visiting Costa Rica and Panama. For names of organizations to contact and publications that can give you more information, *see* Important Contacts A to Z, *above.*

A
AIR TRAVEL

The main tourist season in Costa Rica and Panama, from Thanksgiving to Easter, coincides with vacation times, like Thanksgiving and Christmas. Hence flights are sometimes fully booked well ahead of time. Check through fares from your city to San José, as well as fares from your city to a gateway and from that gateway into San José; the latter can be cheaper. Gateway cities in the United States are Dallas, Houston, Los Angeles, Miami, New Orleans, Orlando, New York, and San Francisco. If your ticket combines airlines, try to get it issued on the ticket stock of the airline that has an office

in San José, making it easier to make changes on the return leg. Also, flexibility on dates makes it more likely that a consolidator (several are listed under Important Contacts A to Z, and your travel agent may know of others) can find you a less-expensive ticket. There are charter flights from Canada, but those from the United States had been suspended at press time.

If time is an issue, **always look for nonstop flights,** which require no change of plane. If possible, **avoid connecting flights,** which stop at least once and can involve a change of plane, even though the flight number remains the same; if the first leg is late, the second waits.

CUTTING COSTS

The Sunday travel section of most newspapers is a good place to look for deals.

Major Airlines> The least-expensive airfares from the major airlines are priced for round-trip travel and are subject to restrictions. Usually, you must **book in advance and buy the ticket within 24 hours** to get cheaper fares, and you may have to **stay over a Saturday night.** The lowest fare is subject to availability, and only a small percentage of the plane's

total seats is sold at that price. It's smart to **call a number of airlines,** and **when you are quoted a good price, book it on the spot**—the same fare may not be available on the same flight the next day. Airlines generally allow you to change your return date for a $25 to $50 fee. If you don't use your ticket, you can apply the cost toward the purchase of a new ticket, again for a small charge. However, most low-fare tickets are nonrefundable. To get the lowest airfare, **check different routings.** If your destination has more than one gateway, **compare prices to different airports.**

From the U.K.> To save money on flights, **look into an APEX or Super-PEX ticket.** APEX tickets must be booked in advance and have certain restrictions. Super-PEX tickets can be purchased right at the airport.

Consolidators> Consolidators buy tickets for scheduled flights at reduced rates from the airlines, then sell them at prices below the lowest available from the airlines directly—usually without advance restrictions. Sometimes you can even get your money back if you need to return the ticket. Carefully read the fine print detailing penalties for changes and cancellations. If you doubt the reliability of a consolidator, **confirm your reservation with the airline.**

ALOFT

AIRLINE FOOD➤ If you hate airline food, **ask for special meals when booking.** These can be vegetarian, low-cholesterol, or kosher, for example; commonly prepared to order in smaller quantities than standard fare, they can be tastier.

SMOKING➤ Smoking is banned on all flights of less than six hours' duration within the United States and on all Canadian flights; the ban also applies to domestic segments of international flights aboard U.S. and foreign carriers. On U.S. carriers flying to Costa Rica and other destinations abroad, a seat in a no-smoking section must be provided for every passenger who requests one, and the section must be enlarged to accommodate such passengers as long as they have complied with the airline's deadline for check-in and seat assignment. If smoking bothers you, request a seat far from the smoking section.

Foreign airlines are exempt from these rules but do provide no-smoking sections; some countries have banned smoking on all domestic flights, and others may not allow smoking on some flights. Talks continue on the feasibility of broadening no-smoking policies.

WITHIN COSTA RICA

Considering the nation's often difficult driving conditions—what may appear to be a small distance on a map of the country can represent hours of driving time on dirt roads pocked with moon-craters—flying can be visually stimulating and convenient, if somewhat expensive. Two domestic airlines serve Costa Rica: **Sansa** and **Travelair.**

Sansa is cheaper (and is willing to carry surfboards under 7 feet long and disassembled mountain bikes for about $15), but its flights fill up early and often leave late. At press time (spring 1996), Sansa flew to the following destinations, with from one to four flights available at different hours on each scheduled day: Barra del Colorado (☉ Tues., Thurs., Sat.), Coto 47 (☉ Mon.–Sat.), Nosara (☉ Mon., Wed., Fri.), Palmar Sur (☉ Mon.–Sat.), Puerto Jiménez (☉ Mon.–Sat.), Quepos (☉ Daily), Samara (☉ Daily), Tamarindo (☉ Daily), and Tambor (☉ Daily), Golfito (☉ Tues., Thurs., Sat.), Puerto Jiménez (☉ Daily). There are also numerous flights available between these destinations, and flights from Liberia to several of the Guanacaste destinations.

At press time, Travelair, which charges extra for surfboards and/or mountain bikes regardless of the availability of

space, had daily flights to the following destinations: Barra del Colorado, Carrillo, Golfito/Puerto Jiménez, Liberia, Nosara, Punta Islita, Quepos (three times daily), Tamarindo (twice daily), Tambor, and Tortuguero. Prices range from $34 for the one-way hop to Jacó up to $136 for the round-trip to Puerto Jiménez. Travelair offers charter flights in addition to their regularly scheduled flights, and there are several other charter companies in San José that will fly you to places where scheduled airlines won't go, such as Limón. For other charter companies check the yellow pages under *taxis aereos* (air taxis).

For more specifics on cost and scheduling, consult the Arriving and Departing and Getting Around sections in individual chapters.

B
BOAT TRAVEL

WITHIN COSTA RICA

Regular passenger and/or car ferries connect Playa Naranjo, Tambor, and Paquera on the south end of the Nicoya Peninsula with Puntarenas. A car and passenger ferry crosses the Río Tempisque, about a one-hour drive north and west from Puntarenas, from 5 AM to 7 PM. During the holidays and the high season car ferries are very crowded, and waits of up to three hours are common. The Arco Iris Passenger Ferry makes daily runs between Golfito and Puerto Jiménez, and the Zancudo's passenger ferry makes a daily round-trip to Golfito. At Río Coto there is continuous service from Golfito to Zancudo and Pavones during daylight hours. To reach Tortuguero and Barra del Colorado from Moín, in the Atlantic Lowlands, there is no formal service except that run by specific lodges for their guests, but boats can be chartered on an informal basis. There are numerous charter options for diving, island visiting, sailing, cruising, and other water sports. For more information on boat travel see the Getting Around section in individual chapters.

WITHIN PANAMA

Water taxis make several trips daily between Almirante and Bocas del Toro, leaving Almirante at 7 AM and 2 PM Sunday through Thursday, 5:30 AM Friday and Saturday, and 4 PM Friday through Monday, returning from Bocas del Toro about 30 minutes later. They also make unscheduled runs if there are enough people. A car ferry departs Almirante for Chiriquí Grande daily at 8 AM, returning at 2 PM, stopping at Bocas del Toro every Friday and Sunday, but water taxis take less time, and there are several departures daily. There are also several ferry trips daily between Panama City and the Island of Taboga.

BUS TRAVEL

WITHIN COSTA RICA

There is reliable, inexpensive bus service throughout much of the country. On longer routes, buses stop midway at inexpensive restaurants. Tickets are sold at the bus station or on the buses themselves. A patchwork of private companies operates out of San José from a variety of departure points. For detailed information, consult the Getting Around sections of individual chapters. Note that although this information was current at press time, it is worthwhile asking the tourist office in San José for an update to make sure. Reservations are not usually necessary and often not possible, but if you want to be sure of a seat (they sell standing room only tickets and the buses frequently fill up), buy your ticket ahead of time and/or get there early. Also note that in some cases buses that list several destinations might not pass through the center of the town but bypass it. (This often happens at Cahuita and Puerto Viejo with the Sixaola bus, for both towns are on dirt roads off the main highway.) If you have burdensome luggage this can be very inconvenient, so try to find out from the driver, the bus station officials, or other passengers if the bus actually goes into the town. Near the ends of their runs many nonexpress buses turn into large taxis, dropping passengers off one

by one once they reach their destinations. To save time, take a *directo* (express bus).

WITHIN PANAMA

The widespread use of microbuses means that there is very regular service between most Panamanian towns. Buses depart about every 30 minutes between Changuinola and Almirante, and slightly less frequently between Changuinola and the border with Costa Rica. There are about five buses a day between Chiriquí Grande and David, from where buses leave every 20 minutes for the Costa Rican border, Volcán and Cerro Punta, and Boquete. Old "Greyhound" buses leave every hour between David and Panama City; it's a seven-hour trip. There is also direct service daily between Panama City and Chiriquí Grande, departing Panama City at 5 AM, and Chiriquí Grande at 1 PM, when the ferry arrives from Almirante.

BUSINESS HOURS

BANKS

Most of Costa Rica's state banks are open weekdays 9–3. Several branches of **Banco Nacional de Costa Rica** (behind the main post office in San José and in the San José suburb of San Pedro) are open until 6. The growing cadre of private banks tend to keep longer hours. Panamanian banks keep similar hours, though many are also open Saturday mornings.

MUSEUMS

Generalizing about Costa Rican museum opening times is unwise, though all public museums—except San José's Jade Museum—are closed Tuesdays. Check for the opening times of the museums in San José in the Exploring section of the San José chapter. Most Panamanian museums are open 9–4, Monday–Friday, though Panama City's anthropology museum and David's José de Obaldía Museum both open Tuesday–Saturday.

SHOPS

Most shops are open weekdays 9–7, though a few older ones still observe the long lunch hour from noon to 2 PM. Most shops open Saturday, though some close at noon. A handful of stores, especially souvenir shops, have Sunday hours.

C

CAMERAS, CAMCORDERS, & COMPUTERS

LAPTOPS

Before you depart, **check your portable computer's battery;** at security you may be asked to turn on the computer to prove that it is what it appears to be. At the airport, you may prefer to **request a manual inspection,** although security X-rays do not harm hard-disk or floppy-disk storage. Also, **register your foreign-made laptop with U.S. Customs.** If your laptop is U.S.-made, call the consulate of the country you'll be visiting to find out whether it should be registered with local customs upon arrival. You may want to **find out about repair facilities at your destination** in case of problems.

Given the oft-bumpy roads, the intense humidity in many areas of Costa Rica, the dry season dust in others, and the possibility of theft, consider carefully whether or not you need your computer, and, if you do, insure it and pack it with extra layers of protection.

PHOTOGRAPHY

If your camera is new or if you haven't used it for a while, **shoot and develop a few rolls of film** before you leave. Always **store film in a cool, dry place**—never in your car's glove compartment or on the shelf under the rear window.

Select the right film for your purpose—**use print film if you plan to frame or display your pictures,** but **use slide film if you hope to publish your shots.** Also, **consider black-and-white film** for different and dramatic images. For best results, **use a custom lab** for processing; use a one-hour lab only if time is a factor.

The chances of your film growing cloudy increase with each pass through an X-ray machine. To protect against this, carry it in a clear plastic bag and **ask for hand inspection at security.** Such requests are virtually always honored at U.S. airports, and are usually accommodated abroad. Don't depend on a lead-lined bag to protect film in checked luggage—the airline may increase the radiation to see what's inside.

Keep a skylight or haze filter on your camera at all times to protect the expensive (and delicate) lens glass from scratches. Better yet, **use an 81B warming filter,** which—unlike skylight or haze filters—really works in overcast conditions and will pump up those sunrises and sunsets.

VIDEO

Before your trip, **test your camcorder, invest in a skylight filter to protect the lens, and charge the batteries.** (Airport security personnel may ask you to turn on the camcorder to prove that it's what it appears to be.) The batteries of most newer camcorders can be recharged with a universal or worldwide AC adapter-charger (or multivoltage converter), whether the voltage is 110 or 220. All that's needed is the appropriate plug.

Videotape is not damaged by X-rays, but it may be harmed by the magnetic field of a walk-through metal detector, so **ask that videotapes be hand-checked.** Prerecorded videotape sold in Costa Rica and Panama is based on the NTSE standard, which will not play back in the United States. Blank tapes bought in Costa Rica can be used for camcorder taping, but they are pricey. Some

U.S. audiovisual shops convert foreign tapes to U.S. standards; contact an electronics dealer to find the nearest.

CAR RENTAL

Renting cars is not common among Central American travelers. The reasons are clear: In capital cities, traffic is bad and car theft is rampant (look for guarded parking lots or hotels with lots); in rural areas, roads are often unpaved, muddy, and dotted with pot-holes; and often the cost of gas is steep. How-ever, with your own wheels you don't have to worry about unreli-able bus schedules and you have a lot more control over your itinerary and the pace of your trip.

Approximately 50 international and local car-rental firms vie for business in San José, at the airport, and in several of the larger towns. In San José most agencies are along the Paseo Colón. Decide which type of vehicle you want to rent: a *doble-tracción* (four-wheel-drive) vehicle is often essential to reach the more remote parts of Costa Rica, espe-cially during the rainy season. They can cost roughly twice as much as an economy car and should be booked well in advance. Most desti-nations are easily reached with a standard vehicle.

CUTTING COSTS

A recent proliferation of companies has led to competitive pricing in Costa Rica. **Look for discount coupons in the tourist papers** (and ads for rentals of privately-owned vehicles as well) and call around for prices.

To get the best deal, **book through a travel agent who is willing to shop around.** Ask your agent to **look for fly-drive packages,** which also save you money, and **ask if local taxes are included** in the rental or fly-drive price. These can be as high as 20% in some destina-tions. Don't forget to find out about required deposits, cancellation penalties, drop-off charges, and the cost of any required insurance coverage.

Also **ask your travel agent about a com-pany's customer-service record.** How has it responded to late plane arrivals and vehicle mishaps? Are there often lines at the rental counter, and—if you're traveling during a holiday period—does a confirmed reservation guarantee you a car?

Always **find out what equipment is standard** at your destination before specifying what you want; automatic transmission and air-conditioning are usually optional—and very expensive.

INSURANCE

When driving a rented car, you are generally responsible for any damage to or loss of the rental vehicle, as well as any property damage or personal injury that you cause. Before you rent, **see what coverage you already have** under the terms of your personal auto insurance policy and credit cards.

If you do not have auto insurance or an um-brella insurance policy that covers damage to third parties, purchas-ing CDW or LDW is highly recommended.

LICENSE REQUIREMENTS

All rental companies will accept your driver's license, as long as it is valid for the entire time you want to rent the car. You will also need a valid passport and credit card.

PARKING

Car theft is rife in Costa Rica and Panama, and at night it is foolish to leave your car in an unguarded parking place. It is one of the idiosyncrasies of insur-ance here that if you do otherwise, you may well be liable to pay for the car. Most hotels, except for the least expensive, therefore offer secure parking with a guard or locked gates.

RULES OF THE ROAD

There are plenty of would-be Mario An-drettis on Costa Rican and Panamanian high-ways; watch out for hare-brained passing on blind corners, tailgat-ing, and failures to signal. Watch out, too, for two-lane roads that feed into one-lane bridges with specified rights of way.

SURCHARGES

Before you pick up a car in one city and leave it in another, **ask about drop-off charges or one-way service fees,** which can be substantial. Note, too, that some rental agencies charge extra if you return the car before the time specified on your contract. To avoid a hefty refueling fee, **fill the tank just before you turn in the car**—but be aware that gas stations near the rental outlet may overcharge.

CHILDREN & TRAVEL

When traveling with children, **plan ahead** and **involve your youngsters** as you outline your trip. When packing, **include a supply of things to keep them busy** en route (☞ Children & Travel *in* Important Contacts A to Z). On sightseeing days, try to **schedule activities of special interest to your children**, like a trip to a zoo or a playground. If you **plan your itinerary around seasonal festivals**, you'll never lack for things to do. In addition, **check local newspapers for special events** mounted by public libraries, museums, and parks.

BABY-SITTING

For recommended local sitters, **check with your hotel desk.**

DRIVING

If you are renting a car, don't forget to **arrange for a car seat when you reserve.** Sometimes they're free.

FLYING

Always **ask about discounted children's fares.** On international flights, infants under 2 not occupying a seat generally travel free or for 10% of the accompanying adult's fare; the fare for children ages 2–11 is usually half to two-thirds of the adult fare. On domestic flights, children under 2 not occupying a seat travel free, and older children are charged at the lowest applicable adult rate.

BAGGAGE➤ In general, the adult baggage allowance applies to children paying half or more of the adult fare. If you are traveling with an infant, **ask about carry-on allowances** before departure. In general, for infants charged 10% of the adult fare you are allowed one carry-on bag and a collapsible stroller; you may be limited to less if the flight is full.

SAFETY SEATS➤ According to the FAA, it's a good idea to **use safety seats aloft** for children weighing less than 40 pounds. Airline policies vary. U.S. carriers allow FAA-approved models but usually require that you buy a ticket, even if your child would otherwise ride free, since the seats must be strapped into regular seats. Foreign carriers may not allow infant seats, may charge a child rather than an infant fare for their use, or may require you to hold your baby during takeoff and landing—defeating the seat's purpose.

FACILITIES➤ When making your reservation, **request children's meals or freestanding bassinets** if you need them; the latter are available only to those seated at the bulkhead, where there's enough legroom. If you don't need a bassinet, **think twice before requesting bulkhead seats**—the only storage space for in-flight necessities is in inconveniently distant overhead bins.

LODGING

Most hotels allow children under a certain age to stay in their parents' room at no extra charge; others charge them as extra adults. Be sure to **ask about the cutoff age.**

CRUISES

To get the best deal on a cruise, **consult a cruise-only travel agency.**

CUSTOMS & DUTIES

IN COSTA RICA

Visitors entering Costa Rica may bring in 500 milligrams of tobacco, 3 liters of wine or spirits, 2 kilos of sweets and chocolates, and the equivalent of $100 worth of merchandise. Two cameras, six rolls of film, binoculars, and electrical items for personal use only are also allowed. Customs officials at the international airport rarely even examine tourists' luggage. If you enter by land, however, customs officials will probably look through your bags.

IN PANAMA

Visitors entering Panama may bring in 500 cigarettes, 3 liters of wine or spirits, two cameras, and personal electronic equipment. Just as in Costa Rica, luggage revision is a rare occurrence with airport arrivals, but standard procedure at land crossings.

IN THE U.S.

You may bring home $400 worth of foreign goods duty-free if you've been out of the country for at least 48 hours and haven't already used the $400 allowance, or any part of it, in the past 30 days.

Travelers 21 or older may bring back 1 liter of alcohol duty-free, provided the beverage laws of the state through which they reenter the United States allow it. In addition, regardless of their age, they are allowed 100 non-Cuban cigars and 200 cigarettes. Antiques and works of art more than 100 years old are duty-free.

Duty-free, travelers may mail packages valued at up to $200 to themselves and up to $100 to others, with a limit of one parcel per addressee per day (and no alcohol or tobacco products or perfume valued at more than $5); on the outside, the package should be labeled as being either for personal use or an unsolicited gift, and a list of its contents and their retail value should be attached. Mailed items do not affect your duty-free allowance on your return.

IN CANADA

If you've been out of Canada for at least seven days, you may bring in C$500 worth of goods duty-free. If you've been away for fewer than seven days but for more than 48 hours, the duty-free allowance drops to C$200; if your trip lasts between 24 and 48 hours, the allowance is C$50. You cannot pool allowances with family members. Goods claimed under the C$500 exemption may follow you by mail; those claimed under the lesser exemptions must accompany you.

Alcohol and tobacco products may be included in the seven-day and 48-hour exemptions but not in the 24-hour exemption. If you meet the age requirements of the province or territory through which you reenter Canada, you may bring in, duty-free, 1.14 liters (40 imperial ounces) of wine or liquor or 24 12-ounce cans or bottles of beer or ale. If you are 16 or older, you may bring in, duty-free, 200 cigarettes, 50 cigars or cigarillos, and 400 tobacco sticks or 400 grams of manufactured tobacco. Alcohol and tobacco must accompany you on your return.

An unlimited number of gifts with a value of up to C$60 each may be mailed to Canada duty-free. These do not affect your duty-free allowance on your return. Label the package "Unsolicited Gift—Value Under $60." Alcohol and tobacco are excluded.

IN THE U.K.

From countries outside the EU, including Costa Rica and Panama, you may import, duty-free, 200 cigarettes, 100 cigarillos, 50 cigars, or 250 grams of tobacco; 1 liter of spirits or 2 liters of fortified or sparkling wine or liqueurs; 2 liters of still table wine; 60 milliliters of perfume; 250 milliliters of toilet water; plus £136 worth of other goods, including gifts and souvenirs.

D

DINING

Costa Rica and Panama are veritable gardens of fresh vegetables and fruit, which means that most cooking is tasty regardless of the recipe. Just don't expect anything spicy, since Costa Rican fare tends to be mild. Typical Costa Rican food is available from the ubiquitous and inexpensive sodas (small cafés). In San José, a string of higher-priced restaurants serve an international smorgasbord of recipes—Italian, French, German, Japanese, Chinese, Korean, you name it. Inexpensive Panamanian food is served in open-air restaurants and food stalls in most cities, where you will also find plenty of Chinese restaurants. Panama City has an even greater selection of international restaurants than San José, as well as an abundance of cafeterias. Normal eating hours in both countries are noon–3 and 7–10.

The typical Costa Rican main course is casado—a plate of rice, black beans, shredded raw cabbage and tomato salad, meat or egg, and sometimes *plátanos* (fried plantains), which is served in most sodas and small restaurants. The national breakfast dish is *gallo pinto*—fried rice and beans, usually served with a fried or scrambled egg, sour cream, and tortillas. Panamanians tend to eat eggs or meat for breakfast, often served with a deep-fried, unleavened bread called *ojaldre*. Maize is a popular staple in both countries, especially for snacks: Options include *guiso de maíz* (corn stew), empanadas (corn turnovers filled with beans, cheese, potatoes, and meat), *gallos* (meat, beans, or cheese in a sandwich of tortillas or maize pancakes), and *elote*, corn on the cob, served *asado* (roasted) or *cocinado* (boiled). Delicious ceviche consists of raw sea bass cured in lime juice with onions and coriander; the acid in the lime juice actually cooks the fish. In Costa Rica, chicken is often roasted using coffee wood; the Panamanians tend to eat chicken *guisado*, served in a red sauce, or in a soup called *sancocho*.

You can find good quality *lomito* (beef tenderloin) at amazingly low prices in both countries. Fried plátanos, *yuca* (cassava), and boiled *pejibaye* (palm fruit that tastes like a cross between avocado, chestnut, and pumpkin) are also popular and often eaten on their own. Common fruits are mango, papaya, *piña* (pineapple), and the ubiquitous banana. Lesser-known and therefore more exciting options include the *marañon* (the orange fruit of the cashew tree), *granadilla* (passion fruit), *guanabana* (soursop), *mamón chino* (similar to a litchi with a spiky red skin), and *carambola* (star fruit). You can get many of these in the form of delicious juices, called *refrescos,* made with either water or milk. Recommended desserts include *tres leches,* a Nicaraguan specialty made of treacle sponge and three kinds of milk; *arroz con leche,* rice pudding; *queque seco* (dry cake), like pound cake; and *flan de coco,* a sweet coconut flan.

DISABILITIES & ACCESSIBILITY

Accessibility in Costa Rica and Panama is extremely limited. Wheelchair ramps are practically nonexistent, and outside major cities, roads are unpaved, making wheelchair travel difficult. Exploring most of the area's attractions involves walking down cobblestone streets and, sometimes, steep trails and muddy paths, though there are some attractions that require little or no walking. Buses are not equipped to carry wheelchairs, so wheelchair users should hire a van to get about and have someone with them to help out. There is a growing awareness of the needs of people with disabilities, and some hotels and attractions in Costa Rica have made the necessary provisions.

When discussing accessibility with an operator or reservationist, **ask hard questions.** Are there any stairs, inside *or* out? Are there grab bars next to the toilet *and* in the shower/tub? How wide is the doorway to the room? To the bathroom? For the most extensive facilities, meeting the latest legal specifications, **opt for newer accommodations,** which more often have been designed with access in mind. Older properties or ships must usually be retrofitted and may offer more limited facilities as a result. Be sure to **discuss your needs before booking.**

DISCOUNTS & DEALS

You shouldn't have to pay for a discount. In fact, you may already be eligible for all kinds of savings. Here are some time-honored strategies for getting the best deal.

LOOK IN YOUR WALLET

When you **use your credit card to make travel purchases,** you may get free travel-accident insurance, collision damage insurance, medical or legal assistance, depending on the card and bank that issued it. Visa and MasterCard provide one or more of these services, so **get a copy of your card's travel benefits.** If you are a member of the AAA or an oil-company-sponsored road-assistance plan, always **ask hotel or car-rental reservationists for auto-club discounts.** Some clubs

THE GOLD GUIDE / SMART TRAVEL TIPS

offer additional discounts on tours, cruises, or admission to attractions. And don't forget that auto-club membership entitles you to free maps and trip-planning services.

SENIOR CITIZENS & STUDENTS

As a senior-citizen traveler, you may be eligible for special rates, but you should mention your senior-citizen status up front. If you're a student or under 26 you can also get discounts, especially if you have an official ID card (☞ Senior-Citizen Discounts *and* Students on the Road, *below*).

DIAL FOR DOLLARS

To save money, **look into "1-800" discount reservations services,** which often have lower rates. These services use their buying power to get a better price on hotels, airline tickets, and sometimes even car rentals. When booking a room, always **call the hotel's local toll-free number** (if one is available) rather than the central reservations number—you'll often get a better price. Ask the reservationist about special packages or corporate rates, which are usually available even if you're not traveling on business.

JOIN A CLUB

Discount clubs can be a legitimate source of savings, but you must use the participating hotels and visit the participating attractions in order to realize any benefits. Remember, too, that you have to pay a fee to join, so **determine if you'll save enough to warrant your membership fee.** Before booking with a club, **make sure the hotel or other supplier isn't offering a better deal.**

GET A GUARANTEE

When shopping for the best deal on hotels and car rentals, **look for guaranteed exchange rates,** which protect you against a falling dollar. With your rate locked in, you won't pay more even if the price goes up in the local currency.

E

ECOTOURISM

Ecotourism, green tourism, environmental tourism: these buzzwords and catch phrases have been flying around Costa Rica for well more than a decade. Many of the hundreds of tour companies currently operating in Costa Rica have evolved a high level of environmental awareness in their business practices. **Find out whether or not a tour company you're interested in practices "eco-friendly" policies,** such as hiring and training local people as guides, drivers, managers, and office workers; teaching people as much as possible about the plant and animal life, the geography, and the history they are experiencing; controlling the numbers of people allowed daily onto a given site; restoring watersheds or anything else damaged by trail-building, visitors, or overuse; or discouraging wildlife feeding or any other unnatural or disruptive behavior (i.e. making loud noises to scare birds into flight). All of this can mitigate the effects of intense tourism; and, after all, it is better to have a hundred people walking through a forest than to cut the forest down.

F

FESTIVALS AND SEASONAL EVENTS

National holidays are known as *feriados;* Costa Rica has 15 each year, while Panama has 11. On these days government offices, banks, and post offices are closed, and public transport is restricted. Religious festivals are characterized by colorful processions. Panama's annual carnival celebrations feature some spectacular costumes. The following is a list of feriados in the two countries:

January 1: New Year's Day; Jan 9: Day of the Martyrs (Panama only); March 19: St. Joseph's Day (San José's patron saint—Costa Rica only); Shrove Tuesday: Carnival Tuesday (Panama); Good Friday–Easter Sunday; April 11: Anniversary of Battle of Rivas (Costa Rica); May 1: Labor Day; June 10: Corpus Christi (Costa Rica); June 29: St. Peter and St. Paul (Costa Rica); July 25: Annexation of Guanacaste (Costa Rica); August 2: Virgin of Los Angeles (Costa Rica's patron saint); August 15: Mother's Day (Costa

Rica); September 15: Independence Day (Costa Rica); October 12: Columbus Day (Día de la Raza); November 3: Independence from Colombia (Panama); November 10: Call for Independence (Panama); November 28: Independence from Spain (Panama); December 8: Immaculate Conception; December 25: Christmas.

For festivals peculiar to each region, see the Pleasure and Pastimes section at the beginning of each chapter.

G

GAY AND LESBIAN TRAVEL

While harassment of gays and lesbians is infrequent in Costa Rica and Panama, so are public displays of affection—discretion is advised. As a result of its history of tolerance, Costa Rica has attracted many gays from other Latin American nations and, consequently, has a large gay community. Panama, on the other hand, doesn't have as extensive a gay population, but gays who practice a little discretion should encounter no problems there.

H

HEALTH CONCERNS

Although the Costa Rican and Panamanian food and water supplies are sanitary for the most part, in rural areas there is some risk posed by the contamination of drinking water, fresh fruit, and vegetables by fecal matter, which causes the intestinal ailment known variously as Montezuma's Revenge (traveler's diarrhea), and leptospirosis (another disease borne on contaminated food or water that can be treated by antibiotics if detected early). In remote areas, **avoid ice, uncooked food, and unpasteurized milk and milk products, and drink only water that has been bottled or boiled for at least 20 minutes.** Mild cases of diarrhea may respond to Imodium (known generically as loperamide) or Pepto-Bismol (which is not as strong), both of which can be purchased over the counter; paregoric, another antidiarrheal agent, does not require a doctor's prescription in Costa Rica and Panama. **Drink plenty of purified water or tea**—chamomile is a good folk remedy for diarrhea. **In severe cases, rehydrate yourself with a salt-sugar solution** (½ tsp. salt and 4 tbsp. sugar per quart/liter of water).

According to the Centers for Disease Control (CDC), there is a limited risk of malaria, hepatitis A and B, dengue fever, typhoid fever, and rabies in Central America. Travelers in most urban or easily accessible areas need not worry. However, if you plan to visit remote regions or stay for more than six weeks, check with the CDC's International Travelers Hotline (☞ Important Contacts). In areas with malaria and dengue, both of which are carried by mosquitoes, **take mosquito nets, wear clothing that covers the body, apply repellent containing DEET, and use a spray against flying insects in living and sleeping areas.** Mild repellents, such as those contained in certain skin softeners, are not adequate for the intense levels of mosquito activity that occur in the hot, humid regions of the Atlantic Lowlands. Also, note that perfume, after-shave, and other body lotions and potions can attract mosquitoes. The CDC recommends chloroquine (analen) as an antimalarial agent; no vaccine exists against dengue.

Though dengue and malaria are less of a problem in Panama, the threat of infection exists there as well, especially in the country's western and eastern extremes and along the Atlantic coast. The threat of malaria is the worst during the May to November rainy season.

Children traveling to Central America should have current inoculations against measles, mumps, rubella, and polio.

DIVERS' ALERT

Scuba divers take note: **Do not fly within 24 hours of scuba diving.**

I

INSURANCE

Travel insurance can protect your monetary investment, replace your luggage and its contents, or provide for medical coverage should you fall ill during your trip. Most tour operators, travel agents, and insurance agents sell specialized health-and-accident, flight, trip-cancellation, and luggage insurance as well as comprehensive policies with some or all of these coverages. Comprehensive policies may also reimburse you for delays due to weather—an important consideration if you're traveling during the winter months. Some health-insurance policies do not cover preexisting conditions, but waivers may be available in specific cases. Coverage is sold by the companies listed in Important Contacts A to Z; these companies act as the policy's administrators. The actual insurance is usually underwritten by a well-known name, such as The Travelers or Continental Insurance.

Before you make any purchase, **review your existing health and homeowner's policies** to find out whether they cover expenses incurred while traveling.

BAGGAGE

Airline liability for baggage is limited to $1,250 per person on domestic flights. On international flights, it amounts to $9.07 per pound or $20 per kilogram for checked baggage (roughly $640 per 70-pound bag) and $400 per passenger for unchecked baggage. Insurance for losses exceeding the terms of your airline ticket can

be bought directly from the airline at check-in for about $10 per $1,000 of coverage; note that it excludes a rather extensive list of items, shown on your airline ticket.

COMPREHENSIVE

Comprehensive insurance policies include all the coverages described above plus some that may not be available in more specific policies. If you have purchased an expensive vacation, especially one that involves travel abroad, comprehensive insurance is a must; **look for policies that include trip delay insurance,** which will protect you in the event that weather problems cause you to miss your flight, tour, or cruise. A few insurers will also sell you a waiver for preexisting medical conditions. Some of the companies that offer both these features are Access America, Carefree Travel, Travel Insured International, and TravelGuard (☞ Important Contacts A to Z).

FLIGHT

You should **think twice before buying flight insurance.** Often purchased as a last-minute impulse at the airport, it pays a lump sum when a plane crashes, either to a beneficiary if the insured dies or sometimes to a surviving passenger who loses his or her eyesight or a limb. Supplementing the airlines' coverage described in the limits-of-liability paragraphs on your ticket, it's expensive and basically unnecessary. Charging

an airline ticket to a major credit card often automatically provides you with coverage that may also extend to travel by bus, train, and ship.

HEALTH

Medicare generally does not cover health care costs outside the United States; nor do many privately issued policies. If your own health insurance policy does not cover you outside the United States, **consider buying supplemental medical coverage.** It can reimburse you for $1,000– $150,000 worth of medical and/or dental expenses incurred as a result of an accident or illness during a trip. These policies also may include a personal-accident, or death-and-dismemberment, provision, which pays a lump sum ranging from $15,000 to $500,000 to your beneficiaries if you die or to you if you lose one or more limbs or your eyesight, and a medical-assistance provision, which may either reimburse you for the cost of referrals, evacuation, or repatriation and other services, or automatically enroll you as a member of a particular medical-assistance company. (☞ Health Issues *in* Important Contacts A to Z.)

U.K. TRAVELERS

You can buy an annual travel insurance policy valid for most vacations during the year in which it's purchased. If you are pregnant or have a preexisting medical condition make sure you're covered before buying such a policy.

TRIP

Without insurance, you will lose all or most of your money if you cancel your trip regardless of the reason. Especially if your airline ticket, cruise, or package tour is nonrefundable and cannot be changed, it's essential that you **buy trip-cancellation-and-interruption insurance.** When considering how much coverage you need, look for a policy that will cover the cost of your trip plus the nondiscounted price of a one-way airline ticket should you need to return home early. Read the fine print carefully, especially sections that define "family member" and "preexisting medical conditions." Also **consider default or bankruptcy insurance,** which protects you against a supplier's failure to deliver. Be aware, however, that if you buy such a policy from a travel agency, tour operator, airline, or cruise line, it may not cover default by the firm in question.

L

Spanish is the official language of both Costa Rica and Panama, although some people speak English, especially along the Caribbean coast. Your stay in Central America will be much better if you learn some basic Spanish before you go and bring a phrase book with you. At the very least, attempt to learn the rudiments of polite conversation such as *por favor* (please) and *gracias* (thank you); your effort is sure to be appreciated.

Hotels are going up fast in Costa Rica, to keep pace with the country's growing popularity as a vacation destination. Development is moving more slowly in Panama, which is still a fairly unknown destination. For Costa Rica's popular beach and mountain resorts, Panama City's best hotels, and the Chiriquí highlands, reserve well in advance for the dry season—send a deposit, too, lest you arrive and find your reservation has disappeared.

Luxury international hotels are found mainly in San José and Panama City. Many visitors will prefer the smaller one-of-a-kind hotels in colonial bungalows with verdant courtyards; these are numerous in and around San José. Except for the northwest beaches of Guanacaste's "Gold Coast," where a number of large scale projects have recently been completed or are in the works, lodging in outlying areas is often in *cabinas* (cabins) or *cabañas,* as they are called in Panama— rustic equivalents of U.S. motels (motels here, by the way, are mostly short-stay sex hotels). Cabinas range from very basic huts with few creature comforts to flashier units with all the modern conveniences. In Costa Rica, there are nature lodges (often within private biological reserves) that cater to naturalist vacationers. Though most of these lodges have only rustic accommodations, a few of the newer ones are luxurious.

Some national parks have campsites with facilities (☞ Chapter 2). Camping at the beach is often possible (many beaches offer no other option), but don't leave belongings unattended in your tent.

APARTMENT & VILLA RENTAL

If you want a home base that's roomy enough for a family and comes with cooking facilities, **consider taking a furnished rental.** This can also save you money, but not always—some rentals are luxury properties (economical only when your party is large). Home-exchange directories list rentals— often second homes owned by prospective house swappers—and some services search for a house or apartment for you (even a castle if that's your fancy) and handle the paperwork. Some send an illustrated catalog; others send photographs only of specific properties, sometimes at a charge; up-front registration fees may apply.

HOME EXCHANGE

If you would like to find a house, an apartment, or some other type of vacation property to exchange for your own while on holiday, **become a** member of a home-exchange organization, which will send you its updated listings of available exchanges for a year, and will include your own listing in at least one of them. Arrangements for the actual exchange are made by the two parties involved, not by the organization.

M
MAIL

Mail from the States or Europe can take 2–3 weeks to arrive in Costa Rica or Panama (occasionally it never does); within these countries, mail service is even less reliable. Outgoing mail is marginally quicker, especially when sent from the capitals. Always use airmail for overseas; it might take anywhere from 5 days to two weeks or more—the rates are low. In 1995, letters sent from Costa Rica to the United States and Canada cost just 50 colones; to the United Kingdom, 60 colones. Letters sent from Panama to the United States cost 35¢; to Canada 40¢; to the United Kingdom, 45¢. Mail theft is a chronic problem, so do not mail checks, money, or anything else of value.

You can have mail sent to your hotel or use poste restante at the post office (Lista de Correos). Most Costa Ricans and Panamanians have to go to the post office to pick up their mail, because of the absence of both street names and any house-to-

house service. *Apartado* (abbreviated *apdo.*), which you will see in many addresses, means post office box.

Anyone with an American Express card or traveler's checks can have mail sent to them at the local American Express office.

A faster and more functional alternative for nonpersonal letters, particularly those confirming reservations and the like, is the fax machine, which is nearly ubiquitous in Costa Rica and Panama. If you need to send important documents, checks or other noncash valuables, you can use one of the courier services, such as Federal Express, DHL, or the less expensive airline courier services (☞ Also Wiring Money, *below*).

MEDICAL ASSISTANCE

No one plans to get sick while traveling, but it happens, so **consider signing up with a medical assistance company.** These outfits provide referrals, emergency evacuation or repatriation, 24-hour telephone hot lines for medical consultation, cash for emergencies, and other personal and legal assistance. They also dispatch medical personnel and arrange for the relay of medical records.

MONEY & EXPENSES

The Costa Rican currency is the colón (plural: colones). The exchange rate floats in

relation to the U.S. dollar, with the colón subject to regular, small devaluations; at press time (spring 1996) the colón had topped 200 to the dollar, and was rising. Panama's national currency is the balboa, which has been out of print for decades, since they use the U.S. dollar instead, and simply call it a balboa. The Panamanian government mints its own coins, which are the same size as U.S. coins, and circulate together with their American counterparts. Since the dollar is currency, and traveler's checks are accepted by most businesses, there is little need to go to the bank. Carry lots of $10 and $20 bills; the abundance of counterfeit dollars has caused many businesses to stop accepting $50 and $100 bills.

Major credit cards are accepted at most of the larger hotels and more expensive restaurants. However, most of the low budget hotels, restaurants, and other facilities in Costa Rica and Panama do *not* accept credit cards, and it is essential, especially when traveling away from San José and Panama City, to have enough cash or traveler's checks. Also, some hotels, restaurants, tour companies, and other businesses will give you a 5%–15% discount if you pay cash.

ATMS

CASH ADVANCES➤ Cirrus, Plus, and many other networks that

connect automated teller machines operate internationally. Chances are that you can **use your bank card, Master-Card, or Visa at ATMs** to withdraw money from an account or get a cash advance. Before leaving home, **check on frequency limits** for withdrawals and cash advances. Also **ask whether your card's PIN must be reprogrammed** for use in Costa Rica or Panama. Four-digit numbers are commonly used overseas. Note that Discover is accepted mostly in the United States.

In San José the Banco Popular near the National Theater and the Parque Central has several 24-hour access ATMs which at press time gave cash advances—in colones—on Visa cards utilizing American PINs. Several of these machines are wired into the Plus system as well. Cash advances are also available through the Credomatic office, on Calle Central between Avenidas 3 and 5.

In Panama, the Banco del Istmo, which has branches in Changuinola, David, and Santiago, gives cash advances on Master-Card and Visa.

TRANSACTION FEES➤ On credit-card cash advances you are charged interest from the day you receive the money, whether from a teller or an ATM. Although fees charged for ATM transactions may be higher abroad than at home, Cirrus and Plus exchange rates are excellent, because they are based on wholesale rates offered only by major banks.

EXCHANGING CURRENCY

For the most favorable rates, **change money at banks.** You won't do as well at exchange booths in airports or rail and bus stations, in hotels, in restaurants, or in stores, although you may find their hours more convenient. To avoid lines at airport exchange booths, **get a small amount of the local currency before you leave home.**

TAXES

AIRPORT➤ A $16.50 airport tax is payable on departure from the José Santamaría Airport. Individuals may offer to sell the exit stamp to departing tourists as they climb out of taxis and buses. Look for properly displayed credentials, and make sure you get the appropriate stamp in exchange for your dollars or colones, thereby avoiding a wait in yet another line within the terminal. The Panamanian airport tax is $20, which must be paid at a booth in the international airport.

TRAVELER'S CHECKS

Whether or not to buy traveler's checks depends on where you are headed; **take cash to rural areas and small towns, traveler's checks to cities.** The most widely recognized checks are issued by American Express, Citicorp, Thomas Cook, and Visa. These are sold by major commercial banks for 1%–3% of the checks' face value—it pays to **shop around.** Both American Express and Thomas Cook issue checks that can be countersigned and used by either you or your traveling companion. So you won't be left with excess foreign currency, **buy a few checks in small denominations** to cash toward the end of your trip. Before leaving home, **contact your issuer for information on where to cash your checks** without incurring a transaction fee. Record the numbers of all your checks, and keep this listing in a separate place, crossing off the numbers of checks you have cashed.

Travelers who have an American Express card and money in a U.S. checking account can purchase traveler's checks at the American Express office in San José, or Panama City; there's a 1% service charge.

WIRING MONEY

For a fee of 3%–10%, depending on the amount of the transaction, you can have money sent to you from home through Money-Gram℠ or Western Union (☞ Money Matters *in* Important Contacts A to Z). The transferred funds and the service fee can be charged to a Master-Card or Visa account.

PACKING FOR COSTA RICA & PANAMA

Pack light: Baggage carts are scarce at airports, and luggage restrictions are tight. Bring comfortable, hand-washable clothing. T-shirts and shorts are acceptable near the beach and in heavily touristed areas. Loose-fitting long-sleeve shirts and pants are good in smaller towns (where immodest attire is frowned upon) and to protect your skin from the ferocious sun and mosquitoes. Bring a large hat to block the sun from your face and neck. If you're heading into the mountains pack a light sweater and jacket because the nights and early mornings can be chilly. Sturdy sneakers or hiking boots are essential if you plan to do a lot of sightseeing and hiking. Sandals or other footwear that lets your feet breathe and are good for strolling about town.

Insect repellent, sunscreen, sunglasses, and umbrellas (during the rainy season) are musts. Other handy items—especially if you will be traveling on your own or camping—include toilet paper, facial tissues, a plastic water bottle, and a flashlight (for occasional power outages or use at campsites). Snorkelers should consider bringing their own equipment unless traveling light is a priority, though gear can be rented at most beach resorts. For long-term stays in remote rural areas, *see* Health Concerns, above.

Bring an extra pair of eyeglasses or contact lenses in your carry-on luggage, and if you have a health problem, **pack enough medication** to last the trip or have your doctor write you a prescription using the drug's generic name, because brand names vary from country to country (you'll then need a duplicate prescription from a local doctor). It's important that you **don't put prescription drugs or valuables in luggage to be checked,** for it could go astray. To avoid problems with customs officials, carry medications in the original packaging. Also, don't forget the addresses of offices that handle refunds of lost traveler's checks.

ELECTRICITY

The electrical current in Central America is 110 volts (AC), and plugs are the same as in the United States.

LUGGAGE

Airline baggage allowances depend on the airline, the route, and the class of your ticket; ask in advance. In general, on domestic flights and on international flights between the United States and foreign destinations, you are entitled to check two bags. A third piece may be brought on board, but it must fit easily under the seat in front of you or in the overhead compartment. In the United States, the FAA gives airlines broad latitude regarding carry-on allowances, and they tend to tailor them to different aircraft and operational conditions. Charges for excess, oversize, or overweight pieces vary.

If you are flying between two foreign destinations, note that baggage allowances may be determined not by piece but by weight—generally 88 pounds (40 kilograms) in first class, 66 pounds (30 kilograms) in business class, and 44 pounds (20 kilograms) in economy. If your flight between two cities abroad *connects* with your transatlantic or transpacific flight, the piece method still applies.

SAFEGUARDING YOUR LUGGAGE➤ Before leaving home, **itemize your bags' contents** and their worth, and label them with your name, address, and phone number. (If you use your home address, cover it so that potential thieves can't see it readily.) Inside each bag, **pack a copy of your itinerary.** At check-in, **make sure that each bag is correctly tagged** with the destination airport's three-letter code. If your bags arrive damaged—or fail to arrive at all—file a written report with the airline before leaving the airport.

PASSPORTS & VISAS

If you don't already have one, **get a passport.** It is advisable that you **leave one photocopy of your passport's** data page with someone at home and keep another with you, separated from your passport, while traveling. If you lose your passport, promptly call the nearest embassy or consulate and the local police; having the data page information can speed replacement.

IN THE U.S.

Although U.S. citizens do not need a valid passport to enter Costa Rica for stays of up to 30 days—a valid tourist card is sufficient—we recommend it: for passage from Costa Rica into Panama, for emergencies, for longer stays, and because it is the most recognizable form of identification for changing money, renting hotel rooms, or any other transaction. U.S. citizens with valid passports are allowed to stay in Costa Rica for 90 days, after which they must leave for at least 72 hours. A valid passport is needed to visit Panama, either with a visa issued by a Panamanian embassy or consulate (free of charge) or on a tourist card that can be purchased at the airport or the tourist board office in Paso Canoas (cost $5). In Costa Rica, you can get a visa from the Panamanian Consul on Avenida Central in the San José suburb of San Pedro; you'll need a round-trip ticket and photocopy of the photo page of your passport; drop it off on a weekday morning, and it will be ready the next work day. If you show up at the Sixaola border without a visa, you'll

have to purchase a $10 immigration stamp in Changuinola or Bocas del Toro.

Application forms for both first-time and renewal passports are available at any of the 13 U.S. Passport Agency offices and at some post offices and courthouses. Passports are usually mailed within four weeks; allow five weeks or more in spring and summer.

CANADIANS

You need only a valid passport to enter Costa Rica for stays of up to 90 days. A 30-day visa for Panama can be purchased for $10 U.S. at a Panamanian consulate (☞ In the U.S. *above* for consulate in Costa Rica). Tourist cards, also good for 30 days, can be purchased for $5 at the airport or Paso Canoas. Passport application forms are available at 28 regional passport offices, as well as post offices and travel agencies. Whether for a first or a renewal passport, you must apply in person. Children under 16 may be included on a parent's passport but must have their own to travel alone. Passports are valid for five years and are usually mailed within two to three weeks of application.

U.K. CITIZENS

Citizens of the United Kingdom need only a valid passport to enter Costa Rica for stays of up to 90 days, and to enter Panama for stays of up to 30 days. Applications for new and

renewal passports are available from main post offices and at the passport offices in Belfast, Glasgow, Liverpool, London, Newport, and Peterborough. You may apply in person at all passport offices, or by mail to all except the London office. Children under 16 may travel on an accompanying parent's passport. All passports are valid for 10 years. Allow a month for processing.

S

SENIOR-CITIZEN DISCOUNTS

To qualify for age-related discounts, **mention your senior-citizen status up front** when booking hotel reservations, not when checking out, and before you're seated in restaurants, not when paying the bill. Note that discounts may be limited to certain menus, days, or hours. When renting a car, **ask about promotional car-rental discounts**—they can net even lower costs than your senior-citizen discount.

STUDENTS ON THE ROAD

Central America is a fantastic place for students and youths on a budget. Although prices are on the rise in Costa Rica, it is still possible to travel on $20 a day. There are youth hostels all over Costa Rica, and though Panama lacks hostels, it has its share of inexpensive hotels. For hotels, any option near the bus station is usually a good bet moneywise. One of the cheapest ways to spend the night is camping. As long as you have your own tent, it's easy to set up camp anywhere. (If it looks like you're near someone's home, it's always a good idea to inquire first.) Central America is popular with adventurous backpackers, so you'll have no problem hooking up with other like-minded travelers in major cities or along popular travel routes. To get good tips and advice on traveling within a budget, chat with other backpackers.

To save money, **look into deals available through student-oriented travel agencies.** To qualify, you'll need to have a bona fide student ID card. Members of international student groups are also eligible (☞ Students *in* Important Contacts A to Z).

T

TELEPHONES

The Costa Rican and Panamanian phone systems are very good by Third World standards. Calls within the country are also very cheap, but you will pay more if you use a hotel's phone, and more still from your room. Many hotels now have fax machines. In rural areas, where pay phones don't exist as such, look for the yellow TELÉFONO PÚBLICO signs, indicating phones from which you can make calls for the same rates as pay phones. You will often find them in the village *pulpería* (grocery). No

area codes exist within Costa Rica and Panama. Call 113 for domestic directory inquiries in Costa Rica, 102 in Panama, and 110 for domestic collect calls in Costa Rica. The country code for Costa Rica is 506; the country code for Panama is 507.

LONG-DISTANCE

The *guía telefónica* (phone book) contains numbers for various services as well as rates for calling different countries. To call overseas direct, dial 00, then the country code (1 for the United States and Canada, 44 for Great Britain), the area code, and the number. It is more expensive to phone from your hotel. Calls through the operator are more than twice as expensive, the only advantage being that if the person you need to speak to isn't in, there is no charge even if somebody answers. Discount times for calling the United States and Canada are weekdays 10 PM–7 AM and weekends; for calling the United Kingdom the only discounted time is between Friday at 10 PM and Monday at 7 AM.

U.S. visitors can call home directly through three telecommunications companies from any phone, including pay phones. You can make collect calls or charge it to your credit card. The companies are AT&T (dial 114 from Costa Rica, 109 in Panama), Sprint International (dial 163 in Costa Rica, 115 in

Panama), and MCI (dial 162 in Costa Rica, 108 in Panama). Operators speak English and Spanish. Before you go, however, find out the local access codes for your destinations.

TIPPING

Meal prices range enormously from the sodas to the sophisticated restaurants of San José and Panama City. In Costa Rican restaurants, a 15% tax and 10% service charge is added to the prices on the menu, so additional gratuity is not expected. In Panamanian restaurants, only the 10% tax is added, which means you are expected to leave at least 10% gratuity.

TOUR OPERATORS

A package or tour to Costa Rica can make your vacation less expensive and more hassle-free. Firms that sell tours and packages reserve airline seats, hotel rooms, and rental cars in bulk and pass some of the savings on to you. In addition, the best operators have local representatives available to help you at your destination.

A GOOD DEAL?

The more your package or tour includes, the better you can predict the ultimate cost of your vacation. Make sure you know exactly what is covered, and **beware of hidden costs.** Are taxes, tips, and service charges included? Transfers and baggage handling? Entertainment and excursions? These can add up.

Most packages and tours are rated deluxe, first-class superior, first class, tourist, or budget. The key difference is usually accommodations. Remember, tourist class in the United States might be a comfortable chain hotel, but in Costa Rica you might share a bath and do without hot water. If the package or tour you are considering is priced lower than in your wildest dreams, **be skeptical.** Also, **make sure your travel agent knows the accommodations** and other services. Ask about the hotel's location, room size, beds, and whether it has a pool, room service, or programs for children, if you care about these. Has your agent been there in person or sent others you can contact?

BUYER BEWARE

Each year a number of consumers are stranded or lose their money when operators—even very large ones with excellent reputations— go out of business. To avoid becoming one of them, take the time to **check out the operator**—find out how long the company has been in business and ask several agents about its reputation. Next, **don't book unless the firm has a consumer-protection program.** Members of the USTOA and the NTA are required to set aside funds for the sole purpose of covering your payments and travel arrangements in case of default. Nonmember operators may instead carry insurance; look

for the details in the operator's brochure— and for the name of an underwriter with a solid reputation. Note: When it comes to tour operators, **don't trust escrow accounts.** Although there are laws governing those of charter-flight operators, no governmental body prevents tour operators from raiding the till.

Next, **contact your local Better Business Bureau and the attorney general's offices** in both your own state and the operator's; have any complaints been filed? Finally, **pay with a major credit card.** Then you can cancel payment, provided that you can document your complaint. Always **consider trip-cancellation insurance** (☞ Insurance, *above*).

BIG VS. SMALL➤ Operators that handle several hundred thousand travelers per year can use their purchasing power to give you a good price. Their high volume may also indicate financial stability. But some small companies provide more personalized service; because they tend to specialize, they may also be more knowledgeable about a given area.

USING AN AGENT

Travel agents are excellent resources. In fact, large operators accept bookings made only through travel agents. But it's good to **collect brochures from several agencies** because some agents' suggestions may be skewed by promotional relationships

with tour and package firms that reward them for volume sales. If you have a special interest, **find an agent with expertise in that area;** ASTA can provide leads in the United States. (Don't rely solely on your agent, though; agents may be unaware of small-niche operators, and some special-interest travel companies only sell direct.)

SINGLE TRAVELERS

Prices are usually quoted per person, based on two sharing a room. If traveling solo, you may be required to pay the full double-occupancy rate. Some operators eliminate this surcharge if you agree to be matched up with a roommate of the same sex, even if one is not found by departure time.

TRAVEL GEAR

Travel catalogs specialize in useful items that can **save space when packing** and make life on the road more convenient. Compact alarm clocks, travel irons, travel wallets, and personal-care kits are among the most common items you'll find. They also carry currency converters and foreign-language phrase books. Some catalogs even carry miniature coffeemakers and water purifiers.

W
WHEN TO GO

The most popular time to visit Costa Rica and Panama is during the dry season, which runs from December through

April. From mid-December until early February you have the combined advantages of good weather and lush vegetation. If you want to visit the beach during the rainy season, it is often dry and sunny in the morning and rainy in the afternoon. Much of the region experiences sunnier weather during July and August, whereas the Caribbean coast around Cahuita and Bocas del Toro tends to enjoy a short dry season from around September to late October, when the Pacific slope is being drenched by daily storms. Remember that hotels are much more likely to be booked up during the dry season.

Despite the fact that temperatures in Costa Rica and Panama vary little from season to season, the dry season (December–April) is referred to as *verano* (summer) and the rainy season as *invierno* (winter). The Caribbean coast tends to be more humid than the Pacific, especially during the dry months. During the dry season, Guanacaste is perhaps the hottest region, with temperatures frequently up in the 90s; during the rainy season, mornings are generally warm and sunny and afternoons cool and wet.

To escape the tourist crowds and prices, visit during the rainy season, which has been promoted in recent years as the "Green" season. Green it is. The vegetation is at its lushest and most gorgeous, but some roads—those without asphalt—are washed out. Visit during either July and August, when the storms let up a bit, or during December, when the rains are tapering off, but the high tourist season has yet to kick in. Keep in mind that during the rainiest months—September and October—some rural hotels simply shut down. The majority stay open, however, and not only are reservations are easy to get, even at top establishments, you'll also have the beaches to yourself.

CLIMATE

Central America's climate varies greatly between the lowlands and the mountains. Tropical temperatures generally hover between 70°F and 85°F. The high humidity, however, is the true sweat culprit. Remember to drink plenty of bottled water to avoid dehydration. The following are average daily maximum and minimum temperatures for cities in Costa Rica.

Climate

GOLFITO, COSTA RICA

Jan.	91F	33C	May	91F	33C	Sept.	91F	33C
	72	22		73	23		72	22
Feb.	91F	33C	June	90F	32C	Oct.	90F	32C
	72	22		73	23		72	22
Mar.	91F	33C	July	90F	32C	Nov.	91F	32C
	73	23		72	22		72	22
Apr.	91F	33C	Aug.	90F	32C	Dec.	91F	33C
	73	23		72	22		72	22

Golfito, which lies at sea level, has a climate similar to that of most coastal and lowland towns, such as Panama City, David, Manuel Antonio, Jacó, Puntarenas, and the better part of Guanacaste.

SAN JOSÉ, COSTA RICA

Jan.	75F	24C	May	80F	27C	Sept.	79F	26C
	58	14		62	17		61	16
Feb.	76F	24C	June	79F	26C	Oct.	77F	25C
	58	14		62	17		60	16
Mar.	79F	26C	July	77F	25C	Nov.	77F	25C
	59	15		62	17		60	16
Apr.	79F	26C	Aug.	78F	26C	Dec.	75F	24C
	62	17		61	16		58	14

San José's average temperatures are similar to those of other highland towns, such as Monteverde and Panama's Boquete and Cerro Punta.

1 Destination: Costa Rica and Excursions to Panama

COSTA RICA: A BRIEF HISTORY

T USED TO BE THAT WHEN YOU ASKED Americans and Europeans where Costa Rica was, the reply would invariably be, "Um. It's that island in the Caribbean. Right?" Times have certainly changed. Mention Costa Rica to someone today and most likely they'll conjure up visions of rain forests, tropical beaches, and exotic wildlife. The reason perceptions about Costa Rica have changed is simple: The country has become one of the hottest destinations on the map.

Tucked away in the Central American isthmus, with Nicaragua to the north and Panama to the south, Costa Rica is about the same size as the state of West Virginia. But packed into this small country are a people who are fiercely proud of their history, culture, and achievements. Ticos, as Costa Ricans call themselves, are also an incredibly polite and peaceful people.

Perhaps what makes Ticos so special is their desire to *"quedar bien"*—"to leave a good impression." Or it could be the exuberant friendliness they express so naturally, with a marked willingness to get to know visitors and help them where they can. Whatever the reason, one thing is for sure—it is a rare visitor who does not return home impressed with the Ticos' warmth and hospitality.

As a tourist destination, Costa Rica offers an incredible wealth of sights and sounds to experience. And its unique history provides a colorful backdrop to every place you will see: sun-drenched Pacific beaches, tropical jungles of the Caribbean coast, and the bustling towns of the Central Valley. Visitors are astonished by the cleanliness of the country, its incredible natural beauty and wildlife, and even by the fact that you can drink water straight from the tap.

Although it formed an integral part of the Spanish empire, the country developed along lines very different from Spain's other colonies in the New World, particularly after independence. This can be seen today by the strong sense of national identity—Ticos pride themselves first on being Costa Ricans rather than Central Americans, or even Latin Americans—and by the fact that the country has largely avoided the political turmoil that has beset so much of Latin America, and Central America in particular.

However, it is a fact that the strife and upheavals in the region conjure up a less than rosy picture in the minds of most Americans and Europeans. People not well-acquainted with Costa Rica often equate the problems in countries such as El Salvador and Nicaragua with all of Central America. In the midst of political unrest, Costa Rica has managed to remain an island of stability and peace. The country has no army, for example—it was abolished in 1949. Costa Rica is also Central America's most stable democracy, and the country has a deep-rooted respect for human rights.

When visiting, you'll hear a wide variety of superlative statistics, such as "Costa Rica has more teachers than policemen," and "The only thing that doesn't grow is what you don't plant," among others. They're all true. In education, for example, Costa Rica ranks with many more developed countries (the literacy rate is a very respectable 93%). Its telecommunications system is generally regarded to be one of the best in the world. The country's most striking feature, however, is the remarkable variety of flora, fauna, landscape, and climate within its frontiers. The country's national parks and biological preserves protect a vast array of habitats, covering more than 13% of the national territory, which should ensure the survival of its 850 species of birds, 205 species of mammals, 376 types of reptiles and amphibians, and more than 9,000 different species of flowering plants, among them 1,200 varieties of orchids. That spectacular biological diversity is distributed through an equally impressive array of landscapes, which include cool mountain valleys, steamy mangrove forests, and massive volcanoes topped with lush forests and desolate craters.

The rivers that wind down the country's valleys churn through steep stretches that are popular white-water rafting routes, whereas others end up as languid jungle waterways appropriate for both animal watching and sportfishing. With mile upon mile of varied beaches backdropped by coconut palms and thick forest, the Caribbean and Pacific coasts are ideal for beachcombers and sun worshippers, and when the sun goes down, many beaches are visited by nesting sea turtles. The oceans that hug those coasts hold intricate coral formations, rugged islands, colorful schools of fish, and plentiful waves, which provide the perfect playground for skin divers, anglers, surfers, and sea kayakers.

History: First Encounters with the Old World

In mid-September 1502, on his fourth and last voyage to the New World, Christopher Columbus was sailing along the Caribbean coast of Central America when his ships were caught in a violent tropical storm. Seeking shelter, he found sanctuary in a bay protected by a small island; ashore, he encountered natives of the Carib tribe, wearing heavy gold disks and bird-shaped gold figures, who spoke of great amounts of gold in the area. Sailing further south, Columbus encountered more natives, also wearing pendants and jewelry fashioned in gold—he was convinced that he had discovered a land of great wealth to be claimed for the Spanish empire. The land itself was a vision of lush greenery; popular legend has it that, on the basis of what he saw and encountered, Columbus named the land Costa Rica, the rich coast.

The Spanish Colonial Era

The first Spaniard to attempt conquest of Costa Rica was Diego de Nicuesa in 1506. But he found serious difficulties due to sickness, hunger, and Indian raids. Similar hardships were encountered by other Spaniards who visited the region. The first successful expedition to the country was made by Gil González de Ávila in 1522. Exploring the Pacific coast, he converted more than 6,000 Indians of the Chorotega tribe to Catholicism. A year later he returned to his home port in Panama with the equivalent of $600,000 in gold, but over 1,000 of his men had died on the exhausting journey. Many other Spanish expeditions were undertaken, but all were less than successful, often because of rivalries between various expeditions. By 1560, almost 60 years after its discovery, no permanent Spanish settlement existed in

Costa Rica (this name was then in general use, although it incorporated an area far larger than its present-day boundaries), and the natives had not been subdued.

Costa Rica remained the smallest and poorest of Spain's American colonies, producing little wealth for the empire. It tended to be largely ignored in terms of the Conquest and instead began to receive a wholly different type of settler—hardy, self-sufficient individuals who had to work to maintain themselves. The population stayed at less than 20,000 for centuries (even with considerable growth in the 18th century), and was mainly confined to small, isolated farms in two highland valleys. Intermixing with the native Indians was not a common practice, and the population remained largely European.

By the end of the 18th century, however, Costa Rica had begun to emerge from isolation. Some trade with neighboring Spanish colonies was carried out—in spite of constant harassment by English pirates, both at sea and on land—and the population had begun to expand across the Central Valley.

Seeds of political discord, which were soon to affect the colony, had been planted in Spain when Napoleon defeated and removed King Charles IV in 1808 and installed his brother Joseph on the Spanish throne. Costa Rica pledged support for the old regime, even sending troops to Nicaragua in 1811 to help suppress a rebellion against Spain. By 1821, though, sentiment favoring independence from Spain was prevalent throughout Central America, and Costa Rica supported the declaration of independence issued in Guatemala on September 15 of that year. Costa Rica, though, did not become a fully independent sovereign nation until 1836, after annexation to the Mexican empire and 14 years as part of the United Provinces of Central America.

Foundations of Democracy

The 19th century saw dramatic economic and political changes in Costa Rica. For the major part of that century, the country was ruled by a succession of wealthy families whose grip was partially broken only toward the end of the century. The development of agriculture included the introduction of coffee in the 1820s and bananas in the 1870s, both of which became the country's major sources of foreign exchange.

In 1899 the first free popular election was held, characterized by full freedom of the press, frank debates by rival candidates, an honest tabulation of the vote, and the first peaceful transition of power from a ruling group to the opposition. This event provided the foundation of political stability that Costa Rica enjoys to this day.

During the early 20th century each successive president fostered the growth of democratic liberties and continued to expand the free public school system, started during the presidency of Bernardo Soto in the late 1880s. By the 1940s economic growth was healthy due to agricultural exports, but the clouds of discontent were again gathering. In 1948 the president refused to hand over power after losing the election; the result was a civil uprising by outraged citizens, led by the still revered José Figueres Ferrer. In a few short weeks the rebellion succeeded and an interim government was inaugurated.

New Beginnings

On May 8, 1948, Figueres accepted the position of president of the Founding Junta of the Second Republic of Costa Rica. One of his first acts was to disband the army, creating in its stead a national police force.

Significant changes took place during the 1950s and 1960s, including the introduction of new social welfare policies, greater expansion of the public school system, and greater involvement by the state in economic affairs. The 1970s saw further growth.

Today the new challenge facing Costa Rica is how best to cope with its booming tourism industry, which has already surpassed coffee and banana exports as the country's top moneymaker. Although tourism provides a much needed injection of foreign exchange into the flagging economy, it has yet to be fully decided which direction it should take. The buzzwords now are "ecotourism" and "sustainable development," and with so much in the way of natural beauty to protect, it is hoped that Costa Rica will find it possible to continue down these roads rather

than opt for something akin to the Acapulco or Cancun style of development.

WHAT'S WHERE

Costa Rica can be divided into five distinct territories—San José, the Central Valley, the Atlantic Lowlands, the northwest, and the southwest—each of which possesses its own unique qualities and defining characteristics. San José, for example, is a bustling, cosmopolitan city with a population of more than a million; it is the political, social, historical, and cultural center of the entire country. Each of the four other regions has its own special features as well, from the northwest with its rolling plains to the cool mountains of the Central Valley and the humid jungles of the Atlantic Lowlands.

Panama, on the other hand, is divided here into two regions, each of which makes for an easy excursion from Costa Rica: the Bocas del Toro Archipelago, islands that boast spectacular reefs and a laid-back way of life, and Chiriquí Province, a largely undiscovered area that is home to raging rivers and protected parks.

Costa Rica

San José

The capital of Costa Rica has several good museums, a surprising and varied cultural calendar, and most of the country's best hotels and restaurants. Thanks to its location in a fertile valley ringed by mountains, San José tends to enjoy warm days and cool nights. From almost any location within the city, you can catch a glimpse of the green hills and volcanoes that surround it—home to traditional agricultural communities and natural attractions that can be visited on a variety of day trips.

The Central Valley

The Meseta Central, or Central Valley, is a broad bowl planted with neat rows of coffee, dotted with traditional towns, and surrounded by a ring of stunning volcanoes and mountains. Its altitude of more than 3,000 feet above sea level assures a pleasant mixture of warm days and cool nights, whereas the upper slopes can often become quite cold. The mountains hold some of the valley's great attractions, such as active volcanic craters, luxuriant cloud forests, and hotels and restaurants with unforgettable vistas. Costa Rica's most accessible volcanoes—Poás and Irazú—define the valley's northern edge, and at their bases stand small towns that preserve historical monuments and provincial charm.

The Atlantic Lowlands

Costa Rica's Atlantic Lowlands region is a world apart, separated from the rest of the country by the towering mountains of the Cordillera Central. Spurned until recently by their brethren to the west, the residents of the Atlantic Lowlands have turned in other directions to find commonality: to the north and south, for the Indians of this side of Costa Rica have more in common with the peoples of eastern Panama and Nicaragua than they do with their countrymen to the west; and east, to the Caribbean, for many of the black Costa Ricans of the region claim Jamaica as their ancestral home. Their language partakes of both English and Spanish, with a little spice provided by regional Indian dialects. The lifestyle is slower, more laidback, reflecting the reality of a hot, wet climate, for this is a land dominated by the intense heat of a tropical sun interspersed with frequent bouts of torrential rain. With the exception of the Cordillera Talamanca in the south, the lowlands country is primarily flat, given over to agriculture—there are miles and miles of banana plantations—or otherwise covered by dense, humid jungle. In the national parks in the northeast corner of the Atlantic Lowlands, and in the rain forests on the eastern slopes of the Cordillera Central, you'll find the most biologically diverse ecosystems of Costa Rica.

The Northwest

The country's driest region, the northwest is a land of contrast: dry cattle ranches and lush river deltas, the fierce and barren beauty of active volcanoes counterpointed by the rain-soaked fecundity of the cloud forests. Along the northwest coast lie most of Costa Rica's most popular beaches, made so by the reliably rain-free dry season; the fine weather, balmy water, and beautiful settings have also turned the northwest's beaches into a "Gold Coast"; and so it is here that development of overscale resorts most threatens the country's tranquil way of life and magnificent scenery. But there are still miles and miles of uncrowded beach; the national parks are endowed with an abundance of flora and fauna, and some are remote and little-visited. There are party towns like Montezuma, Coco, and Tamarindo, but it's easy to get away and find a secret place, an uncrowded shore, a mountain trail through a forest full of howler monkeys and raccoonlike coatis. In a sense the region is a microcosm for the whole country, because everything that Costa Rica has to offer, from rain forest to seashore to volcanic peak, can be found here.

The Southwest

The southwest corner of Costa Rica is a wild and varied region, containing diverse ecosystems that range from the cloud forests of the Talamanca Mountains to the lowland rain forests of the Osa Peninsula. Its attractions include two of the country's most popular beach resorts; one of the best botanical gardens in Latin America; several vast, isolated national parks; private biological reserves; and world-class conditions for fishing, hiking, birdwatching, skin diving, white-water rafting, and surfing. These natural wonders are complemented by some of the country's finest accommodations, most of which are surrounded by rain forest and overlook the blue Pacific.

Panama

Bocas del Toro

The islands in the archipelago of Bocas del Toro off the northeast coast of Panama are among the most remote places in the Americas, for since the once-thriving town of Bocas del Toro lost its prominence in the economic life of the country, this isolated region has been forgotten. Recently rediscovered, primarily by European expatriates leaving Costa Rica to renew visas, Bocas del Toro may become another hot spot on the international vagabond circuit because it has much to offer: great beaches ringing jungle-covered islands, friendly indigenous peoples, low priced (admittedly few in number and rather shabby) hotels, and, best of all, an abundance of pristine coral reefs for skin and scuba divers to explore. With much of it protected within the confines of Bastimentos Island National Marine Park, the coral and sea life around the islands adds up to one great diving adventure, for those willing to take the time to get there. And now is the time to go, because it appears that these quiet, neglected little islands may soon be overtaken by tourism. The town is in serious need of a face-lift, and it will probably take tourist dollars to make it happen—but the tourists with the dollars will forever change this charming place.

Chiriquí Province

The Panamanian province of Chiriquí boasts a varied ecology and traditional cultures. The Talamanca Mountains, which stretch out of Costa Rica to the southeast, are largely covered with pristine forest, which is home to everything from jaguars to resplendent quetzals. The mountains' lower slopes and valleys contain affluent agricultural communities and Guaymí Indian villages. The mountain forests are the perfect playground for hikers and birders, and the rivers that flow from them are exciting white-water-rafting routes. But probably the best thing about western Panama is the fact that it is still relatively undiscovered, so you won't have to share its attractions with crowds of tourists.

PLEASURES AND PASTIMES

Archaeological Treasures

Though Costa Rica was never part of the Maya empire, and has nothing to compare with the ruins of Guatemala and Mexico, it was home to some sophisticated cultures prior to the arrival of Christopher Columbus. Those people may never have erected temples to rival those of Tikal and Palenque, but they left behind a treasure trove of gold, jade, ceramics, and stone work, which can be admired at several San José museums. Pre-Colombian Costa Rica was home to some incredibly talented artisans, and thanks to good laws prohibiting the export of their works, museums such as the Jade Museum and the Gold Museum house collections that could be envied by the nations of the former Maya realm. Though the country's most impressive pre-Columbian heritage is found in the museums, there is one noteworthy archaeological site: Guayabo National Monument, a partially excavated city of 20,000 that is surrounded by protected rain forest.

Horseback Riding

Because horses remain one of the most common forms of transportation in Costa Rica, there are opportunities to ride just about everywhere in that country. Experienced equestrians should be pleased with the spirit of the horses in Costa Rica, but even if you can't remember when you were last in the saddle, exploring a bit of the countryside on horseback is recommended. Horses are available for rent at most of the popular beach towns and mountain resorts, and guided trail rides often head to waterfalls, scenic overlooks, and other landmarks that you might otherwise never visit. However, the most interesting places to ride are the many farms and ranches that have been converted to nature lodges, several of which border national parks. There are also dozens of day trips available out of San José, which usually take you up into the mountains for a morning of trail riding followed by a typical Costa Rican lunch.

Nature's Bounty

Costa Rica and Panama possess an almost unfathomable wealth of natural treasures, with more species of plants and animals than scientists have been able to count, and a variety of scenery that ranges from barren mountain peaks to luxuriant lowland forests. Because Costa Rica is such a small country, it is easy to visit many different ecosystems, and see some of the plants and animals that are contained in them, in a short period of time. Costa Rica particularly has made a concerted effort to preserve its natural heritage, and it has paid off: Over 13% of Costa Rica's national territory is under the aegis of the parks system, which contains nearly all of the country's ecosystems. The most pristine of those protected areas lie in remote locations, which can take some time and effort to reach, but whether you hike in, take a four-wheel-drive vehicle, or board a boat or small plane, the trip there is often half the adventure. There are also a growing number of private nature reserves, many of which are just as wild and beautiful as the national parks, and which often offer better facilities and easier access.

Skin Diving

COSTA RICA➤ The options for observing Costa Rica's rich and varied marine life range from simple snorkeling sessions off the beach near your hotel to a full-fledged scuba diving safari. Coastal reefs submerged off the southern Caribbean coast are home to colorful coral gardens and hundreds of species of fish and invertebrates. The country's most extensive reef is protected within Cahuita National Park, but there are several other good diving spots spread between Puerto Viejo and Manzanillo. The Pacific coast has less coral diversity, but more big animals, such as manta rays, sea turtles, and even whale sharks. The northwest is a popular diving area, with dozens of diving spots in sheltered Bahía Culebra (Snake Bay) and around Santa Catalina and Bat Islands, all of which can be visited from the area's beach resorts. The snorkeling is good off such popular beaches as Montezuma and Manuel Antonio, but the best diving spot along the Pacific coast is Caño Island, in the southwest. Even better diving, however, is found at distant Cocos Island, some 530 kilometers (330 miles) southwest of the mainland. Two commercial boats offer 10-day trips to Cocos, which feature three daily dives, and the opportunity to swim with hammerhead sharks, dolphins, and occasional whales.

PANAMA➤ In the Bastimentos Island National Marine Park near the faded colonial town of Bocas del Toro in northeast Panama, the reefs are pristine, the tropical fish are bountiful, and there are at least 25 different kinds of coral to gawk at. Much of the water is shallow, precluding the need for the complications of scuba equipment (although here as in any good diving area a regulator and a set of tanks open up a whole new world), and it is fairly easy to book a ride to the best snorkeling sites—around the two Zapatilla Cays—in a motorized dugout canoe out of Bocas del Toro. There are dive shops and snorkeling equipment available for rent in Bocas, the only town of any size in all the islands, and there were, at press time, only about 50 hotel rooms in town, not one of them priced over $25, and most under $20. The Zapatillas and the other 20 or so minor and 5 major islands in the Archipelago de Bocas del Toro, separating the Bay of Almirante from the Caribbean, are an isolated wonderland, not much frequented by tourists, with indigenous Indian villages on several islands, fantastic bird-watching, and, above all, the diving, with or without scuba gear.

Sportfishing

Anglers have long flocked to Costa Rica, drawn by phenomenal offshore fishing all along its Pacific coast and the abundance of snook and tarpon in the rivers and coastal canals of the northern Caribbean. The Pacific charter fleet is scattered along the ports and beach towns from Playa del Coco, in the northwest, to Zancudo, deep within the Golfo Dulce, making sportfishing possible from almost every resort on the west coast. Those fully equipped boats usually head a few miles out to troll for marlin and sailfish, but they also catch plenty of tuna, dolphin, wahoo, and roosterfish. Though the Pacific fishing is good year round, it drops off a bit during the rainiest months: September through November. The balmy Caribbean offers a more languid type of angling—casting into the murky waters of canals and rivers, where silvery snook and tarpon lurk, waiting to burst into the air when hooked. Several lodges in the northeast specialize in fishing packages. The best months for tarpon are January to August, whereas the snook fishing is best from September to February.

Surfing

Both Costa Rica and Panama's east and west coasts are dotted with innumerable surfing spots, from the radical, experts-only reef break of Salsa Brava near Puerto Viejo on the Atlantic Coast to the mellow waves off the town of Tamarindo in northern Guanacaste. Of appeal to easygoing, noncompetitive, long-board-riding older surfers are the good-for-learning beach and rivermouth breaks of Tamarindo itself, and the more intense beach break in front of the Hotel Las Tortugas at Playa Grande just to the north. You can tell from the small army of grizzled 40- and 50-something California surf veterans paddling about in the Tamarindo surf almost any day during dry season that it's a special place, with waves enough for all. Even if they aren't always perfect—Tamarindo's waves don't generally have the best shape—the beauty of the sea and landscape, the easygoing camaraderie, and the relaxed atmosphere combine to make this beach town a paradise for graying surfers. Or ford the rivermouth (not a problem with a surfboard to paddle); a 45-minute walk up Playa Grande will take you to a more shapely and more radical beach break, where you can find out whether you still have it in you to drop into a steep, fast-breaking, 8-foot wave. There are dozens of other surf spots, ranging from easygoing to radical, or "gnarly," as the surfers would say, up and down both sides of Costa Rica—and in Panama as well.

Volcanoes

Volcanic activity was one of the principal forces in the geological process that created Costa Rica, and volcanoes remain a predominant part of the country's landscape. Those volcanoes range from sleeping giants, such as the extinct Barva Volcano, to hyperactive Arenal, whose perfectly conical form towers over the lake of the same name. The easiest ones to visit are Irazú and Poás, both of which have paved roads leading up to the edges of their craters, each just a 90-minute drive from San José. Irazú's crater bears the scars of an active period that ended three decades ago, whereas the active crater of Poás regularly emits a plume of sulfuric smoke. Volcanoes that can only be ascended on foot or horseback include nearby Barva and Turrialba, and Rincón de la Vieja, in Guanacaste Province. One peak that only lunatics try to ascend is Arenal, the country's most active volcano, which regularly spews lava and incandescent boulders into the air—an incendiary performance that is quite spectacular when viewed by night.

White-Water Rafting

Costa Rica is a rafter's paradise; it is no coincidence that several Olympic kayaking teams include its rivers as part of their winter training schedule. Nevertheless, the warm weather, spectacular river scenery, and the wide variety of runs make it a worthy destination for neophytes as well as experts. The most popular rafting river is the Reventazón, on the Atlantic side of the Cordillera Central, which has an excellent first-time run and many intense Class IV and V rapids. The fastest stretches of the Reventazón are for experts only! The Pacuare, which runs parallel to it, is the most beautiful rafting river in Costa Rica, and surely one of the most beautiful in the world. With its breathtaking mix of rain forest and gorge views, swimmable (water temperature averages about 70°F) stretches between lively Class III and IV rapids, and bird-watching delights, it is a fantastic place to experience white water for the first time. It can be run in one day or, preferably, in two, with a camp-out or lodge stay breaking up the days. There are a couple of lodges and camping areas of varying degrees of rusticity run by rafting companies, and an overnight stay in the Pacuare gorge is highly recommended. Less navigated rivers are the Savegre, near Manuel Antonio; the Sarapiquí (which has nice smooth stretches, ideal for families, as well as some class II and III rapids) in the Northern Zone; and the Corobicí, not far from Lake Arenal in Guanacaste, which is a very mellow, easily floated river enlivened with an abundance of very visible animal life.

Windsurfing

Although there are a limited number of spots (really only one, if you're a serious windsurfer) to practice the sport, windsurfing has reached legendary proportions in Costa Rica. A combination of natural and man-made events have conspired to produce one of the best freshwater windsurfing sites in the Western Hemisphere at Lake Arenal. It was ICE, Costa Rica's national electric agency, that in the 1970s turned tiny Lake Arenal into the large, dammed, electricity-producing reservoir-lake that it is today, and it is nature in the form of trade winds passing from the Atlantic to the Pacific sides of Costa Rica through a conveniently located gap in the Cordillera Central that, coupled with the venturi effect, produce the powerful 20- to 50-mile-an-hour winds that rip across the northwest end of the lake. Surrounded by rolling green hills long ago cleared for cattle pasture, this northern end of Lake Arenal has been compared to such windsurfing meccas as the Columbia River Gorge and Italy's Lake Garda. (The wind is so consistent that a couple of firms are in the running to install wind generators run by windmills to be placed on the hills above the north end of the lake.) And here, if the timing is right, you can watch a volcano erupt while you're tacking across the lake. You'll find serious windsurfers here from December to April, and there are often good, if unpredictable, winds in other months. There's a well-supplied rental shop run by the Hotel Tilawa on the shore, and the launch site is into side-shore wind off a neat little peninsula—an ideal arrangement. Arenal is not a particularly good place to learn the sport, however. The water is exceedingly choppy due to the lake's narrowness, and during the season the wind is just too strong for beginners. While fanatics head straight for Lake Arenal, other good, less demanding windsurfing sites, and some rental equipment, can be found off many of the beaches of northern Guanacaste.

NEW AND NOTEWORTHY

In April 1996 the controversial $15 admission price for foreigners to all Costa Rican national parks, biological reserves, national monuments, and other protected areas was reduced to $6. The government has also made it a priority to repair the roads and signs leading to major tourist destinations.

FODOR'S CHOICE

Archaeological Sites

Costa Rica

★**Guayabo National Monument.** This ancient city, once home to 20,000 inhabitants, was abandoned in the 1400s and not rediscovered until 1968.

Dining

Costa Rica

★**Ambrosia, San José.** Tucked into a small shopping center on the east end of San Pedro, a 15-minute drive from downtown San José, this restaurant has long been popular among local epicureans, thanks to its menu of delicious culinary inventions. $$$

★**Barba Roja, Manuel Antonio.** The panoramic setting, chic clientele, and wonderful food at this hilltop restaurant have given it the reputation of being one of Costa Rica's best. $$–$$$

★**Chubascos, Poás Volcano.** Whether you prefer the brisk mountain air, the delicious fresh fruit drinks, the green surroundings, or the platters packed with traditional Costa Rican taste treats, this spot on the road to Poás Volcano offers a winning combination. $$

★**Edith Soda y Restaurant, Cahuita.** Ticos and outsiders alike flock to this restaurant for the outrageous Caribbean menu, which includes a variety of vegetarian dishes and herbal teas that owner Miss Edith claims will remedy whatever ails you. $$

★**San Remo, San José.** This Italian-owned, downtown eatery is a popular lunch spot with residents, thanks to its delicious daily specials and ample portions, but a well-balanced menu makes it a good dinner choice as well. $–$$

Lodging

Costa Rica

★**Hotel La Mariposa, Manuel Antonio.** This elegant, white, Spanish-style villa is high on a promontory with excellent views of both the shoreline and the inland hills. $$$$

★**Lapa Rios, Cabo Matapalo.** Perched on a ridge in a private rain forest reserve, with an unforgettable view of the surrounding jungle and ocean beyond, Lapa Rios is a small luxury hotel that provides close contact with tropical nature without ever skimping on the amenities. $$$$

★**Villa Caletas, Tárcoles.** Each of these exquisite bungalows scattered over a forested promontory seems to enjoy a better view than the rest. Though isolation and natural beauty would seem to be this hotel's strongest points, the architecture, interior decorating, and cuisine are equally impressive. $$$$

★**Grano de Oro, San José.** Built at the turn of the century, this pink, wooden house has been transformed into one of the capital's finest hotels, with interior gardens, a sundeck, and first-class restaurant. $$$–$$$$

★**Fonda Vela, Monteverde.** Spacious rooms crafted using local hardwoods have plenty of windows for enjoying the surrounding forest and distant Gulf of Nicoya, whereas the restaurant not only features great food to match the view, but is also the venue for Monteverde's annual music festival. $$$

★ **Le Bergerac, San José.** The deluxe rooms and large bathrooms at this friendly hotel in a quiet neighborhood have rightfully given it the reputation as one of the city's best. *$$$*

Special Moments

Costa Rica

★ **Arenal Volcano erupting at night.** If you have never seen an active volcano, then this will be a spectacular first—the perfect conical profile dominates the southern end of Lake Arenal, in northwest Costa Rica, where it thrills visitors with regular incendiary performances.

★ **A simian encounter.** Whether you listen to the roar of a howler monkey reverberating through the forest canopy, or come face to face with a playful troop of spider monkeys, it's hard not to be fascinated by the local monkey business.

★ **Turtle watching on the beach.** Several different types of turtles lay eggs on a number of different beaches throughout Costa Rica during the year, but one of the most amazing sights is that of a leatherback the size of a large sofa (or a small car) dragging herself up the beach (the trail she leaves looks like a bulldozer's) to delicately dig a hole and drop her eggs in. Then she will painstakingly refill the hole, covering the eggs with sand, utilizing her flippers with the skill of a surgeon; and then rough up the sandy surface to camouflage it, making it appear as if nothing has occurred.

Finally she lumbers back down the beach and out to sea for another year of roaming—only she will be back next year, riding in on a high tide in the dark, to repeat the act. Watching this miracle occur in the middle of the night on a Costa Rican beach can be a most amazing and moving experience—something you will remember all your life.

Costa Rica/Panama

★ **Navigating a jungle river.** Many Costa Rican and Panamanian rivers are actually excellent routes into the rain forest, and the river trips available range from an invigorating paddle down the Pacuare to the lazy navigation of Costa Rica's Caribbean Canals.

★ **Quetzal spotting in the cloud forest.** One of the New World's most beautiful creatures, the quetzal—with metallic green feathers, a bright crimson stomach, and long tail streamers—is best observed in the forests of San Gerardo de Dota, in the southwest, and Monteverde, in the northwest, and Panama's Chiriquí highlands.

★ **Watching a Pacific sunset.** The suggestion that sunsets are more beautiful on the Pacific coasts of Costa Rica and Panama than in other parts of the world may seem ridiculous, but there is something about the cloud formations, colors, and venues that make them exemplary crepuscular productions.

2 National Parks and Biological Reserves

An in-depth look at Costa Rican and Panamanian protected areas—what you can expect to see, how to get there, and where to stay nearby.

Updated by
David
Dudenhoefer
and Justin
Henderson

BOTH COSTA RICA AND PANAMA POSSESS an almost unfathomable wealth of natural assets. The
breathtaking scenery of the two countries, for ex-
ample, encompasses barren mountain peaks, lush forests, and vibrant,
multihue coral reefs. Equally fantastic is the native wildlife population,
more species of plants and animals than scientists have been able to
count.

Moreover, the governments of both nations have had the foresight to
protect a significant portion of that ecological wealth within national
parks and biological preserves. There are also wildlife refuges, forest
reserves, and Indian reservations where the flora and fauna benefit from
some degree of conservation.

Although the protected areas contain some spectacular scenery and
wildlife, including such endangered species as jaguars, tapirs, and giant
anteaters, don't be disappointed if you don't come face to face with
one of these animals during your visit. Despite their frequent appear-
ances in advertisements and brochures, jaguars, for example, are practically impossible to see in the wild, given their scarcity, shyness, and
nocturnal schedules. Don't give up hope, though: If you take the time
to explore a few protected areas, you should be able to see some monkeys, iguanas, sloths, parrots, toucans, and dozens of other interesting critters.

Travelers are often surprised by how difficult it can be to spot animals
in the rain forest. The low density of mammals combined with the fact
that thick vegetation often obstructs your view, means that you have
to be patient and attentive to see things. River trips can provide some
excellent animal observation, and because the tropical dry forest is less
overgrown, it is one of the best life zones for animal observation.

Costa Rica and Panama have done a remarkable job of conserving part
of their natural heritage, especially when you consider that they are
relatively poor countries with limited resources. Just three decades ago,
there was hardly a protected area in either nation. Today Costa Rica's
parks cover about 13% of the national territory, and Panama's national
parks and reserves cover 17% of their national territory, although the
Panamanian areas tend to be less protected than those in Costa Rica.
Thanks to the foresight of local conservationists, and ample assistance
from abroad, those parks and reserves now contain examples of nearly
all the ecosystems that exist in the region. Natural environments protected within Costa Rica and Panama include mangrove estuaries,
lowland rain forests, tropical dry forests, pristine beaches, coral reefs,
cloud forests, caves, fresh-water swamps and lagoons, active volcanic
craters, transition forests, and various marine ecosystems.

Though the tropical flora and fauna they preserve is nothing short of
spectacular, Panamanian and Costa Rican national parks have very little infrastructure compared with protected areas in northern nations.
Many of the parks require four-wheel drive to reach them, only a few
have paved roads, and some can only be visited by boat, on horseback,
or on foot. Most parks still don't have visitor centers, and trails often
aren't well-marked—but getting in and out of the less accessible protected areas can be half the adventure.

During the first decades of those nations' park systems, conservationists raced against rampant deforestation to protect as much of the country's vital wildlands as possible. Parks were created and maps were
drawn, but protecting the flora and fauna within them turned out to

be a daunting task for the underfunded government agencies responsible for conservation. The Costa Rican National Parks Service and the Panamanian environmental institute, Institute of Renewable Natural Resources (INRENARE), are now concentrating on consolidating management of the parks created during the last three decades and improving their infrastructure. Though most of Panama's parks still receive very few visitors, Costa Rica is facing a new conservation challenge—controlling the crowds of visitors that flock to its most famous protected areas.

In August 1994, Costa Rica's National Parks Service raised the cost of entry for foreign visitors into all national parks, biological reserves, and national monuments from 200 colones to $15 per person per day. That controversial decision infuriated many in the tourism industry, but it has allowed the Parks Service to work toward two important goals: raising the money needed to effectively patrol the parks and improve infrastructure, and decreasing the traffic into some of the more heavily visited parks. In April of 1996, however, the price of admission to the Costa Rican national parks was reduced to $6 regardless of whether tickets were purchased in advance or no. At press time (mid-1996), the Panamanians still weren't charging people to enter their national parks, but that could change at any time.

Admission tickets to the parks are sold at the **National Parks Foundation** on Avenida 15 at Calle 23 in San José (☎ 506/257–2239; ☯ Weekdays 8–4). For specific information on Costa Rican parks call the **Sistemas de Areas de Conservación** (✉ C. 25 between Avdas. 8 and 10, ☎ 506/283–8004) or call the **National Parks toll-free hot line** (☎ 192).

In Panama, **INRENARE** can send written permission to visit a park and can contact a local guide for you, if you fax the main office in Paraíso, outside Panama City (☎ 507/232–4325, FAX 232–4083). They can also inform you if they have instituted entrance fees. It is, however, easiest to simply go to the park; the rangers are happy to help visitors, who are still somewhat scarce.

Some Costa Rican parks, on the other hand, receive so many visitors during the high season that it can be worth your while to head to less popular protected areas, where you'll be treated to a more private and natural experience. In addition to the national parks and preserves, there are a growing number of private nature reserves that are open to the public, many of which have their own lodges. Nearly all tour companies offer trips to the national parks and reserves, although certain ones have more experience in ecological tourism (☞ Tour Operators *in* Important Contacts A to Z *and* Tour Companies *in* individual country chapters).

In Costa Rica and Panama, economic pressures still cause people to cut down trees and hunt endangered animals. Citizens of both those countries are slowly coming to realize that conservation pays, and when you visit one of those parks or reserves, you are sending a positive message to both that government and the marketplace. But your contribution to the protection of the wilderness that you visit can go well beyond the payment of entrance fees. Whether you travel on your own or with a tour group, make sure your visit benefits the people who live near the wilderness areas: use local guides or services, visit local restaurants, and buy local handicrafts or fruits. To ensure that these areas will be preserved for future generations, you can also make donations to local conservation groups; tour operators in each country may be able to make suggestions. A few foreign environmental organizations, including Conservation International, the Nature Conservancy, and the World Wildlife Fund, are also aiding ecological efforts in Costa Rica and Panama.

COSTA RICA

The Central Valley

Since the Central Valley was one of the first parts of Costa Rica to be settled, and is now home to more than half of its burgeoning population, Mother Nature has had to retreat to the region's mountaintops and a few isolated river valleys. Most of the wilderness that remains has been declared protected, so there are several parks that can be easily visited on day trips from San José. The Central Valley parks have good access, with paved, albeit somewhat potholed, roads leading to all of them, and most (all but Guayabo, Tapantí, and the Barva sector of Braulio Carrillo) are accessible for people who can't walk far. Because the floor and lower slopes of the Central Valley are covered with coffee plantations and cities and towns, the region's parks are predominantly high-elevation, cloud forest ecosystems—extremely luxuriant and often shrouded in thick mist.

Braulio Carrillo

This amazing, accessible expanse of pristine wilderness is one of Costa Rica's largest protected areas (110,000 acres). Stretching from the misty mountaintops north of San José to the Atlantic Lowlands, **Braulio Carrillo National Park** protects a series of ecosystems that range from the cloud forests covering the park's upper slopes to the tropical wet forest of the Magsasay sector. The Guápiles Highway, the main route to the Atlantic coast, cuts through one of Braulio's most precipitous areas, passing countless breathtaking views of the rugged landscape. There is a ranger station just after the Zurquí Tunnel, where a short trail loops through the cloud forest. Another trail leads into the forest to the right about 17 kilometers (10 miles) after the tunnel, where it follows the Quebrada González, a stream with a cascade and swimming hole, into the rain forest. The vegetation is beautiful around the highway, and you may see a few of the 350 bird species that inhabit the park. (Although Braulio is home to most of the mammals found in Costa Rica, they tend to avoid the forest near the highway.) There are no camping areas in this part of the park.

Hikers will want to explore the Barva Volcano sector of Braulio Carrillo, with its trail that leads through the cloud forest to two crater lakes. Camping is allowed at the Barva ranger station, which is far from any traffic and thus is a good area to spot birds and animals. Quetzals can be seen in the area during the dry season, which is the only time you'll want to camp there, but it's a good place for a morning hike just about any time of year. Stay on the trail when hiking anywhere in Braulio; it's easy to get lost in the cloud forest, and the rugged terrain makes wandering through the woods very dangerous.

GETTING THERE

By Car. The Guápiles Highway passes the Zurquí and Quebrada González sectors of the park, whereas the Barva sector lies to the north of Heredia. The route to Barva heads north out of Heredia through the communities of Barva, San José de la Montaña, Paso Llano, and Sacramento. At Sacramento the paved road turns to dirt, growing worse as it nears the ranger station. A four-wheel-drive vehicle can make it all the way to the ranger station during the dry season.

By Bus. Buses from San José to Guápiles will drop you off in Braulio Carrillo; they depart every 40 minutes from Calle 12 between Avenidas 7 and 9. Buses from Heredia go to Paso Llano, about 6 kilometers (4 miles) from the park.

Guayabo

Although the ruins here don't compare with those of Guatemala and Mexico, **Guayabo National Monument** is Costa Rica's most significant archaeological site. Most of the original buildings were made of wood, so today only their bases remain. Rangers give guided tours (in Spanish) of the ruins, which include stone roads and a communal well fed by a pre-Columbian aqueduct. On your own, you can hike along a trail that loops through the surrounding rain forest, where you can do some bird-watching. Camping is permitted near the ranger station.

GETTING THERE

By Car. Guayabo sits on the lower slopes of Turrialba Volcano and is most easily reached by taking the old Atlantic Highway to the town of Turrialba, then heading 19 kilometers (12 miles) north to Guayabo.

By Bus. Hourly buses head from San José to Turrialba, where you can hire a cab to Guayabo. There is only one bus a day between Turrialba and Guayabo, which leaves Turrialba at 9:30 AM.

Irazú Volcano

Irazú Volcano National Park protects little more than the summit of Irazú Volcano (11,260 feet), the country's highest. The landscape at the top of the crater is bleak but beautiful, still scarred from the volcano's violent eruptions between 1962 and 1965, when several feet of ash covered the Central Valley. It's best to head up Irazú as early in the morning as possible, before the summit becomes enveloped in clouds, so that you can catch a glimpse of its cream-of-asparagus crater lake and, if you're lucky, views of nearby mountains and of either the distant Pacific or Caribbean. There are no trails or visitor center at the summit, but a paved road leads all the way to the top, past pastoral landscapes that resemble the Alps more than what you'd expect to see in Central America.

GETTING THERE

By Car. Head east from San José on the Inter-American Highway. At the Cartago intersection, veer left, and follow the signs to the summit.

By Bus. An excursion bus departs San José for Irazú every Saturday and Sunday at 8 AM, from Avenida 2, between Calles 1 and 3.

Poás Volcano

A vast and desolate crater dominates **Poás Volcano National Park,** one of the country's most popular and best developed preserves. The park protects the summit of a mildly active volcano, which regularly spews a plume of sulfuric smoke, and the surrounding cloud forest. A paved road leads all the way to the crater, and there are well-maintained trails and an elaborate visitor center. The road that heads off the parking lot ends at a nearby overlook of the active crater, which is usually at least partially hidden by clouds. Two short trails lead into the forest to the right of that road; the first is a nature trail with a series of signs displaying nature poetry, and the second leads to Laguna Botos: an inspiring turquoise lake in an extinct crater surrounded by lush vegetation. The visitor center, near the parking lot, has an extensive exhibit (in Spanish) about volcanoes that includes information about Poás's history and the park's flora and fauna. During the rainy season, it's best to visit Poás as early in the morning as possible. Camping is not permitted.

By Car. Take the Inter-American Highway to the turn-off for Alajuela; head through the center of town, continue north up into the mountains, and turn left at Poasito.

By Bus. An excursion bus departs San José for Poás every Sunday at 8:30 AM from Calle 12 between Avenidas 2 and 4.

Tapantí

The Grande de Orosí River flows through the middle of **Tapantí National Park,** a protected cloud forest that covers the mountain slopes at the southern end of the Orosí Valley. The emerald waters of that boulder-strewn river pour into some brisk but inviting swimming holes near the park's picnic area. There's a modest visitor center by the entrance, and 1½ kilometers (1 mile) up the road is a parking area with trails that head into the woods on both sides of the street. The Sendero Oropéndola trail leads to two loops, one that passes the picnic and swimming areas and another that winds through the forest nearby. The trail across the road does a loop along a forested hillside, and La Pava trail, 2½ kilometers (1½ miles) farther up on the right, leads down a steep hill to the riverbank. Several kilometers farther up the road from La Pava is a view of a long, slender cascade on the far side of the valley. Camping isn't permitted in Tapantí, but it's the perfect destination for a morning swim and a picnic, although it tends to get cloudy and cool in the afternoon.

By Car. Head east on the Inter-American Highway to Cartago. Drive through town, and take the road to Paraíso, turning right when you reach that town's central park. The road into the valley passes through the town of Orosí, after which you'll reach a fork where you veer right to Tapantí. The road is paved all the way into the park, although the last few kilometers have quite a few potholes.

Central Valley Dining and Lodging

Braulio Carrillo is easy to visit on a day trip from San José, or on your way between the Central Valley and the Atlantic Lowlands. It can also be combined with a visit to the **Rain Forest Aerial Tram** (☞ Chapter 5), which has a small restaurant. The **Hotel El Pórtico** (☞ Barva Volcano Dining and Lodging *in* Chapter 4) is the closest lodge to the Barva sector of Braulio Carrillo. Though most of Braulio's wilderness is practically inaccessible, both **La Selva** and **Rara Avis** biological reserves are contiguous with the lower reaches of the park, which means that you can experience the area's biological diversity from those convenient lodges (☞ Rara Avis and La Selva Reserve Dining and Lodging *in* Chapter 5). Guayabo lies very close to the **Turrialba** hotels (☞ Turrialba Dining and Lodging *in* Chapter 5), and there are some simple lodges with restaurants in the community of **Guayabo.** There are neither hotels nor restaurants near Irazú, but since the volcano's summit is just a 90-minute drive from San José, it is usually visited as a morning excursion from the capital. **La Providencia Lodge** (☞ Poás Volcano Dining and Lodging *in* Chapter 4) offers rustic accommodations and a private nature reserve that is contiguous with the forests of Poás Volcano National Park. But since the park lies just over an hour by car from San José, most people visit it as a day trip from the city. The **Río Palomo Lodge** (☞ The Orosí Valley Dining and Lodging *in* Chapter 4) has the closest accommodations to Tapantí and is a good spot to enjoy a meal after a morning in the park.

The Atlantic Lowlands

The parks of the Caribbean slope—with their humid, greenhouselike climate and lush vegetation—are the kind of wilderness one would expect to see upon hearing the word "jungle." In these Atlantic forests live South American species that you won't find in the rest of Costa Rica—poison dart frogs, the crab-eating raccoon, and the great green macaw.

The Atlantic region's most popular protected areas are its coastal parks, where the rain forest meets the beach—in these protected areas you'll find marine wonders as well as the flora and fauna of the jungle. Aside from the surf and sand, the prime natural attractions along the southern Caribbean coast are coral reefs, whereas the northern beaches are famous for the sea turtles that come here by night to lay their eggs in the sand.

The protected areas on the Caribbean side have the added convenience of being close to good dining and lodging; in some cases restaurants and hotels stand just a stone's throw from the park entrance. And the trip there can be an adventure in its own right, since the Atlantic Highway passes through the heart of Braulio Carrillo National Park, and the boat trip up the canals to Tortuguero is one of the best opportunities to see wildlife in Costa Rica.

Cahuita

The 600-acre coral reef that surrounds Cahuita Point is a natural treasure, and **Cahuita National Park** was set up to protect its 35 species of coral and even greater number of sponges and seaweeds, which provide food and refuge for the myriad colorful tropical fish and crustaceans. The reef alone would be ample attraction for visitors; most, however, come for Cahuita's luxuriant coastal forest and idyllic palm-lined beaches, which have stepped, seemingly, straight out of a travel poster.

The 7-kilometer (4-mile) path that winds in and out of the forest along the beach, from the town of Cahuita around the point to Puerto Vargas, offers a good look at the park's coastal and jungle wonders. The hike can be completed in a few hours if you don't stop to swim and enjoy the scenery. The forest and swamps are home to troops of monkeys, kingfishers and herons, sloths, snakes, crabs, and lizards. The beach nearest the town of Cahuita has a regular rip tide, so swim farther into the park, where the beach curves toward the point. This is also a good snorkeling area, although the best diving is off the point. Unfortunately, the park's coral reef is slowly being killed by sediment, run off from deforested areas such as the banana plantations in the nearby Estrella Valley. This process was intensified by the earthquake of 1991, as many riverbank trees in the nearby jungle foothills were downed by the quake, exposing riverbank soil to the erosive effect of tropical deluges, sending trees, soil, leaves, shrubs, and everything else seaward. As of February 1995, local divers were estimating that the reef was 80% dead, but don't despair, there is still good snorkeling to be had. Just use a local guide to find the best reefs, and don't dive for a few days after it rains when the water is sure to be murky.

GETTING THERE

Cahuita National Park starts at the southern edge of Cahuita, which is served by bus from San José; there is also regular service to Puerto Viejo (☞ The Atlantic Lowlands A to Z *in* Chapter 5). Five kilometers (3 miles) south of Cahuita on the left is the road to Puerto Vargas, the ranger station, and the camping area. If you stay in town, you can take a bus or catch a ride into Puerto Vargas and hike back around the point in the course of a day. If you camp at Puerto Vargas, you can also hike south along the beach to Puerto Viejo and bus or taxi it back to the park. Be sure to bring plenty of water, food, and sunscreen on these hikes. At the park entrance in Cahuita there are currently no rangers on duty and no one is collecting the entry fee.

Caño Negro

Caño Negro Wildlife Refuge has a river trip that can be an interesting alternative to the Tortuguero canal trip—Caño Negro is most easily accessed from the Nuevo Arenal/La Fortuna area (☞ Chapter 6). Another lowland rain-forest reserve, Caño Negro has suffered severe deforestation over the years, but most of the Frío River remains lined with trees, so the boat trip up the river to the reserve provides an opportunity to see a variety of wildlife. The lagoon at the heart of the reserve also attracts numerous waterfowl from November to January.

GETTING THERE

By Boat. Boats can be hired for trips to Caño Negro in the town of Los Chiles, near the Nicaraguan border. The larger hotels in the Arenal–La Fortuna area offer day tours to the refuge.

Gandoca-Manzanillo

Although less pristine than Cahuita National Park, **Gandoca-Manzanillo Wildlife Refuge** stretches along the southeastern coast from the town of Manzanillo to the border of Panama, offering plenty of rain forest and many good dive spots. Because of weak laws governing the conservation of refuges and the value of coastal land in the area, Gandoca-Manzanillo has suffered steady environmental degradation over the years and continues to be developed. For now, the easiest way to explore it is by hiking along the coast south of Manzanillo, which also has some good snorkeling offshore. You can hike back out the way you came in, or arrange in Puerto Viejo to have a boat pick you up at Monkey Point (a 3- to 4-hour walk from Manzanillo) or Gandoca (6–8 hours from Manzanillo). Boat trips to dive spots and beaches in the refuge can also be arranged in Puerto Viejo, Punta Uva, and Manzanillo. In Punta Uva, Jake at **Caribbean Adventures** (☎ ⒻⒶⓍ 506/221–3397), 5 kilometers (3 miles) south of Puerto Viejo, offers daily diving excursions, certification dive courses, and kayaking in rivers, lagoons, and surf. For snorkeling trips out of Manzanillo, Javier is a gifted boatman and knows the local reefs as well as anyone. Ask for him at the **Maxi Restaurant** near the end of the road in Manzanillo.

GETTING THERE

By Car. Take the Atlantic Highway to Moín, then the Coastal Highway south to the Puerto Viejo turnoff. Continue through Puerto Viejo and head south via Punta Uva to Manzanillo.

By Bus. There is sporadic bus service to Manzanillo from Puerto Viejo on both local buses and buses coming through Limón to San José.

Juan Castro Blanco

On the upper level of the Atlantic plain, where foothills mark the transition from the coastal lowland to the central mountains, most of the once-jungle-covered land has been cleared for cattle and dairy farming. There are, however, a number of biological preserves here and at least one new national park, **Juan Castro Blanco National Park.** East of Ciudad Quesada (locally known as San Carlos), the 35,232-acre park was created to protect large tracts of virgin forest around the headwaters of the Platanar, Tora, Aguas Zarcas, Tres Amigos, and La Vieja rivers. There are no facilities of any kind in the park at present.

By Bus. The park is near the bustling, hillside market town of Ciudad Quesada (also known as San Carlos) which is served by regular bus service, both local and direct, from San José. By car, follow the main highway northwest out of San Jose, and just past the Alajuela exit turn right at the Naranjo and Ciudad Quesada (or San Carlos) turnoff. You'll wind upward through miles of coffee plantations, with spectacular views of the mountains, and come down the other side to the city of Ciudad Quesada. There are some hair-raising roadside chasms, particularly on the east slope of the mountains, but the road is paved all the way. The drive should take roughly 2½ to 3 hours.

Tortuguero and Barra del Colorado

The Spanish word for turtle is *tortuga,* so it isn't surprising that **Tortuguero National Park** was created to protect the sea turtles that nest by the thousands on its beach. The park comprises a variety of ecosystems, including lowland rain forest, estuaries, and swampy areas covered with *yolillal* palms. The park's palm-lined beach stretches off as far as the eye can see; you can wander there alone, but rip currents make swimming dangerous and there are rumors of sharks as well. This spectacular beach is even more intriguing at night, when four species of endangered sea turtles nest there. If you want to watch them, contact your hotel or the parks office to hire a certified local guide. (You won't be permitted to use a camera on the beach and flashlights must be covered with red plastic, since the lights may deter the turtles from nesting.)

The jungle-lined canals that lead to Tortuguero have been called the Amazon of Costa Rica, and the boat trip up to the park, which leaves from the docks at Moín, is an excellent opportunity to see the area's wildlife, including several species of kingfishers and herons, sloths, monkeys, and crocodiles. Hire a dugout canoe with guide to explore some of the rivers that flow into the canal; these waterways contain less boat traffic and often have more wildlife. You can also continue up the canals to the **Barra del Colorado Wildlife Refuge,** an immense protected area that is connected with the park via a biological corridor. Barra del Colorado is a less-visited area that protects significant expanses of wilderness.

Although there are no roads to Tortuguero, getting there is easy enough—either with a tour (☞ The Atlantic Lowlands A to Z *in* Chapter 5) or by flying or taking a bus to Moín then catching a boat up (☞ The Atlantic Lowlands A to Z *in* Chapter 5). There are fewer boats to Barra del Colorado, but you can also fly there directly from San José. Plenty of companies offer tours there, and all the big hotels provide transportation to the park. It is also possible—albeit expensive—to hire a boat in Puerto Viejo de Sarapiquí to travel the San Juan River to Barra del Colorado or Tortuguero.

Atlantic Lowlands Dining and Lodging

Cahuita, at the northern edge of the park of the same name, offers a variety of dining and lodging options (☞ Cahuita Dining and Lodging *in* Chapter 5). Caño Negro is best explored on a day trip from the Arenal-Fortuna area, which also has plenty of hotels and restaurants (☞ Arenal Dining and Lodging *in* Chapter 6). The **Gandoca-Manzanillo Reserve** actually has some hotels and restaurants within its borders, and there is a wide range of dining and accommodations in the nearby **Puerto Viejo de Limón** area (☞ Puerto Viejo de Limón Dining and Lodging *in* Chapter 5). Use San José as your base from which to visit Juan Castro Blanco or stay in **La Fortuna, Ciudad Quesada,** or at the **El Tucano resort.** Several lodges and *cabinas* (cabins) can be found near **Tortuguero,** north of Tortuguero National Park (☞ Tortuguero Dining and

Lodging *in* Chapter 5). **Costa Rica Expeditions** (☎ 506/257–0766, FAX 257–1665) has its own lodge at the northern border of Tortuguero National Park.

The Northwest

The several parks in the province of Guanacaste protect some of the last remnants of the Mesoamerican tropical dry forest that once covered the Pacific lowlands from Costa Rica to the Mexican state of Chiapas. Because Spanish colonists found the climate on the Pacific slope of the isthmus more hospitable than its humid Atlantic side, most of the development that followed the conquest of Central America took place at the cost of the Pacific forests, and today hardly any wilderness remains on that half of the land bridge. The protected dry forests of Guanacaste are, consequently, of extreme importance to conservationists.

During the rainy season, the tropical dry forest looks very much like the lowland forests in other parts of the country, but as soon as the daily deluges subside in December, the landscape enters a transition: As the dry season progresses, most of the trees drop their foliage and the region resembles a desert. Many trees flower during the dry season, however, and the yellow, white, and pink blossoms of the *tabebuia* add splashes of color to the leafless landscape.

Because of the sparse foliage and partial deforestation, Costa Rica's dry forest parks are some of the best places in the country to see wildlife. Many animals native to North America are common in Guanacaste's protected areas—white-tailed deer, coyotes, magpie jays, diamondback rattlesnakes—but they are also home to predominantly South American animals, such as collared peccaries, armadillos, parrots, and broad-beaked hawks called caracaras.

Perhaps due to the wide-open spaces one encounters in the Northwest, the region's parks tend to lie away from bus routes, which means you're better off visiting most of them in rental cars or on tours. The big tour companies in San José offer trips to northwest parks: **Guanacaste Tours** (☎ 506/666–0306, FAX 666–0307) in Liberia knows the region best; **Horizontes** (☎ 506/222–2022, FAX 255–4513) has the best guides; **Fantasy Tours** (☎ 506/220–0127, FAX 220–0125) offers a boat tour to Palo Verde on Saturday.

Barra Honda

Rocky hills that contain an extensive network of caves dominate **Barra Honda National Park,** an area of protected dry forest farther south. Local guides lower spelunkers into the caverns using ropes and a climber's ladder—a descent into darkness that is not for the fainthearted but is rewarding for the adventurous. If you're not up for the drop, you can trek into the forest-covered hills, which are full of wildlife and where scenic overlooks offer views of the Gulf of Nicoya and surrounding countryside. The Cascada Trail begins near the ranger's office and makes a loop near the caves that should take two or three hours to walk; serious hikers will want to continue on to the Boquete Trail, which, together with the Cascada Trail, takes the better part of a day to hike down and back. A community tourism association provides guides and climbing equipment and runs a simple restaurant and lodge, called **Las Delicias,** by the park entrance. Camping is permitted.

GETTING THERE

By Car. Take the Inter-American Highway northwest from San José and turn left for the Tempisque Ferry. The turnoff to Barra Honda is on the right shortly after you cross the river.

By Bus. There is regular bus service to Nicoya from San José; in Nicoya, take a taxi to Barra Honda.

Guanacaste National Park

Contiguous with Santa Rosa National Park and comprised of a mosaic of ecologically interdependent protected areas, parks, and refuges, this relatively new park (dedicated in 1989) stretches from the Pacific coast across the Inter-American Highway and east to the cloud forests atop Cacao Volcano. Although the park is still in fragments, the ultimate goal is to create a single enormous, Guanacaste Megapark that will accommodate the natural migratory patterns of myriad creatures, from jaguars to tapirs, and birds of all kinds. There are 300 different birds and over 5,000 species of butterflies in the park. Camping is reportedly possible at the biological stations, and there are a couple of very rustic lodges. Call ahead to the **Santa Rosa Park Headquarters** (☎ 506/695–5598) to verify camping and lodge availability.

GETTING THERE

By Bus or Car. Head north on the Inter-American Highway to the entrance of Santa Rosa National Park. Guanacaste Park is administered from the Guanacaste Regional Conservation Unit Headquarters there.

Las Baulas

Another important turtle nesting beach is Playa Grande, protected within Las Baulas Marine National Park, near the resort town of Tamarindo. Las Baulas, dedicated in 1991 and officially made a park in 1995, is visited by thousands of leatherback turtles—the world's largest—every year during the October–March nesting season. The adjacent Tamarindo Wildlife Refuge, although under some developmental pressure, protects a mangrove estuary that is an excellent bird-watching area. Just south of the town of Tamarindo and accessible by dirt road is the San Francisco River, with its own estuary system. Beyond this river lies Playa Langosta, recently added to the protected-areas list but as of yet not nearly as well organized as Las Baulas (meaning the turtle tours are less formal and less expensive). The San Francisco estuary is rich in bird life and (unlike the Tamarindo Wildlife Refuge) free of motorboats. Playa Langosta, like Playa Grande–Las Baulas, is a leatherback turtle nesting site.

GETTING THERE

By Bus. Buses leave San José at 5 and 7:45 AM and 4:15 PM for Peñas Blancas, passing the entrance to Santa Rosa about 5 hours later.

By Car. Las Baulas lies north of Tamarindo, on the other side of an estuary; take the Inter-American Highway north to Liberia and from there head south to Santa Cruz, then west to the coast.

Palo Verde National Park/Lomas Barbudal Biological Reserve

Adjoining Guanacaste National Park, **Palo Verde National Park** and **Lomas Barbudal Biological Reserve** protect some significant expanses of dry forest, and because both areas receive fewer visitors than Santa Rosa, they offer a more natural experience. Palo Verde's major attraction is the swampland, which becomes the temporary home for thousands of migratory birds toward the end of the rainy season. An important part of these lagoons lies near the ranger station, where a raised platform has been built for bird-watchers. From December to March you can spot dozens of species of aquatic birds in the area, including several kinds of herons, ducks, wood storks, and elegant roseate spoonbills.

Palo Verde's forests are home to most of the species you can find in Santa Rosa, and the road that leads to the ranger station from the town of Bagaces passes some wooded patches where you're bound to spot birds and mammals if you drive slowly. There are also trails that head away from the ranger station—one short path into the hills behind it, and a longer one that goes to the river. The road south from Bagaces is long and rough and passes a lot of pasture before it gets to the park. An alternative route between Palo Verde and the Inter-American Highway passes through Lomas Barbudal—meaning it traverses more forest—though it's a longer haul. The ranger station in Lomas Barbudal stands by the Cabuya River, which has a small swimming hole nearby, and the road that crosses the stream becomes a trail that winds around the forested hillside. The road that heads north from Lomas is pretty bad, but it's only 15 kilometers (9 miles) to the highway. Camping is permitted at Palo Verde.

GETTING THERE

By Boat. During the nesting season, another option is to hire a motorboat to take you up into Palo Verde. This way you'll get a closer look at **Bird Island,** home to thousands of birds from January to March. Boats are available on the west bank of the Tempisque River, to the right of the ferry dock as you disembark. The trip takes roughly 45–60 minutes. The price is negotiable but will probably be high, in the range of 10,000 colones ($55). However, along with spotting the birds on the island, you may see alligators, howler monkeys, and other wildlife on the way. Bring something soft to put on your plank seat and something waterproof to wear—these are small fishing boats, not tour boats, and the river ride can be windy, bumpy, and wet.

By Car. Both Palo Verde and Lomas Barbudal are best reached by car. The road to Palo Verde heads south off the Inter-American Highway at Bagaces. The turnoff from the Inter-American Highway to Lomas Barbudal is about 15 kilometers (9 miles) south of Liberia.

Rincón de la Vieja

Rincón de la Vieja National Park was created to protect the upper slopes of the volcano of the same name, with forests that stay greener than those in the drier lowland and a series of steam geysers, bubbling mud pots, hot springs, and several cascades. This extensive protected area has entrances at Hacienda Santa María and Las Pailas. There's a camping area by the old farmhouse of Santa María, and a 2-kilometer (1¼-mile) hike away is Bosque Encantado, where the Zopilote River pours over a cascade in the forest, forming an enticing pool. Three kilometers (2 miles) farther is a hot sulfur spring that is a popular spot for a dip, and 4 kilometers (2½ miles) beyond that are boiling mud pots and fumaroles in an area called Las Pailas. Respect the fences, and don't get too close to the mud pots; their edges are brittle, and several people have slipped in and been severely burned. The trail to the summit of the volcano heads into the forest above Las Pailas, but it's a trip for serious hikers, best done in the dry season (and by those prepared for cold weather at the top). The nearby **Rincón de la Vieja Mountain Lodge** (☞ Rincón de la Vieja Dining and Lodging *in* Chapter 6) offers horseback tours of the park. The lodge has its own network of trails that lead to the park's trails, and it has turned a sulphur spring along one path into a lovely rock-lined, hot-water bathing pool.

A less strenuous (and less expensive) option for visiting the park is to buy a ticket (1,600 colones) good for access to a 3-kilometer (2-mile) loop where you will see fumaroles, a *volcancito* (baby volcano), and Las Pailas, a series of bubbling mud pots. Along the trail you might also see armadillos, howler monkeys, and semidomesticated, raccoonlike coatis looking for handouts (which you should ignore: a cardinal rule of wildlife encounters is not to feed the animals).

By Car. Take the Inter-American Highway northwest from San José to Liberia and drive through town to the dirt road that leads to the Santa María sector of the park. The road to the Las Pailas sector and the Rincón de la Vieja Mountain Lodge heads east from the Inter-American Highway just a few kilometers north of Liberia. A four-wheel-drive vehicle is recommended, though not essential, for either of these bone-rattling 1- to 1½-hour rides.

Santa Rosa

Santa Rosa National Park combines a variety of attractions, which makes it one of the country's most impressive protected areas. The dry forest that covers much of the park draws biologists and nature lovers, and whereas one of the park's beaches (Nancite) is a vital nesting area for the olive ridley sea turtle, the beach next to it (Naranjo) is well-known among the surfing cognoscenti for its world-class waves.

The forested slopes of Orosí Volcano, which are protected within Guanacaste National Park, can be seen from the Inter-American Highway as you approach the entrance to Santa Rosa. A couple of kilometers after you enter Santa Rosa, there is a scenic overlook on the right that offers the first good look at the park's dry forest. La Casona, an old farmhouse and former battle site, houses a small museum that includes exhibits about the battle between ill-equipped Costa Ricans and American mercenary William Walker and the area's ecology. A small nature trail loops through the woods near La Casona, and there is a large camping area nearby. The road that passes the campground heads to Playa Naranjo, a spectacular, pristine beach with great animal-watching and surfing. There is a camping area at Playa Naranjo, but no potable water, and it can only be reached in a four-wheel-drive vehicle or by taking a 12-kilometer (7-mile) hike from La Casona. Be aware that Santa Rosa's campgrounds sometimes fill up during the dry season, especially during the first week of January and Holy Week (Palm Sunday–Easter Sunday).

If you don't have time to go to Playa Naranjo, there are two good animal-watching trails that head off the road before it becomes too steep for anything but four-wheel-drive vehicles. The Patos Trail, on the left a few kilometers after the campgrounds, heads through the forest past a water hole and several scenic overlooks. A kilometer farther down the road on the right is a short trail that leads to an overlook from which you can see distant Playa Naranjo, and the massive Witch's Rock, which stands offshore.

Nancite, to the north of Naranjo, is an important turtle-nesting beach. The *arribadas*—mass nestings—that Nancite is famous for can also be seen at **Ostional Wildlife Refuge,** near Nosara.

By Car. Take the Inter-American Highway north all the way to Santa Rosa National Park; the park is west of the highway at Km 269.

By Bus. Buses leave San José at 5 and 7:45 AM and 4:15 PM for Peñas Blancas, passing the entrance to Santa Rosa about 5 hours later.

The Northwest Dining and Lodging

Liberia is the most convenient town from which to visit Guanacaste's parks, but nearby beach resorts such as Coco and Ocotal are almost as close and much more comfortable. Ostional Wildlife Refuge lies near Nosara and Carrillo. Barra Honda is close to Nicoya and can be easily visited from Carrillo and Nosara, but there is a small, community-run lodge called **Las Delicias** near the park entrance, which has several simple, comfortable rooms for rent. (There's no phone, so you'll have to show up and see if there's a vacancy.) Las Baulas is easy to visit from Tamarindo and Flamingo, but **Hotel Las Tortugas** is right there, as is the new **Villa Baulas** (☞ Las Baulas Dining and Lodging *in* Chapter 6).

The Southwest

The southwest is a vast and wild region, where the ecosystems range from the reefs off Caño Island to the highland *páramo*—a landscape of shrubs and herbs—of Chirripó peak. There are animals in this region that you won't see in other parts of the country, such as scarlet macaws and squirrel monkeys, as well as species that are found in other regions but are easier to observe in the southwest's parks. Although it has some of the country's largest expanses of pristine wilderness, it also has a couple of parks that receive more visitors than they probably should.

Carara

The **Carara National Park,** on the road between Puntarenas and Jacó Beach, protects one of the last remnants of a transition zone between the dry forests of the northern Pacific lowlands and the humid forests of the southwest. Its tall trees don't drop their foliage during the dry season, but the sylvan scenery is much less luxuriant than what you'll encounter farther south. Carara is one of two areas in the country where you can see scarlet macaws, which are easiest to spot in the early morning or late afternoon. The Tárcoles River, which defines the park's northern border, is a good place to see crocodiles, and you may also encounter monkeys, coatis, and an array of birds as you explore the reserve's forests.

Unfortunately, Carara's proximity to San José and several resort beaches has made it one of the country's most popular protected areas, which means tour buses of visitors arrive there on a daily basis during the high season. For independent travelers, the presence of tour buses usually means that most of the animals have been frightened deeper into the forest, but if you catch Carara when there are few visitors—very early or late in the day—you can see a lot. The trail that starts near the ranger station makes a loop through the forest that should take an hour to hike. A longer trail, several kilometers to the north, is better for animal-watching, but cars parked at the trail head have been broken into. Camping isn't permitted at Carara.

GETTING THERE

By Bus. Buses from San José to Jacó and Quepos can drop you off at Carara; they leave from the Coca-Cola bus station on an almost hourly basis.

By Car. From San José, take the Inter-American Highway west past the airport to the turnoff for Atenas, la Garita de Alajuela, and the Zoo Ave bird museum. Turn left there, and follow the signs for Jacó. Carara will be on the left immediately after crossing the Tárcoles River.

GUIDED TOURS

Most of the San José travel agents offer tours to Carara as well as **Fantasy Tours** in Jacó.

Chirripó

Surrounding Costa Rica's highest peak, **Chirripó National Park** is a wild and scenic area that is different from what you'll find anywhere else in the country. It is also so remote that there is no easy way in; hikers usually spend one night in San Gerardo de Rivas, which has several inexpensive lodges, and can be reached by bus from San Isidro. From San Gerardo, it's a grueling climb up to the park—6–10 hours, depending on your physical condition. There is a cabin near the top, so you don't have to pack a tent, but you will need to bring food, a camp stove, a good sleeping bag, and warm clothes. It's best to head out of San Gerardo with the first light of day. You first hike through pastures, then forests, and then the burnt remains of forest fires. Bring plenty of water and snacks along for this demanding trek. You'll want to spend at least two nights at the cabin, since you have to hike up from there to explore the peaks, glacier lakes, and páramo—a highland ecosystem common to the Andes that consists of shrubs and herbaceous plants. Trails lead to the top of Chirripó and the nearby peak of Terbi, both of which have unforgettable views, weather permitting. Camping isn't allowed at Chirripó, and reservations for the cabin must be prepaid at the **parks office** in San José or San Isidro (☎ 506/771–3155). The cabin holds only 40 people; 25 of those spaces can be reserved at the San José office, whereas 15 are assigned by the San Isidro office. Reservations must be made well ahead of time during the dry season. Be prepared for very cold weather on top!

GETTING THERE

By Bus. There are hourly buses from San José to San Isidro, where buses depart for San Gerardo de Rivas at 5 AM and 2 PM.

By Car. Take the Inter-American Highway south to San Isidro (136 kilometers, or 84 miles), where a road heads north to the town of San Gerardo de Rivas (15 kilometers, or 9 miles). You'll have to leave your car there.

Corcovado

An expanse of wilderness covering one-third of the Osa Peninsula, **Corcovado National Park** is among the most impressive and pristine of Costa Rica's protected areas, safeguarding virgin rain forest, deserted beaches, jungle-edged rivers, and a vast, inaccessible swamp. Corcovado is home to all the big animals—boa constrictors, jaguars, anteaters, tapirs—and if you're lucky enough to come face to face with one of those rare creatures in Costa Rica, it is most likely to happen here. You will definitely see flocks of scarlet macaws, troops of spider monkeys, colorful poison dart frogs, toucans, agoutis, and other interesting animals.

The reason that the park's tropical nature has survived intact is because it is remote, meaning that you have to spend either a good bit of money or time and energy to go there. The easiest way to visit the park is on a day trip from one of the lodges in the nearby Drake Bay area, but if you have a backpack and strong legs, you can spend days deep within its wilderness. Only 35 people are allowed to camp at any given ranger station. You have to register and prepay for your time in the park, either in **Puerto Jiménez** (☎ 506/735–5036) or **San José**. There are bunks available at the **Sirena station**, where you can also get meals, but reservations are necessary well ahead of time.

There are several trails into the park, along the beach starting from La Leona or San Pedrillo ranger stations, or through the forest from Los Patos ranger station. Although hiking is always tough in the tropical heat, the forest route is easier than the beach hikes, which can be done only at low tide. The longer hike between San Pedrillo and Sirena can be undertaken only during the dry season, because the rivers become too high to cross during the rainy months. You can hire a boat in Sierpe to take you to San Pedrillo or Drake Bay; from Drake it's a 3-hour hike to San Pedrillo. You can hire a taxi in Puerto Jiménez to take you most of the way to Los Patos, and shared taxis leave every morning at 6:00 for Carate, which is a short hike from La Leona. It's an all-day hike between any two stations, and you'll want at least a day to rest between hikes. There is potable water at every station, but don't drink stream water. Be sure to bring plenty of insect repellent, sun block, rain gear, a pair of good boots, a first-aid kit, and either a mosquito net and sheets, or a tent and sleeping bag. Finally, try to pack light!

GETTING THERE

By Bus. Buses leave San José for Puerto Jiménez from Calle 12 between Avenidas 7 and 9 at 6 AM and noon; the trip takes 8 hours. Buses to Puerto Jiménez, Golfito, and San Vito stop in Palmar Norte, where you can hire a taxi to Sierpe, the port for boats to Drake Bay.

By Car. It's a 7-hour drive from San José to Puerto Jiménez, which lies near the two main Corcovado trailheads. From there it's an hour with four-wheel drive to Carate, and 20 minutes to the Rincón River, which is a 2-hour hike from Los Patos, but you'll have to leave your car at a farm if you want to spend a night in the park. To reach Puerto Jiménez, take the Inter-American Highway south to Piedras Blancas, where you turn right for the rough road into the Osa Peninsula.

By Plane. Since Corcovado lies so far from San José, flying is the best way to get near it, if you can afford to. Two airlines, Sansa and Travelair, fly to Puerto Jiménez and Palmar Sur on a daily basis. From those two airports you can taxi and/or boat to points near the park. You can also charter a plane in Puerto Jiménez to fly you directly to Sirena, in the heart of the park; Alfa Romeo Aerotaxi (☎ 506/735–5178, FAX 735–5112).

GUIDED TOURS

The hotels in the Drake Bay area run regular boat trips to San Pedrillo, and Lapa Rios also offers guided tours to the park, though you can see most of the same wildlife in the forest that surrounds the hotel (☞ Cabo Matapalo Dining and Lodging *in* Chapter 7).

Manuel Antonio

The popularity of **Manuel Antonio National Park** is not surprising when you contemplate its exuberant forests, idyllic beaches, and coral reefs. But the assets of that beautiful patch of wilderness may have made the area too popular for its own good. The road between the town of Quepos and Manuel Antonio is lined with hotels, and when their guests head to the park, its magic wanes. In an attempt to manage the crowd, the parks service only allows 600 visitors to enter per day, which means you might not get in during the afternoon in high season. It is also closed Monday.

Because it is a relatively small, protected area, Manuel Antonio isn't home to a great deal of wildlife, but it is one of only two areas of the country, together with Corcovado, where you can see squirrel monkeys. It is also a good place to see agoutis, sloths, and capuchin monkeys, which have been fed by visitors, and get so close that they sometimes bite people who attempt to pet them. Unfortunately, a tropical storm that hit Manuel Antonio several years ago toppled many of the park's largest trees. There is also plenty to see in the park's coves, which hold submerged rocks, coral formations, and abundant marine life.

The park entrance is on the beach just across a little estuary (don't swim there—it's polluted) from the end of the road. A trail heads through the forest just behind the beach, but you can also walk on the sand. Another trail that does a loop on Punta Catedral, the steep point at the end of the beach, offers a good look at the rain forest and a fantastic view of nearby islands. The second beach, on the other side of the point, is in a deep cove that is safe for swimming and has good snorkeling. From the simple visitor center here, one trail leads to the nearby cove of Puerto Escondido and a lookout point beyond; a second, the Perezoso, heads back through the forest to the park's entrance. Camping is not permitted.

GETTING THERE

By Bus. Express buses depart San José from the Coca Cola bus station at 6 AM, noon, and 6 PM.

By Car. From San José, take the Inter-American Highway west past the airport to the turnoff for Atenas and the Zoo Ave (Bird Zoo). Turn left there, and follow the signs for Jacó, continuing south along the coastal highway to Quepos, from where it's a 15-minute drive south to the park.

By Plane. Sansa and Travelair have daily flights from San José to Quepos, 15 minutes by taxi from Manuel Antonio.

GUIDED TOURS

Most of the companies in San José offer tours to Manuel Antonio.

Southwest Dining and Lodging

Carara is on the east side of the coastal highway, 20 minutes north of Jacó (☞ Tárcoles Dining and Lodging *in* Chapter 7) and 30 minutes south of Puntarenas (☞ Puntarenas Dining and Lodging *in* Chapter 6). The hotels **Villa Lapas** and **Villa Caletas** are just to the south of the reserve. There are several rustic pensions and inexpensive restaurants in **San Gerardo de Rivas,** but you'll need your own food, stove, and sleeping bag while you're in the park. The nature lodges in **Drake Bay** on the Osa Peninsula (☞ Drake Bay Dining and Lodging *in* Chapter 7) offer day trips to Corcovado that bring you back to a comfortable room in time for a hearty dinner. **Costa Rica Expeditions** (☎ 506/222–0333) has a tent camp, Corcovado Lodge, on the park's southern border. The parks service also provides bunks and basic meals at the **Sirena ranger station,** although space and supplies are limited, and must consequently be reserved ahead of time. Manuel Antonio lies near more lodging and dining options than you'll find anywhere else in the country (☞ Quepos Dining and Lodging *in* Chapter 7).

PANAMA

Panama's national park system protects an array of ecosystems as impressive as Costa Rica's, but since Panamanian tourism lags far behind that of its neighbor nation, the country's parks tend to have rather limited infrastructure. The good thing is that you don't have to share Panama's protected areas with the kinds of crowds that sometimes descend on Costa Rican parks. At press time, there were no admission fees for Panamanian parks, but that could change at any time. The country's parks are managed by the Renewable Resources Institute, **INRENARE** (☎ 507/232–4325, ℻ 232–4083) which is based in Paraíso, near Panama City.

Chiriquí Province

The Talamanca Mountain Range extends from eastern Costa Rica into western Panama, and much of that massive cordillera is protected within a series of parks and reserves that together form the Amistad Biosphere Reserve. Although most of the biosphere reserve covers the mountain range's Atlantic slope, its most accessible areas are found on the Pacific side, and several of those are in the mountains of western Panama. The trails and roads that wind into the mountains of Chiriquí, Panama's southwest province, not only pass unforgettable panoramas, they lead to luxuriant cloud forests inhabited by quetzals, toucans, tiny venomous toads, and other colorful creatures.

La Amistad

The single largest protected area within the Amistad Biosphere Reserve is Panama's **La Amistad National Park,** which covers more than 2,000 square kilometers, extending from cloud forests down to sultry lowland jungles. The name Amistad, which means friendship in Spanish, refers to its role as half of a binational park—it is contiguous with Costa Rica's La Amistad National Park, which is slightly smaller than its Panamanian twin, and more difficult to visit. The ranger station at Las Nubes, in the hills above Cerro Punta, is the park's main entry point. It is a quiet spot at the edge of the forest, with a couple of houses and a grassy area where you can camp. A 2-kilometer (1.2-mile) trail does a loop through the forest near the ranger station, and a second trail heads to a nearby waterfall. The bird-watching is good in the area—you may spot the violet saberwing, emerald toucanet, collared redstart, or, with much luck, the resplendent quetzal. Camping is permitted, and there is sometimes space available in one of the houses, but you should fax a request to spend the night, including your fax number, to the **INRENARE office** (☞ Panama introduction, *above*). Another area of the park can be explored by visiting the private Los Quetzales Reserve, most of which is within the national park. You can hike the reserve's trails accompanied by one of their guides ($3 per hour) or rent one of two cabins in the cloud forest.

GETTING THERE

By Bus. There is regular bus service between David and Cerro Punta, where you can hire a four-wheel-drive taxi to take you to the park entrance.

By Car. La Amistad is a 20-minute drive along a dirt track that heads into the mountains above Cerro Punta (☞ Chiriquí Province *in* Chapter 8). Turn left after the Hotel Cerro Punta, and left at the next intersection, then follow that road to the park; you'll need four-wheel drive to make it all the way there.

GUIDED TOURS

The **Hotel Bambito** (☏ 507/771–4265) can arrange guided tours to the park, either in a Jeep or on horseback. **Los Quetzales** (☏ 507/771–2182) provides guided tours of their sector of the park.

Barú Volcano

Barú Volcano, an 11,450-foot, long-extinct peak, dominates the Chiriquí countryside, inviting hiking and bird-watching enthusiasts to ascend. The upper slopes and summit of that massive volcano are protected within Barú Volcano National Park, which comprises significant patches of cloud forest and a rugged peak. The cloud forest is home to a wealth of bird life, including three-wattled bellbirds and resplendent quetzals, whereas the heights are home for the rare volcano junco. There are two routes to the summit: a foot path that winds up the western slope from near the town of Volcán, and a road (you'll need a four-wheel-drive vehicle for this) that heads up the eastern slope from Boquete. There is also a dirt road through the forest between Cerro Punta and Boquete, along the volcano's northern slope, which makes for a good one-day hike. There are no visitor facilities at the summit, and although camping is allowed, you'll need plenty of water and warm clothes—it freezes regularly up top.

By Bus. Regular bus service connects David to Volcán and Boquete, both of which lie near routes to the summit. Hikers can hire taxis in Volcán to drop them off at the trailhead early in the morning—the Hotel Dos Ríos (☞ Volcán Dining and Lodging *in* Chapter 8) can arrange transportation.

By Car. The lower slopes of Barú Volcano are easy to reach in any car, by driving from David to either Volcán or Boquete. A four-wheel-drive vehicle can make it all the way to the summit from Boquete.

GUIDED TOURS
Since none of the routes to the summit are marked, and the hike takes the better part of a day, it is best to hire a guide. The Dos Ríos Bambito (☞ Bambito Dining and Lodging *in* Chapter 8) and Cerro Punta hotels (☞ Cerro Punta Dining and Lodging *in* Chapter 8) and the **Río Monte** tour company (☎ 507/720–1536) can all arrange hiking trips up Barú. For those who aren't up to making the hike, Río Monte will take you up in a Jeep to watch the sunrise from the summit.

Chiriquí Dining and Lodging
The closest accommodations to La Amistad National Park are found at **Los Quetzales,** although it can easily be visited from the **Hotel Cerro Punta** or the **Hotel Bambito** or any of the lodges in **Volcán** (☞ Chiriquí Dining and Lodging *in* Chapter 8). Since Barú Volcano towers over the communities of **Boquete, Volcán,** and **Cerro Punta,** it is practically surrounded by accommodations (☞ Chiriquí Dining and Lodging *in* Chapter 8).

The Bocas del Toro Archipelago

Although most of this isolated province remains covered with jungle, and much of that jungle is protected within national parks, forest reserves, and Indian reservations, the majority of it is barely accessible. Although adventurers with jungle gear and time to spare may want to head back into mountain refuges such as the Palo Seco Forest Reserve, the Teribe Indian Reservation, and the Atlantic sector of La Amistad National Park—Ecotours de Panama (☎ 507/263–3076) can arrange trips into that wilderness—most tourists will have to settle for the region's most accessible protected area, Isla Bastimentos.

Bastimentos Island National Marine Park
Bastimentos Island National Marine Park, on and around Bastimentos Island in the Bocas del Toro province of northeastern Panama, is a pristine jewel of a park, comprised primarily of underwater coral reefs, with nearly two dozen islands of varying sizes thrown in, too. Among the things to do and see there: fantastic diving, as yet unexplored potential for windsurfing and surfing, charming little towns and remote, indigenous Indian villages, wildlife, great birding, and swatches of virgin beach on islands that have rarely seen tourists. Although there are communities on its western and eastern ends, most of Bastimentos Island remains covered with lush forests that are home to ospreys, iguanas, parrots, and tiny poison dart frogs. The long, palm-lined beaches of its northern coast are as beautiful as they are ecologically important, and the calm waters to the south of the island hold some extensive coral reefs. The best area for skin diving within the park, however, is in the waters that surround the Cayos Zapatillas—two atolls to the southeast of Bastimentos. When the ocean is calm, the visibility is quite good around the cayos, where you might see eagle rays, moray eels, dolphins, and colorful tropical fish.

The area seemingly was about to go tourist-mad in early 1996, as Europeans and Americans with fat wallets and well-oiled check-writing pens were roaming the streets of the capitol town of Bocas del Toro looking for people who could sell them land, but for the moment at least, if you hit a week there when the sun is out you will find a snorkeling and scuba diving paradise (it's about an hour by boat from town to the best diving areas in the park), numerous islands to explore, and some funky, falling-down charm (sadly, the town was devastated by the earthquake of 1991 and has never really been rebuilt) in the once-grand, now faded Bocas del Toro. There are dozens of examples of lovely, if earthquake-skewed, turn-of-the-century wooden buildings, a couple of decent restaurants, and an island that sank a few years ago resting a foot under water 300 yards offshore. For more on Bocas del Toro and Bastimentos, and dining and lodging in the area (☞ Chapter 8).

GETTING THERE

By Bus, Boat, and Plane to Bocas del Toro. There's a daily, relatively direct bus from San José to Changuinola in Panama (it only makes a few stops). The $4, one-way, 8-hour trip (there is a daily return bus out of Changuinola as well) includes climbing off the bus to cross the border, via a railroad bridge—converted, with planks, into a road—over the Sixaola River, and then climbing back on. From Sixaola take a bus to Almirante, or find a couple of people to share a cab—it should cost around $20, and take under an hour. From Almirante the water taxis run hourly to Bocas del Toro. For the super-budget-minded, the free "workingman's ferry" runs from Bocas to Almirante every morning, returning to Bocas every evening. There are also buses from Puerto Viejo to Sixaola, where after you've hiked across the border bridge, cabs will take you to Changuinola for a couple of bucks, or all the way to Almirante for $20. In November 1995 the Bocas del Toro Airport reopened after several years, and service will be forthcoming from Changuinola, David, and Panama City.

By Boat from Bocas del Toro to the Bastimentos Island Marine National Park. The only way to get to Bastimentos is by boat, almost always from the town of Bocas del Toro. If you find a boat heading over to the community of Bastimentos, you can usually get a ride for $1, but if you hire one, it may cost $2 or $3 per person. From Bastimentos, it's a 40-minute hike across the island to the first beach; from there it takes almost 4 hours to walk east to Playa Larga, the main turtle-nesting beach. Boats can also be hired to take you directly to the Cayos Zapatillas, but it can be expensive if you don't have people with whom you can split the cost.

GUIDED TOURS

Two dive shops, a yacht, and several local fishermen all offer one-day excursions to the Cayos Zapatillas. The dive shops—**Bocas Dive Shop** (☎ 507/757–9541) and **Turtle Divers** (☎ FAX 507/757–5954) can provide snorkeling and scuba equipment.

Bocas del Toro Dining and Lodging

Bocas del Toro has a decent selection of inns and restaurants, and there are two rustic rooms for rent at the only restaurant in the town of **Bastimentos,** on the western end of the island (☞ Bocas del Toro Archipelago Dining and Lodging *in* Chapter 8).

3 San José

Most visits to Costa Rica begin and end in San José, the capital, which is home to several excellent museums and cultural institutions as well as some of the country's best hotels, restaurants, and nightlife. Since you'll only need a day or two to cover the city, we suggest that you use San José as a base. Head out and explore: Climb the lush, green hills surrounding the city, raft the rivers of the Atlantic Lowlands, and relax on the tropical Pacific coast.

DOWNTOWN SAN JOSÉ IS A BUSY grid-plan city—
population estimates range from 300,000 to more
than a million, depending on how many suburbs

Updated by
David
Dudenhoefer

you include—with a rather untidy pastiche of building styles ranging
from mirrored-glass high-rises to elegant stuccoed bungalows. On one
block you'll find dull, prefabricated office blocks and then, only a street
away, brightly colored terraces of one- and two-story wood and adobe
houses. In the affluent suburbs at the edges, middle-class, bungalow-
dwelling Ticos (as Costa Ricans call themselves) tend their tidy gardens behind high-security metal fencing.

San José's best assets are its location and climate. The city stands in a
broad fertile bowl at an altitude of more than 3,000 feet, bordered to
the west by the jagged Cerros de Escazú and to the north by the twin
volcanoes of Barva and Poás. These green uplands are almost never
out of view; on clear days you can make out the lofty Irazú Volcano
in the east. The climate is excellent, with cool nights and daytime temperatures ranging from 15°C–26°C (59°F–79°F). The rainy season
lasts from May to December, although mornings are often sunny and
brilliantly clear.

The city was founded in 1737 and replaced nearby Cartago as the country's capital in 1823 shortly after independence from Spain. San José
remained relatively small for more than a century, before the coffee and
banana industries caused it to mushroom after World War II. Today,
San José truly dominates national life and nearly one-third of the
country's population lives within its metropolitan area. The national
government, diplomats, industry, and agribusiness have their headquarters here, and all the institutions required of a capital city—good
hospitals, schools, the main university, theaters, restaurants, and night-
clubs—flourish within its limits.

Pleasures and Pastimes

Day Tripping

San José's central location and relative proximity to both the coast and
the mountains means that travelers can see plenty by making day trips
into the surrounding countryside. Also, many of the tours—some of
which head out of the Central Valley—will pick you up and return you
to your San José hotel the same day. One of the most popular of these
trips is the cruise to Tortuga Island, near the tip of the Nicoya Peninsula. This tour begins with an early-morning bus trip to Puntarenas
and continues with a short Pacific cruise, several hours of leisure time
on the island's white-sand beach, and a lunch buffet served in the shade
of palm trees. A shorter but more exhilarating excursion is the sunrise
hot-air balloon ride over the countryside near Grecia, to the northwest
of San José.

Though the Reventazón and Pacuare rivers are on the Atlantic slope,
white-water rafting trips down them almost always leave from the capital. Another Atlantic attraction that can easily be experienced on a
day trip is the Rain Forest Aerial Tram, which carries people through
the treetops of a private biological reserve on the eastern border of Braulio
Carrillo National Park. Near the Pacific coast, the Carara Biological
Reserve can also be visited on day-long trips from San José. Dozens
of companies offer one-day Central Valley horseback tours, most of
which take place on private ranches. Guided tours to the summits of

Poás and Irazú volcanoes are also popular one-day excursions, and the trip up Irazú can easily be combined with visits to the Jardín Lankester botanical gardens or the scenic Orosí Valley. Another popular option is the nighttime tour of Arenal Volcano, which entails leaving San José after lunch and returning near midnight.

Dining

Costa Rican specialties include *arroz con pollo* (chicken with rice), *ensalada de palmito* (heart of palm salad), *sopa negra* (black bean soup), *casados* (plates of rice, beans, fried plantains, salad, cheese, and fish or meat), and *gallo pinto* (rice and black beans). Tico food, however, is often bland, so luckily, the capital is home to a smorgasbord of international restaurants.

Wherever you go, dress is casual. Remember that meals tend to be taken earlier here than in many Latin American countries—few restaurants serve past 10 PM. Also note that 25% is added to all the prices on the menu—15% for tax and 10% for the service. Because the gratuity is included, there is no need to tip, but if service is good, it's nice to add a little money to the obligatory 10%. Caveat: Except for those in hotels, nearly all restaurants close during Holy Week (Palm Sunday to Easter Sunday).

Festivals

The International Arts Festival takes place for two weeks in late March and attracts dancers, theater groups, and musicians from around the world. They perform in dozens of venues throughout the San José area. A dance festival is held in April and May at the Teatro Melico Salazar. There is a carnival parade down Avenida 2 every December 26 and a horse parade December 27. During Semana Universitaria (University Week), beginning about April 20, students at the Universidad de Costa Rica cast off academics to spend the week drinking and dancing. The Día de la Virgen de Los Angeles, which honors Costa Rica's patron saint, is celebrated on August 2 with processions and a huge mass. On the night before, nuns, athletes, families, and friends walk *el romaría,* a 22-kilometer (14-mile) trek down the highway from San José to Cartago.

Lodging

San José offers the full range of accommodations, from luxury to bare necessity. You'll find massive, contemporary, luxury hotels with all the modern conveniences and amenities; historic buildings with more atmosphere but fewer creature comforts; and even smaller, less glamorous establishments. Dozens of former residences in the city's older neighborhoods, especially the Barrio Amón, have been converted to B&Bs, most of which are in the middle to upper price ranges.

EXPLORING SAN JOSÉ

Great Itineraries

San José is home to several interesting museums and other cultural attractions, and serves as a comfortable base for day trips into the surrounding countryside. Popular day trips within the Central Valley include excursions to either Irazú Volcano and Cartago or to Poás Volcano and Alajuela. You may want to explore the Orosí Valley and stop at Jardín Lankester botanical gardens or visit Heredia and the slopes of Barva Volcano. If you are visiting San José during the rainy months, head into the countryside in the morning and return to the city to shop and visit museums during the afternoon. There are also a number of popular one-day tours available out of San José (☞ *See* Day Tripping, *above*).

IF YOU HAVE 3 DAYS

On day one you'll definitely want to explore San José and visit at least one or two of its many museums. The walking tour included in this chapter provides a good introduction to the city and lets you know where the main museums are located. On day two you may want to spend the morning horseback riding in the mountains above town, visiting a butterfly farm, or touring the Britt coffee plantation, saving the afternoon for another museum. On day three you'll no doubt want to head up a volcano, or, if it's cloudy, explore the Orosí Valley.

IF YOU HAVE 5 DAYS

San José really deserves two days' exploration, since it has excellent museums, plentiful shopping, and an enticing enough nightlife to make you want to sleep in. One museum a day is enough for many people, which is why we suggest heading into the countryside during the morning and hitting a museum when you return in the afternoon. On day three you'll definitely want to climb either Poás or Irazú, stopping in at the nearby towns of Alajuela and Cartago. The Orosí Valley is a good destination for day four and should include a morning in Tapantí National Park and an afternoon touring the valley. On day five you may want to take advantage of one of the excursions from San José, whether it be an early morning balloon flight or an all-day rafting trip on the Pacuare River.

IF YOU HAVE 7 DAYS

Spend day one getting acquainted with the city and visit at least one museum. On day two, hit at least one museum and the serpentarium, the zoo, or the butterfly farm. On day three, try a horseback riding trip or coffee plantation tour in the morning and return to San José in the afternoon for a museum or the menagerie. On day four, visit the Orosí Valley. By day five, you'll be ready to head to the top of either Poás or Irazú. Though only hikers can reach the summit of Barva Volcano, anyone can drive along its green slopes and visit historic Heredia. Dedicate day six to a far-flung excursion, either white-water rafting, or the cruise to Tortuga Island. The Guápiles Highway enters Braulio Carrillo National Park (☞ The Atlantic Lowlands *in* Chapter 5), a short drive from San José, and makes for an excellent day trip for day seven.

Downtown and Environs

The Costa Rican capital is laid out on a grid: *avenidas* (avenues) run east and west; *calles* (streets), north and south. Avenidas that are north of the Avenida Central have odd numbers whereas those to the south are even. Avenidas 2 and Central merge in the west and become the Paseo Colón. Calles to the east of Calle Central have odd numbers; those to the west are even. Calle 3 to the north becomes the Guápiles Highway, which wanders off toward the Atlantic coast. Avenidas Central and 2 pour into the Inter-American Highway on the eastern and western ends of the city. Usually Ticos don't use avenue–street descriptions when giving directions but will instead say that a destination is "two blocks north of the *Correos* (Post Office), and two blocks east, next to the Mercedes garage" or else that a destination is "so many feet or yards from a certain church or other landmark."

Downtown San José is surrounded by numerous suburbs including the following: Barrio Amón/Barrio Atoya, which is full of historic buildings that are being transformed into charming hotels; Los Yoses/San Pedro, east of downtown and the home of the University of Costa Rica and numerous bar and restaurants catering to students; and Escazú, in the hills west of downtown, with its relaxed ambience and numerous small inns and B&Bs.

A Good Walk

Numbers in the text correspond to numbers in the margin and on the San José map.

Start in the **Plaza de la Cultura** ①, beneath which you'll find the Instituto Costarricense de Turismo (ICT), the Costa Rican tourist office, where you can pick up a city map. Next door is the **Gold Museum**, which deserves an hour or two visit. After wandering around the bustling plaza, slip into the **Teatro Nacional** ② for a look at the elegant interior and perhaps a cup of coffee in the lobby café. When you leave the theater, the city's main east–west corridor, Avenida 2, will be to your left. Walk 1½ blocks west along it to the **Parque Central** ③ and the **Catedral Metropolitana.** After checking out the park and cathedral, cross Avenida 2 and head north on Calle Central, walking one block to the small plaza next to the **Banco Central** ④. Turn left and walk two blocks west along the Avenida Central pedestrian zone to the **Mercado Central** ⑤, where you can do a bit of shopping or simply look around. After exploring the market, head back two blocks on the Avenida Central, then turn left and walk one block north to the white stuccoed **Correos** ⑥ (central post office building). From there, return to the Avenida Central and walk east along the mall to the Plaza de la Cultura.

From the eastern end of the Plaza de la Cultura, near the Tourist Office, walk two blocks north to the corner of the **Parque Morazán** ⑦. Walk northeast across the park, crossing busy Avenida 3 on the way, to the shady **Parque de España.** On the northern side of the park is the modern National Insurance Institute (INS) building with its 11th-floor **Museo de Jade** ⑧, which houses an interesting collection and offers some great views of the city. When you leave the INS building, walk north some two blocks up Calle 7 to the **Parque Zoológico Simón Bolívar** ⑨ to see some of the country's incredible wildlife. Abutting the Parque Zoológico is the **Spyrogyra Butterfly Garden (Jardín de Mariposas)** ⑩, with its 30 species of butterflies. (Note, however, that the museum is most easily accessed from the other side of the Barrio Tournon; *see* Spyrogyra *in* Sights to See, *below.*) Head back to the INS building then walk one block east and one block south, to the corner of the **Parque Nacional** ⑪. Three blocks east of the Parque Nacional is the **Serpentarium** ⑫ where you can peer at both homegrown and exotic snakes, including the deadly *terciopelo* (fer-de-lance viper). Walk one block south to the Avenida Central and three blocks east to the terraced **Plaza de la Democracia** ⑬. Nearby is the **Museo Nacional** ⑭, housed in the old Bellavista Fortress. From here it's about a five-block walk west back to the starting point of the tour, the Plaza de la Cultura.

Sights to See

Numbers in the margin correspond to points of interest on the San José map.

❹ **Banco Central.** The country's federal reserve bank is an unattractive modern building that looms between Avenidas Central and 1 and Calles 2 and 4. Note the 10 sculpted figures of bedraggled *campesinos* (peasants) outside the western facade of the bank. The small plaza south

San José

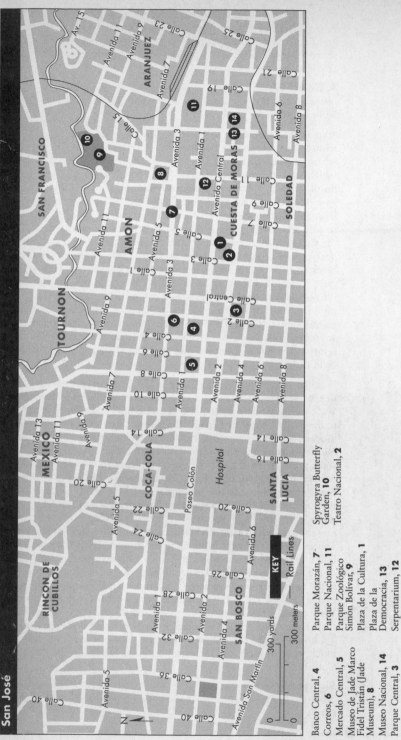

Banco Central, **4**
Correos, **6**
Mercado Central, **5**
Museo de Jade Marco Fidel Tristán (Jade Museum), **8**
Museo Nacional, **14**
Parque Central, **3**

Parque Morazán, **7**
Parque Nacional, **11**
Parque Zoológico Simón Bolívar, **9**
Plaza de la Cultura, **1**
Plaza de la Democracia, **13**
Serpentarium, **12**

Spyrogyra Butterfly Garden, **10**
Teatro Nacional, **2**

KEY

— Rail Lines

300 yards
300 meters

of the bank is a popular spot with hawkers, money changers, and retired men, and is a good place to get a shoe shine and listen to street musicians. Beware: the money changers here are notorious for circulating counterfeit bills and using doctored calculators to shortchange customers.

6 **Correos.** The ornate facade of the handsome central post office building is tough to miss amidst the insipid architecture surrounding it. It faces Calle 2 between Avenidas 1 and 3. Upstairs is a display of first-day stamp issues. Also, here's your opportunity to look down on the activity of loading *apartado* (post office) boxes. A pretty dull pastime you say? Not for the locals. Since street addresses hardly exist in this country, Ticos fall over themselves to get one of the hard-to-come-by post office boxes here. Opposite the post office is a small park shaded by massive fig trees and lined with the stalls of flower vendors. Behind it stands the marble facade of the exclusive Club Unión (members only). ✉ *C. 2 between Avdas. 1 and 3.* ☼ *Post office: Weekdays 8 AM–8 PM, Sat. 8–noon.*

5 **Mercado Central.** San José's Central Market is a warren of dark, narrow passages flanked by stalls selling exotic spices (some labeled according to their medicinal uses), fish, fruit, vegetables, and wood and leather handicrafts. The mercado feels like the melting pot of San José. The unassuming building covers a city block between Avenidas 1 and Central and Calles 6 and 8 at the western end of the Avenida Central pedestrian zone.

★ **8** **Museo de Jade Marco Fidel Tristán (Jade Museum).** On the 11th floor of the tall, modern INS building, the Jade Museum contains the world's largest collection of American jade. When it was produced in pre-Columbian times, from around 300 BC to AD 700, in the Nicoya and South Pacific or Diquis regions, jade was considered more valuable than gold. Most-often carved into pendants depicting human and animal figures, jade was also used for more mundane purposes such as tooth fillings and decorating pots and vases. A series of drawings explains how this extremely hard stone was cut using string saws with quartz and sand abrasive. The museum also contains other pre-Columbian artifacts, such as polychrome vases and three-legged metates (low tables for grinding corn). The final room on the tour displays a startling array of carved fertility symbols. ✉ *11th floor of INS building, Avda. 5 between C. 9 and 11,.* ☎ *223–5800, ext. 2584.* ✉ *Free.* ☼ *Weekdays 8–4:30.*

Across the street from the INS building is one of the capital's most pleasant spots, the **Parque de España,** with its statue of a conquistador perched at one end and lovely tiled guard house at the other. The yellow compound to the east of the park was a government liquor factory until 1994, when it was converted into the **National Culture Center.** Covering an entire block, the complex includes two theaters, an extensive modern art museum, and the offices of the Ministry of Culture. To the west of the park is a two-story, metal-sided building that houses the colonial **Casa Amarilla,** once owned by steel magnate Andrew Carnegie and now used by the Foreign Ministry to impress visiting dignitaries. If you ask at the door they might just let you in to see the elegant series of patios, elaborate plasterwork, and hardwood floors. A few doors to the east is the elegant **Mexican Embassy,** which is equally worth a quick look.

14 **Museo Nacional.** Housed in the whitewashed colonial interior of the **Bellavista Fortress,** the National Museum gives visitors a quick and insightful lesson about Costa Rican culture from pre-Columbian times to the present. Rooms are devoted to pre-Columbian artifacts, period costumes, colonial furniture, and photos of Costa Rican life through the ages. Outside, there's a veranda and pleasant manicured courtyard garden. ⊠ *C. 17 between Avdas. Central and 2,* ☎ *257–1433.* ▣ *150 colones.* ⊙ *Tues.–Sat. 8:30–5, Sun. 9–5.*

❸ Parque Central. Technically the city's nucleus, this simple tree-planted square has a gurgling fountain and benches—the perfect spot from which to watch the world go by. In the center of the park is a spiderlike, avocado-colored kiosk donated by former Nicaraguan dictator Anastasio Somoza. When the park was remodeled several years ago, a referendum was held to decide whether to demolish the despot's gift, and the citizens voted to preserve the bandstand for posterity. Across Avenida 2, to the north, stands the **Melico Salazar Theater,** San José's other leading venue. The venerable **Soda Palace,** a restaurant-cum-black market exchange, is on the western end of that block. ⊠ *Avda. 2 between C. 2 and Central.*

To the east of the park stands the **Catedral Metropolitana,** with its mostly uninteresting neoclassical exterior and corrugated tin dome; inside, however, the cathedral has patterned floor tiles and framed polychrome basreliefs. The interior of the small chapel on the north side of the cathedral is much more ornate than the main building, but it is usually closed. The cathedral is undergoing an ambitious 3-year restoration project that is scheduled for completion in 1998, but the building remains open. ⊙ *Daily 8–8.*

❼ Parque Morazán. Centered around a neoclassical bandstand, downtown San José's largest park is slightly barren and dull—the park does, however, have a more uplifting annex with a large fountain across busy Avenida 3. Two blocks north of the Plaza de la Cultura, the park is a serene place popular with young lovers and families by day, even though a steady stream of traffic flows noisily along its northern edge. At night you should avoid it, because the park then plays host to hookers and drunks. Near the park's northwest corner stands the Aurola Holiday Inn, a mirror-skinned monstrosity, which, at 17 stories, is downtown San José's tallest building. Along the park's southern edge are a public school and two lovely old mansions, both with beautiful facades (one is a private residence and the other is a prostitute pickup bar). ⊠ *Bordered by Avda. 5 and C. 5 and 9.*

★ ⓫ Parque Nacional. A large and leafy downtown park, the Nacional is centered around a monument commemorating the nation's battle against American invader William Walker in 1856. It's a pleasant block of downtown greenery, dominated by tall trees that often have colorful parakeets high in their branches. It's a great spot to relax by day, but it gets very dark at night, when it becomes a haven for lovers and pickpockets. Across from the southwest end of the park is the Mudéjar **Legislative Assembly building,** home to Costa Rica's congress. You can look around, although there isn't much to see apart from a chart recording the more momentous events in Costa Rican history. Next door is the **Casa Rosada,** a colonial-era residence now home to bureaucrats, and behind it is a more modern one-time home used by the government for parties and special events. The two former schools that cover the block to the east have long been occupied by government offices. The massive red building to the west of the park houses the National Registry and the Electoral Tribunal. ⊠ *Between Avdas. 1 and 3 and C. 15 and 19.*

👋 ⑨ **Parque Zoológico Simón Bolívar.** Bearing in mind the country's mind-boggling diversity of wildlife, San José's zoo appears rather modest in scope. It will, however, introduce you to the animals that you may or may not see when you venture out into the jungle. The park is set in a forested ravine in historical Barrio Amón, and provides soothing green space in the heart of the city. The best way to find the zoo is to walk north along Calle 7 to the bottom of the hill, then turn right. ⊠ *Avda. 11 and C. 11,* ☎ *233–6701.* 🎫 *150 colones.* ☉ *Daily 9–4:30.*

★ ❶ **Plaza de la Cultura.** One of the most popular loitering spots in San José, this plaza is somewhat sterile—it's basically a large cement square between busy Avenidas Central and 2 and Calles 3 and 5. Surrounded by shops and fast food restaurants, the plaza is a pleasant spot to feed the pigeons, buy some souvenirs, or simply soak up the sun. It is also a favored performance spot for local marimba bands, clowns, jugglers, and colorfully dressed South Americans playing Andean music. The stately ☞ **Teatro Nacional** dominates the Plaza's southern half, whereas its western edge is defined by the venerable **Gran Hotel Costa Rica,** whose 24-hour Parisienne café offers some of the best people-watching in town.

Need a map? Want some help with hotel reservations? Head for the country's main tourist office, the **ICT** tucked beneath the eastern end of the plaza. The people who work there are usually friendly and informative, and they can give you map and bus schedule information. ☎ *222 1090.* ☉ *Weekdays 9–5, Sat. 9–1.*

Next to the tourist office is the dazzling, modern **Gold Museum,** which contains the largest collection of pre-Columbian gold jewelry in Central America: 20,000 troy ounces of gold in more than 1,600 individual pieces—all owned by the Banco Central. ⊠ *Entrance is next to tourist office at eastern end of Plaza de la Cultura,* ☎ *223–0528.* 🎫 *$5.* ☉ *Tues.–Sun. 10–4:30.*

⑬ **Plaza de la Democracia.** President Oscar Arias built this terraced open space to the west of the Museo Nacional to mark 100 years of democracy and to receive visiting dignitaries during the 1989 hemispheric summit. It will look much better once the trees grow, but the view west toward the jagged Cerros de Escazú is already mesmerizing. Along the western edge of the plaza are a number of stalls where vendors sell jewelry, T-shirts, and handicrafts from Costa Rica, Guatemala, and South America. Standing over the eastern side of the plaza is the coral-color Bellavista Fortress—home to the ☞ **Museo Nacional**—with its bullet-scarred turrets, reminders of the 1948 Civil War.

👋 ⑫ **Serpentarium.** Don't be confused by the absence of motion within the display cases here—all of the snakes and lizards are very much alive. Most notorious is the terciopelo, which is responsible for more than half the poisonous snakebites in Costa Rica. The menagerie also features boa constrictors, Jesus Christ lizards, poison dart frogs, iguanas, and an aquarium full of deadly sea snakes. In addition to the many local species, there are also such exotic creatures as king cobras and Burmese pythons. ⊠ *Avda. 1 between C. 9 and 11,* ☎ *255–4210.* 🎫 *500 colones.* ☉ *Daily 9–6.*

★ 👋 ⑩ **Spyrogyra Butterfly Garden.** An hour or two spent at this magical garden will prove entertaining and educational for travelers of all ages. Visit when it's sunny, since that's when butterflies are most active. Self-guided tours provide information about butterfly ecology and a chance to observe the winged jewels close up. Visitors watch a 15-minute video, then guide themselves through screened-in gardens following a numbered trail given in a booklet. Some 30 species of colorful butterflies flutter around the gardens, together with several types of hummingbird. Though the garden abuts the northern edge of the Parque Zoológico Simón Bolívar, its entrance is on the outskirts of the Barrio Tournon, near the El Pueblo shopping center. ⊠ *55 yds. west and 164 yds. south of brick church of San Francisco, Guadelupe,* ☎ *222–2937.* ☞ *1,000 colones.* ⊙ *Daily 7:30–3:30.*

❷ Teatro Nacional. Easily Costa Rica's most enchanting building, the National Theater stands at the southwest corner of the Plaza de la Cultura, catercorner from the Gran Hotel Costa Rica's Parisienne café. The sandstone facade is decorated with statues of odd bedfellows Beethoven and 17th-century Spanish Golden Age playwright Calderón de la Barca, marble columns with bronze capitals, and Italianate arched windows. The Muses of Dance, Music, and Fame are silhouetted in front of a maroon iron cupola. Chagrined that touring prima donna Adelina Patti bypassed San José in 1890, wealthy coffee merchants raised export taxes in order to pay for the Belgian architects, cast iron, Italian marble, and decorators to construct the theater. It's not surprising, then, given the provenance of the building funds, that frescoes depicting coffee and banana production grace the stairway. The theater was inaugurated in 1894 with a performance of Gounod's *Faust,* starring an international cast. The sumptuous baroque interior sparkles owing to a two-year restoration project undertaken after the theater was damaged in a 1991 earthquake. Check the box office on the east side of the theater for upcoming performances; performance tickets are often as cheap as admission to the building itself. ⊠ *On the Plaza de la Cultura,* ☎ *221–1329.* ☞ *400 colones.* ⊙ *Mon.–Sat. 9–5:30.*

NEED A   The **National Theater Café** off the lobby of the Teatro Nacional has a
BREAK?   stunning Belle Epoque setting and serves up exotic coffees, good sandwiches, and exquisite pastries.

DINING

$$$$ ✕ **Le Chandelier.** In terms of decor, ambience, and cooking, this is San
  ★   José's classiest restaurant. The Swiss chef, Claude Dubuis, has been delighting businesspeople and visitors alike for the past 14 years. Dubuis's gourmet menu, which changes weekly, might include such unique creations as corvina in a *pejibaye* (peach palm) sauce or the more familiar *pato a la naranja* (duck à l'orange). The wicker chairs, tile floor, original paintings, and formal service all complement the cooking. ⊠ *San Pedro, from ICE, 1 block west and 109 yds. south,* ☎ *225–3980. AE, DC, MC, V. Closed Sun., and Dec. 24–25. No lunch Sat.*

$$$$ ✕ **L'Ile de France.** Proprietor-chef Jean-Claude Fromont, who hails from
  ★   Paris, has overseen this intimate downtown restaurant for 18 years. The design is simple but elegant, with a tile floor, wood paneling, padded leather chairs, and white walls adorned with framed Toulouse-Lautrec posters. The sauce-based cooking is superb, and there is a very extensive list of French wines. ⊠ *C. 7 between Avdas. Central and 2,* ☎ *222–4241. AE, DC, MC, V. Closed Sun., Sat. lunch, and Dec. 23–Jan 4.*

$$$–$$$$ ✕ **La Masía de Triquell.** San José's most authentic Spanish restaurant is appropriately located in the Casa España, a Spanish cultural center two blocks north of La Sabana park (the Paseo de Colón deadends at the park). Since the death of Catalunya native Francisco, the original

owner, his widow (Emerita) and son (also named Francisco) have kept the restaurant on the same course. The dining room has a tile floor; wood beams; red, green, and yellow walls; white tablecloths; and leather-and-wood Castilian-style chairs. Start with *champiñones al ajillo* (mushrooms sautéed with garlic and parsley), and, as a main course, try the *camarones Catalana* (shrimp in a tomato, onion, and garlic cream sauce). The wine list is long and international and strongest in the Spanish and French departments. ⊠ *Sabana Norte,* ☎ *296–3528. AE, DC, MC, V. Closed Sun., and Dec. 25–Jan. 2.*

$$$ ✕ **Ambrosia.** A navy-blue canopy at the entrance of an open-air shop-
★ ping mall heralds this chic restaurant in San Pedro. The menu is international and includes salads, soups, pasta, and fish. Start with the *sopa Neptuna* (a mixed fish soup with tomato, onion, bacon, and cream); follow with either the light fettuccine ambrosia (with white sauce, cheese, ham, and oregano) or corvina *troyana* (steamed, covered with a sauce of mushrooms, shrimp, and tarragon, and served with rice and vegetables). The atmosphere is relaxed and informal, and the decor is well-chosen to complement the adventurous cooking: watercolors, wood and cane chairs, and plants. ⊠ *Centro Comercial de la Calle Real, San Pedro,* ☎ *253–8012. AE, DC, MC, V. Closed Sun. evenings.*

$$$ ✕ **La Cocina de Leña.** In the charming El Pueblo shopping center,
★ which was designed to resemble a colonial village, La Cocina serves up traditional Costa Rican fare. The white walls are hung with old tools and straw bags—it's supposed to give guests the feeling that they are down on the farm. Popular Tico dishes such as black bean soup, ceviche, tamales, ox tail with yucca, and plantains cost more here than in the Mercado Central, but the quality and hygiene are more attuned to the standards of the North American palate and stomach. The restaurant presents folk dancing and music several nights a week during the high season. ⊠ *Centro Comercial el Pueblo, Barrio Tournon,* ☎ *223–3704. AE, DC, MC, V.*

$$–$$$ ✕ **Balcón de Europa.** Italian-owned and in existence since 1909, this is San José's oldest restaurant. The cuisine is international and wide-ranging, although not always consistent; especially good are the many pasta dishes. The paneled interior features a hardwood floor, white-and-green tablecloths, ceiling fans, and abundant plants. Old sepia photos of Costa Rica, including some of the first ones ever taken in San José, cover the walls. The ambience is relaxed. ⊠ *Avda. Central and C. 9,* ☎ *221–4841. No credit cards. Closed Sat.*

$$–$$$ ✕ **Machu Picchu.** On a quiet street just north of Paseo Colón, this small restaurant set in a converted house is *the* place for excellent Peruvian cuisine or a good *pisco sour* (lime juice, pisco brandy, and sugar). A few Peruvian travel posters and some fishnets holding crab and lobster shells are about the only concessions the management makes to decor. The food, however, is anything but plain. The *pique especial de mariscos* (special seafood platter), which is big enough for two people, contains shrimp, conch, and squid cooked four ways. The *causa limeña,* a lemon-accented potato salad with shrimp, is a good starter. A blazing Peruvian hot sauce served on the side adds zip to any dish. ⊠ *C. 32, 136 yds. north of Kentucky Fried Chicken, Paseo Colón,* ☎ *222–7384. AE, DC, MC, V. Closed Sun.*

$$ ✕ **Fulusu.** Some like it hot: This Chinese place across from L'Ile de France is one of the very few restaurants in the entire country where you can get spicy food. The decor is mundane, with red-and-white tablecloths and Chinese prints on the walls, but the *vainicas con cerdo* (green beans with pork) and pollo *estilo sichuan* (Szechuan) are among the best hot-

San José Dining and Lodging

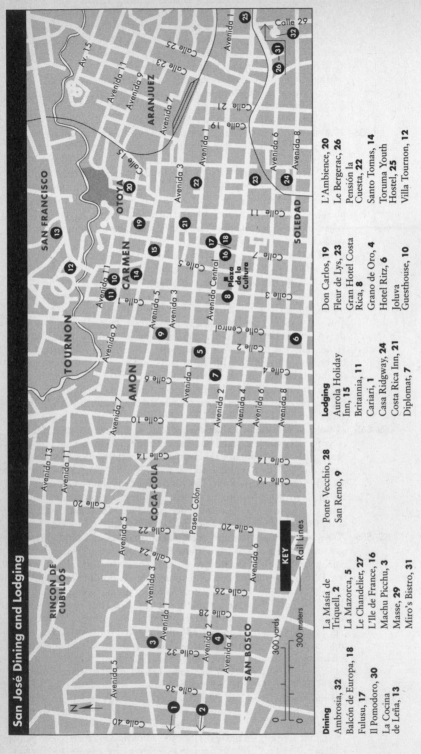

Dining
Ambrosia, **32**
Balcón de Europa, **18**
Fulusu, **17**
Il Pomodoro, **30**
La Cocina
de Leña, **13**

La Masía de
Triquell, **2**
La Mazorca, **5**
Le Chandelier, **27**
L'Ile de France, **16**
Machu Picchu, **3**
Masse, **29**
Miro's Bistro, **31**

Ponte Vecchio, **28**
San Remo, **9**

Lodging
Aurola Holiday
Inn, **15**
Britannia, **11**
Cariari, **1**
Casa Ridgway, **24**
Costa Rica Inn, **21**
Diplomat, **7**

Don Carlos, **19**
Fleur de Lys, **23**
Gran Hotel Costa
Rica, **8**
Grano de Oro, **4**
Hotel Ritz, **6**
Joluva
Guesthouse, **10**

L'Ambience, **20**
Le Bergerac, **26**
Pensión la
Cuesta, **22**
Santo Tomas, **14**
Toruma Youth
Hostel, **25**
Villa Tournon, **12**

KEY
—— Rail Lines

food plates in town. ⊠ *C. 7 between Avdas. Central and 2,* ☎ *223–7568. Reservations not accepted. MC, V. Closed Sun.*

$$ ✕ **Il Pomodoro.** In San Pedro, a few doors north of the church, is San José's best pizzeria. The pizza menu is long—the *capricciosa* (with artichokes, ham, sausage, and olives) is especially good—and you'll find a medium-size pizza ample for two. Alternatives to the humble pie are calzone, focaccia, spaghetti, and lasagna. The maroon-and-white tiled floor, dark paneling, round wooden tables, and low-hanging lamps give the Pomodoro a charming bistrolike ambience. ⊠ *100 yds. north of San Pedro Church,* ☎ *224–0966. DC, MC, V. Closed Dec. 15–Jan. 3.*

$$ ✕ **Miro's Bistro.** In a brick building by the railroad tracks, Miro's has
★ long been popular with locals. Croatian-born Miro spent most of his life in Italy, and the menu reflects the cuisine of both nations: goulash, eggplant Parmesan, and various types of tortellini. Miro, who has run this tiny restaurant for more than a decade, often greets guests, takes orders, and cooks. The decor is very red, with a few watercolors on the walls and simple pine tables and chairs. It's a bit cramped, especially at the three-stool bar tucked away in the corner, but the terrific food and prices make it worth your while. ⊠ *Barrio Escalante, 333 yds. north and 27 yds. east of Pulpería de la Luz,* ☎ *253–4242. Reservations not accepted. MC, V. Closed Sun.*

$$ ✕ **Ponte Vecchio.** Affable chef-owner Tony D'Alaimo has applied what he learned in his New York Italian restaurant to this popular, cozy San Pedro spot. The garish sign in the colors of the Italian flag belies the tasteful interior's soft lighting, candles, and silk flowers on coral-pink tablecloths. The menu isn't particularly creative, but fresh local meats and vegetables, homemade pasta, and imported cheeses help create high-quality classic Italian cuisine. Start out with antipasti, followed by the rich cheese ravioli, and finish things off with veal saltimbocca. ⊠ *216 yds. west and 27 yds. north of San Pedro Church,* ☎ *283–1810. AE, DC, MC, V. Closed Sun.*

$–$$ ✕ **San Remo.** Owned and managed by expatriate Italian Eugenio
★ Favron, the San Remo has long been popular with locals and travelers alike. The big draw is the lunch special, which usually features a choice of meat, fish, or pasta, but which also has an impressive à la carte selection. The decor is rustic, with lots of wood and posters of Costa Rica's natural wonders, and the wooden chairs and tables are small and packed in tight. The food is excellent, the portions big, and the prices very reasonable. ⊠ *C. 2 between Avdas. 3 and 5,* ☎ *221–8145. Reservations not accepted. No credit cards. Closed Sun.*

$ ✕ **La Mazorca.** The name means "ear of corn," referring to the restaurant's commitment to health food. La Mazorca's bakery produces a variety of whole-wheat goods, and the menu, although predominantly vegetarian, does include both chicken and corvina. In an old brick building a few blocks from the University of Costa Rica, it's a popular lunch spot with students and professors, and it maintains a somewhat bohemian atmosphere. Come here for the inexpensive, delicious food, not the decor—long wooden tables and benches and bare brick walls. ⊠ *1 block north and 2 blocks east of San Pedro Church,* ☎ *224–8069. Reservations not accepted. AE, MC, V. Closed Sun.*

$ ✕ **Masse.** This popular locale, in the university neighborhood, is a great people-watching spot. It serves a good and cheap *plato del día* (daily special), but Masse's is known for its pollo *al carbón* (cooked on charcoal and marinated with lemon, onions, and garlic). A neon Rex cigarette sign and striped canopy out front ensure that you'll find the place. Patrons favor the leafy terrace, decorated with primary-color chairs, wooden tables, and jolly murals. ⊠ *150 yds. north of San Pedro Church,* ☎ *234–1645. Reservations not accepted. MC, V. Closed weekends and Dec. 20–Jan. 3.*

LODGING

$$$$ 🏨 **Aurola Holiday Inn.** The upper floors of this 17-story mirrored-glass building, three blocks north of Plaza de la Cultura, have the best views in town. Rooms are decorated with cream-stripe wallpaper, pale burgundy carpets, patterned bedspreads, and attractive local prints. The wide beds are a real treat. Ask for a room facing south or, better still, for one on the southwest corner from where you can see the city and the Cerros de Escazú beyond. The Aurola's public areas are high-ceilinged, modern, and airy. ⊠ *Avda. 5 and C. 5, Apdo. 7802–1000,* ☎ *233–7233 or 800/465–4329 in the U.S.,* FAX *255–1036. 188 rooms with bath, 12 suites. Restaurant, bar, cafeteria, indoor pool, hot tub, sauna, exercise room. AE, DC, MC, V.*

$$$$ 🏨 **Cariari.** The modern, low-rise Cariari is popular because of its wide range of facilities, which include a private, 18-hole golf course. Bedrooms have blue carpets, white walls, watercolor paintings, sloping wood ceilings, and beds with striped covers and bulging circular headboards. Restaurants range from the relaxed poolside bar, with cane chairs and mustard tablecloths, to posh Los Vitrales, whose green velvet chairs overlook a tropical rock garden. There is always something going on at this out-of-town property (it's on the highway to the airport), meaning you can stay put if you like. Many visitors do. ⊠ *Autopista General Cañas, Intersección San Antonio de Belén, Apdo. 737–1007,* ☎ *239–0022 or 800/227–4274 in the U.S.,* FAX *239–2803. 220 rooms with bath. 3 restaurants, bar, cafeteria, pool, hot tub, tennis, golf. AE, DC, MC, V.*

$$$–$$$$ 🏨 **Britannia.** On a busy corner in the Barrio Amón neighborhood, this pink house with a tiled porch appears to have changed very little since its construction in 1910. On closer inspection, however, you'll discern a row of new rooms on the far side of the property; the old cellar, too, has been remodeled and converted into an intimate restaurant. Rooms in the new wing are slightly small, with carpeting and hardwood furniture. Deluxe rooms and junior suites in the old house are spacious, with high ceilings and windows on the street side—they're worth the extra money. The cellar restaurant has brick walls and arches and overlooks the interior gardens that separate the old and new wings. It's only open for breakfast and dinner, serving dishes such as cream of pejibaye soup and tenderloin in béarnaise sauce. ⊠ *C. 3 and Avda. 11, Apdo. 3742–1000,* ☎ *223–6667,* FAX *223–6411. 19 rooms with bath, 5 junior suites. Restaurant. AE, MC, V.*

$$$–$$$$ 🏨 **Grano de Oro.** This turn-of-the-century wooden house, on a quiet
★ side street on the western edge of San José, is one of the city's most charming inns. The former home underwent an extensive remodeling, which included the addition of new rooms, a restaurant, and indoor gardens. The older rooms are the nicest, especially the Garden Suite, with its hardwood floors, high ceilings, and private garden. The standard rooms are a bit small, but tasteful. The restaurant overlooks an interior patio, and the kitchen is run by a French chef. The hotel's sundeck has a spiffy view of both the city and the far-off volcanoes. ⊠ *C. 30 between Avdas. 2 and 4, Box 025216, SJO 36, Miami, FL 33102-5216,* ☎ *255–3322,* FAX *221–2782. 32 rooms with bath, 3 suites. Restaurant, fans, hot tubs, sundeck. AE, MC, V.*

$$$–$$$$ ⊞ **L'Ambience.** L'Ambience, an elegant, restored, colonial manor
★ house, is in a quiet, upscale, residential neighborhood five blocks from
the city center. Each of this hotel's rooms overlooks the central court-
yard, where potted tropical plants spill onto multicolor glazed tiles.
The antique furniture, gilt mirrors, and old prints in the rooms are from
the owner's personal collection. The Presidential Suite has a large
drawing room attached to it. The food in the restaurant has a markedly
French accent. Try the tournedos *Dijonnaise* (with mustard cream
sauce). ⊠ *C. 13 at Avda. 9, Apdo. 1040–2050 or c/o Interlink 179,
Box 526770, Miami, FL 33152;* ☎ *222–6702,* FAX *223–0481. 6 rooms
with bath, 1 suite. Restaurant, bar. No credit cards.*

$$$ ⊞ **Don Carlos.** A rambling gray villa houses this eclectically decorated
hotel-cum-crafts shop. Public areas are a split-level maze of polished
hardwood floors, greenery-draped courtyards, and tile patios, some
adorned with colorful crafts sold in the on-site shop. Room sizes vary
greatly: Those in the Colonial Wing cost $10 extra per night and have
polished wood floors, high white ceilings, and heavy furniture. Another
$10 buys even more space. Breakfast included. ⊠ *C. 9 between Avdas.
7 and 9, Box 025216, Dept. 1686, Miami, FL 33102–5216,* ☎ *221–
6707,* FAX *255–0828. 33 rooms with bath, 6 suites. Restaurant, bar,
breakfast room. AE, MC, V.*

$$$ ⊞ **Fleur de Lys.** Although it's run by Swiss International Hotels, you
would never guess that this elegant, chic hotel is part of a chain. Guest
rooms in this restored lavender-colored mansion are small but bright,
with big closets, floral bedspreads, Tiffany-style lamps, and paintings
by Costa Rican artists; junior suites are more spacious. The Fleur de
Lys has a prime location on a quiet street between the National Mu-
seum and the Plaza de la Cultura. A buffet breakfast, served in the in-
timate restaurant in back, is included in the price. The chef has won
accolades for his Swiss-Italian creations, including chicken with wine
and herbs, and shrimp flambéed with whiskey. Fish lovers who are tired
of corvina will applaud specialties such as sole cooked with tomato
and basil and squid in champagne sauce. ⊠ *C. 13 between Avdas. 2
and 4, San José, Apdo. 10736–1000,* ☎ *223–1206,* FAX *257–3637.
18 rooms with bath, 1 suite. Restaurant, bar, parking. AE, DC, MC,
V.*

$$$ ⊞ **Gran Hotel Costa Rica.** Opened in 1930, the dowager of San José
hotels remains a focal point of the city. All bedrooms have beige walls,
pastel-pattern bedspreads, subdued carpets, and individual abstract watercolors. Rooms that overlook the Plaza de la Cultura are noisy but
have the best views. The bathrooms have old-fashioned taps and modern comfort. There is one drawback here: The hotel's size combined
with the flow of nonguests who frequent the glitzy ground-floor casino
and bars reduce the intimacy quotient to zero. ⊠ *Avda. 2 at C. 3, Apdo.
527–1000,* ☎ *221–4000,* FAX *221–3501. 106 rooms with bath, 13 suites.
Restaurant, 24-hr cafeteria, bars, 24-hr casino. AE, DC, MC, V.*

$$$ ⊞ **Le Bergerac.** Set in a quiet residential neighborhood east of down-
★ town, Le Bergerac occupies what was once a couple of private homes
and is the cream of a growing crop of small upscale San José hotels.
Public areas are furnished with antiques; guest rooms have custom-made
stone-and-wood dressers and writing tables along with tropical-print
bedspreads. Deluxe rooms, which cost an extra $10, have garden ter-
races or balconies and large bathrooms. There's a patio complete with
lawn chairs where a complimentary breakfast is served. ⊠ *Los Yoses,
Apdo. 1107–1002,* ☎ *234–7850,* FAX *225–9103. 18 rooms with bath.
Meeting room. DC, MC, V.*

$$$ ⌷ **Santo Tomas.** Step back to the days of the coffee barons at this restored, turn-of-the-century plantation house elegantly decorated with mahogany floors and handmade tile. Select an upstairs room for a view north toward Heredia, although tall people may find the eaved ceilings dangerous. The downstairs rooms have white walls, elegant fittings, and higher ceilings than those above. Request a room with a window, because those that open onto the corridor are gloomy. If you want peace and quiet, ask for a room in the back. Complimentary breakfast is served. ⊠ *Avda. 7 between C. 3 and 5, Box 025216, SJO 1314, Miami, FL 33102–5216,* ☎ *255–0448,* ☒ *222–3950. 20 rooms with bath. Bar. MC, V.*

$$$ ⌷ **Villa Tournon.** Just a few minutes' walk north of downtown or a
★ two-block jaunt from El Pueblo shopping center, the Tournon is a modern businessperson's hotel, noted for its true-value accommodations. Sloping wooden ceilings and bare, redbrick walls recall the construction of a ski chalet. Bright landings lead to snug rooms painted in pastel shades and adorned with prints. The restaurant serves a wide variety of meat and fish dishes, brought to the tables by white-jacketed waiters. The small garden is attractively laid out with lawns, shrubs, and a kidney-shaped pool. ⊠ *Barrio Tournon, Apdo. 69–2120,* ☎ *233– 6622,* ☒ *222–5211. 80 rooms with bath. Restaurant, pool. AE, MC, V.*

$$ ⌷ **Diplomat.** This colorless place on a commercial street half a block from the busy Avenida 2 is popular among bargain hunters who want to be in the middle of the action. With tan walls, worn carpets, twin beds, and tiny bedside tables, the boxlike rooms have all the warmth of an army barracks, but they're quiet and impeccably clean. The sitting areas on each floor have more flair owing to their huge tropical murals. ⊠ *C. 6 between Avdas. Central and 2, Apdo. 6606–1000,* ☎ *221–8744,* ☒ *233–7474. 30 rooms with bath. Restaurant, bar. MC, V.*

$$ ⌷ **Joluva Guesthouse.** This small B&B caters primarily to a gay clientele, but the accommodations and price make it attractive regardless of your sexual orientation. It would be easy to pass by this white cement building, on one of the quieter streets of Barrio Amón, since it is marked by only a small sign. A narrow entrance, flanked by white columns detailed in gold, leads to a high-ceiling common area with a colorful tile floor, couches, armchairs, and a TV. Rooms have hardwood floors, rugs, firm beds with pastel quilts, and small baths; the two cheapest rooms share a bath. Complimentary Continental breakfasts are served in a bright room at the back of the hotel. ⊠ *C. 3b between Avdas. 9 and 11, Apdo. 1998–1002,* ☎ *223–7961 or 619/298–7965 in the U.S.,* ☒ *257–7668. 6 rooms with bath, 2 without. Breakfast room. AE, MC, V.*

$$ ⌷ **Pensión la Cuesta.** The eight rooms of this laid-back, centrally lo
★ cated, wooden villa on Cuesta de Nuñez have comfortable wicker chairs, hardwood floors, and brightly painted walls. Rooms in back are darker but quieter than those in front, since the pensión faces a busy street. Guests can lounge, read, and swap traveler's tales in the sunken sitting area (also used as the breakfast room), which has a high ceiling and a wall of windows. Breakfast is included in the price of the room, and guests are welcome to use the kitchen to prepare other meals. ⊠ *Avda. 1 between C. 11 and 15, 1332,* ☎ *255–2896,* ☒ *257–2272. 8 rooms share 3 baths. Breakfast room. DC, MC, V.*

$–$$ ⌷ **Costa Rica Inn.** Although its entrance faces a busy bus stop, the inn's rooms are far enough removed that you could easily forget you're in the heart of the city. The lobby, in an old house, has a long, arched hallway with beige couches and armchairs. The reception area doubles as a bar, and across from it is a small sitting area. Rooms are off a narrow corridor in a new addition, behind the old house. The room's linoleum floors, Formica furniture, and pale green walls aren't going to win any decorating awards, but the rooms are clean, comfortable, well-situated (across from Parque Morazán), and very reasonably priced. ⊠ *C. 9 between Avdas. 1 and 3, Apdo. 10282–1000,* ☎ *222–5203,* ℻ *223–8385. 15 rooms with bath. Bar. MC, V.*

$ ⊞ **Casa Ridgway.** Affiliated with the Quaker Peace Center next door,
★ Casa Ridgway is the budget option for itinerants concerned with peace, the environment, and social issues in general. In an old villa on a quiet street, the bright, clean premises include a planted terrace, a lending reference library, and kitchen where you can cook your own food. There are rooms for couples and bunk dormitories for larger groups and individuals. ⊠ *Avda. 6 B off C. 15, Apdo. 1507–1000,* ☎ *233–6168,* ℻ *224–8910. 6 rooms share 2 baths. Kitchen, workshop/lecture area, library. No credit cards.*

$ ⊞ **Hotel Ritz.** Inexpensive accommodations in a safe neighborhood are the selling points of this Swiss-owned hotel a couple blocks south of the Parque Central. You get what you pay for: The rooms are clean but very basic, with wood floors and soft beds—rooms in back are quiet but gloomy. The hotel's ground floor is actually the "Pensión Centro Continental," which has even cheaper rooms, all of which share a bath. There's a common area upstairs where breakfast is served, and there's a tour desk in the lobby. ⊠ *C. Central between Avdas. 8 and 10, Apdo. 6783–1000,* ☎ *222–4103,* ℻ *222–8849. 25 rooms, 7 with bath. Travel services. AE, MC, V.*

$ ⊞ **Toruma Youth Hostel.** The headquarters of Costa Rica's expanding hostel network is housed in an elegant colonial bungalow in the suburb of Los Yoses, near the university. Though practically destroyed by the 1991 earthquake, the building was renovated and expanded to include more rooms. The tiled lobby and veranda are ideal spots for backpackers to hang out and exchange travel tips. The open bunks in the slightly more expensive new section are preferable to the coffinlike boxes toward the back. An on-site information center offers discounts on tours. ⊠ *Avda. Central between C. 29 and 31, Apdo. 1355–1002,* ☎ ℻ *224–4085. 105 beds with shared bath. Dining hall, kitchen area. MC, V.*

NIGHTLIFE AND THE ARTS

Nightlife

Bars and Discotheques

Blending white walls, bare brickwork, and timber, **La Esmeralda** (⊠ Avda. 2 between C. 5 and 7) is a late-night mariachi bar where visitors are serenaded and can gaze at paintings depicting old scenes of San José. The food here isn't bad either. A trendy place to see and be seen is **El Cuartel de la Boca del Monte** (⊠ Avda. 1 between C. 21 and 23), a large, low-ceiling bar, where young artists and professionals gather to eat *bocas* (appetizers) and sip San José's fanciest cocktails. **Río** in the Los Yoses suburb is always rocking and crowded with young Ticos on weekends. In San Pedro, lively bars line the streets around the university. **El Pueblo** is a shopping arcade in the style of a quaint Spanish village and home to a range of bars, restaurants, and discos. Recommended are **Cocoloco,** which often has a live salsa band, and **La Plaza,** across the street, with its huge dance floor. Gay and lesbian travelers can hit the following bars and dance clubs: **Buenas Vibraciones** (⊠ Paseo de los Estudiantes); **El Churro Español** (⊠ Avda. 8 and C. 11); **Déja Vù** (⊠ C. 2 between Avdas. 14 and 16a), a mostly gay, techno-heavy disco with two dance floors; and **La Avispa** (⊠ C. 1 between Avdas. 8 and 10).

Cabaret
Josephine's (⊠ Avda. 8 between C. 2 and 4, ☎ 257–2269) is a Vegas-style nightclub presenting a cabaret show called "San José Nights." It is open from 9 PM until 3 AM.

Casinos
The **Casino Colonial** (⊠ Avda. 1 between C. 9 and 11) is open 24 hours a day. Most of the country's larger hotels have casinos, including the **Aurola Holiday Inn** (the view from the casino is breathtaking), **Cariari,** and **Gran Hotel Costa Rica** (☞ Lodging, *above*).

The Arts

Theater and Music
The Baroque **Teatro Nacional** (⊠ Plaza de la Cultura, ☎ 221–1329) hosts performances of the excellent National Symphony Orchestra, whose season runs from April to the end of December, with concerts on Thursday and Friday evenings. The Nacional also stages performances from visiting opera companies and dance troupes. The other main theater is the **Teatro Melico Salazar** (⊠ Avda. 2 between C. Central and 2, ☎ 221–4952). Dozens of theater groups, including two that perform in English, put on shows at smaller theaters around town; check the English-language *Tico Times* for theater ads.

Cinemas
Dubbing is rare in Costa Rica, so moviegoers can see films in their original language, usually English, and brush up on their Spanish by reading the subtitles. The film scene is dominated by U.S. movies, which reach San José about a month after their release in the United States. **Sala Garbo and Laurence Olivier** (⊠ Avda. 2 and C. 28) and **Cine Variedades** (⊠ C. 5 between Avdas. Central and 1) are San José's only arts cinemas. Check the local papers for listings.

OUTDOOR ACTIVITIES AND SPORTS

Golf

Nine-hole courses are open to nonmembers at the **Costa Rica Country Club** in Escazú and **Los Reyes Country Club** in La Guácima (southwest of Alajuela). Unfortunately, you have to be a guest at the Cariari hotel to play the **Cariari Country Club's** 18-hole course.

Gyms

Luxury hotels like the **Aurola Holiday Inn** and the **Cariari** (☞ Lodging, *above*) have modern gyms attached. For others, look under "Gimnasios" in the *Páginas Amarillas* (*Yellow Pages*).

Horseback Riding

The city's abundant travel agencies offer a variety of one-day horseback tours, most of which head to farms on the slopes of nearby volcanoes, which usually means panoramic views of the Central Valley. Tours include round-trip transportation from your hotel, lunch, and sometimes breakfast.

Jogging

Parque La Sabana, at the end of the Paseo Colón, once the airport but now a eucalyptus-shaded park, is the best place to jog in San José, with 5-kilometer (3-mile) routes along cement paths.

Tennis

Public tennis courts can be found at the country clubs referred to under Golf, *above*. Hotels with courts include the **Cariari** (☞ Lodging, *above*) and the **Bougainvillea** (☞ Barva Volcano Dining and Lodging *in* Chapter 4) but the facilities are not available to nonguests.

White-Water Rafting

White-water trips down the **Reventazón, Pacuare,** and **General rivers** all leave from San José, but the action takes place in other parts of the country (☞ Outdoor Activities and Sports *in* Chapters 5 and 7).

The Reventazón's class II and IV–V runs are both day trips, whereas the General is descended on three-day camping trips, and the Pacuare can be run in either one or two days; accommodations are either in a tent or a rustic lodge, depending on the outfitter.

SHOPPING

Antiques

Antigüedades Amon (⊠ Avda. 3A between C. 3 and 5, ☎ 223–9552) and **Antigüedades Mónaco** (⊠ C. 5 between Avdas. 3 and 3B, no phone) both sell high-quality antiques from the postcolonial era.

Arts and Crafts

The **central market** has the best range and prices for hammocks and leather bags, belts, and shoes, but shop around and haggle before digging out your wallet. The best place for bags and belts at the market is near the northwestern entrance. The **Centro Comercial El Pueblo,** on the northern edge of Barrio Tournon, is an open-air shopping center designed to look like a colonial village, and most of its shops cater to tourists. **Boutique Annemarie** in the lobby of the Don Carlos Hotel (☞ Lodging, *above*) is particularly strong in small wooden objects and imitation pre-Columbian stoneware. **La Casona** (⊠ C. Central between Avdas. Central and 1) is an indoor market selling almost every craft typical of Central America. **Atmósfera** (⊠ C. 5 between Avdas. 1 and 3, ☎ 222–4322) is good for jewelry, masks, wall hangings, and dishes with bright, primitive designs. **Magia** (☎ 233–2630), a few doors north, specializes in fine woodwork. **Suráska** (⊠ C. 5 and Avda. 3, ☎ 222–0129) has an interesting selection of wooden crafts, ceramics, and paintings.

Books and Maps

The Bookshop (⊠ Avda. 11 between C. 1 and 3, no phone) sells a wide selection of books in English as well as magazines, cards, and local crafts. It also functions as a coffeehouse. **Chispas Books** (⊠ C. 7 between Avdas. Central and 1, ☎ 256–8251) specializes in ecological themes. **Universal** (⊠ Avda. Central between C. Central and 1, ☎ 222–2222) has some books in English, as well as a stock of large-scale topographical maps.

Coffee and Liquor

Coffee can be purchased in souvenir shops and supermarkets; Britt and Tarrazú are the names to look for. The country's best rum is the aged Centenario, and it costs about $5 a bottle. **Yamuni** (⊠ Avda. 2 and C. 7) is San José's largest liquor store; it's a good place to buy local liqueurs, picnic gear, and kitchenware.

SAN JOSÉ A TO Z

Arriving and Departing

By Bus

San José has no central bus station. For arrival and departure depots for various destinations, *see* Getting Around, *below.*

By Car

San José is the hub of the national road system. Paved roads fan out from Paseo Colón left to Escazú, or right to the airport, the Pacific coast, Guanacaste, and Nicaragua. Calle 3 runs into the highway to Limón and the Atlantic coast; and if you follow Avenida 2 east through San Pedro you'll enter the highway to Cartago, Turrialba, the Southwest, and Panama.

By Plane

AIRPORTS AND AIRLINES

All international and some domestic flights arrive at **Juan Santamaría Airport,** 16 kilometers (10 miles) northwest of downtown San José. Other domestic flights depart from **Tobias Bolaños Airport** in the suburb of Pavas, 3 kilometers (2 miles) west of downtown San José. (For airlines serving San José, *see* Air Travel *in* Smart Travel Tips A to Z.)

BETWEEN THE AIRPORT AND DOWNTOWN

Taxis from the airport to downtown cost around $10. Beware of taxi drivers eager to take you to a hotel they know, which no doubt pays them a hefty commission. Far cheaper and almost as quick, is the bus marked "Ruta 200 San José," which will drop you at the west end of Avenida 2, close to the heart of the city. The other option is to pick up a vehicle from one of the car-rental offices. Driving time is about 20 minutes, but allow 40 minutes to be safe. Note that some hotels provide a free shuttle service—inquire when you book.

Getting Around

By Bus

Bus service within San José is absurdly cheap (around 30 colones per ride) and easy to use. For Paseo Colón and La Sabana take buses marked SABANA-CEMENTERIO from the stop on Avenida 3 and Calle 2. For the university-vicinity suburbs of Los Yoses and San Pedro take those marked SAN PEDRO, CURRIDABAT, or LOURDES from Avenida 2, between Calles 5 and 7.

By Car

Almost all the streets in downtown San José are one-way. Traffic gets surprisingly congested at peak hours, when it's ill-advised to drive through the city.

By Taxi

Taxis are a good deal in the capital. You can hail them in the street or call them directly. Companies include **San Jorge** (☎ 221–3434),

The best places to travel may be the best places to get hepatitis A.

You can pick up hepatitis A when traveling to high-risk areas outside of the United States. From raw shellfish or water you don't think is contaminated. Or from uncooked foods — like salad — prepared by people who don't know they're infected. At even the best places.

Symptoms of hepatitis A include jaundice, abdominal pain, fever, vomiting and diarrhea. And can cause discomfort, time away from work and memories you'd like to forget.

The U.S. Centers for Disease Control and Prevention (CDC) recommends immunization for travelers to high-risk areas. *Havrix*, available in over 45 countries, can protect you from hepatitis A. *Havrix* may cause some soreness in your arm or a slight headache.

Ask your physician about vaccination with *Havrix* at your next visit or at least 2 weeks before you travel. And have a great trip.

Please see important patient information adjacent to this ad.

Havrix®
Hepatitis A Vaccine, Inactivated

The world's first hepatitis A vaccine

For more information on how to protect yourself against hepatitis A, call

1-800-HEP-A-VAX (1-800-437-2829)

Manufactured by
SmithKline Beecham Biologicals
Rixensart, Belgium

Distributed by
SmithKline Beecham Pharmaceuticals
Philadelphia, PA 19101

HA8590   © SmithKline Beecham, 1996

Havrix is a registered trademark of SmithKline Beecham.

Hepatitis A Vaccine, Inactivated
Havrix®

See complete prescribing information in SmithKline Beecham Pharmaceuticals literature. The following is a brief summary.

INDICATIONS AND USAGE: *Havrix* is indicated for active immunization of persons ≥ 2 years of age against disease caused by hepatitis A virus (HAV).

CONTRAINDICATIONS: *Havrix* is contraindicated in people with known hypersensitivity to any component of the vaccine.

WARNINGS: Do not give additional injections to patients experiencing hypersensitivity reactions after a *Havrix* injection. (See CONTRAINDICATIONS.)

Hepatitis A has a relatively long incubation period. Hepatitis A vaccine may not prevent hepatitis A infection in those who have an unrecognized hepatitis A infection at the time of vaccination. Additionally, it may not prevent infection in those who do not achieve protective antibody titers (although the lowest titer needed to confer protection has not been determined).

PRECAUTIONS: As with any parenteral vaccine (1) keep epinephrine available for use in case of anaphylaxis or anaphylactoid reaction; (2) delay administration, if possible, in people with any febrile illness or active infection, except when the physican believes withholding vaccine entails the greater risk; (3) take all known precautions to prevent adverse reactions, including reviewing patients' history for hypersensitivity to this or similar vaccines.

Administer with caution to people with thrombocytopenia or a bleeding disorder, or people taking anticoagulants. Do not inject into a blood vessel. Use a separate, sterile needle or prefilled syringe for every patient. When giving concomitantly with other vaccines or IG, use separate needles and different injection sites.

As with any vaccine, if administered to immunosuppressed persons or persons receiving immunosuppressive therapy, the expected immune response may not be obtained.

Carcinogenesis, Mutagenesis, Impairment of Fertility: *Havrix* has not been evaluated for its carcinogenic potential, mutagenic potential or potential for impairment of fertility.

Pregnancy Category C: Animal reproduction studies have not been conducted with *Havrix*. It is also not known whether *Havrix* can cause fetal harm when administered to a pregnant woman or can affect reproduction capacity. Give *Havrix* to a pregnant woman only if clearly needed. It is not known whether *Havrix* is excreted in human milk. Because many drugs are excreted in human milk, use caution when administering *Havrix* to a nursing woman.

Havrix is well tolerated and highly immunogenic and effective in children.

Fully inform patients, parents or guardians of the benefits and risks of immunization with *Havrix*. For persons traveling to endemic or epidemic areas, consult current CDC advisories regarding specific locales. Travelers should take all necessary precautions to avoid contact with, or ingestion of, contaminated food or water. Duration of immunity following a complete vaccination schedule has not been established.

ADVERSE REACTIONS: *Havrix* has been generally well tolerated. As with all pharmaceuticals, however, it is possible that expanded commercial use of the vaccine could reveal rare adverse events.

The most frequently reported by volunteers in clinical trials was injection-site soreness (56% of adults; 21% of children); headache (14% of adults; less than 9% of children). Other solicited and unsolicited events are listed below:

Incidence 1% to 10% of Injections: Induration, redness, swelling; fatigue, fever (>37.5°C), malaise; anorexia, nausea.

Incidence <1% of Injections: Hematoma; pruritus, rash, urticaria; pharyngitis, other upper respiratory tract infections; abdominal pain, diarrhea, dysgeusia, vomiting; arthralgia, elevation of creatine phosphokinase, myalgia; lymphadenopathy; hypertonic episode, insomnia, photophobia, vertigo.

Additional safety data

Safety data were obtained from two additional sources in which large populations were vaccinated. In an outbreak setting in which 4,930 individuals were immunized with a single dose of either 720 EL.U. or 1440 EL.U. of *Havrix*, the vaccine was well-tolerated and no serious adverse events due to vaccination were reported. Overall, less than 10% of vaccinees reported solicited general adverse events following the vaccine. The most common solicited local adverse event was pain at the injection site, reported in 22.3% of subjects at 24 hours and decreasing to 2.4% by 72 hours.

In a field efficacy trial, 19,037 children received the 360 EL.U. dose of *Havrix*. The most commonly reported adverse events were injection-site pain (9.5%) and tenderness (8.1%), reported following first doses of *Havrix*. Other adverse events were infrequent and comparable to the control vaccine Engerix-B® (Hepatitis B Vaccine, Recombinant).

Postmarketing Reports: Rare voluntary reports of adverse events in people receiving *Havrix* since market introduction include the following: localized edema; anaphylaxis/anaphylactoid reactions, somnolence; syncope; jaundice, hepatitis; erythema multiforme, hyperhydrosis, angioedema; dyspnea; lymphadenopathy; convulsions, encephalopathy, dizziness, neuropathy, myelitis, paresthesia, Guillain-Barré syndrome, multiple sclerosis; congenital abnormality.

The U.S. Department of Health and Human Services has established the Vaccine Adverse Events Reporting System (VAERS) to accept reports of suspected adverse events after the administration of any vaccine, including, but not limited to, the reporting of events required by the National Childhood Vaccine Injury Act of 1986. The toll-free number for VAERS forms and information is 1-800-822-7967.

HOW SUPPLIED: 360 EL.U./0.5 mL: NDC 58160-836-01 Package of 1 single-dose vial.

720 EL.U./0.5 mL: NDC 58160-837-01 Package of 1 single-dose vial; NDC 58160-837-02 Package of 1 prefilled syringe.

1440 EL.U./mL: NDC 58160-835-01 Package of 1 single-dose vial; NDC 58160-835-02 Package of 1 prefilled syringe.

Manufactured by **SmithKline Beecham Biologicals**
Rixensart, Belgium
Distributed by **SmithKline Beecham Pharmaceuticals**
Philadelphia, PA 19101
BRS–HA:L5A

Havrix is a registered trademark of SmithKline Beecham.

Coopetaxi (☎ 235–9966), and **Taxis Unidos** (☎ 221–6865). A 3-kilometer (2-mile) ride costs around 200 colones. Taxis parked in front of expensive hotels charge about twice the normal rate. By law, all cabbies must use their meters; if one refuses, negotiate a price before going anywhere.

Contacts and Resources

Car Rentals

There is an overabundance of rent-a-car companies in San José, ranging from the big international firms to dozens of local operations. **Avis, Budget, Hertz,** and **Thrifty** all have offices in the country (☞ Car Rental *in* Important Contacts A to Z), and their cars can be reserved before traveling to Costa Rica. Costa Rican companies with toll-free U.S. numbers include **Ada** (☎ 800/570–0671) and **Elegante** (☎ 800/582–7432; Canada ☎ 800/283–1324). Once in the country, you can look in the *Yellow Pages* under "Alquiler de Automóviles," or look in the *Tico Times* or *Costa Rica Today* for ads offering discounts. Note: It is practically impossible to rent a car in Costa Rica from December 20 to January 3.

Doctors and Dentists

Your embassy can provide you with a list of recommended doctors and dentists. Hospitals open to foreigners include **Clínica Bíblica** (⊠ Avda. 14 between C. Central and 1, ☎ 257–0466) and **Clínica Católica** (⊠ Guadelupe, attached to San Antonio Church on C. Esquivel Bonilla St., ☎ 225–5055).

Embassies

U.S. (⊠ Pavas, ☎ 220–3939). **Canadian** (⊠ Sabana Sur, next to tennis club, ☎ 296–4146). **U.K.** (⊠ Centro Colón, Paseo Colón between C. 38 and 40, ☎ 221–5566).

Emergencies

In just about any emergency you can dial **911,** but the following are some additional useful numbers: **Police** (☎ 117, or 127 outside cities), **Traffic Police** (☎ 222–9330), and **Fire** (☎ 118).

English-Language Bookstores

See Shopping, *above* for English-language bookstores.

Guided Tours

ADVENTURE TOURS

Serendipity Adventures (☎ 450–0318) offers sunrise flights in hot air balloons, mountain biking, river rafting and other outdoor tours. The country's most experienced rafting outfitters are: **Costa Rica Expeditions** (☎ 222–0333, FAX 257–0766), **Costa Sol Rafting** (☎ 293–2151, FAX 293–2155), **Ríos Tropicales** (☎ 233–6455, FAX 255–4354), and **Aventuras Naturales** (☎ 225–3939, FAX 253–6934). Ríos Tropicales also offers sea kayaking expeditions. **Ecotreks** (☎ 289–8191), Ríos Tropicales, and Aventuras Naturales also feature mountain biking tours. **Motoaventura** (☎ 255–4174) arranges motorcycle and Jet Ski tours. **Tropical Bungee** (☎ 233–6378) runs bungee jumps near San José on weekends.

EXCURSIONS

The seemingly hundreds of travel agents in San José all sell the same basic day trips. Many of the hotels listed above have in-house travel agents or book trips at the front desk. Companies that run cruises to Tortuga Island include **Calypso** (☎ 256–2727, FAX 233–0401) and **Bay Island Cruises** (☎ 296–5551, FAX 296–5095). **Café Britt** (☎ 260–2748, FAX 238–1848) runs a popular coffee tour, which presents the history of coffee via skits, a tour of a coffee farm, and coffee tastings. Among the many operators that offer horseback tours (☞ Outdoor Activities and Sports, *above*) are: **Magic Trails** (☎ 234–2530, FAX 225–6143), **Sacramento Lodge** (☎ 237–2116, FAX 237–2976), and **Tipical Tours** (☎ 233–8486, FAX 257–5433).

NATURAL HISTORY TOURS

Although everyone is selling ecological tours, there are a few companies that have more experience than the majority, among them **Cosmos Tours** (☎ 234–0607, FAX 253–4707), **Costa Rica Expeditions** (☎ 222–0333, FAX 257–0766), **Geotur** (☎ 234–1867), **Horizontes** (☎ 222–2022, FAX 255–4513), **Sun Tours** (☎ 255–2011), and **Tikal Ecoadventures** (☎ 223–2811).

Late-Night Pharmacies

The Clínica Bíblica (☞ Doctors and Dentists, *above*) operates a **24-hour** pharmacy.

Travel Agencies

Galaxy (✉ C. 3, Avdas. 5 and 7, ☎ 233–3240), **INTERTUR** (✉ Avda. 1, C. 3 and 5, ☎ 233–1400), and **TAM** (✉ C. 1, Avdas. Central and 1, ☎ 223–5111).

Visitor Information

The main tourist office (**ICT,** ☎ 222–1090) for the entire country is beneath the Plaza de la Cultura. Walk down the steps across from the Burger King on Calle 5. It's open weekdays 9–5 and Saturdays 9–1. There is also a tourism information desk at Juan Santamaría International Airport (◷ Daily 6 am–9 pm).

4 The Central Valley

A ring of spectacular volcanoes defines the boundaries of the Meseta Central, or Central Valley. This is a densely populated agricultural area, heavily planted with neat rows of coffee. The valley surrounds San José—when you tire of the hustle bustle of the capital city, head here for one of the many exciting, daylong excursions. Peer into the crater of a volcano; wander amidst lush tropical plants; visit colonial-era towns; or tour a coffee plantation and discover the important economic role of the grano de oro (golden bean).

S YOU DRIVE OUT OF SAN JOSÉ, the bungalowed, grid-plan suburbs of the city quickly give way to arable land and vast coffee plantations. Coffee has come to symbolize the prosperity of both the Central Valley and of the nation as a whole; as such, this all-important cash crop has developed a certain amount of cultural mystique and folklore. Costa Rican artists, for example, have long venerated coffee workers, and the painted ox-cart, once used to transport coffee to Puntarenas on the coast, has become a national symbol. As you explore the hills of the region, you may still see one of these quaint oxcarts in use or parked next to a farm-house.

Updated by
David
Dudenhoefer

Looming above these coffee plantations are the Meseta's sentinel-like volcanoes, three of which are now national parks. Irazú Volcano, Costa Rica's highest, is less than two hours away from the capital; the barren landscape surrounding the crater is a grim reminder of the destructive eruptions of the early 1960s. Poás, whose crater is often eerily hidden by clouds, spews dramatic puffs of noxious sulfuric smoke. On a clear day you'll be awestruck by the jewel-like blue-green lake nestled in the crater's center. Hike to the summit of Barva Volcano, a difficult trek but one well worth it; arrive early before the hordes of tourists descend and you may catch a brief glimpse of the rare, multicolored quetzal.

The Central Valley is also home to charming, historical towns and hamlets. Though most of the region's colonial architecture has been destroyed by earthquakes and the ravages of time and a tropical climate, there are several smaller cities here that preserve a bit more history than San José. The central squares of Alajuela and Heredia, for example, are quite charming, surrounded by an architectural mixture of the old and new. Cartago, the country's first capital, has the impressive Basílica de los Angeles, as well as the ruins of a cathedral that was under construction when an earthquake hit the city. There are also a number of smaller communities in the hills around San José with lovely churches and adobe houses with coffee growing in their backyards—such as Escazú, to the west, Barva, near Heredia, and Grecia.

Pleasures and Pastimes

Dining
Since most travelers explore the Central Valley from San José, they can enjoy the capital's selection of Costa Rican and international cuisine (☞ Chapter 3). Out in the valley you'll find few places offering more than local fare—nevertheless, you will find some excellent restaurants, where the hearty meals are enhanced by the natural surroundings.

Festivals
April 11 is Juan Santamaría Day, celebrated in Alajuela with marching bands, majorettes, and parades. In Alajuela, the Festival of Mangoes involves nine days of music, parades, markets, and general merrymaking in July. The second Sunday in March is Día del Boyero (Oxcart Driver Day), when a colorful procession of carts parades through San Antonio de Escazú.

Lodging
The accommodations scattered across the Central Valley range from the rustic *cabinas* (cabins) of La Providencia to the elegant suites of

the Hotel Tara. Regardless of their luxuriousness or lack thereof, all of the properties have pleasant views and lush, natural surroundings. Most travelers tend to stay in San José, since its central location makes it possible to visit all the Central Valley's attractions on day trips. Though the city has an ample selection of hotels and restaurants, it also has the crime, noise, and pollution that accompany crowds and traffic, which can make rural lodging a much more attractive option.

Volcanoes

Costa Rica's most accessible volcanoes define the northern edge of the Central Valley, two of which, Poás and Irazú, have paved roads right to their summits. Poás is the more popular, since it has an extensive visitors' center and an enchanting crater lake set in the middle of a dwarf forest. Irazú is topped by a more desolate landscape, the result of violent eruptions in the early 1960s, but on a clear day, the view is incomparable. Barva, which requires some strenuous hiking, offers more exposure to the flora and fauna of the cloud forest. All three volcanoes can be visited on day trips from San José; Poás and Irazú require only a morning, whereas you'll need a full day to hike into Barva.

Exploring the Central Valley

Great Itineraries

Most travelers explore the Central Valley from San José, which has the most varied selection of dining and lodging options. Dozens of towns and small cities surround the capital and beyond them lie countless coffee farms and pastures. Most of these towns stand in the shadows of the volcanoes, so include a stop at one or two of these towns during your itinerary. To reach Poás, for example, you have to drive through Alajuela, while Heredia lies on the road to Barva, and Cartago sits at the foot of Irazú. To simplify matters, we have divided the region into two areas: the eastern Central Valley and the western Central Valley, everything to the west and north of San José.

IF YOU HAVE 2 DAYS

Numbers in the text correspond to numbers in the margin and on the Central Valley map.

Start by ascending ▣ **Poás Volcano** ⑤, where you can settle in for the night, or drive back to San José. Next day, head to the **Orosí Valley** ③ with a stop at the spectacular Jardín Lankester.

IF YOU HAVE 4 DAYS

On day one, head north to **Heredia** ⑥ and the nearby coffee communities, continuing up the slopes of **Barva Volcano** ⑦ for a picnic lunch in the cool mountain air. Energetic travelers may want to dedicate a day to hiking in to see the crater lakes atop the volcano. Spend the next day exploring the ▣ **Orosi Valley** ③, starting with a morning in Tapantí National Park. You may want to spend a night in the valley, visiting Jardín Lankester and **Cartago** ① the next day. Or you may wish, instead, to start the next day with an ascent up **Irazú Volcano** ②, after which you can visit **Cartago** ① and the Jardín Lankester. On the fourth day, climb **Poás Volcano** ⑤ and stop in at nearby **Alajuela** ④ and the towns of Sarchí and Grecia.

IF YOU HAVE 5 DAYS

Start by exploring the colonial town of **Escazú** ⑧, then go horseback riding, tour a traditional coffee community, or hike in the cloud forest. On day two, visit the summit of ▣ **Poás Volcano** ⑤ and spend the night either here or near ▣ **Escazú** ⑧. Dedicate day three to a horse-

The Central Valley

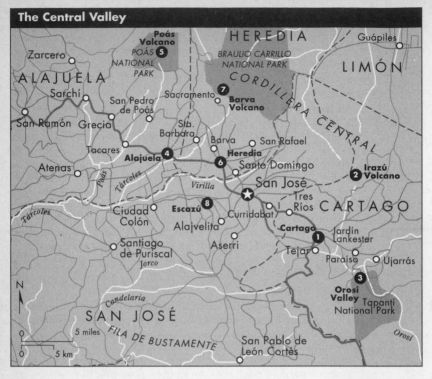

back tour or a visit to the Zoo Ave, the bird zoo. Head for the **Orosí Valley** ③ on the following day, where you should start by visiting Tapantí National Park. The fifth day should begin with a trip up **Irazú** ②, after which you can wander through **Cartago** ① and Jardín Lankester or head to San José for some shopping.

When to Tour the Central Valley

The Central Valley experiences the same annual dry and rainy seasons found along the entire length of the Pacific slope. From January to May it tends to be sunny and breezy on an almost daily basis; after mid-May skies begin to cloud up and rain almost every afternoon. Regular afternoon downpours are consistent during May and June, dropping off a bit between mid-July and mid-September. The afternoon showers are most plentiful from September to December, when the season changes again.

Though it rains for days on end a few times during the rainy season, this is nevertheless a pleasant time to explore the region. The reason is simple—few tourists visit during this period, so you'll have the place mostly to yourself. This also means that advance reservations probably won't be necessary during those months. The region is spectacularly beautiful, too, when, in mid-May, the coffee bushes burst into white blossom, the closest it comes to snowing in Costa Rica. There are many dry days scattered throughout the rainy season, and normally it only storms a few hours every afternoon. The Central Valley is swathed in green during the rainy months, but come January the sun begins to beat down, and by April the countryside is parched.

It rains very little in December, but it can be almost impossible to rent a car during the last two weeks of the year, because Costa Ricans reserve them all for the holidays. From December to February, you may come across people harvesting coffee in the farms of the Central Valley. You'll want to head for the volcanoes at the crack of dawn during the rainy months; in the dry season, the summits sometimes stay cloud-free all day long. Since it can also be very difficult to get a room anywhere outside San José during the week preceding Easter, you'll want to make your reservations well in advance.

EASTERN CENTRAL VALLEY

Cartago, Jardín Lankester, Irazú Volcano, and the Orosí Valley

Numbers in the margin correspond to points of interest on the Central Valley map.

The eastern half of the Central Valley contains Costa Rica's highest volcano and the remains of its oldest church. There are actually several interesting churches in the area, two of them in the scenic Orosí Valley, as well as the many ecological attractions of a botanical garden and protected cloud forest. Travelers could feasibly explore this area in one day but only if they want to be on the road from dawn until well past dusk. For a more leisurely pace, dedicate two days to this end of the valley, visiting Irazú Volcano and Cartago one day, and tackling the Orosí Valley on another. Lankester Gardens could be easily included in either trip.

Cartago

❶ *22 km (14 mi) southeast of San José.*

The country's original capital is much older than San José, but since earthquakes have destroyed most of its colonial structures, only a 17th-century basilica remains as a testimonial to the city's former architectural glory. Cradle of Costa Rican culture and capital for 260 years until 1823, Cartago lost almost all its historic buildings as a result of the above-mentioned 1841 and 1910 earthquakes. The last of these prevented completion of the central cathedral, whose Romanesque ruins (Las Ruinas) now form a pleasant garden cultivated with pines and bougainvillea. You'll spot a few attractive old buildings as you head through town, most of which were erected after the 1910 quake—the majority of the city's architecture, however, is bland. Exception: Cartago's most impressive landmark, the gaudy Basílica, on the eastern edge of town.

The spectacular **Basílica de Nuestra Señora de Los Angeles** (Basilica of Our Lady of the Angels) is a hodgepodge of styles from Baroque to Byzantine with a dash of Gothic thrown in. It is also the focus of an amazing annual pilgrimage from San José: During the night of August 1 and well into the early-morning hours of the 2nd, the road from the capital clogs with people on their way to celebrate the 1635 appearance of La Negrita (Black Virgin), Costa Rica's patron saint, at the spring behind the church. The faithful come here to fill bottles with the supposedly curative waters. Miraculous healing powers are attributed to the saint; and the devoted have placed thousands of symbolic crutches, ears, eyes, and legs next to her diminutive statue in recognition of her gifts. The constant arrival of tour buses and school groups, along with shops selling candles and bottles of holy water in the shape of the saint, add a bit of a circus atmosphere to the scene. La Negrita has twice been stolen, most recently in 1950 by José León Sánchez, now one of Costa Rica's best known novelists, who spent 20 years on the prison island of San Lucas for his crime. At the edge of town, 10 blocks east of the central square. ⊠ *C. 16 between Avdas. 2 and 4.*

Duck into **Pops** (☎ 551–7878), a half block north of the market on the main street, for an ice cream or a cool drink and a view of the always-bustling strip.

Anyone interested in plants, especially orchids, should visit **Jardín Lankester** (Lankester Botanical Gardens), minutes from Cartago. Created in the 1940s by the English naturalist Charles Lankester to help preserve the local flora, it is now under the auspices of the University of Costa Rica. The lush garden and greenhouses contain one of the world's largest orchid collections, more than 800 species, both native and introduced. Orchids, by the way, are mostly epiphytes, meaning they use other plants for support without damaging them in the process. The best time to visit the always-interesting garden is March–May, when the orchids are in full bloom. Bromeliads and aroids also abound, along with 80 species of trees, including hardwoods, fruit, bamboo, and cacti; this diversity of plants attracts a wide variety of birds as well. To reach the gardens, drive through the center of Cartago, passing the Basílica on your left, and take the road to Paraíso. The road isn't well marked, so ask a passerby if in doubt. After 6 kilometers (4 miles), an orange sign on the right-hand verge marks the turn to Jardín Lankester. ⊠ *Dulce Nombre, Cartago.* ☎ *551–9877.* ▩ *500 colones.* ☉ *Daily 8:30–3:30; visitors admitted every hr on the ½ hr.*

Irazú Volcano

② *31 km (19 mi) northwest of Cartago to the summit.*

Irazú Volcano is Costa Rica's highest at 11,260 feet, and its summit has long been protected as a national park (☞ Central Valley National Parks *in* Chapter 2). The mountain looms high above Cartago, and its eruptions have dumped a considerable quantity of ash on the city over the years. The most recent were from 1962 through 1965, beginning on the day that John F. Kennedy arrived in Costa Rica for a presidential visit. Boulders and mud rained down on the countryside, damming rivers and causing serious flooding. Although farmers who cultivate Irazú's slopes live in fear of the next eruption, they are also grateful for the soil's richness, a direct result of the volcanic deposits.

The road up to the summit climbs past vegetable fields, pastures, and native oak forests. You'll pass through the villages of **Potrero Cerrado** and **San Juan de Chicoá,** both with lookout points, before reaching the bleak, gaping **crater** at the summit. Although currently dormant, gases and steam billow out from fumaroles on Irazú's northwestern slope, scarcely visible from the crater lookouts. The gray, moonscape peak of Irazú is one of the few places from which both the Pacific Ocean and the Caribbean Sea can be seen, although clouds frequently obscure both from view. **The Area Recreativa de Prusia,** halfway down, has hiking trails for beautiful walks through oak and pine forest. Picnic areas are available if you want to bring your own supplies; warm, waterproof clothing is advisable for the summit. Leave San José very early in the day so as not to be thwarted by low clouds. Bear left where Irazú is signposted, 4 kilometers (2½ miles) short of Cartago, to bypass the city. Driving time from San José to the summit is just short of 1½ hours. *For more information, call the Sistemas de Areas de Conservación in San José,* ☎ *283–8004, or the National Parks toll-free number,* ☎ *192.* ☉ *Daily 8–4.*

The Orosí Valley

❸ *Orosí: 30 km (19 mi) southeast of San José.*

The Orosí Valley, an area of breathtaking views and varied attractions, contains remnants of the colonial era and of the tropical forest that covered the country when the Spanish first arrived. The valley was one of the earliest parts of Costa Rica to be settled by Spanish colonists, as ruins and a colonial church attest. The rich soil and proximity to San José have made it an important agricultural area, with extensive plantations of coffee, chayote (a pale-green, native squash), and other vegetables. Fed in the west by the confluence of the Navarro and Orosí rivers and drained in the east by the ferocious Reventazón, the valley was dammed in the east for hydroelectricity, forming the Cachí Reservoir. Two roads descend into the valley from the town of Paraíso, looping around the lake then continuing on to wind past the tidy patchworks of cultivated crops and pass over the Cachí Dam.

The lakeside **Charrara Recreation Area** is a popular weekend spot on the shore of the Cachí Reservoir, in the heart of the Orosí Valley. Families flock here on weekends, gathering at covered picnic shelters, complete with barbecue pits; after lunch, they head for the basketball courts, the soccer field, and the swimming pool. There's also a trail through the planted pine forest to the edge of the reservoir. The restaurant has a view of the pool, reservoir, and green hills beyond and serves a predictable selection of meat and seafood dishes. ⊠ *1 km (½ mi) east of Ujarrás,* ☎ *574–7557.* ☒ *250 colones, plus 200 colones for your car.* ☉ *Daily 9–5.*

The town of **Orosí,** in the heart of the valley of the same name, has but one tourist attraction: a beautiful restored **colonial church.** Built in 1743, the structure has a squat, whitewashed facade; the roof is made of cane overlaid with terra-cotta barrel tiles. Inside, canvases depict the Stations of the Cross. The museum in the cloister annex houses old religious regalia and multicolored wood carvings. Opening times fluctuate, but should you find it closed, ask around and somebody will probably open it up for you. South of town there are some **thermal pools** fed by a hot spring, which are open to the public for a nominal fee.

NEED A BREAK?	The **Hotel Río Palomo,** between the Cachí Dam and Orosí, has a restaurant that overlooks the Orosí River and two pools that nonguests can use for 200 colones (☞ Dining and Lodging, *below*).

Paraíso (Paradise), an unattractive town east of Cartago, has few heavenly attributes, but it is the gateway to the beautiful Orosí Valley. The two main roads into the valley are reached by turning right just before the town's shady central park. If you turn left at the *bomberos* (fire station), which houses some splendid old-style fire engines, you'll head to Ujarrás and the Charrara Recreation Area. Go straight, and you'll be on the road to the town of Orosí and Tapantí National Park. Both roads snake down into the valley through coffee plantations, passing miradors (vantage points) where you should definitely stop for a view of one of the prettiest valleys in Costa Rica. Both roads lead into a loop around the Cachí Reservoir.

Tucked into a steep valley to the south of Orosí you'll find **Tapantí National Park,** an 11,600-acre cloud forest preserve that is home to abundant bird life and refreshing swimming holes (☞ Chapter 2). The National Parks Service oversees this humid forest refuge where 211 species of bird reside. The graceful, shy, and endangered **quetzal** nests here in late spring; look into the laurel trees to the left of the road near the entrance and you may spot one. Courtesy of the hydroelectric power station, the 10-kilometer (6-mile) track to Tapantí is paved. That track follows the course of the Orosí River past coffee plantations, elegant *fincas* (farmhouses), and seasonal barracks for coffee workers before being hemmed in by the steep slopes of thick jungle. The green rangers' office on the left is where you stop to pay the entry fee. The road continues through the reserve, and you can leave your vehicle at the start of the various trails, one of which leads to a swimming spot on the Orosí. Since the park tends to cloud up in the afternoon, it's best early in the day or during the dry season (December to early May). Taxis, carrying up to six people, make trips to the reserve from beside the soccer field in the town of Orosí for about $10 per round-trip. *Call Amistad Atlántico (☎ 758–3996), a regional branch of the National Parks Service, for more info.* 🗺 *$6.* ⊙ *Daily 7–4.*

The ruins of the **country's oldest church** stand in a small park in the town of **Ujarrás** on the floor of the Orosí Valley, down the hill from Paraíso. Built between 1681 and 1693 in honor of the Virgin of Ujarrás, the church, together with the surrounding village, was abandoned in 1833 after a series of earthquakes and floods. An unlikely victory by the Spaniards over a superior force of invading British pirates was attributed to a prayer stop here. Today it is a pleasant monument surrounded by well-kept gardens and large trees that often attract flocks of parakeets and parrots. Ujarrás is about 10 kilometers (6 miles) northeast of Orosí. ⊙ *Daily 8–5.*

Dining and Lodging

$ ✕🖬 **Río Palomo Lodge.** Next to the bridge across the Orosí, the restaurant at this hotel enjoys close proximity to the stony river of the same name. The large open-sided dining room has a cane ceiling, a tile floor, and spindly white metal chairs. Foodwise, the best bet is probably the fresh fish. Outside, there's a large pool with a high diving board (open to nonresidents/diners for 200 colones). Farther along the riverbank you come to the secluded modern cabinas with white walls, wood ceilings, and modern furniture. Larger units have well-equipped kitchens. ✉ *Apdo. 220–7050, Cartago,* ☎ *533–3128,* 🖷 *533–3057. 7 cabinas with bath. [df]Restaurant, bar, pool. AE, DC, MC, V.*

Outdoor Activities and Sports
HIKING

There are several short trails that let you explore the cloud forest in Tapantí National Park (☞ *Exploring, above*).

Shopping
In the Orosí Valley, between the Cachí Dam and Orosí, the **Casa del Soñador** sells wooden sculptures.

WESTERN CENTRAL VALLEY

Alajuela, Poás Volcano, Heredia, Barva Volcano, and Escazú

Numbers in the margin correspond to points of interest on the Central Valley map.

Costa Rica's coffee heartland lies predominantly to the west and north of San José. Two of the country's most important cities, Alajuela and Heredia, are found here and combine a few rare architectural treasures with provincial charm. They owe much of their prosperity to the grano de oro, the "golden bean," grown on the fertile slopes of Poás and Barva volcanoes, which tower to the north of Alajuela and Heredia respectively. The upper slopes of both these volcanoes are too cold for coffee and have thus been dedicated to dairy cattle, strawberries, and ferns. The roads that climb these mountains afford spectacular views of the Central Valley, and their summits are draped in lush cloud forest protected within national parks. This area deserves at least two days: one for Poás Volcano and Alajuela and one for Heredia and Barva Volcano, whereas Escazú lies close enough to San José to be visited in a morning or afternoon. Since there are some pleasant lodges in the hills above these towns, an overnight or two could let you stretch your exploration of this compact area out to several days.

Alajuela

4 *20 km (13 mi) northwest of San José.*

Although it is Costa Rica's second largest city (population 50,000), and only a 30-minute bus ride from the capital, Alajuela has a definite provincial feel. Architecturally it differs little from the bulk of Costa Rican towns: A low-rise grid plan with structures painted in primary colors is the norm, but its picturesque **Parque Central** is well worth having a look at. Dominated by royal palms and mango trees (home to three-toed sloths), the plaza has cement benches where the locals gather to chat and a lovely fountain imported from Glasgow. Surrounding the plaza is a mix of charming old buildings and insipid cement boxes. The large, neoclassical **cathedral** to the east, badly damaged by the 1990 earthquake, has interesting capitals decorated with local produce motifs and a striking red dome. Although spacious, the interior is rather plain, except for the ornate dome over the altar. To the north of the park stands the **old jail,** which now houses the local offices of the Ministry of Education—an appropriate metaphor for a country that claims to have more teachers than police.

Alajuela was the birthplace of Juan Santamaría, the national hero who lost his life in a battle against the mercenary army of U.S. adventurer William Walker who invaded Costa Rica in 1856 (☞ Santa Rosa National Park *in* Chapter 6). There is a statue of Santamaría in a plaza one block south of the Parque Central, and his deeds are celebrated in the **Museo Juan Santamaría,** one block north of the central square. The museum contains maps, compasses, weapons from both sides, and paintings, including one of Walker's men filing past to lay down their weapons. The colonial building that houses it is more interesting than the displays, however. ✉ *Corner of C. 2 and Avda. 3,* ☎ *441–4775.* ⊠ *Free.* ☉ *Tues.–Sun. 2–9* PM.

NEED A
BREAK?

The **Café Soda Torcaz** serves up traditional Costa Rican specialties in an airy, skylighted space. Try one of the cooling fruit *batidos* (milk shakes).

☼ A good stop for animal lovers of all ages is the **Zoo Ave,** or bird zoo, which actually has a lot more than birds on display. Spread over the lush grounds is a collection of large cages holding macaws, toucans, hawks, and parrots, as well as crocodiles and monkeys. The zoo is running a breeding project for rare and endangered birds, only about 30% of which are ever on display. It can be reached by heading west from the center of Alajuela past the cemetery then turning left after the stone church in Barrio San José. ⊠ *La Garita de Alajuela,* ☎ *433–8989.* ⊠ *1,550 colones.* ☉ *Daily 9–5.*

☺ The **Butterfly Farm** in La Guácima, Alajuela, features a presentation about the ecology of those delicate animals as well as a chance to observe and photograph them up close. The farm contains a variety of habitats holding 40 rare species of butterfly and an apiary exhibit; there is also a restaurant. It's best to visit the farm when it is sunny, since that's when butterflies are most active. The easiest way to reach it is to turn south at the Cariari Hotel, right at the church of San Antonio de Belén, left shortly thereafter, and then follow the signs with butterflies on them. ☎ *438–0115*. ☞ *$10*. ☉ *Daily 9–3*.

OFF THE
BEATEN PATH

SARCHÍ/GRECIA – Not far from Alajuela are two towns worthy of a quick visit: Sarchí and Grecia. Sarchí, one of the country's principal crafts centers, produces the brightly-colored toy oxcarts (oxcarts were once used to transport coffee to the coast) that have come to symbolize the country. Also noteworthy here is the 20th-century church decorated with colored angels and ornaments. Grecia, down a winding road from Alajuela, houses a prefabricated iron Gothic church that was imported from Belgium in the 1890s. The pieces of metal were sent piece by piece from Antwerp to Limón then transported by train to Alajuela—from there, the church was carried, appropriately, by oxcarts.

Dining and Lodging

$$$ ✕▥ **Orquídeas Inn.** Set amidst gardens and tall trees, in the heart of the coffee country west of Alajuela, the Orquídeas occupies what was once a home. The Spanish-style residence, complete with arches and barrel-tile roof, now houses a restaurant, gift shop, and a couple of suites. A new building next door has 20 standard rooms, whereas a third suite sits beneath a geodesic dome. Rooms have red tile floors and white stuccoed walls, with Guatemalan fabrics on the beds and paintings by Central American artists. The Marilyn Monroe bar has an impressive collection of posters and photos of old Norma Jean and is a popular watering hole for American expatriates. Five acres of wooded grounds are inhabited by pet toucans, parrots, and macaws, which means there's lots of squawking by the light of day. ✉ *Apdo. 395, Alajuela (3 km/2 mi west of Barrio San José)*, ☎ *433–9346*, ℻ *433–9740. 20 rooms with bath, 3 suites. [df]Restaurant, bar, pool. MC, V.*

Shopping
Buy one of the multicolor miniature oxcarts in Sarchí—most of the souvenir shops are south and north of the town's center.

Poás Volcano

❺ *37 km (23 mi) north of Alajuela (to the summit).*

The massive active crater, idyllic lake, and highland forests that top Poás Volcano are the main attractions, but one of the reasons that it receives so many visitors is that a paved road winds its way all the way to the top of the 8,800-foot summit. The road up from Alajuela winds past coffee fields, pastures, the shaded houses of a large fern plantation, and, near the summit, forests. The volcano's multicolored active crater, at nearly 1½ kilometers (1 mile) across and 1,000 feet deep, is said, by guides, to be one of the largest in the world, and the sight of the smoking fumaroles and greenish-turquoise sulfurous lake at the bottom is breathtaking. All sense of scale is absent here because of the lack of vegetation within the crater. The summit is frequently enshrouded in mist, and many who come up see little beyond the lip of the crater. But wait a while, especially if there is some wind, because the clouds can disappear quickly. If you're lucky, you will see the famous geyser in action, spewing a column of gray mud high into the air. Poás last erupted properly in 1953 and is thought to be approaching another active phase; at any sign of danger it is closed to visitors. The earlier in the day you go, the better. And since it can be very cold and wet at the summit, dress accordingly; if you come ill-equipped, you can duck under the plant commonly known as the poor man's umbrella. Bring a handkerchief, because the sulfurous gases can play havoc with your eyes. It is forbidden to venture down the side of the crater.

The 14,000-acre **Poás Volcano National Park** (☞ Chapter 2) protects epiphyte-laden cloud forest on the volcano's slopes and dwarf shrubs near the summit. One trail, which leads off to the right of the main crater trail, winds through shrubs and dwarfed trees toward the large and eerie **Botos Lake,** which occupies an extinct crater some 15 minutes away. Another leads from the car park through a taller stretch of cloud forest; boards along the way feature sentimental ecopoetry. Mammals are almost absent because of the volcano's recent active cycle, but you should see various birds, including insect-size hummingbirds and the abundant sooty robins. On occasion, quetzals have also been spotted in the park. On Sunday, audiovisual displays can be viewed in the auditorium near the parking area. A last note of warning: This is a popular site, and because of the crowds, is not a good choice for those who like solitude. ⊠ *From San José, take Hwy. 3 to Alajuela, and then Hwy. 130 to Poás, following the signs. For more information, call the Sistemas de Areas de Conservación in San José,* ☎ *283–8004, or the National Parks toll-free number,* ☎ *192.* ☉ *Daily 7–4.*

Dining and Lodging

$$ ✕ **Chubascos Restaurant.** Set amidst tall pines and colorful flowers on
★ the upper slopes of Poás Volcano, this popular restaurant has a limited menu of traditional Tico dishes. There is a full selection of *casados* (plates of white rice, beans, fried plantains, salad, cheese, and meat or fish) and platters of *gallos* (a mixture of rice and black beans), with a variety of fillings served on homemade tortillas. The *refrescos* (fresh fruit drinks) are top-drawer, especially the locally grown *fresas* (strawberries) and *moras* (blackberries) in milk. If it's warm, you can sit out on the porch, and enjoy a view of the surrounding flowers, trees, and the volcano's summit in the distance. ⊠ *West side of road to Poás National Park, between Fraijanes and Poasito,* ☎ *482–2069. Reservations not accepted. AE, MC, V.*

$$ ✕🛏 **La Providencia Lodge.** The view from this rustic lodge, perched
★ on the northern edge of Poás National Park, is breathtaking—encompassing the agricultural valley of Bajos del Toro and the forested domes of several extinct volcanoes. The visibility is best first thing in the morning, and you can enjoy scenery while you eat your breakfast, since the restaurant's walls are mostly glass. The seating is in narrow wooden booths, the floor is made of volcanic gravel, the cooking is done on a wooden stove, and the menu is simple but authentic. Cabins are scattered along the hillside, with red cement floors, colorful quilts, and hot water, although two of them don't have electricity. Hiking trails wind through the lodge's 500-acre forest reserve, where you may spot quetzals, and a three-hour horseback tour heads to the back side of the volcano, where you can see waterfalls and the destruction caused by the last eruption. Alcohol is prohibited. It can get very cold at night, so you'll need a sweater. ⊠ *Apdo. 10240–1000, San José (on left after entering Poás National Park),* ☎ *232–2498,* ℻ *231–2204. 6 cabins with bath. [df]Restaurant, hiking, horseback riding. MC, V.*

Outdoor Activities and Sports

HIKING

Although the foot paths in Poás National Park are rather short, the nearby **La Providencia Lodge** has more extensive trails for hiking through the forest (☞ Dining and Lodging, *above*).

HORSEBACK RIDING

La Providencia Lodge offers a 3-hour horseback tour that heads to the back side of Poás Volcano to view waterfalls and charred forests. You don't need to be a guest to take part, but you should reserve your horses at least one day ahead of time.

Shopping

There are a number of **roadside stands** on the way up Poás that sell strawberry jam, *cajeta* (a pale fudge), and corn crackers called *biscoche*. The **Neotrópica Foundation** has a store in the visitors' center of Poás National Park, which sells a variety of T-shirts, cards, and posters with natural themes—a portion of the profits are spent on conservation projects.

Heredia

⑥ *9 km (6 mi) north of San José.*

Perhaps Costa Rica's best-preserved colonial town, Heredia bears witness to just how little that means in an earthquake-prone country: Heredia has lost nearly all its colonial structures but a few. The **Parque Central,** for example, still retains a bit of its colonial charm. At its eastern end stands an impressive **stone church,** which dates back to 1797, whose thick walls, small windows, and squat buttresses have kept it standing through the tremors. Unfortunately, the church's stained glass work has not fared as well as the walls. The park itself is sparsely landscaped with a simple kiosk and a cast iron fountain imported from England in 1897. Surrounding the park are some interesting buildings such as the Spanish tile roofed **Casa de la Cultura,** the **Correos,** the **Escuela República de Argentina,** and the brick **Municipalidad,** behind which stands a strange, decorative tower called the **fortín.**

With a population of around 30,000, Heredia is the capital of one of the country's most important coffee producing provinces, and, consequently, is a fairly affluent town. It is also the seat of the **Universidad Nacional,** the modern campus of which lies at the east end of town.

Although there are some adobe buildings scattered throughout Heredia, the bedroom communities of Barva, Santo Domingo, and San Rafael possess much more provincial charm. The church in **San Rafael,** to the northeast of Heredia, is lovely, while Santo Domingo, to the southeast, contains quaint adobe homes.

Although a small community, **Barva de Heredia** has a pleasant **central plaza** surrounded by old Spanish-tiled adobe houses on three sides, and a white stuccoed **church** to the east that dates from the late 18th century; on a clear day, you can see massive Barva Volcano to the north.

A worthwhile stop between Heredia and Barva is the **Museo de Cultura Popular** (Popular Culture Museum), which is run by the Universidad Nacional. A turn-of-the-century farmhouse constructed with an adobe-like technique called *bahareque* has been furnished with antiques and is surrounded by a small garden and coffee fields. There is also an inexpensive, open-air restaurant that serves authentic Costa Rican cuisine. The restaurant sometimes features live music and folk dancing, mostly on the weekends. ⊠ *Between Heredia and Barva (right turn is marked, follow signs)*, ☎ *260–1619*. 🖾 *300 colones*. ☉ *Daily 8–4 (restaurant schedule varies; no credit cards)*.

Barva Volcano

❼ *20 km (12 mi) north of Heredia.*

North of the community of Barva, the road becomes narrow and steep, as it winds its way up the verdant slopes of Barva Volcano. Long extinct, Barva is massive in size: its lower slopes are almost completely covered with coffee fields, interspersed between about a dozen small towns. The upper slopes consist of pastures divided by exotic pines, and the occasional oak and cedar, which give way to the botanical diversity of the cloud forest near the top. Although any vehicle can make the trip above San Rafael to the Monte de la Cruz, or the loop above Barva via San José de la Montaña, you'll need four-wheel drive or else be ready to hike if you want to get much higher than that. The air is usually cool at the top; coupled with the pines and pastures, the atmosphere is a surprise for those who expect only rain forest, bananas, and coffee beans to grow in Costa Rica.

Hikers will want to head up to the 9,500-foot summit of extinct Barva Volcano, which is the highest point in the **Braulio Carrillo National Park** (☞ Chapter 2). This misty, luxuriant area is the only part of the park where camping is allowed, and it is an area where you may see a quetzal, if you camp or arrive in the early morning. Because of its difficult access, Barva receives a mere fraction of the visitors that flock to the summits of Poás and Irazú, which makes it a much more pristine experience. A 30-minute hike in from the ranger station will bring you to the main crater, which is about 200 yards across. Its almost vertical sides are covered in poor man's umbrellas and oak trees laden with epiphytes. At the bottom of the crater is a dark lake; farther down the track into the forest lies another crater lake. Buses go as far as San José de la Montaña, leaving a four-hour hike to the crater. A four-wheel-drive vehicle will get you to the park entrance during the dry months. Bring rain gear, boots, and stay on the trails; even experienced hikers who know the area have lost their way up there. *For more information, contact the Sistemas de Areas de Conservación in San José, ☎ 283–8004, or the National Parks toll-free number, ☎ 192. 🖾 $6. ☉ Daily 7–4.*

Dining and Lodging

$$$ ✕🖾 **Hotel Bougainvillea.** As you stroll through this hotel's tranquil gar-
★ dens, you'll easily forget that you're just 15 minutes from San José. Set amidst the coffee farms of Santo Domingo de Heredia, the hotel has an extensive private garden surrounded by tall trees. Spacious, carpeted rooms make nice use of local hardwoods, with large closets, desks, tables, and tiled baths complete with tub and hair drier. All rooms have large balconies; those in back overlook the garden, those in front enjoy a view of San José and distant mountains. The lobby and restaurant are decorated with paintings by local artists and pre-Columbian pieces. A small bar features picture windows on the garden side, and the restaurant has an excellent reputation. ⊠ *Apdo. 69–2120, San José (from San José: Guápiles Hwy. to Tivas exit then take road to Santo Domingo—follow signs from there)*, ☎ *244–1414*, 🖷 *244–1313. 44 rooms with bath. [df]Restaurant, bar, pool, sauna, tennis court. AE, MC, V.*

$$ ✕⌑ **Hotel El Pórtico.** The small red brick hotel's long sloping roof is vaguely reminiscent of a Swiss chalet; the interior decor blends brick, hardwood, and terra-cotta tiles to achieve a rustic effect, and soft leather chairs, sofas, and a log fire warm the public areas. Bedrooms have carpeting, paneled walls, and patterned bedspreads. The food is good, although portions tend to be on the small side. Surrounding the hotel is a garden with pine trees and geese—a great place for hiking and bird-watching or just relaxing in the fresh mountain air. ✉ *Apdo. 289–3000, Heredia (9 km/5½ mi up a steep, battered, sometimes paved track from Barva and 27 km/16 mi from San José),* ☎ 260–6000, ℻ 260–6002. *13 rooms with bath.* [df]*Restaurant, bar, pool, hot tub, sauna. AE, MC, V.*

Nightlife and the Arts

Heredia's **Casa de la Cultura,** on the north side of the Parque Central, puts on many art exhibits. The **Museo de Cultura Popular,** between Heredia and Barva, can be a lively spot on weekends, when the food is sometimes complemented by marimba music and folk dancing (☞ Exploring, *above*).

Outdoor Activities and Sports

HIKING

Hiking trails wind through the cloud forest in the Barva sector of Braulio Carrillo National Park, but if you don't have a four-wheel-drive vehicle, you face a tough uphill hike just to reach the park entrance (☞ Exploring, *above*).

HORSEBACK RIDING

Horseback tours along the upper slopes of Barva Volcano can be booked through the **Hotel El Pórtico,** the **Sacramento Lodge** (☎ 237–2116), near the Braulio Carrillo National Park, or at almost any San José travel agent.

TENNIS

The **Hotel Bougainvillea** (☞ Dining and Lodging, *above*) has a tennis court, for guests only.

Escazú

❽ *5 km (3 mi) southwest of San José.*

A short drive to the west of San José lies Escazú, a traditional coffee-farming town at the foot of a small mountain range that has become a bedroom community of the capital. Known as the "city of witches," since local lore has it that it has always been a popular spot with those spell-casting women, Escazú has an ancient church facing a small plaza, and plenty of adobe homes nearby. Scattered amidst the coffee fields that cover the steep slopes above town are well-tended farmhouses, often painted blue and white, with tidy gardens and the occasional oxcart parked in the yard. There are also plenty of fancy homes between those humble farm houses, since Escazú has long been popular among wealthy foreigners and Ticos. High in those hills stands the tiny community of **San Antonio de Escazú,** famous for its annual oxcart festival, held on the second Sunday of March. The view of the Central Valley is impressive from San Antonio, but for even greater drama head higher: roads wind up into the mountains, toward **Pico Blanco,** the highest point in the Cordillera.

Dining and Lodging

$$$$ ✕⌑ **Tara Resort Hotel.** Scarlett never had it so good: Patterned after
★   the house of the same name in *Gone with the Wind* and decorated in antebellum style, this hotel near the top of Pico Blanco may be the coun-

try's most luxurious. Hardwood floors throughout the three-story, white-and-green building are covered with patterned area rugs. A 10-foot-wide veranda encircles the second floor, offering 180-degree views of the Central Valley. Guest rooms are decorated with floral spreads and lace curtains; French doors open onto the veranda. The Presidential Suite has a canopied bed, a large dressing room, and a fireplace. The Atlanta Dining Gallery restaurant serves up such specialties as beef tenderloin in green pepper sauce and chicken Tara in a mango-avocado sauce. There is an extensive wine list with a good choice of French reds and California whites. ✉ *Apdo. 1459–1250, Escazú (from central church in Escazú head south and follow signs),* ☎ 228–6992, 𝖥𝖠𝖷 228–9651. *12 rooms with bath, 1 suite, 1 bungalow. Restaurant, pool, hot tub, massage, spa. AE, DC, MC, V.*

$$–$$$ 🏨 **Costa Verde Inn.** Rooms at this B&B outside of Escazú make nice use of local hardwoods. South American art adorns the main building, where a large sitting area has comfortable chairs and a fireplace. The inn is surrounded by gardens, and at night you can see the lights of San José twinkling to the east. Complimentary breakfast is served on the shady patio. ✉ *SJO 1313, Box 025216, Miami, FL 33102–5216 (from cemetery in Escazú: 110 yds. to the west and 333 yds. to the south),* ☎ 228–4080, 𝖥𝖠𝖷 289–8591. *9 rooms with bath. Pool, hot tub, tennis. MC, V.*

THE CENTRAL VALLEY A TO Z

Arriving and Departing

By Car
San José is the hub of the Central Valley; for arrival and departure information *see* Chapter 3.

By Plane
All international flights arrive in Costa Rica at **Juan Santamaría Airport,** 2 kilometers (1 mile) south of Alajuela. There are no domestic flights within the Central Valley (For airlines serving San José, *see* Air Travel *in* Smart Travel Tips A to Z).

Getting Around

By Bus
Bus service to the Central Valley from San José is listed here according to destination point, followed by information on the appropriate bus's departure point in the capital, telephone numbers for the bus company, time schedules, and length of ride, in this order: to the **airport** and **Alajuela,** departures from Avenida 2 between Calles 12 and 14 (TUASA, ☎ 222–5325) daily every 10 minutes 5:30 AM–7 PM (20-minute ride), every 40 minutes 7 PM–midnight, every hour midnight–5 AM; to **Cartago,** departures from Calle 5 and Avenida 18 (SACSA, ☎ 233–5350) daily every 10 minutes (45-minute ride); however, it is more convenient to catch it on Calle 9 at Avenida Central; to **Escazú,** departures every 10 minutes from Avenida 6 between Calles 12 and 14; to **Heredia,** departures every 10 minutes (25-minute ride) from Calle 1 between Avenidas 7 and 9; to **Irazú Volcano,** departures from Avenida 2 between Calles 1 and 3, outside the Gran Hotel Costa Rica (Metropoli, ☎ 272–0651) at 8 AM and returning at 1 PM Saturday and Sunday (90-minute ride); to **Lankester Gardens,** take the Paraíso bus, which departs from the south side of the Parque Central Park in Cartago daily every 30 minutes 4:30 AM–10:30 PM; to **Orosí Valley,** departures from one block east and three blocks south of Las Ruinas in Cartago (Mata, ☎ 551–6810) weekdays every 90 minutes (every hour on weekends) 6 AM–10

PM; to **Poás Volcano,** departures from Calle 12 between Avenidas 2 and 4 on Sunday at 8:30 AM and returning at 2:30 PM (90-minute ride); to **Sacramento** (Barva Volcano), take Paso Llano bus from Heredia (first bus 6:30 AM), get off at Sacramento crossroads (note: some go only as far as San José de la Montaña, adding an hour to the hike; check first).

By Car

All of the Central Valley's attractions lie just a short drive from San José. To reach **Cartago,** follow Avenida 2 east through San Pedro to reach the highway; a traffic light shortly before the city marks the beginning of the road up **Irazú,** with traffic to Cartago veering right. For the **Orosí Valley** and **Lankester Gardens,** head straight through Cartago to Paraíso. The Paseo Colón ends at La Sabana park, on the west end of San José; turn right there for **Alajuela** and **Heredia.** For **Heredia,** turn right off the highway just before it heads up an overpass, where the Hotel Irazú stands on the right; turn left when you reach the Universidad Nacional to reach the center of Heredia, or continue straight for the town and volcano of Barva. For **Alajuela,** take the highway all the way out to the airport, where you turn right. The road to **Poás** heads through the center of town, skirting the western edge of the Plaza Central. To reach **Escazú,** turn left at the western end of Paseo Colón, take the first right, get off the highway at the first ramp, and turn right at the traffic light.

By Taxi

Taxis parked near the central plazas of Alajuela, Cartago, and Heredia can take you to up Poás, Irazú, and Barva volcanoes, but the trips will be quite expensive, unless you can get a small group together. There are a few taxis in Orosí that will run you down to Tapantí National Park. Taxis in San José can also be hired by the day, but it's usually less expensive to rent a car.

Contacts and Resources

Car Rentals

For information on car rentals, *see* the San José A to Z *in* Chapter 3.

Emergencies

In just about any emergency you can dial **911,** but the following are some additional useful numbers: **Police** (☎ 117), **Traffic Police** (☎ 222–9330), and **Fire** (☎ 118).

Guided Tours

Travel agencies in San José offer a variety of one day tours to the Central Valley's attractions (☞ Guided Tours *in* San José A to Z *in* Chapter 3).

Travel Agencies

For information about Travel Agencies *see* San José A to Z *in* Chapter 3.

Visitor Information

See San José A to Z *in* Chapter 3.

5 The Atlantic Lowlands

Inhabited by a lively mix of Afro-Caribbean, Spanish, and indigenous peoples, Costa Rica's coastal plain is home to some of the country's densest jungles and wildest places. Too hot and humid to be anything but laid back, the isolated Atlantic Lowland slope is a world unto itself. It is also a region of tremendous natural beauty: The lowlands boast endless miles of coral-fringed beaches, good for swimming, snorkeling, and surfing; quiet, easygoing towns; rapid-filled rivers; and enchanting national parks.

Updated by
Justin
Henderson

ADJACENT TO THE CARIBBEAN SEA and separated from the Central Valley by the lofty spine of the Cordillera Central (Central Mountains), the Atlantic Lowlands lie between the provinces of Limón and Heredia, scenically dominated by sprawling banana plantations and thick tropical jungle. A widespread, largely untamed region, the Lowlands stretch from the dense rain forests of the Sarapiquí area northeast of San José, home to the private La Selva and Rara Avis reserves, east through banana-growing areas, and down to the pristine beaches at Cahuita and Puerto Viejo on the southern Caribbean Sea. In between are the untouched jungle of Braulio Carrillo National Park and Costa Rica's most important archaeological site, Guayabo National Monument.

The distinctive and colorful Afro-Caribbean character of this region is what most obviously sets it apart from the rest of the country. Roughly a third of Limón province's population are Afro-Caribbeans, descendants of early 1800s turtle fishermen and the West Indians who arrived in the late 1800s to construct the Atlantic Railroad and then remained to work on banana and cacao plantations. These immigrants had to withstand extreme hardship—some 4,000 Jamaicans are reputed to have died from yellow fever, malaria, and snakebites during the construction of the first 40 kilometers (25 miles) of railroad to San José. They were paid relatively well, however, and gradually their lot improved. By the 1930s many had obtained their own small plots of land, and when the price of cacao rose in the 1950s, they emerged as comfortable landowners employing migrant, landless Hispanics. However, until the Civil War of 1948, Afro-Caribbeans were forbidden from crossing to the Central Valley, for fear of upsetting the country's racial balance, and they were thus prevented from following work when United Fruit abandoned many of its blight-ridden plantations in the 1930s for green-field sites on the Pacific plain. Although Jamaican immigrants brought some aspects of British colonial culture along with them, such as maypole dancing and cricket, these habits have long since given way to reggae, salsa, and baseball. Many of the Atlantic coast Ticos are bilingual, speaking fluent English as well as Spanish, and to the south, around Puerto Viejo, you'll even hear some phrases that derive from the language of the indigenous peoples, among them the Kekoldi, the BriBri, and the Cabecar.

Some of the cocaine flowing from Latin America into the United States has spilled into the Limón area, resulting in a drug-related crime problem. The situation came to a head in December 1994, when an American woman was killed by bandits; the government responded by quickly deploying more police in the area. It should be noted, however, that the crime problem here is still minor when compared to that in an American city and should not affect plans to visit the area—although the city of Puerto Limón is possibly the roughest in Costa Rica and not worth visiting except on a brief, pass-through basis anyway.

To the north is the Tortuguero region, whose centerpiece is Tortuguero National Park, where turtles arrive by the thousands to lay their eggs on the beaches and the jungles resound with the cries of myriad birds and howler monkeys. The occasional caiman can be spotted here, sunning on a bank or drifting like a log down a jungle waterway. And farther north still, sportfishing fans will find tarpon and snook aplenty to detain them off the shores of Barra del Colorado.

Laid-back coastal villages worthy of a visit include Cahuita, with its readily accessible protected rain forest and coral reef, and Puerto Viejo, renowned as a surfer's paradise. Locals and travelers in these two towns amble about the dirt streets, between brightly painted wooden bungalows, barefoot or in flip-flops, exchanging the odd "Wh'appen man?"

In coastal Talamanca farming and fishing have given way to tourism as the predominant economic force. During the 1970s a blight caused by the monilia fungus completely devastated the cacao industry; and a severe earthquake in April 1991, followed by widespread flooding in August of that same year, came as a cruel blow to the already fragile economy of the region. Although locals still speak in awe of the earthquake, most of the damaged bridges and roads have been repaired and repaved, making access to Talamanca the best it's ever been.

Between Cahuita and Puerto Limón the paved road turns inland, winding upward through banana plantations toward the Indian town of BriBri in the Cordillera Talamanca. This region is home to three indigenous tribes, each with its own reserve—the BriBri, the Cabecar, and the Kekoldi—all three of which have been able to maintain a fairly strong grip on traditional language and culture. With a little extra effort a visit to one of these Indian reserves can be arranged out of Puerto Viejo. The terrain mingles the industrial agriculture of banana plantations with virgin jungle on the hills and heights. It's a short hop from BriBri to the Sixaola River bordering Panama; and just a few hours away are the Panamanian islands of the Bocas del Toro archipelago—islands difficult to reach from the population centers of Panama but an easy jaunt from the Atlantic side of Costa Rica. This quiet corner of Panama is home to the Bastimentos Island National Marine Park, one of the great undiscovered diving spots in the Caribbean (☞ Bocas del Toro *in* Chapter 8).

Pleasures and Pastimes

Beaches

The Atlantic coast is characterized by long swaths of palm-fringed white sand fronting laid-back villages like Cahuita and Puerto Viejo. The black sand Playa Negra, on the other hand, which is between Cahuita National Park and Puerto Viejo, is somewhat more frenetic: It is often overrun by the surfing fraternity, so should the beach be overcrowded, head south—you'll find some great beaches just north of Punta Uva.

Dining

Although a few upscale hotels, lodges, and restaurants have opened in recent years, introducing a more varied international cuisine, much of the cooking along the Caribbean coast derives from old Jamaican recipes. Rondon, for example, is a traditional Jamaican stew that requires hours of preparation, so if you crave some, be sure to notify your restaurateur well in advance. Rice and beans are flavored with coconut, meat is fried with hot spices to make *paties* (pies), and fish or meat, yams, plantains, breadfruit, peppers, and spices are boiled in coconut milk to prepare a "rundown." Among baked goods, johnnycakes and *panbón* (a heavy spicy fruit bread) are both popular with locals. Various medicinal herbal teas are another ubiquitous feature in the Lowlands. Seafood is, of course, readily available, as is a wide variety of fresh fruit. Dress is casual everywhere.

Festivals

May Day is celebrated in Limón with cricket matches, quadrille dances, and domino playing. During the week of October 12, the Limón Carnival features street dances, concerts, and a spectacular New Orleans–style parade finale.

Fishing

World-class tarpon and snook attract serious sportfishermen to the northern Caribbean shore in and offshore of the National Parks of Tortuguero and Barra del Colorado. January through May is the best time for tarpon, August through November for snook.

Hiking and Jungle Boating

From the rough and ready ecotourism of the Rara Avis preserve to the more leisurely jungle boat cruises arranged by the lodges near Tortuguero National Park, the opportunities for plunging into tropical jungle and rain forest are myriad in the Atlantic Lowlands and the eastern side of the Cordillera Central. Only an hour out of San José, the cloud and rain forested mountains of Braulio Carrillo National Park offer some of the most scenic hiking in the country. Closer to the sea, private and public reserves like Rara Avis, La Selva, and Cahuita National Park contain sterling examples of the many varied environments that can be described by the word "jungle."

Lodging

With only a few exceptions, the Atlantic Lowlands have little in the way of luxury hotels. Most of the places to stay are either rustic cabinas (cottages) or nature lodges. Often isolated in the jungle and reached only by boat or strenuous hike, some of the lodges are rough, bare-essentials kinds of places; others verge on the luxurious. Given the difficulty inherent in getting supplies in to these "luxe" lodges, you will find that you'll have to pay a hefty price for the comforts of a hot shower and a cold beer in the jungle.

Snorkeling and Scuba Diving

Cahuita has Costa Rica's largest coral reef, and although it has been severely damaged by pollution, there is plenty still to admire. Other dive spots include the coral reef at Isla Uvita off Limón, and the sea caverns off Puerto Viejo. The water is clearest during the dry season. In and around Bastimentos Island National Marine Park near Bocas del Toro in Panama, the snorkeling and diving are magnificent (☞ Chapter 8).

Surfing

Although some point breaks were badly affected by coastal uplift in 1991, other new ones were created—a left at Cocles and a right at Punta Uva. Puerto Viejo's famous and formidable Salsa Brava is still ridable, but its spectacular waves are really only for the practiced and/or fearless surfer. Other, perhaps less hair-raising spots include Playa Negra, Cahuita, Playa Bonita north of Limón, and Isla Uvita, 20 minutes from Limón by boat. Many of the beach breaks are also excellent for body surfing and boogie-boarding, although one must always beware of rip tides. Farther south, off the coast of Panama, there are great reef breaks as yet to be discovered in the Bocas del Toro archipelago. December to March and June to August are the best times for surfing this coast.

White-Water Rafting and Kayaking

The Atlantic side of the Cordillera Central is Costa Rica's white-water heartland. The Reventazón River is the fiercest, with many Class IV and V (most advanced skills required) rapids, suitable only for more experienced rafters and kayakers. The Pacuare River, which runs parallel to it, has Class III and IV rapids, ideal for adventurous beginners in guided boats, and passes through a spectacularly beautiful gorge en route to the lowland plain. For rafters seeking gentler waters, try the Sarapiquí—its banks are rich with wildlife.

Exploring the Atlantic Lowlands

The region described herein includes parts of both the eastern slope of the Cordillera Central, Costa Rica's primary mountain range, and the Cordillera Talamanca to the southeast. Below these cloud and rain forested mountains lie fertile agricultural plains, with the roadless primary and second growth jungles of Barra del Colorado and Tortuguero to the northeast, and enormous remnants of primary tropical jungle still evident in the foothills and flatlands of the agricultural plains. Although much of the land has been cleared and given over to farming and ranching, and although most beaches are within walking distance of the road, vast expanses of this region are still inaccessible by car. For this reason, and because the basics of getting around in Costa Rica can be so time-consuming, we suggest a number of alternative itineraries.

Great Itineraries

You need at least a week to cover this territory, but even three days are enough to sample the charms of Costa Rica's Caribbean side if you plan your time judiciously. In addition to the difficulties of getting around, it should be emphasized that the Atlantic Lowlands and the mountains above them offer a wide selection of activities requiring different levels of physical endurance and commitment, ranging from seashore lounging to rain forest trekking. If your time, energy, and willingness to put up with discomfort (mud, mosquitoes, and rain, for starters) are limited, you'll have to make choices. The Rara Avis preserve, for example, is a wonderful place to visit, but the difficulty of getting there—a 2- to 4-hour tractor haul into the park—explains the two-night minimum stay requirement. Similarly, reaching Bastimentos Island National Marine Park in Panama takes roughly 6 hours from Puerto Viejo de Limón via a sequence of buses, taxis, and water taxis. The bus rides are interesting for the landscapes as well as the people onboard—the faces of the Indians and the old country people of the area are utterly compelling—but at the end of a 6-hour haul you might want to spend at least a couple of days in the Bocas del Toro before facing the long trek back (☞ Chapter 8). As you contemplate these itineraries, keep in mind that you have to be selective, for you may not have time to do it all.

Be honest with yourself: do you want to spend your vacation roughing it in Rara Avis, or would you rather see the jungle from the comfort of a motorized launch, cruising through the canals of Tortuguero National Park, then finishing the day with a well-cooked meal at the elegantly rustic Tortuguero Lodge? Similarly, Puerto Viejo is a fun, funky little town, but if you're not a surfer/hippie/backpacker type, there's probably no reason to visit there for more than an hour or two, en route to one of the better hotels on the beach at Punta Uva or Punta Cocles. Just remember, these itineraries are meant to be mixed and matched: we're giving you ideas, but you can improvise and combine them in whatever way suits you best.

Keep in mind that there are two towns called Puerto Viejo in this region. One, Puerto Viejo de Sarapiquí, is a former river port that lies in the Northern Lowlands; the other, Puerto Viejo de Limón, is a laid-back coastal town not far from the border with Panama. Keeping these towns straight can be confusing, since locals often refer to both of them merely as "Puerto Viejo" without the clarifying "de Sarapiquí" and "de Limón."

IF YOU HAVE 3 DAYS

Numbers in the text correspond to numbers in the margin and on the Atlantic Lowlands map.

This, as with many journeys in Costa Rica, begins in San José. On day one, take a white-water rafting trip down the Río Pacuare. Class III and IV rapids (you'll get thrills but not a heart attack), swimmably warm water, and spectacular scenery make this a must for the moderately adventurous traveler. You'll be starting and finishing the day at your hotel in ⊞ **San José,** with transportation through **Turrialba** ⑤ to the rafting put-in provided by your white-water tour company. On the second day take the earliest possible flight to ⊞ **Tortuguero** ⑦ or ⊞ **Barra del Colorado** ⑧, then spend the day exploring the labyrinthine jungle waterways of either park by boat, and stay the night at one of the lodges near either of the parks. An alternate here could be a one-day fishing trip from Parismina, Tortuguero, or Barra del Colorado. Or you could visit the Rain Forest Aerial Tram for an amazing, treetop level ride through the rain forest, or stop in **Braulio Carrillo National Park** ① for a day hike—from either location take the bus or tour company van back to San José. Another option would be to fly out of Tortuguero back to San José early and take a bus or van to **Braulio Carrillo** ① or the Rain Forest Aerial Tram. Finish the day back at your hotel in ⊞ **San José.**

IF YOU HAVE 3 DAYS AND LOVE THE RAIN FOREST

Wake early in San José and drive or bus over the Guápiles Highway to hike **Braulio Carrillo National Park** ① or ride the Rain Forest Aerial Tram—get there early, since the people in the first gondolas into the forest will see the most wildlife. Then drive or bus to ⊞ **La Selva** ③ (it's a 2-kilometer/1.2-mile walk from the road to the La Selva entrance, so pack light if you're taking public transportation) and spend the afternoon hiking its network of trails. Spend the night there (reservations essential) or at one of the lodges in the Sarapiquí area, and early the next morning bus or drive back to Las Horquetas in time (9 AM) to meet the tractor, which will take you in to ⊞ **Rara Avis** ② for two days and nights (two-night minimum stay, reservations essential). Bus or drive back to San José.

IF YOU HAVE 3 DAYS AND LOVE THE BEACH BUT WANT A MIX

Hop on an early flight from San José to ⊞ **Tortuguero** ⑦ or **Barra del Colorado** ⑧ for jungle boat tours. Next morning take the boat down to Moín, and head south by car; or take the boat to Moín and then taxi from Moín to Limón, and bus or drive from Limón south to ⊞ **Cahuita** ⑩ and/or ⊞ **Puerto Viejo de Limón** ⑪. In or near either of these towns you can either relax on the beach or spend the day playing in the surf, snorkeling, and hiking through the Cahuita National Park. Camp at ⊞ **Puerto Vargas** or stay one or two nights in any one of dozens of hotels or cabinas ranging from grungy to first class in ⊞ **Cahuita,** ⊞ **Puerto Viejo de Limón,** ⊞ **Punta Uva,** or farther south along the beach road, which terminates at the bird-filled jungles and deserted beaches of the **Gandoca-Manzanillo Wildlife Refuge** ⑫.

An alternative with appeal for archaeology buffs would start with an early trip by car through **Turrialba** ⑤ to the **Guayabo National Mon-**

ument ⑥, Costa Rica's primary site for pre-Columbian ruins. From there the road follows the Río Reventazón east; stop at the Centro Agronómico Tropical de Investigación y Enseñanza (CATIE) to admire the grounds and the tropical plant research and to do some bird-watching. From there head down from the mountains to meet the main highway at Siquirres. Drive east, bypass **Limón** ⑨, and head south for two days of beach, jungle, surf, and sun at **Cahuita** ⑩, **Puerto Viejo de Limón** ⑪, and the miles of beaches between and beyond.

IF YOU HAVE 5 DAYS

Start in San José. Raft the **Pacuare** or visit **Guayabo National Monument** ⑥ and CATIE, then overnight it back in ⊡ **San José.** Fly to ⊡ **Tortuguero** ⑦ or ⊡ **Barra del Colorado** ⑧ for a day and a night, with an early morning flight back to San José, where you pick up a car (or bus) and head to **Braulio Carrillo National Park** ① or the **Rain Forest Aerial Tram.** From there travel to ⊡ **La Selva** ③ for an afternoon and overnight, then choose between two nights at ⊡ **Rara Avis** ② or exploring the lodges, jungles, preserves, and rivers in the ⊡ **Puerto Viejo de Sarapiquí** ④ area. An alternative to the two nights in this area would be to head east and then south to ⊡ **Cahuita** ⑩, ⊡ **Puerto Viejo de Limón** ⑪, and environs, for a jungle/beach scenario.

IF YOU HAVE 7 DAYS OR MORE

After exploring any or all of the above in whatever fashion you find most congenial (some variations: the Pacuare raft trip can last two days with an overnight in a river lodge or campsite; ⊡ **La Selva** ③ may be worth two days; fishing trips out of ⊡ **Barra del Colorado** ⑧ or ⊡ **Tortuguero** ⑦ can run one, two, three days, or more). You might want to arrange to visit the BriBri, Cabecar, or Kekoldi Indian reservations in the hills west of **Puerto Viejo de Limón** ⑪ or hike into the remote

Hitoy Cerere Biological Preserve. Finally, if you love snorkeling amidst pristine coral reefs block out two or three days to visit ⛴ **Bocas del Toro** and Bastimentos Island National Marine Park in Panama. From Changuinola, two hours by water taxi and bus gets you to and from Bocas, and an eight-hour bus ride gets you back to San José (☞ Chapter 8).

When To Tour the Atlantic Lowlands

In three words: the dry season. This is a realm that absorbs 200 or more inches of rain a year, so unless you are planning to view the turtles laying eggs on the beach (each species has its own schedule), you'll want to avoid the worst of it. Chances are you'll be rained on no matter when you go, but your best bet for good weather is the "dry" season that runs from December through March, possibly stretching into November and April. If you don't mind the rain, go in the rainy season: you may stay soaked your entire visit, but at least you'll find lower prices and few tourists.

BRAULIO CARRILLO AND THE NORTHERN LOWLANDS

Rara Avis, La Selva, and Puerto Viejo de Sarapiquí

Numbers in the margin correspond to points of interest on the Atlantic Lowlands map.

The immense Braulio Carrillo National Park, northeast of San José, extends toward the Caribbean coast. The park protects virgin rain forest on either side of the highway to Guápiles; you can get some idea of it as you pass through on the highway, but inside is another world. Everywhere you look, green things sprout, twist, and bloom. Bromeliads and orchids cling to arching trees while white-faced monkeys and blue morpho butterflies creep, climb, and flutter. Adjacent to the park is the Rain Forest Aerial Tram, a private reserve, where you can explore the flora and fauna of the rain-forest canopy via gondolas.

After visiting Braulio Carrillo the road branches at Santa Clara just after the Guápiles Highway has completed its descent onto the Caribbean plain. To the right, the highway continues on to Puerto Limón and the Caribbean coast; to the left, the recently paved road leads through flat, deforested pasture toward two spectacular preserves, Rara Avis and La Selva. Continue farther north to reach the old river port town of Puerto Viejo de Sarapiquí.

Braulio Carrillo National Park

❶ *30 km (19 mi) north of San José.*

In a country where deforestation has been and still is rife, Braulio Carrillo National Park (☞ Chapter 2) provides the rare opportunity to see dense primary tropical cloud forest as far as the eye can see. The park owes its foundation to the public outcry provoked by the construction of the highway through the region in the late 1970s, when the government bowed to pressure from environmentalists. With the highway running through it, the park's rain forest is the most accessible in Costa Rica for travelers from the San José area. It is well worth a visit, even if seen only through a car window. Covering 110,000 acres, the park's extremely diverse terrain extends from 100 to more than 9,500 feet above sea level; the park reaches from the central volcanic range down the Atlantic slope to La Selva research station near Sarapiquí. Six thousand tree species, 500 different birds, and 135 types of mammals have been cataloged here.

Braulio Carrillo's **Zurquí ranger station** is to the right of the road, 500 yards before the Zurquí tunnel. Ascents start here and are steep, so the paths inevitably involve a lot of ups and downs. Note: Before you head out on one of the trails, put on boots to protect you from the mud and possible snakes. The main mile-long trail through primary forest culminates in a mirador (vantage point); unfortunately the highway is included in the view. An early start, preferably before 8 AM, lessens the risk of the mist that can obscure your view. Monkeys, tapirs, jaguars, kinkajous (a nocturnal tree-living, raccoon-like mammal), sloths, raccoons, margays (a small spotted cat similar to the ocelot), and porcupines all live in the forest, although most animals are very shy. Resident birds include the quetzal and the eagle. Orchids, bromeliads, heliconias, fungi, and mushrooms can be seen throughout.

From the **Carrillo ranger station,** 22 kilometers (14 miles) down the highway from Zurquí, the trails are less steep and make for an easier jaunt. For access to the 9,500-foot Barva Volcano, you need to start from Sacramento, north of Heredia. The walk to the crater takes two to three hours, but your efforts will be rewarded by great views. *For more information call the Sistemas de Areas de Conservación in San José, ☎ 283–8004, or the National Parks toll-free hotline, ☎ 192. ▨ $6. ⊘ Daily 7–4.*

Helpful hint: It is perfectly legal and much cheaper—free, in fact—to get into the park by way of numerous informal trails rather than those that start at either of the ranger stations. Stop at any of the roadside turn-outs and look for a trailhead.

Adjacent to Braulio Carrillo National Park is a 1,000-acre private preserve that houses the **Rain Forest Aerial Tram.** A privately owned and operated engineering marvel consisting of a series of gondolas strung together in a modified ski-lift pulley system (to lessen the impact on the jungle, the support pylons were flown into place by helicopter, with the chopper and pilot rented from neighboring Nicaragua's Sandinista Army), it provides students, researchers, and tourists with a new way of seeing the rain-forest canopy—with its spectacular array of epiphyte plant life and birds—from close above, hitherto possible only if you climbed the trees yourself. The founder, Dr. Donald Perry, developed a more primitive system of canopy touring at nearby Rara Avis. Of the two, this is the easier-to-use, commercialized version, and though purists might complain that it treats the rain forest like an amusement park ride, it is entertaining and educational—a great way to enlighten people as to the beauty and value of rain forest ecology.

The gondolas hold five people, including a bilingual guide who is also a biologist. The guides are equipped with walkie-talkies so that they can request brief stops for viewing or photography. The 2½-kilometer (1½-mile) ride takes between 1 and 1½ hours, depending on the number of stops. There are simple accommodations for researchers and students and a breakfast and lunch cafe on site. The price includes a biologist-guided walk through the area, for ground-level orientation prior to the tram ride. The walks commence at 6 AM, and the tram rides begin at 8 AM. San José pickups can be arranged, and there is a regular bus service (on the Guápiles line) every half hour. ☎ 257–5961,

FAX *257–6053 for reservations.* ✉ *$47 (guided walk and tram).* ☉ *Mon. 9ᴀᴍ–2ᴘᴍ, Tues.–Sun. 6ᴀᴍ–2ᴘᴍ.*

Rara Avis

❷ *100 km (62 mi) north of San José.*

Toucans, tapirs, sloths, green macaws, howler and spider monkeys, vested anteaters, and tapirs may be on hand to greet you when you arrive at Rara Avis, one of Costa Rica's most popular private reserves and an inspiring example of ecotourism at work. The town of **Las Horquetas** is the jumping-off point for the 3,300-acre private reserve. The 16-kilometer (10-mile) journey from Horquetas to the reserve is accomplished in three hours on horseback, two to three hours by tractor, or one hour by Jeep (the tractor leaves daily at 8:30 ᴀᴍ). The trails are steep and rugged, but seeing the flora and fauna is worth the hard work. Rara Avis was started by an ecologist named Amos Bien with the intent of combining research, tourism, and the sustainable extraction of forest products. Bilingual guides are on hand to take visitors along the muddy trails and to help spot wildlife; the guides will also convincingly explain their means of harvesting: a process that minimizes forest destruction. Bring a camera: The reserve's lacy double waterfall is one of Costa Rica's most photographed sites. The site is open only to overnight guests.

Dining and Lodging

$$$$ ✕⊡ **Rara Avis.** Rara Avis is tough to get to but the struggle is well worth
★   it. A number of research projects under way there are studying sustainable uses for the rain forest. The Waterfall Lodge, named for the 180-foot waterfall nearby, contains hardwood-paneled corner rooms with chairs, firm beds, balconies, and hammocks. El Plástico Lodge used to be a prison and has coed bunk rooms and reductions for International Youth Hostel Federation members, students, and scientists. All rates include transport from Horquetas, guides, and three meals daily. Management requires a two-night minimum stay. ✉ *Apdo. 8105–1000, San José (from Braulio Carrillo, turn left at signs for Puerto Viejo de Sarapiquí, travel 17 km/10.5 mi to town of Las Horquetas),* ☎ *710–6872. (Reservations office in San José:* ☎ FAX *253–0844.) 8 rooms with bath, 5 rooms with shared bath. Dining room. AE, MC, V.*

La Selva Reserve

❸ *14 km (9 mi) west of Rara Avis.*

La Selva is a biologist's paradise, a 3,700-acre reserve at the confluence of the Puerto Viejo and Sarapiquí rivers, which is not far from the Rara Avis preserve. La Selva is a much more agreeable locale than Rara Avis for those who prefer to see wildlife without sweating or getting dirty—the reserve is also home to the beautiful **Selva Verde Lodge.** This OTS (Organization for Tropical Studies) biological research station is designed for scientists but welcomes visitors in the daytime and also overnight when space permits—January–March and June–July are the busiest times. Extensive and well-marked trails and swing bridges connect habitats as varied as tropical wet forest, swamps, creeks, rivers, secondary regenerating forests, and pasture. Sundry plants are tagged along the route, and there is plenty of wildlife. Buy one of the superb self-guide pamphlets based on ongoing scientific research at park headquarters at the main entrance. The OTS has a van that can transport visitors here from San José, or else you can arrive by public bus or rental car. ✉ OTS▶ *Apdo. 676–2050, San Pedro (look for sign for Sarapiquí Ecoadventure Lodge on left some 14 km/9 mi farther on from Rara Avis which will lead you to La Selva),* ☎ *240–6696 in San José or 710–1515 on-site.* 🍴 *$20 per day, including lunch.*

Dining and Lodging

$$$ ✕🏠 **Selva Verde Lodge.** This expanding rancho-style complex is on the edge (across the Sarapiquí River) of a 500-acre private reserve of tropical rain forest and caters primarily to retirees on natural-history tours. The river lodge stands on stilts over the Sarapiquí River. All the buildings have wide verandas strung with hammocks, and bedrooms come with polished wood paneling, fans, and mosquito blinds. Activities include fishing, horseback riding, boat trips, rafting, mountain biking, canoeing, and guided walks. The rates include three meals per day in the hotel restaurant. ✉ *Apdo. 55, Chilamate, Heredia (7 km/4.3 mi west of Puerto Viejo in Chilamate),* ☎ *766–6077,* 📠 *766–6011. (Reservations office in San José:* ☎ *240–6696.) 47 rooms with bath, 7 rooms without bath. Restaurant, library. MC, V.*

Puerto Viejo de Sarapiquí

④ *6½ km (4 mi) north of La Selva.*

During the last century Puerto Viejo de Sarapiquí was a thriving river port and the only link with the Barra del Colorado Wildlife Refuge and Tortuguero National Park. Fortunes nosedived with the construction of the coastal canal from the town of Moín, and today Puerto Viejo has a slightly rundown air. The activities of the Contras also made this a dangerous zone during the 1980s but with the political situation now improved, boats once again ply the old route up the Sarapiquí River to the San Juan River on the Nicaraguan frontier. There's really not much here to grab the attention of tourists, although a couple of companies now offer river tours, with up to Class III rapids, plus there is plenty of wildlife in the area.

Dining and Lodging

$$$ ✕🏠 **El Gavilán Lodge.** The lodge, the erstwhile hub of a fruit and cat-
★ tle farm, is two stories high and is fronted by a veranda. The comfortable bedrooms have white walls, terra-cotta floors, fans, and decorative *artesanía* (crafts); some of the rooms have flashy purple bathrooms. Beautiful manicured gardens run down to the river, and colorful tanagers (a brightly colored woodland bird) and three types of toucan feast in the citrus trees. The food, *comida típica* (typical Costa Rican fare), has a good reputation. Most people come here as part of a tour with pickup in San José. Activities include fishing, horseback jungle treks, and boat trips up the Sarapiquí River toward the San Juan River and the border with Nicaragua. ✉ *Apdo. 445–2010, Zapote, San José (a few km southeast of Puerto Viejo; watch for the sign on the road from Horquetas),* ☎ *234–9507,* 📠 *253–6556. 12 rooms with bath, 3 without bath. Dining room, hot tub. MC, V.*

$ ✕🏠 **Rancho Leona.** This ranch has small rustic dormitories designed for kayaking trips. The restaurant has a varied menu with Italian specialties like eggplant parmesan and chicken cacciatore as well as numerous vegetarian dishes. The restaurant and rooms were built to accommodate customers on kayaking tours, but owners Ken and Leona Upcraft have opened the restaurant to the public and say they'll put you up if there's room. Activities include kayaking on the Sara-

piquí, hiking to a beautiful 30-foot waterfall, and river swimming. ⊠
*La Virgen de Sarapiquí, Heredia (17 km/10.5 mi southwest of Puerto
Viejo de Sarapiquí in La Virgen),* ☎ FAX *761–1019. 5 bunk rooms with
shared bath. Restaurant, library, No credit cards.*

TURRIALBA AND GUAYABO NATIONAL MONUMENT

*Numbers in the margin correspond to points of interest on the Atlantic
Lowlands map.*

After leaving San José, you'll pass through Cartago, Pacayas, and
Santa Cruz: Take the Irazú road and turn right just before Cot, next
to a large white statue of Jesus (signaling the continental divide). The
road is twisty, but the hillside scenery is stunning. Pollarded jaul trees
line the road to form formal avenues, and white girder bridges cross
crashing streams. From Santa Cruz a track leads up to within hiking
distance of the 10,900-foot summit of Turrialba Volcano. As you begin
the descent to Turrialba, the temperature rises and neatly farmed coffee crops cover the slopes.

Turrialba

⑤ *58 km (36 mi) east/southeast of San José.*

Turrialba is a relatively well-to-do grid-plan agricultural center with
a population of 30,000 that suffered when the main San José–Limón
route was diverted through Guápiles. The demise of the famous Jungle Train that used to travel between San José and Puerto Limón has
been an additional blow to the town. Although lively enough, Turrialba itself doesn't have much to offer, but there are still interesting places
to investigate. Kayakers and white-water rafters, for instance, flock here
to ride the Reventazón and Pacuare rivers; serious aficionados, including
the white-water Olympic kayaking teams from a handful of countries,
stay all winter. The put-in for the Pacuare is just a few miles from town;
your guide will lead the way.

Rafting the **Río Pacuare** is an unforgettable experience: exhilarating,
beautiful, and great fun! You'll learn the teamwork of white-water rafting; a good guide—and there are many—will teach you not only how
to ride the rapids but also about the natural history, the geography,
and the geology of the area, which is astoundingly beautiful (stretches
of the Pacuare stood in for Africa in the otherwise eminently forget-
table 1995 film *Congo*). You'll see numerous exotic birds—toucans,
assorted kingfishers, aracaris, and oropéndolas among them—along
with blue morpho butterflies, and maybe the odd river otter, sloth, or
coati as well, especially if you're first down the river. Currently threatened with the possibility of sinking forever behind a new hydroelectric dam, the Pacuare's 20-odd miles of white-water runs (for those who
know about these things, the gradient averages 48 feet per mile, and
the volume of water ranges from 1,400 up to 4,000 cubic feet per second) include a series of Class III and IV rapids with evocative nick-
names such as Double Drop, Upper Huacas, Lower Huacas, Toucan,
Magnetic Rock, and Dos Montañas (where two mountains nearly
meet—the potential site of the dreaded dam). There are half a dozen
licensed operators currently running the Pacuare, and a couple of them
have built lodges halfway down the run, making it possible to overnight
in great comfort on the riverbank. The runs terminate near Siquirres,

and from there it is a lovely drive back through Braulio Carrillo to San José.

Not far from the town of Turrialba, on the way to Siquirres, is **CATIE** (☎ 556–6431), one of the world's leading tropical research centers. The 2,000-acre property includes pristine white offices, landscaped grounds, seed conservation chambers, greenhouses, orchards, experimental agricultural projects, and lodging for students and teachers. CATIE is also a good bird-watching spot; a trail leads from behind the administration building to the Reventazón River and around the lagoon. With some luck you might catch sight of the brilliant, yellow-winged jacana spinosa. Phone ahead for more information; the center has presently suspended guided tours but these may again be available in the future.

Dining and Lodging

$$$$ ✕⌨ **Albergue Volcán Turrialba.** In the foothills of the volcano and reachable only by four-wheel drive (the lodge will arrange transport for a fee), the Volcán has comfortable rooms with hot-water baths. You'll eat well, too: The proprietors serve healthy, Costa Rican–style meals cooked up on a wood-burning stove. More compelling are the tours they offer: one goes deep into the Turrialba crater; a second visits the fumaroles and thermal waters of Volcán Irazú; mountain biking, horseback riding, and a 10-hour trek from the Turrialba Volcano to Guápiles via Braulio Carrillo National Park can also be arranged. ✉ *Apdo. 1632–2050, San José (5 km/3 mi from Irazú crater up posted access road),* ☎ FAX *273–4335. 9 rooms with bath. Dining room, bar, library. AE, MC, V.*

$$$$ ✕⌨ **Rancho Naturalista.** This 125-acre private reserve offers guided horseback and bird-watching tours. Three hundred species of birds, several varieties of the Morpho butterfly, and thousands of different types of moths live nearby. The two-story lodge is rustically decorated throughout. Good home cooking is served in both the indoor and outdoor dining rooms. ✉ *Dept. 1425, Box 025216, Miami, FL 33102–5216 (southeast of Turrialba, 2½ km/1½ mi up a dirt track from village of Tuís),* ☎ FAX *267–7138. 5 rooms with bath, 2 with shared bath. Dining room. No credit cards.*

$ ✕⌨ **Turrialtico.** Eight kilometers (5 miles) out of Turrialba on the Limón road, a hedged drive winds its way up to this dramatically positioned, open-sided hotel-restaurant. The new second-floor rooms, handsomely designed with Guatemalan spreads on the firm beds and wooden floors, could be the country's best bargain. Try to get a room on the west side for a dazzling view toward Turrialba and, if you're in luck, Irazú Volcano. Although the restaurant's menu isn't extensive, the cooking is tasty: Casado (rice, beans, salad, and meat or fish) is a safe bet. A possible minus is that the place is a stopover for tour/rafting buses: About three per week come here to eat. ✉ *Apdo. 121, Turrialba (Carretera to Limón km 8),* ☎ FAX *556–1111. 12 rooms with bath. Restaurant, bar. No credit cards.*

Outdoor Activities and Sports

RAFTING AND KAYAKING

At least six licensed companies operate similar rafting and kayaking trips out of San José of varying length and grade on the Pacuare and other rivers with their headwaters in the Turrialba area. Among the more experienced ones are: **Costa Rica Whitewater** (☎ 257–0766), **Ríos Tropicales** (☎ 233–6455), **Aventuras Naturales** (☎ 225–3939), **Pioneer Raft** (☎ 225–8117 and 225–4735, FAX 253–4687), and **Costa Rica**

Raft (☎ 224–0505, FAX 253–6934). The cost is around $70 for one day. Call around to price two-day packages with overnight stays.

Guayabo National Monument

❻ *19 km (12 mi) north of Turrialba.*

Nestled on the slopes of the Turrialba Volcano is the Guayabo National Monument, Costa Rica's most significant archaeological site. In 1968 a local landowner was out walking her dogs when she discovered what she thought was a tomb. A friend, archaeologist Carlos Piedra, began excavating the site and unearthed the base wall of the chief's house in what eventually turned out to be a large city (around 20,000 inhabitants) covering 49 acres. The city was abandoned in AD 1400, probably due to disease and/or starvation. A guided tour (in Spanish only) takes you through rain forest to a mirador (lookout) from where you can see the layout of the excavated circular buildings. Only the raised foundations survive, since the conical houses themselves were built of wood. As you descend into the city ruins, observe the well-engineered surface and covered aqueducts leading to a drinking-water trough that still functions; next you'll pass the end of an 8-kilometer (5-mile) paved walkway used to transport the massive building stones. Carved abstract patterns on the stones continue to baffle archaeologists, although some clearly depict jaguars, which were revered by the Indians as deities. The hillside jungle setting is captivating, and the trip is further enhanced by the bird-watching possibilities; sacklike nests of *oropéndolas* (golden orioles) hang from many of the trees. *Call the National Parks Service for information toll-free at* ☎ *192.* ⬚ *$6.* ☉ *Daily 8–3.*

Dining and Lodging

$$$ ✕⬚ Albergue La Calzada. Young eucalyptus trees surround this bucolic bird-watchers' lodge 400 yards before the national monument. The bedrooms are in a pondside cabin with views of the wooded hills and distant Caribbean. Best views are from upstairs, but these rooms, although cheaper, share a bath and have drafty corrugated-iron roofs, noisy when it rains. All rooms have firm wooden beds, paneling, flimsy curtains, and bedside lamps. Beware the snapping, unfriendly geese outside. ⬚ *Apdo. 260–7150, Turrialba,* ☎ *556–0465,* FAX *556–0427. 4 rooms without bath. Restaurant, bar. AE, MC, V.*

TORTUGUERO AND BARRA DEL COLORADO

Numbers in the margin correspond to points of interest on the Atlantic Lowlands map.

Tortuguero means "turtle region," and this area, tucked into northeastern Costa Rica, remains one of the world's prime spots for viewing the awesome although excruciatingly difficult life cycle of sea turtles. The stretch of beach between the Colorado and Matina rivers was first mentioned as a nesting ground for sea turtles in 1592, in a Dutch chronicle, and due to the area's isolation—there isn't a road there to this day—the turtles were able to get on with their nesting virtually undisturbed for centuries. By the mid 1900s, however, the harvesting of eggs and catching of turtles had increased to such an extent that the turtles faced extinction. In 1963 an executive decree regulated the hunting of turtles and the gathering of eggs, and in 1970 the govern-

It helps to be pushy in airports.

Introducing the revolutionary new TransPorter™ from American Tourister.® It's the first suitcase you can push around without a fight. TransPorter's™ exclusive four-wheel design lets you push it in front of you with almost no effort–the wheels take the weight. Or pull it on two wheels if you choose. You can even stack on other bags and use it like a luggage cart.

Stable 4-wheel design.

TransPorter™ is designed like a dresser, with built-in shelves to organize your belongings. Or collapse the shelves and pack it like a traditional suitcase. Inside, there's a suiter feature to help keep suits and dresses from wrinkling. When push comes to shove, you can't beat a TransPorter™. For more information on how you can be this pushy, call 1-800-542-1300.

Shelves collapse on command.

Your passport around the world.

- Worldwide access
- Operators who speak your language
- Monthly itemized billing

MCI Calling Card

415 555 1234 2244
J.D. SMITH

Use your MCI Card® and these access numbers for an easy way to call when traveling worldwide.

American Samoa	633-2MCI (633-2624)
Antigua †	#2
(Available from public card phones only)	
Aruba ⁂	800-888-8
Argentina ★†	001-800-333-1111
Bahamas (CC)†	1-800-888-8000
Barbados	1-800-888-8000
Belize	815 from pay phones
	557 from hotels
Bermuda ⁂ †	1-800-888-8000
Bolivia ◆	0-800-2222
Brazil (CC)†	000-8012
British Virgin Islands ⁂	1-800-888-8000
Cayman Islands†	1-800-888-8000
Chile (CC)†	
To call using CTC ■	800-207-300
To call using ENTEL ■	123-00316
Colombia (CC)◆†	980-16-0001
Costa Rica◆†	0800-012-2222
Dominica	1-800-888-8000
Dominican Republic (CC)	1-800-888-8000
Ecuador (CC)⁂†	999-170
El Salvador ◆	800-1767
Grenada ⁂	1-800-888-8000

Guatemala ◆	189
Guyana	177
Haiti (CC) ⁂	001-800-444-1234
Honduras ⁂	122
Jamaica	1-800-888-8000
(From Special Hotels only)	873
Mexico▲†	95-800-674-7000
Netherlands Antilles (CC)⁂†	
	001-800-950-1022
Nicaragua (CC)	166
(Outside of Managua, dial 02 first)	
Panama†	108
Military Bases	2810-108
Paraguay ⁂	008-11-800
Peru	170
Puerto Rico (CC)†	1-800-888-8000
St. Lucia ⁂	1-800-888-8000
Trinidad & Tobago ⁂	1-800-888-8000
Turks & Caicos ⁂	1-800-888-8000
Uruguay	00-412
U.S. Virgin Islands (CC)†	1-800-888-8000
Venezuela ⁂◆	800-1114-0

To sign up for the MCI Card, dial the access number of the country you are in and ask to speak with a customer service representative.

http://www.mci.com

† Automation available from most locations. ⁂ Limited availability. ★ Not available from public pay phones. (CC) Country-to-country calling available. May not be available to/from all international locations. (Canada, Puerto Rico, and U.S. Virgin Islands are considered Domestic Access locations.) ◆ Public phones may require deposit of coin or phone card for dial tone. ■ International communications carrier. ▲ When calling from public phones use phones marked LADATEL.

ment established the Tortuguero National Park (☞ Chapter 2). The area is also home to watery Barra del Colorado Wildlife Refuge.

Tortuguero

❼ *50 km (31 mi) northwest of Puerto Limón.*

Four species of turtle nest at **Tortuguero National Park:** the green turtle, the hawksbill, the loggerhead, and the giant leatherback. Green turtles reproduce in large groups, and Tortuguero is one of the sites they choose for nesting from July to October every year. They lay eggs on average every two to three years and produce two or three clutches each time. In between, green turtles feed as far away as Florida and Venezuela. Their meat is considered the best of all turtle species, and there have been many attempts to breed them artificially. Hawksbills are small in comparison with other sea turtles and are threatened by hunters because of their shells, a transparent brown that is much sought after to make jewelry in countries like Japan. Loggerheads, as their name implies, have outsized heads as well as shorter fins; they are very rare at Tortuguero, though, and you will be extremely unlikely to see one. The giant leatherback is the largest of all turtle species; individuals grow up to 6½ feet long. They have a tough outer skin instead of a shell, hence their name. From mid-February through April, leatherbacks nest mainly in the southern sector of the park. At the right time of year, there is no reason why you shouldn't witness firsthand the remarkable spectacle of this mass emergence. Most nesting turtles come ashore at night, plowing an uneven furrow with their flippers to propel themselves to the high-tide line, beyond which they employ their hind flippers to scoop out a hole in which to lay their eggs. A couple of months later, the hatchlings struggle out of the nests and make their tortuous, danger-ridden way to the sea.

Freshwater turtles live in the rivers at Tortuguero, as do crocodiles, which are most prevalent in the Agua Fría River, and the endangered *vacas marinas,* or manatees. Manatees, which consume huge quantities of aquatic plants, are endangered mainly because their lack of speed renders them easy prey for hunters. Inhabitants of the forests include tapirs (watch for these in the jolillo groves), jaguars, anteaters, ocelots, howler monkeys, collared and white-lipped peccaries, raccoons, otters, skunks, and coatis. There are also some 350 species of bird and countless butterflies (including the iridescent blue morpho) in the area.

To the north of Tortuguero National Park, the hamlet of **Tortuguero,** with its 600 inhabitants, two churches, three bars, and two souvenir shops is a pleasant little place to spend an hour or two if one is in the area for more than a day. Be sure to visit the new headquarters of the **Caribbean Conservation Corporation** (☞ Ecotourism, *below*), check out the information kiosk on the park, turtles, wildlife, etc., in the center of town, and take a stroll along the 20 odd miles of beach—although swimming here is not recommended due to strong riptides and the presence (although, according to locals, no one has ever actually been attacked) of large numbers of nurse sharks and barracuda.

The tiny town of **Parismina** sits on a narrow strip between canal and Caribbean not far from the south entrance of Tortuguero National Park. There is nothing particularly noteworthy here, except for a couple of lodges in the area. In the high season it might serve as a base for getting into areas of the park that are less crowded—in the Tortuguero area certain waterways see heavy traffic during the high season.

The three-hour trip by boat through the combination of natural and man-made **canals** between Tortuguero and Moín is an adventure in itself, a kind of real-life amusement park adventure ride. As you swoop through the sinuous turns of the natural waterways, your driver/guide will point out monkeys, snakes, caiman, mud turtles, sloths, and dozens of different birds, including flocks of bright, noisy parrots, kingfishers, aracaris, and assorted herons. The jungle along these waterways is awesome—the densely layered greenery is highlighted by brilliantly colored flowers—and the visual impact is doubled by the jungle's reflection in the mirror smooth surface of the water. One should definitely plan on either leaving or arriving by boat.

Dining and Lodging

$$$–$$$$ ✕☲ **Mawamba Lodge.** This lodge is the perfect place to kick back and relax. Once whisked from Moín in a fast launch (2½ hours), guests stay in comfortable rustic cabinas with fans and dine in the spacious dining room. Activities include tours of the jungle, canals, and turtle-laying beaches. ⊠ *Apdo. 10980–1000, San José (1 km/½ mi north of Tortuguero on ocean side of canal),* ☎ 710–7282. *(Reservations office in San José:* ☎ 223–2421, FAX 255–4039.) *36 rooms with bath. Dining room. MC, V.*

$$$ ✕☲ **Tortuga Lodge.** Costa Rica Expeditions owns this thatched river-
★   side lodge, renowned for its tarpon and snook fishing. The second-largest tarpon ever caught in Costa Rica, weighing 182 pounds, was reeled in here in 1987. The bedrooms are comfortable and have fans, mosquito blinds, and hot water. Wander through the landscaped garden with its lush lawns, orchids, and tropical trees. There are a couple of short hiking trails from the property that lead into the nearby jungle, where bright red poison dart frogs and other interesting critters can be observed. Wear your repellant and long sleeves; the mosquitoes can be voracious! Considering that the majority of the food is flown in, the chefs do an excellent job, producing voluminous quantities of hearty, well-prepared food. The Tortuga Lodge is across the river from the airstrip, 2 kilometers (1 mile) from Tortuguero. Most guests come as part of a tour. ⊠ *Apdo 6941–1000, San José (20 mins north by boat from Tortuguero National Park or 35 mins by plane from San José),* ☎ FAX 710–6861. *(Reservations office in San José:* ☎ 257–0766, FAX 257–1665.) *25 rooms with bath. Dining room, bar, fishing. AE, MC, V.*

$$ ✕☲ **El Manatí.** The friendly owners, Fernando and Lilia Figuls, followed the rough-hewn wood and cane indigenous architectural style when they carved this comfortable lodge out of the jungle. The sparkling-clean wood-paneled rooms have firm beds, mosquito screens, and fans. The terraces look across a narrow lawn to the river. Chestnut-beaked toucans, poison arrow frogs, and three types of monkey hang out in the jungle that looms behind the rooms. ⊠ *(across river and about 1 km/½ mi north of Tortuguero),* ☎ 233–3333 *(leave message with answering service). Dining room. No credit cards.*

Ecotourism

Deep in the Tortuguero jungle the **Canadian Organization for Tropical Education and Rainforest Conservation** has set up a small station, where a couple of volunteers are running a butterfly farm, cataloging plants and animals, and exploring sustainable forest practices.

In the town of Tortuguero, the **Caribbean Conservation Corporation (CCC)** opened a **Visitor's Center and Museum** in late 1994 that's worth a visit. Actor Cliff Robertson narrates the video history of the area, and the exhibits include excellent animal photos as well as detailed discussions of what's going on in the area, ecologically speaking, and what one can do to help. There's a souvenir shop next door, and at least one other store in Tortuguero sells locally produced crafts. ⊠ *Apdo. 246–2050, Att: Tortuguero, San Pedro (head to beach and walk north along path next to beach—watch for sign),* ☎ *710–0547 or* ☎ *224–9215 (San José office).* ⊙ *Daily 10* AM–*noon, 2* PM–*5:30.*

For the committed ecotourist, the **Casa Verde Green Turtle Research** Station has camping areas as well as dormitory style quarters with a communal kitchen. If you're interested in a deeper involvement in the life of the turtles, you can arrange a stay through the CCC. ⊠ *By the airport, across the canal from Tortuga Lodge,* ☎ *352/373–6441 in the U.S.*

Barra del Colorado

❽ *25 km (16 mi) northwest of Tortuguero.*

Farther up the coast from the town of Moín, bordered in the north by the San Juan River and the frontier with Nicaragua, is the vast 228,000-acre **Barra del Colorado Wildlife Refuge** (☞ Chapter 2). Approach is by air or boat from San José or Tortuguero, and transport once you get there is almost exclusively waterborne; there are virtually no paths in this swampy terrain. Apart from the route via Tortuguero, another possibility is to come from Puerto Viejo up the Sarapiquí and San Juan rivers. The list of species that you are likely to see from your boat is virtually the same as that for Tortuguero; the main difference here is the greater feeling of being more off the beaten track. Most travelers who make it as far as this are attracted by the sportfishing potential. The hamlet of Barra del Colorado with its stilted, plain wooden houses, and dirt paths, remains without motorized land vehicles, although some locals have added outboard motors to their hand-hewn canoes.

Dining and Lodging

$$$$ ✕⌂ *Rain Goddess.* Dining, lodging, and everything else is self-contained on Dr. Alfredo López's 65-foot long *Rain Goddess,* a small floating luxury hotel that travels up the San Juan River and around the Barra del Colorado area, offering guests an opportunity for nature cruising and deep sea fishing—there are two seaworthy fishing and excursion boats in tow—depending on their own preferences. The emphasis is on fishing, but the amenities include first-class food, hot showers, air conditioning, handcrafted furnishings, color TV with a video library, and covered decks. Currently offering five- to seven-day packages, with pickup in San José by van for transport to speedboat at Puerto Viejo de Sarapiquí and a fast trip downriver to the Rain Goddess, waiting on the Río San Juan. ⊠ *Apdo. 850–1250, San José,* ☎ *231–4299 (San José office) or 800/308–3394 in the U.S.,* ⅁ *231–3816. Sleeps up to 12 in 6 staterooms. AE, MC, V (7% credit card charge).*

$$$ ✕⌂ **Río Colorado Lodge.** This jungle lodge caters almost exclusively to sportfishing folk, as the property runs a modern fleet of 16- and 23-foot sportfishing vessels. Bedrooms have twin beds with patterned bedspreads, paneled ceilings, white curtains, and basket lampshades. Expensive all-inclusive tours include the flight here from San José, all meals, and fishing. ⊠ *Apdo. 5094–1000, San José (35-min flight from San José via Travelair),* ☎ *232–8610 (San José office) or 800/243–9777 in the U.S.,* ⅁ *231–5987. 18 rooms with bath. Restaurant, bar. AE, MC, V.*

COASTAL TALAMANCA

Numbers in the margin correspond to points of interest on the Atlantic Lowlands map.

The quickest route from San José to the Atlantic coast runs through the magnificent cloud forest of Braulio Carrillo National Park before reaching the Caribbean Sea and the lively—and sometimes dangerous—port town of Limón. The 160-kilometer (100-mile) trip along the Guápiles Highway to the coast takes about 2½ hours, with all going well—the highway, carved out of mountainous jungle, is susceptible to landslides. Make sure it's not blocked before heading out.

As the highway descends and straightens toward Guápiles, you will enter Limón province, where cloud forest gives way to banana plantations and partially deforested pastureland. This region is also home to farms that harvest cocoa, exotic export plants, and macadamia nuts. Many of the crystal-clear green rivers that run through the area have bathing pools. After passing through villages with names like Bristol, Stratford, and Liverpool, you arrive in the provincial capital, Limón.

Puerto Limón

❾ *130 km (81 mi) southeast of Braulio Carrillo.*

Puerto Limón's promontory setting, overlooking the Caribbean, is inherited from an ancient Indian village, Cariari, which lay close to the Isla Uvita, where Christopher Columbus lay anchor on his final voyage in 1502. The colorful Afro-Caribbean flavor of Costa Rica's most important port (population 50,000) gives visitors their first glimpse of life on Costa Rica's east coast. Puerto Limón is a lively town with a 24-hour street life. The wooden houses are brightly painted, but the grid-plan streets have a somewhat worn appearance, largely due to the damage caused by the 1991 earthquake.

On the left of the highway as you enter Limón is a large **Chinese cemetery:** Chinese made up a large part of the ill-starred railroad construction team that worked here. Follow the railroad as far as the palm-lined **promenade** that runs around the Parque Vargas. From the promenade you can see the raised dead coral left stranded by the quake. Nine Hoffman's two-toed sloths live in the trees of **Parque Vargas;** ask a passerby to point them out, as sighting them requires a trained eye. From here, find the lively **market** on Avenida 2, between Calles 3 and 4, where you can buy fruit for the road onward. Staying overnight in Limón is not recommended: Street crime is common.

The docks at neighboring **Moín** are a logical next stop, especially if you want to take a boat north to explore the Caribbean coast. Possibly you can also negotiate a waterway/national park tour with a local guide, and if you're lucky or made a call in advance you'll find the man considered the best guide on the Caribbean coast. His name is Modesto Watson, and he is legendary for his bird- and animal-spotting skills as well as his howler monkey calls.

Dining and Lodging

$–$$ ✕ Springfield. Protected from the street by a leafy conservatory, this Caribbean kitchen whips up tasty rice and bean dishes. Decor consists of wood paneling, red tablecloths, and a white tile floor. Bring your dancing shoes: out back there's a huge dance floor that creaks to the beat of soca, salsa, and reggae on weekends. ⊠ *On left of road that runs north from Puerto Limón to Portete, opposite hospital,* ☎ *758–1203. Reservations not accepted. AE, MC, V.*

$$$ ✗⚏ **Hotel Maribú Caribe.** Perched on a cliff overlooking the Caribbean
★ Sea, between Limón and Portete, these white, conical thatched huts have great views, air-conditioning, and hot water. Green lawns, shrubs, palm trees, and a large, kidney-shaped pool dominate the lovely gardens. The poolside bar does away with the need for any added exertion. ⊠ *Apdo. 623–7300, San José (Carretera to Portete),* ☎ *758–4010,* FAX *758–3541. 52 rooms with bath. Restaurant, bar, snack bar, pool. AE, MC, V.*

Nightlife

Limón starts hopping after dark—there are popular dance floors at the **Hotel Acón** and at the **Springfield** restaurant (☞ Dining and Lodging, *above*).

Cahuita

⑩ *44 km (27 mi) southeast of Puerto Limón.*

Heading south from Limón, the Caribbean character of the Atlantic Lowlands becomes powerfully evident, in the surf rolling shoreward on your left; in the hot, humid stir of the Caribbean tradewinds; in the laid-back pace of the people you meet. This is tropical Central America, and it feels like another country, its slow, somewhat sultry atmosphere far removed from the business and hustle of San José. Often visible from the road, the coast is lined with gorgeous black and white sand beaches fringed with palm trees. Way offshore, you can see whitewater breaks where the waves crash over coral reefs. Following the nearly ruler-straight coastline, the road is smooth, well-paved, with a few indents and curves reflecting similar shifts in coastal geography. You'll occasionally spot banks of dead coral exposed above the surface, thrust there by the big quake of 1991. Passing through cleared forests of banana plantations and stands of primary jungle, now and then you'll cross a recently rebuilt bridge over a slow green river, its peaceful waters belying the fierce flooding that has washed out the lowland bridges—those that survived the big earthquake—time and time again.

Watch carefully for the left turn to Cahuita about 44 kilometers (27 miles) out of Limón; it is quite easy to miss. Turn right at the end of the first of three entrance roads to get to Cahuita's main dirt street, flanked by wooden-slat cabins. The turquoise Salón Vaz in Cahuita emits lively reggae, soca, and samba 24 hours a day; the assemblage of dogs dozing on its veranda sums up the laid-back pace of life here. Cahuita is a backpackers' holiday town with something of a druggy reputation, a hippie hangout with a dash of Afro-Caribbean spice tossed in.

At the southern end of Cahuita's main street is the start of **Cahuita National Park** (☞ Chapter 2). This entrance is preferable to Puerto Vargas (☞ *below*) because there is no entry fee here. Lush rain forest extends to the brink of the completely undeveloped curving white-sand beach that stretches for 3 kilometers (2 miles). A 7-kilometer (4-mile) trail follows the coastline within the forest to Cahuita point, which is encircled by a 600-acre coral reef. Here you'll find blue parrot fish and angelfish that weave their way among the various equally colorful species of coral and sponge. The reef escaped the 1991 earthquake with little damage, but biologists are worried that the coral has stopped growing due to silt and plastic bags washed down the Estrella River from banana plantations upstream. Glass-bottom-boat tours that operate out of Cahuita visit this aquatic garden. Visibility is best in September and October. To snorkel independently, swim out from the beach on the Puerto Vargas side.

The trail extends as far as **Puerto Vargas,** the park's main headquarters. Along the trail there are opportunities for spotting howler monkeys, coatis, armadillos, and raccoons. Some stretches of beach have much worse currents than others; ask the rangers at Puerto Vargas for advice. There are campsites carved out of the jungle along the beach at Puerto Vargas.

Dining and Lodging

$$ ✕ **Edith Soda y Restaurant.** Miss Edith is revered for her outrageous
★ Caribbean cooking, vegetarian meals, and herbal teas for whatever ails you. Don't expect to get anything in a hurry; most of her dishes are made to order. But her rondon and smoked chicken are worth the wait. Her restaurant is at the north end of town, near the guardia rural (police station). ✉ *From bus station, follow main road north, turn right at police station. No phone. No credit cards. Closed Tues. No lunch Sun.*

$ ✕ **Vista del Mar.** The main attraction of this open-air, aluminum-roof eatery is its proximity to Cahuita National Park. After a hard day of sunbathing, you need walk only about 10 steps past the park exit to sample the Vista's traditional Costa Rican food and seafood. The *pescado en salsa* (fish in sauce) is always fresh and delicious. ✉ *South of bus stop, next to park entrance. No phone. No credit cards.*

$$$ ✕🏨 **Jaguar.** These white cabinas on Playa Negra provide the roomi-
★ est accommodations plus the classiest cooking in Cahuita. The naturally ventilated cabins have high ceilings, large wooden beds, mosquito blinds, and terra-cotta floors, and you'll be delighted by the assortment of fruit trees and the virtual menagerie of exotic birds on the 17-acre grounds. The rooms nearest the road enjoy a view of the Caribbean through palm trees. The owners tend an herb garden whose produce they use in their most popular recipe, *dorada en salsa de hierbas* (dorado fish in an herb sauce). Phone ahead to see if transportation is available from Limón. ✉ *Apdo. 7046–1000, San José (from football field, 326 yds. to the north; across from Playa Negra),* ☎ *755–0238, or 226–3775 (San José office),* FAX *226–4693. 45 rooms with bath. Restaurant, bar, pool. MC, V.*

$$$ ✕🏨 **Magellan Inn.** This group of bungalows is the most elegant choice
★ of accommodations around. The white-walled rooms have original artwork, custom-made wooden furniture, ceiling fans, wall-to-wall carpets, and tiled terraces with wicker chairs and tables. Feast on French and Creole specialties in the candlelit restaurant, or groove to the jazz playing in the open-air bar. ✉ *Apdo. 1132, Limón (2 km/1.2 mi north of Cahuita at far end of Playa Negra),* ☎ FAX *755–0035. 6 rooms with bath. Restaurant, bar, pool. AE, DC, MC, V.*

$$$ 🏨 **Atlántida.** Atlántida's main assets are its attractively landscaped grounds, the beach across the road, and its large swimming pool. Up the street from Jaguar, the yellow bedrooms of this hotel are quite small and have heavy wood furniture, fans, and mosquito blinds. They encircle a thatched restaurant that provides breakfast with the price of the room. You can also cook your own food. The managers cultivate a younger and trendier ambience than Jaguar's. ✉ *(next to soccer field at Playa Negra),* ☎ *758–1515, ext. 213,* FAX *228–9467. 30 rooms with bath. Restaurant, pool. AE, MC, V.*

$$$ ▣ **Aviarios del Caribe.** Luís and Judy Arroyo have built this lodge and
★ bird-watching sanctuary from the rubble of the 1991 earthquake.
More than 285 species of bird have been spotted on the property, many
with the help of the telescope on the wide second-floor deck. The spa-
cious guest rooms have white walls, blue tile floors, and fresh flowers.
Buttercup, the resident three-toed sloth, oversees the proceedings from
her spot on the couch of the airy sitting room–library, and Koko the
crocodile will arrive on demand to tangle with birds over morsels of
cheese. ✉ *Apdo. 569–7300, Limón (head south from Limón and fol-
low myriad hotel signs on Estrella River delta, 9 km/5 mi north of
Cahuita), no phone,* 🖷 *798–0374. 5 rooms with bath. Breakfast
room.*

$ ▣ **Seaside Jenny.** The eponymous owner of this inn retains her Cana-
dian lilt after 16 years in Cahuita. Book here if proximity to the sea is
what you crave. Near the main part of Cahuita, the modern two-story
structure is just 10 yards from the very audible water's edge. The cab-
ins upstairs are $5 more but worth it for their sea views, balconies,
and extra light; the ones downstairs are rather dingy. There are more
beds in some—a good pointer for groups to keep in mind. Fans keep
the rooms cool, and hammocks strung on the terraces catch Caribbean
breezes. Furnishings are traditional. You won't find any mosquito nets
here because the pests miraculously avoid the sea around these parts.
There are two new rooms in a building behind the main house. ✉ *(head
straight to the shore from bus stop),* ☎ *758–1515, ext. 256. 9 rooms
with bath. No credit cards.*

Puerto Viejo de Limón

⑪ *16 km (10 mi) south of Cahuita.*

Puerto Viejo de Limón is quieter than Cahuita but offers a greater choice
of accommodations—dozens of cabinas (cottages) and hotels. Watch
for the left turn 8 kilometers (5 miles) before BriBri; the last 6 kilo-
meters (4 miles) are unpaved. Many visitors come here with only one
thing on their mind: surfing. Waves are at their best between Decem-
ber and April and again in June and July. A decent dirt road leads south
from Puerto Viejo to Punta Cocles and Punta Uva, where some of the
region's first luxurious tourism developments have opened in the last
few years, and on to Manzanillo.

Dining and Lodging

$$–$$$ ✕ **The Garden.** Transplanted to Costa Rica from Trinidad by way of
★ Toronto, the Garden's owner/chef Vera Mabon incorporates her In-
dian heritage into her recipes. The beautifully prepared and presented
Asian-Caribbean food reflects a multicultural background, and for the
traveler looking for a first-class meal to break up the monotonous, if
satisfying, daily casado routine, this is the place to go. The decor is so-
phisticated hippie with candlelight, linen, and flowers; the staff is
pleasant and competent, and the food is wonderful. The restaurant oc-
cupies a round, wood- and thatch-roofed open air building buried in
a flowering garden. ✉ *A few blocks off beach—follow signs, no phone.
No credit cards, but Vera will take traveler's checks or dollars.*

$–$$ ✕ **Bambú.** This funky little bar and restaurant, with a view of the world-
class surf of Salsa Brava, is owned and operated by the same two Ger-
mans who've been building the El Sueño guesthouse down the road
(☞ *below*). One German is a doctor, and rumor has it the room behind the bar has been used for surgery more than once. The other German performs another kind of operation, making powerhouse margaritas

and other mixed drinks. The food is simple, but sound: daily fresh fish specials, casados, and sandwiches. ⊠ *Outside of town on ocean road, no phone. No credit cards.*

$ ✕ **Elena Brown Soda y Restaurant.** This unpretentious place serves excellent fresh fish dishes. ⊠ *Along road from Puerto Viejo to Punta Uva, no phone. No credit cards.*

$$–$$$ ✕⊞ **El Pizote.** El Pizote observes local architectural mores while offering more than most in the way of amenities. Rooms have polished wood paneling, reading lamps, mirrors, mats, firm beds, and fans. Some rooms share a bathroom; others, in individual huts, have their own. A two-room bungalow accommodates six people. The restaurant serves breakfast, dinner, and drinks all day. Guanabana and papaya grow on the grounds; hiking trails lead off into the jungle. Children under 8 aren't welcome. ⊠ *Apdo. 230–2200 (set back on right of road that runs into Puerto Viejo),* ☎ ℻ *229–1428. 8 rooms with shared bath, 6 bungalows with bath. Restaurant, bar, volleyball. MC, V.*

$$$ ✕⊞ **Yaré.** The sound of the jungle is overpowering, especially at night, as you relax in your charming, brightly-painted cabin at the Yaré hotel. The cabinas have fans, hot water, and private baths. The in-house restaurant is open for breakfast, lunch, and dinner. The owner organizes all kinds of tours. ⊠ *(4 km/2.5 mi on right of road to Gandoca),* ☎ ℻ *284–5921,* ☎ *232–7866 (San José office). 8 cabins and 10 rooms with bath. Restaurant, horseback riding, fishing. AE, MC, V.*

$$ ✕⊞ **Playa Chiquita Lodge.** These wooden cabinas are tastefully furnished and set in thick jungle 200 yards back from the beautiful Chiquita beach, near Punta Uva. It is popular with bird-watchers, so in the evenings you can swap sightings. ⊠ *(10 km/6 mi on left of road from Puerto Viejo),* ☎ ℻ *223–7479. 11 rooms with bath. Restaurant, bar. No credit cards.*

$$$–$$$ ⊞ **Villas del Caribe.** Undoubtedly one of the most elegant places in Costa Rica east of San José, this villa complex is right on the beach north of Punta Uva. Each multiroom villa has a blue-tile-lined kitchen with stove and refrigerator, a small sitting room with low-slung couches, a plant-filled bathroom, and a patio with sea views. Upstairs are one or two spacious bedrooms with a wooden deck and a view of the Caribbean. Although they serve coffee at the reception counter, the nearest restaurant is several hundred yards away—that may not seem far, but when it rains it pours, and the road is unlit and full of potholes. But if you bring your own edibles you're set, since the hotel rents all kinds of watersports equipment and will arrange any kind of tour. ⊠ *Puerto Viejo, Limón,* ☎ *233–2200,* ℻ *221–2801. 12 villas with bath. AE, DC, MC, V.*

$$–$$$ ⊞ **Miraflores Lodge.** It's not difficult to tell that this was a flower farm before a hotel was built on the property in 1990. The collection of bromeliads and heliconias and the intricate landscaping are a dead giveaway. The buildings, designed in the indigenous style, with peaked thatched roofs and cane walls, make you feel as if you're off the tourist trail. The proprietor sells local artwork in an attempt to infuse some tourism money directly into the local economy. ⊠ *Playa Chiquita, Puerto Viejo, Limón,* ☎ ℻ *233–2822. 5 rooms with bath, 5 with shared bath. Breakfast room. No credit cards.*

$$ ⊞ **El Sueño.** "The Dream" is a four-story Caribbean confection, an architectural "cabina de fantasía" spun from the minds of its two German owners. It may remain an ongoing project for years to come, but the first 4 of 15 planned rooms are available now, and every one is unique. If you'd like to sleep in a treehouse two minutes from the sea, here's your chance. Complimentary bicycles, snorkeling gear, and rides to the better beaches in the area come with the package. Make reservations through Talamanca Association for Ecotourism and Conservation

(ATEC, Puerto Viejo, ☎ FAX 798–4244). ✉ *10-min walk south from Puerto Viejo, no phone. 4 rooms with bath. Snorkeling, bicycles. No credit cards.*

$ 🏠 **Cabinas Black Sands.** This beachside cabina is of BriBri Indian design—bamboo, laurel wood, thatch, and stilts—and is surrounded by tropical foliage. Its isolated position, a 20-minute walk from Puerto Viejo, ensures privacy and tranquillity. The same can't be said for the rooms, whose dividing walls don't quite reach the ceiling. A basic kitchen is shared by all guests; bring your own food. ✉ *Ken Kerst, Lista de Correos, Puerto Viejo de Limón, Talamanca (go left at Violeta's Pulpería—ask bus driver to drop you here—just before reaching Puerto Viejo, and Black Sands is 400 yds away, signposted), no phone. 3 double rooms with shared bath. No credit cards.*

Ecotourism

Perhaps the single most influential person in Puerto Viejo these days is a woman named **Damaris Patterson.** A graduate of the University of Oklahoma, Patterson runs **ATEC** out of a small office in the middle of Puerto Viejo. ATEC, which in addition to its increasingly important role in the ecotourism movement, also serves as a fax and phone center, a post office, and a general information center for the town and the region. Under ATEC's auspices the following tours and activities can be pursued: Afro-Caribbean culture and nature walks; indigenous culture and nature walks; rain forest hikes; coral reef snorkeling or fishing trips; bird and night walks; and adventure treks. Remember, ATEC is not a profit-making tourist agency but a grass-roots organization promoting ecotourism in Talamanca; the idea is to encourage tourism through small-scale, locally owned businesses—tour guides, cabinas, restaurants, and so on. Fifteen percent to 20% of money collected for tours booked through ATEC goes to local organizations and wildlife refuges. In Puerto Viejo, visit the office, or call 798–4244. Even if you're not using their services, they could use a donation.

Outdoor Activities and Sports

BICYCLING

You can bike through the national park, although the trail gets pretty muddy at times. Nevertheless, mountain bikes are a wonderful way to get around on the dirt roads and trails surrounding Cahuita, Puerto Viejo, and points south. They can be rented at a number of different places in the region, such as **Moray's Tour Office** in Cahuita. At the convergence of the two beach roads, Moray's makes reservations, rents surfboards, bicycles, and snorkeling gear, and arranges horseback and other tours.

SNORKELING

Cahuita National Park's reefs comprise just one of several high-quality dive spots in the area. Snorkeling gear can be rented in Cahuita or Puerto Viejo or through your hotel. Most hotels will organize dive trips. Or contact the **ATEC** office (☞ Ecotourism, *above*) in the middle of Puerto Viejo to make arrangements. It's a good idea to work with a guide because the number of good dive spots is limited, and they are not necessarily close to town or close to shore.

SURFING

Surfing is the name of the game in Puerto Viejo. There are a number of breaks here, the most famous being **Salsa Brava.** Salsa Brava breaks rather far offshore and there are some tricky currents and reefs to maneuver just to get out there. It's a hollow, primarily right-breaking wave over a shallow reef; when it gets big, it is one "gnarly" wave, as the surfers would say. Talk to **Patrick Abrams** at the Hogfish Ranch (ask around town; you'll find him and his pack of happy dogs wandering about) for advice on where to go, locally, if Salsa Brava is too big, or not big enough; or call 220–2026 for a forecast of wave conditions all over the country. The operators claim about an 80% success rate, which isn't too bad; the cost is about 50¢ per minute. There are also plenty of good waves, especially at Punta Uva and Punta Cocles, for bodysurfing and boogie boarding.

Shopping

Shopping is not the star attraction of the Atlantic Lowlands. The owners of **Rancho Leona** make and sell stained glass, necklaces, earrings, and painted T-shirts. The town of Tortuguero has at least one **craft shop,** and there's a **souvenir shop** at the Caribbean Conservation Corporation's new headquarters. On the track running north from Cahuita to Playa Negra, the **Tienda de Artesanía** is a women's craft cooperative producing painted T-shirts and jewelry. There are also jewelry and crafts for sale from **streetside vendors** in Puerto Viejo.

Gandoca-Manzanillo Wildlife Refuge

12 *15 km (9 mi) south of Puerto Viejo.*

The Gandoca-Manzanillo Wildlife Refuge protects *orey* and *jolillo* swamps, 10 kilometers (6 miles) of beach where four species of turtle lay their eggs, and 741 acres of *cativo* forest and coral reef (☞ Chapter 2). The Gandoca estuary is a nursery for tarpon and a wallowing spot for crocodiles and caimans. The administrators of the park, Benson and Florentino Grenald, can tell you more and recommend a local guide. If you ask when you enter Manzanillo village, residents will point you toward them.

From the frontier with Panama, retrace your steps to the main road and head left through BriBri to Sixaola, the border town. There are Indian reserves in the area protecting the domains of the BriBri, Cabecar, and Kekoldi Indians.

OFF THE   **HITOY CERERE BIOLOGICAL RESERVE** – The remote 22,600-acre Hitoy
BEATEN PATH   Cerere Biological Reserve occupies the head of the Valle de la Estrella.
The park's limited infrastructure was badly damaged by the 1991 quake, whose epicenter was precisely there. Paths that do exist are very overgrown due to their limited use—visitors scarcely ever get here. Jaguars, tapirs, peccaries, porcupines, anteaters, and armadillos all live in the forest, along with more than 115 species of birds. Watch for the so-called Jesus Christ lizards, which can walk on water. The moss-flanked rivers have clear bathing pools and spectacular waterfalls. To get there, take a Valle de la Estrella bus from Limón and get off at Finca Seis; hire a Jeep and you'll be able to get within 1 kilometer (½ mile) of the reserve for $5. Check beforehand with the park service in San José if you want to stay overnight.

THE ATLANTIC LOWLANDS A TO Z

Arriving and Departing

By Bus

Bus service to the Atlantic Lowlands from San José includes daily service to Limón from Avenida 3 between Calles 19 and 21 (☎ 223–7811) every half hour between 5:30 AM and 7 PM (2½-hour trip); to Cahuita and Sixaola from Avenida 11 between Calles Central and 1 (☎ 221–0524) daily at 6 AM and 1:30 and 3:30 PM (four-hour trip); to Turrialba from Calle 13 between Avenidas 6 and 8 (☎ 556–0073) daily every hour between 5 AM and 10 PM; to Río Frío and Puerto Viejo de Sarapiquí via Braulio Carrillo from Avenida 11 between Calles Central and one daily at 7 and 9 AM and 1, 3, and 4 PM (four-hour trip); to Braulio Carrillo every half hour between 7:30 AM and 7 PM from Calle 12, Avenidas 7 and 9; to Puerto Viejo at 3:30 PM and Sundays at 8 AM from Calle Central, Avenida 11. Make sure your bus to Puerto Viejo is not heading to Sixaola without actually going into Puerto Viejo—otherwise you'll face a 2-mile hike into town from the drop-off point where the dirt road to Puerto Viejo begins.

By Car

The paved two-lane Guápiles Highway runs from Calle 3 in San José to Limón, a distance of about 160 kilometers (100 miles). South of Limón, a paved road goes for about 40 kilometers (25 miles) to Cahuita, then past the Cahuita turnoff and proceeds for roughly 16 kilometers (10 miles) toward Puerto Viejo. The paved main road turns inland and heads up to BriBri and Sixaola a couple of miles before it reaches Puerto Viejo, but the dirt road remains navigable as far as Punta Uva year-round. The roads in the Sarapiquí area of the Atlantic Lowlands are mostly paved, with the usual rained-out dirt and rock sections—road quality depends on the time of year, the last pass of the infrequent road crews, or the amount of rain dumped by the latest tropical storm. Four-wheel drive is always preferable, but for the most part the major roads in this region are passable by any kind of car.

By Plane

Currently neither of the two domestic airlines flies to Puerto Limón on a scheduled basis, although a charter is certainly possible because there is a good landing strip just south of town. **Travelair** flies to Tortuguero and Barra del Colorado daily, with flights departing at 6 AM. **Sansa** flies to Barra del Colorado on Tuesday and Thursday through Saturday at 6 AM. Several tour companies, such as **Costa Rica Expeditions** (☏ 222–0333, ℻ 257–0766) offer regular or charter flights into Tortuguero and/or Barra del Colorado in conjunction with stays in their lodges in the area.

Getting Around

By Boat

Many private operators will take you from the docks at Moín, just outside of Limón, to Tortuguero, but there is no scheduled public transportation. **Modesto Watson** (☞ Guided Tours, *below*), an eagle-eye Miskito Indian guide, will take you upstream if he has room on his boat. You can hire boats to travel between Tortuguero and Barra del Colorado, but prices are quite high. Boats leave Puerto Viejo de Sarapiquí to travel upstream, but times vary—contact **El Gavilán Lodge** (☞ Dining and Lodging, *above*), or negotiate your own deal on the dockside.

By Bus

Buses leave from in front of Distribuidora Tropigas Victor Chin on the west side of Calzado Mary in Limón for **Cahuita, Puerto Vargas, Puerto Viejo,** and **Sixaola** daily at 5, 8, and 10 AM and 1, 4, and 6 PM.

By Car

There are no roads to Tortuguero (☞ By Boat, *above*). At press time (mid-1996) the paved road running down the Talamanca coast was in good shape all the way to the border, although past Cahuita it turns inland to the border at Sixaola and the coast road south from there is dirt all the way to Manzanillo, where it terminates.

By Train

The famous **Jungle Train** from San José to Limón via Turrialba is out of operation, taking with it the last rail transportation in the area. **Swiss Travel's** one-day tour, which includes a train trip between Siquirres and Guápiles, is also out of operation.

Contacts and Resources

Emergencies

Police (☎ 117 in towns or ☎ 127 in rural areas). **Traffic Police** (☎ 227–8030). **Fire** (Bomberos, ☎ 118). **Ambulance** (Cruz Roja, ☎ 128).

Guided Tours

Tortuguero National Park tours are usually packaged with one- or two-night stays in local lodges. **Cotur's** (✉ Paseo Colón and C. 34/36, ☎ 233–0155) offers three-day, two-night tours with a bus to Port Hamburgo, a canal trip, and accommodations at the Jungle Lodge for $210. **Mawamba** (☎ 223–2421) offers a slightly more expensive version of the same tour, with the nights spent at the Mawamba Lodge, or a less expensive version with nights at Cabinas Sabina. **Costa Rica Expeditions** (✉ C. Central and Avda. 3, ☎ 222–0333) flies you directly to their rustically charming Tortuga Lodge for three days, two nights, for about $300. **Fran and Modesto Watson** (☎ 226–0896) know the history and ecology of the area best. They offer a two-day, one-night tour for $125. **Atlántico Tours** (Contact ATEC, ☎ FAX 798–4244), based in Puerto Viejo, offers tours to Tortuguero and Barra del Colorado as well as more local tours of Cahuita National Park, Hitoy Cerere Biological Reserve, Gandoca-Manzanillo Wildlife Refuge, and other destinations. They also rent surfboards, bicycles, kites, and snorkeling gear. The ATEC office offers tours to local Indian preserves as well as every known, and some unknown, destinations in the area. Most of the hotels in the Puerto Viejo area will organize tours of almost any kind—hikes, horseback, bicycle, fishing, and so on. We recommend working with ATEC or other local people, because locally based tourism is in the sustainable, ecotourism mode.

Visitor Information

The tourist office in San José has information covering the Atlantic Lowlands (☞ Contacts and Resources *in* Chapter 3). The ATEC office in Puerto Viejo is a great source of information on local tours, guides, and interesting activities. You can probably find out here if it is possible to hire a boat to take you down to Panama from here as well (☞ Chapter 8). Rumor has it that it can be done. ATEC (☎ FAX 798–4244) is right in town.

6 The Northwest

In the northwestern province of Guanacaste, Costa Rican cowboys graze their cattle on the dry plains, while expatriate California surfers wander the golden beaches of the Nicoya Peninsula, searching for the perfect wave. Inland, world-class windsurfers sail across Lake Arenal while ecotourists explore the lush cloud forests and preserves around Monteverde.

Updated by
Justin
Henderson

WITH ABOUT 65 INCHES OF RAINFALL per year, Costa Rica's wild west is the country's driest region. The northwest is also home to countless natural wonders: Six semiactive volcanoes, large areas of wet and dry forest, limestone caverns, several large lakes, and mile upon mile of sparkling beaches.

Guanacaste, Costa Rica's westernmost province, at the border of Nicaragua and the Pacific Ocean, derives its name from the broad earpod trees, the guanacaste, that give well-needed shade to the lounging white Brahman cattle so prevalent in the region. An independent province of Spain's colonial empire until 1787 when it was ceded to Nicaragua, Guanacaste became part of Costa Rica in 1814. After independence in 1821, both Nicaragua and Costa Rica claimed Guanacaste for their own; the Guanacastecos themselves were divided: provincial capital Liberia wished to return to Nicaragua whereas rival city Nicoya favored Costa Rica. Nicoya got its way, helped by the fact that at the time the vote was taken, Nicaragua was embroiled in a civil war.

In appearance, the Guanacastecos more closely resemble their darker Nicaraguan neighbors than they do the Cartagos, their Central Valley neighbors, whose perceived sense of cultural and racial superiority they resent. The Guanacastecos, descendants of the Chorotegan Indians and early Spanish settlers, started many of the traditions that are now referred to as typically Costa Rican, and a strong folkloric character pervades the region. As you travel through the region, watch for traditional costumes, folk dancing, music, and recipes handed down from colonial times.

Because of the region's dry climate, the beaches here are popular during the rainy season. Development is so far mostly low-key, but the area is being targeted for huge amounts of investment. Large luxury resort and condominium projects are currently under way in Tambor and Flamingo; the Hotel Playa Tambor, for example, which opened in 1992, has come under intense scrutiny and criticism for allegedly violating environmental laws. Thousands of homes, hotel rooms, and tourism facilities are planned for Papagayo as well, and although environmentalists oppose the massive development, it appears that ground will soon be broken.

A golf-course with luxury housing is in the early stages of construction adjacent to Las Baulas National Marine Park, and there are now two hotels open directly behind the park's Playa Grande turtle preserve. To the north, a consortium of Italians and Costa Ricans are planning an "ecosensitive" low-rise luxury resort behind the exquisite Playa Rajada just south of Bahía Salinas, near the Nicaraguan border. New hotels have opened at Playa Langosta, Playa Panama, Punta Islita near Carrillo, and on many other beaches, while a kind of land-sale frenzy is ongoing in Tamarindo and heating up in Nosara and at Playa Negra. The future for nesting turtles and wild birds remains uncertain, although it is doubtful they will be able to exist in ecological harmony with golf courses and luxury hotels, despite the assurances of the developers, most of whom appear more concerned by the greenness of their dollars than that of the environment.

Most but not all. It would be unfair to accuse every developer in Guanacaste of craven, insensitive behavior, when so many of them are doing their best to keep the turtles and the monkeys happy along with the investors and the tourists. Several of the new hotels we've added to this edition of the book have been designed and constructed with at least a modicum of environmental awareness. But there is more at stake now—more money, more land for sale, more pressure on the environment and the economy. It will prove interesting to see how the promoters of ecotourism in the area contend with the onslaught of luxury development as it intensifies in the next few years. In the end, the paradoxes of Costa Rican ecotourism will be impossible to ignore: bright lights and nesting turtles simply do not mix.

Pleasures and Pastimes

Beaches

The shrubby dry forest vegetation of the northwest coast contrasts sharply with the tropical beach backdrops that you'll encounter farther south. The great advantage here is the climate, which is far more reliable (drier) during the rainy season. Swimmers, however, should be careful of riptides, which are quite prevalent. What follows is a brief appraisal of selected beaches from north to south; use this listing to select the beach that is most right for you: Bahía Rajada, near Bahía Salinas, is an unspoiled jewel of white sand. Near Coco, which is rather dirty, both the beaches of Ocotal (in a very pretty cove with snorkeling potential and good views) and of Hermosa (a curving gray-sand beach hemmed in by rocky outcrops) are recommended strands. Pan de Azúcar offers good snorkeling and is deserted, but it's rather stony in the rainy season. Flamingo is the nearest thing to a built-up resort; despite a few condos and the Flamingo Beach Hotel it is still relatively low-key, and the beach is white and handsome. Brasilito allows you to observe the goings-on of fishing-village life. Conchal is famous for its tiny shells. Playa Grande, a restricted-access (at night) turtle-nesting beach stretching north from Tamarindo for 5 kilometers (3 miles), is safest for swimming, except in the surfing area near the Hotel Las Tortugas, and Tamarindo itself has a long white strand backed by good bars. Playa Langosta, adjacent to a bird sanctuary, has good surfing waves, nesting turtles at night, and few people. Nosara has a long beach that is overlooked by the apartments of foreign retirees but it is, nevertheless, backed by dense jungle where you might see wildlife. Guiones has a coral reef suitable for snorkeling, while Carrillo is on a very picturesque and deserted half-moon bay. Montezuma has several colorful, shell-strewn beaches, some of them long and some short. Tambor, in Bahía Ballena, offers calm waters for swimming.

Dining

Guanacaste's traditional foods derive from dishes prepared by pre-Columbian Chorotegan Indians. Typical dishes include *frito guanacasteco* (similar to the traditional *gallo pinto* dish of beans, rice, vegetables, and meat), *pedre* (a mixture of carob beans, pork, chicken, onions, sweet peppers, salt, and mint), *sopa de albóndigas* (meatball soup with chopped eggs and spices), and *arroz de maíz* (not actually rice but ricelike corn). Meat lovers rejoice: The northwest, whose plains are covered with cattle ranches, produces the country's best steak. Most of the places listed in this chapter serve international as well as local dishes, so you can take your pick.

Festivals

Santa Cruz celebrates its patron-saint day from January 15 onward with marimba music, folk dances, and Tico-style bullfights. On July 16 you can see a colorful regatta and carnival in Puntarenas in honor of its patron saint. The annexation of Guanacaste is celebrated July 17–25 with folk dances, bullfights, and rodeos in Liberia. The festival of La

Yeguita in Nicoya on December 12 features a solemn procession, dancing, fireworks, and bullfights.

Lodging

The northwest has a good mix of quality hotels, nature lodges, and more basic *cabinas* (cottages). It is wise to book ahead during the dry season, especially for weekends, when Ticos can fill beach hotels, especially, to bursting. A number of luxury hotels, both large and small, have opened recently along the coast, catering to a more upscale clientele.

Spelunking

For the modern-day troglodyte, the caves in Barra Honda National Park offer the opportunity to make a serious plunge into the underworld. The 60-foot Terciopelo Cave, in particular, contains a vast assortment of oddly-shaped rock formations; some stretches of the cave system are reputedly unexplored to this day.

Surfing

With its miles of coastline indented with innumerable points, rock reefs, river-mouth sandbars, and other wave-shaping geological configurations, it comes as no surprise that Guanacaste is a surfer's paradise—warm water, beautiful beaches, cheap beer, and uncrowded waves. What more could an aging California boy or girl ask for? Costa Rica was "discovered" in the '60s surf film classic, "The Endless Summer," and revisited in the recent sequel. Boca Barranca near Puntarenas has one of the world's longest lefts, but the water is dirty from the nearby river. Tamarindo is a good base for the five reef breaks, three river mouths, a couple of point breaks, and the superb 5-kilometer (3-mile) Playa Grande beach break nearby. The best waves at Playa Grande can be found just south of the Hotel Las Tortugas. Inquire at Iguana Surf, the surfboard shop in Tamarindo, to find out where the waves are breaking. Sámara and Nosara both have decent beach breaks. Roca Bruja (Witches Rock), in the Santa Rosa National Park, accessible by car only in summer, has a right river mouth. For well-heeled wave riders, there's a good break directly in front of the Hotel Tango Mar. Playa Negra, about an hour south of Tamarindo (four-wheel drive recommended), is also "gnarly"—in surferspeak—having been featured in "Endless Summer II." Playa Langosta, just south of Tamarindo, has a good river-mouth wave, and Playa Avellana, a few miles farther south, is rumored to have one of the best rights in Nicoya. Mal País, just above Cabo Blanco, is home to some of the largest waves in Costa Rica. At all of these spots you should be careful of the riptides.

Turtle Watching

Difficult to reach but worth it: Playa Nancite in Santa Rosa National Park and the Ostional Refuge near Nosara are prime for watching the mass nestings, or *arribadas,* of the olive ridley turtles. More accessible Playa Langosta to the south and Playa Grande to the north—they bookend the resort town of Tamarindo—provide wonderful opportunities for viewing the nesting rituals of the enormous, ponderous, and yet exquisitely dignified leatherback turtles, who arrive with high tide to dig holes and deposit their eggs.

Windsurfing

When winter settles in up north, serious American windsurfers look south. These days many of them look to Arenal, the man-made lake that lies to the north and west of Arenal Volcano, which many world champion windsurfers have called "one of the world's top five windsurfing spots." Trade winds from the Caribbean sneak through a pass in the Cordillera Central, crank up to 50 miles an hour or more from

December through April, and blow from the east toward the northwest end of the lake, creating perfect conditions for high wind fresh-
water sailing. The scenery here, too, is unmatched: watch the frequent
volcanic eruptions while you glide across the lake.

Exploring the Northwest

The area described herein includes the dry, partially deforested plains
of Guanacaste (crossed by the Nicaragua-bound Inter-American Highway); the foothills and the mountains of the Cordillera Central, with
its active and semiactive volcanoes and cloud and rain forests; and the
plains of Guanacaste, which give way to the golden beaches and lively
surf of the Nicoya Peninsula. Throughout, caverns, lakes, river deltas,
and dry forests add variety to the landscape, providing shelter and sus-
tenance for myriad animal and bird species.

Great Itineraries

The northwest has a couple of "must-see" destinations, but once
you've visited Monteverde and watched the Arenal Volcano in action,
time spent in the region (which for our purposes includes the province
of Guanacaste and parts of Puntarenas and Alajuela as well) can be
comfortably divided between lazy days on the beach, swimming in the
surf, and hiking/visiting a number of appealing or unusual sites: caverns, volcanoes, forests, estuaries, and turtle-watching beaches. Given
a week, one could spend two days in the Monteverde area, a day and
night at Arenal, and then travel back and forth between the beaches,
the mountains, and the mixed terrain that divides them, exploring at
leisure the most interesting sites.

Bear in mind, however, that aside from the Inter-American Highway
many of the roads in the region are of the pitted, pocked, and rock-
and-dirt variety, with the occasional river rushing over, rather than under,
the pavement. As a result, covering seemingly short distances can require long, grueling hours behind the wheel, and four-wheel drive is
often essential. For this reason, we highly recommend flying, when possible and affordable, if any of the beach resorts you plan to visit have
nearby air strips, as do Tamarindo, Carrillo, and Tambor. Also, many
of the northern beach resorts can be most easily reached from Liberia,
where an international airport has been operational for a couple of years.
Lacsa now flies to Liberia every Sunday from Miami before continuing on to San José; return flights to Miami are Wednesday and Friday.
Costa Rica's domestic carriers both fly to Liberia from San José.

The beach towns and resorts can be clustered into three loose geo-
graphical groups based, in part, on location and, in part, on the routes
you must take to reach them: those on the south end of the Nicoya
Peninsula, accessible by ferry from Puntarenas or by plane to Tambor,
and those in the central Nicoya Peninsula, reachable by plane to Punta
Islita, Carrillo, and Nosara, or by car via the Tempisque Ferry and the
roads through Carmona, Curime, and Nicoya, and those in the northern Nicoya Peninsula, accessible by plane to Tamarindo or Liberia, or
by car through Liberia and Comunidad, Santa Rosa National Park, or
La Cruz. These three loose clusters of beaches have a lot in common,
but there are distinct differences as well: if your time is limited and you
have to make a choice, consider whether you want, for example, lively
surf or calm waters; turtle-watching options at night; an isolated resort or a more active beach town.

IF YOU HAVE 3 DAYS AND NO INTEREST IN THE BEACH
*Numbers in the text correspond to numbers in the margin and on the
Northwest map.*

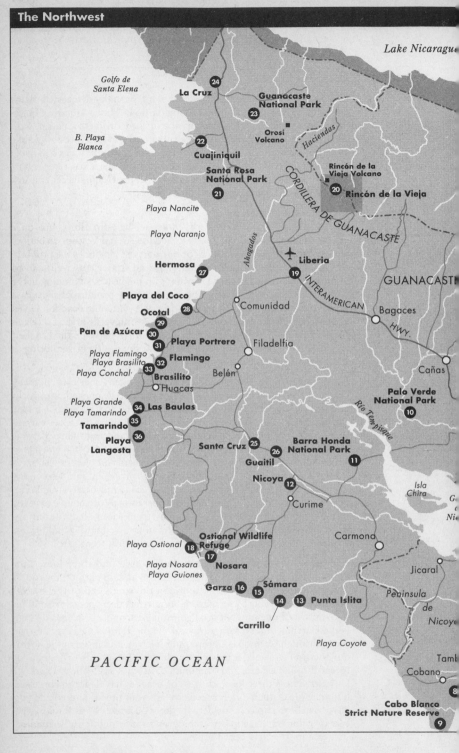

Lake Nicaragu[a]

Golfo de Santa Elena

24 **La Cruz**

Guanacaste National Park

23

B. Playa Blanca

Orosí Volcano

Haciendas

22 **Cuajiniquil**

Rincón de la Vieja Volcano

Santa Rosa National Park

CORDILLERA DE GUANACASTE

20 **Rincón de la Vieja**

21

Playa Nancite

Ahogados

Playa Naranjo

GUANACAST[E]

Hermosa

Liberia

27

19

INTERAMERICAN

Playa del Coco

Comunidad

Bagaces

Ocotal

28

HWY.

29

Pan de Azúcar

30

Cañas

31 **Playa Portrero**

Filadelfia

Playa Flamingo
Playa Brasilito

32 **Flamingo**

Belén

33

Playa Conchal

Palo Verde National Park

Brasilito

Huacas

Rio Tempisque

Playa Grande
Playa Tamarindo

34 **Las Baulas**

10

35 **Tamarindo**

Playa Langosta

36

Santa Cruz **25**

Barra Honda National Park

26

Guaitil

11

Nicoya

12

Isla Chira

Curime

*G[...]
[...]
Ni[...]*

Ostional Wildlife Refuge

Carmona

Playa Ostional **18**

17

Playa Nosara
Playa Guiones

Nosara

Jicaral

Garza **16** **15**

Sámara

Península de Nicoy[a]

14 **13** **Punta Islita**

Carrillo

Playa Coyote

PACIFIC OCEAN

Tam[...]

Cobano

8

Cabo Blanco Strict Nature Reserve

9

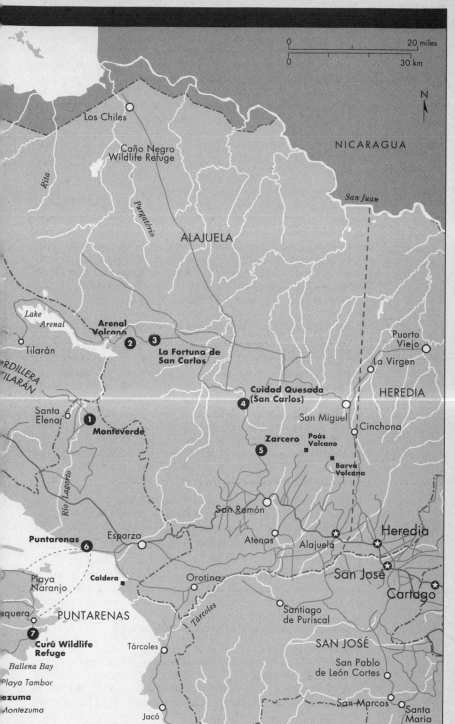

Starting from San José, most trips through the northwest commence with a visit to the cloud forest preserve at ⛰ **Monteverde** ①. From here it is a short distance on the map, but a 2½- to 3-hour drive (by either of two routes), to Tilarán, near the shores of Lake Arenal, and another two hours will take you on a scenic drive around the lake to the dam, quite close to the very active **Arenal Volcano** ②. The best places from which to see the volcano include resorts and hotels in and around the town of ⛰ **La Fortuna de San Carlos** ③, where you should spend your first night. From La Fortuna to **San Carlos** (a.k.a. **Ciudad Quesada**) ④ it is a short drive; just outside Ciudad Quesada is the relatively new Juan Castro Blanco National Park and, for a last, healing night, the wondrously invigorating thermal waters of the El Tucano Resort.

<u>IF YOU HAVE 3 DAYS AND WANT TO DO IT ALL</u>

To fit a day at the beach into this short itinerary: After a day at ⛰ **Monteverde** ① and at Tilarán viewing **Arenal Volcano** ② or windsurfing, rather than heading east around the lake to approach the volcano you can head west, returning to the Inter-American Highway at Cañas. From there drive north to **Liberia** ⑲, and from Liberia head southwest through Comunidad and choose a beach: ⛰ **Ocotal** ㉙, ⛰ **Playa del Coco** ㉘, or ⛰ **Hermosa** ㉗; or go farther south from Comunidad to Filadelfia and from there west to the beach at ⛰ **Flamingo** ㉜, ⛰ **Brasilito** ㉝, or ⛰ **Tamarindo** ㉟, for a day in the sun and surf, and a night of turtle watching (in season only) at **Las Baulas Marine National Park** ㉞.

<u>IF YOU HAVE 3 DAYS AND LOVE THE BEACH</u>

After a day and night at ⛰ **Monteverde** ①, travel back to San José and fly to ⛰ **Tambor**, ⛰ **Punta Islita** ⑬, ⛰ **Carrillo** ⑭, ⛰ **Nosara** ⑰, or ⛰ **Tamarindo** ㉟, for a two-night stay at one of the dozens of beach resorts on the Nicoya Peninsula. From Tambor or **Montezuma** ⑧, a short drive takes you to Cabo Blanco, where you can hike the trail through the **Cabo Blanco Strict Nature Reserve** ⑨ to deserted Playa Cabo Blanco, where hundreds of pelicans dive and frolic, or visit the **Curú Wildlife Refuge** ⑦, or surf at Tango Mar Hotel, if you are a hotel guest, or at Mal País, just north of Cabo Blanco, which reputedly has the largest surfing waves in Costa Rica.

If lounging on the sand isn't enough, you can stay up late to watch the arribada of the olive ridley turtles at **Ostional Wildlife Refuge** ⑱. Remember, the turtles' arrival is seasonal: if you want to see them you must visit at the right time of year. It's also a good idea to check with locals for time and tide information.

At ⛰ **Tamarindo** ㉟, there are numerous intermediate quality surfing and excellent swimming beaches, a lively bar and restaurant scene (perhaps best if you're under 30, but fun for all ages), and great surfing just up the beach at Playa Grande; in season, you can watch the leatherback turtles come in at night at **Las Baulas** ㉞.

<u>IF YOU HAVE 5 DAYS</u>

Begin with a day and night at ⛰ **Monteverde** ①. Then return to San José and leave again early the next morning, driving up through the coffee plantations into the mountains around **Zarcero** ⑤, en route to ⛰ **La Fortuna de San Carlos** ③ or **Ciudad Quesada** ④. Spend a day at the Juan Castro Blanco National Park near Ciudad Quesada and a night soaking in the healing thermal waters at nearby El Tucano Resort. Next day, drive the back route to **Arenal Volcano** ② by way of ⛰ **La Fortuna** ③ and Nuevo Arenal. From there, consider a one-day foray north, to the waters of the Caño Negro Wildlife Refuge. Then continue north by northwest around Arenal Lake, with a stop at

Tilarán or one of the lakeview hotels for a day of windsurfing, hiking, mountain biking, or volcano viewing. From Tilarán head down to Cañas, and from Cañas north to **Liberia** ⑲. From Liberia you can go north, and then east to hike the volcano trails in **Rincón de la Vieja** ⑳ or **Guanacaste National Park** ㉓, or west to **Santa Rosa National Park** ㉑. You can also choose to go southwest from Liberia, and spend a night or two at one of the beaches that lie between ⌖ **Tamarindo** ㉟ and **Hermosa** ㉗.

This five-day itinerary can be reversed very easily, for those who need immediate doses of sea and sun; and the beaches of the central or southern Nicoya Peninsula can be substituted for those of the north.

IF YOU HAVE 7 DAYS

Spend one day and night at ⌖ **Monteverde** ①, then return to the Inter-American Highway and follow signs to the Tempisque River. Catch the ferry across and do some bird-watching on the river or in **Palo Verde National Park** ⑩; or spend a few hours spelunking in **Barra Honda National Park** ⑪. Continue on through **Nicoya** ⑫ and **Santa Cruz** ㉕ and overnight it in ⌖ **Tamarindo** ㉟ or at one of the beach resorts north of there. Spend a day or two on the beach, and a night watching turtles at **Las Baulas** ㉞ (in season only), then head back to the highway via **Liberia** ⑲, and continue north. Here, make a choice: camping in ⌖ **Santa Rosa National Park** ㉑, ⌖ **Guanacaste National Park** ㉓, or ⌖ **Rincón de la Vieja National Park** ⑳, depending on your preferences (☞ Chapter 2), or stay in ⌖ **La Cruz** ㉔ to explore the pristine beaches of the far north; or in one of the several ranch or lodge-style hotels in or near the national parks. Head south on the Inter-American Highway and east at Cañas, and spend a night at one of the lake- and volcano-view hotels near **Arenal Volcano** ②. Next day make the trip around the lake, stopping for the night at ⌖ **La Fortuna de San Carlos** ③, which should provide a night of volcano viewing. Next day make the drive around the back of the volcano to ⌖ **Ciudad Quesada** ④, and visit Juan Castro Blanco National Park briefly before stopping for the night at nearby El Tucano Resort. The next day's drive over a spectacular if at times hair-raising mountain road back to San José via topiary-rich **Zarcero** ⑤ should take roughly two hours, and a bit less if you're headed for the airport.

When to Tour the Northwest

Although the dry season from December to April is considered the best time to visit any and all Costa Rican destinations, if there is one part of the country that is possibly more appealing during the rainy season it is the northwest. The Guanacastecos have renamed the rainy season the "green" season, and that it is: the rain falls for a couple of hours each day, and the countryside, tending toward brown during the dry season, remains lush and green, yet warm and sunny every day before and after the rain. The roads are muddy, but there are far fewer people, and the prices go down everywhere. For the seasonal activities of windsurfing and turtle watching, you have to go during dry season, but for most other activities in the northwest, you can go at almost any time of year. A good bet would be traveling in November or April–May, around the edges of the dry season, when the crowds are gone, the prices are lower, and the weather is "transitional."

INLAND: MONTEVERDE AND ENVIRONS

Numbers in the margin correspond to points of interest on the Northwest map.

To reach Monteverde from San José, travel north approximately 125 kilometers (78 miles) on the Inter-American Highway to the Río Lagarto turnoff. From here, an unpaved 30-kilometer (19-mile) track to the reserve snakes dramatically up through hilly farming country; it takes 1½ hours to negotiate it, faster by four-wheel drive. At the junction for Santa Elena, bear right for the reserve. The Monteverde settlement has no real nucleus; houses and hotels flank a 5-kilometer (3-mile) road at intervals until you arrive at the reserve's entrance.

Monteverde Cloud Forest Biological Reserve

❶ *167 km (104 mi) northwest of San José.*

In close proximity to several fine hotels, Monteverde Cloud Forest Biological Reserve is one of the country's best-kept reserves, with well-marked trails, lush vegetation, and a cool climate. The area's first residents were a handful of Costa Rican families, fleeing the rough-and-ready life of nearby gold-mining fields during the 1940s. They were joined in the 1950s by Quakers from Alabama who came in search of peace, tranquility, and good grazing, but the cloud forest that lay above their dairy farms was soon to attract the attention of ecologists.

The collision of moist winds with the continental divide here creates a constant mist whose particles provide nutrients for plants growing at the upper layers of the forest. Giant trees are enshrouded in a cascade of orchids, bromeliads, mosses, and ferns, and, in those patches where sunlight penetrates, brilliantly-colored flowers flourish. The sheer size of everything, especially the leaves of the trees, is very striking. No less astounding is the variety: 2,500 plant species, 400 species of birds, 500 types of butterflies, and more than 100 different mammals have so far been cataloged at Monteverde. A damp and exotic mixture of shades, smells, and sounds, the cloud forest is also famous for its population of resplendent quetzals, which can be spotted feeding on the *aguacatillo* (like an avocado) trees; best viewing times are early mornings from January until September, especially in April and May, during mating season. Other forest-dwelling inhabitants include hummingbirds and multicolored frogs. For those who don't have a lucky eye, a **short-stay aquarium** is in the field station; captives here stay only a week before being rereleased into the wild. Although the reserve limits visitors to 100 people at a time, Monteverde is one of the country's most popular destinations and gets very busy, so get there early and allow a generous slice of time for leisurely hiking in order to see the forest's flora and fauna; longer hikes are made possible by some strategically placed overnight refuges along the way. At the entrance to the reserve you can buy self-guide pamphlets and rent gum boots, and a map is provided when you pay the entrance fee. ☎ *645–5122.* 🎫 *$8 (reserve); $15 (guides).* ☉ *Daily 7–4.*

Several conservation areas have sprung up near Monteverde and make attractive day trips for reserve visitors, particularly if the Monteverde reserve is too busy. The **Santa Elena Reserve** (🎫 *$8.50*), a 900-acre forest 5 kilometers (3 miles) north of the town of Santa Elena, just west of Monteverde, has a series of trails that can be walked alone or with a guide.

Visit the office of the **Children's Eternal Cloud Forest** which currently encompasses nearly 50,000 acres of primary forest on three sides of the Monteverde Reserve.

The Monteverde cloud forest can be visited from high in the air compliments of **Canopy Tours,** which has three platforms up in the trees and, along with its cable and harness traversing system, offers a 40-foot climb inside a strangler fig to reach the newest platform. The tours last 2½ hours. With a base at the Cloud Forest Lodge, Canopy Tours charge $40. ✉ *Apdo. 751–2350, San José,* ☎ *645–5243. (Reservations office in San José:* ☎ 🗚 *257–5149.)*

🕐 **The Butterfly Garden** (✉ $5; 🕓 Daily 9:30–4), near the Pensión Monteverde Inn, has hundreds of tropical butterflies on display in three enclosed botanical gardens from which there are stunning views of the Gulf of Nicoya. A guided tour helps visitors understand the stages of a butterfly's life. The private bird farm (✉ Nominal fee; 🕓 Daily 9–4) next door has several trails through secondary forest. More than 90 bird species have been sighted here, from the crowned motmot to the spectacular quetzal.

The Monteverde Conservation League's 1.5 kilometer (1 mile) **Bajo del Tigre trail** (follow signs along the highway on the way to Monteverde) makes for a pleasant, 1½-kilometer (1-mile) hike through secondary forest.

NEED A
BREAK? **Stella's Bakery,** halfway between Santa Elena and Monteverde, serves everything from chocolate brownies to hearty breakfasts in a warm, wood-paneled room decorated with Stella's oil paintings and her daughter Meg's stained-glass windows. You can also sip coffee on the backyard patio.

Dining and Lodging

$$$ ✕🗔 **El Sapo Dorado.** Having started its life as a nightclub, El Sapo Dorado (The Golden Toad) became a popular restaurant and graduated into a very pleasant hotel. Geovanny's family arrived here to farm 10 years before the Quakers did, and he and his wife, Hannah, have built secluded hillside cabins with polished paneling, tables, open fires, and rocking chairs. Ten new rooms feature spectacular views of the Gulf of Nicoya. The restaurant is renowned for its pasta, pizza, vegetarian dishes, and fresh sailfish from Puntarenas; the dance floor is still put to use with live music on weekends; and the 6-kilometer (4-mile) distance from the park entrance isn't a problem if you enjoy hiking or have a car. ✉ *Apdo. 09–5655, Monteverde,* ☎ 🗚 *645–5010. 20 rooms with bath. Restaurant, bar, massage, bicycles. No credit cards.*

$$$ ✕🗔 **Fonda Vela.** The most innovatively designed of Monteverde's hotels is also one of the closest to the reserve entrance. Owned by the Smith brothers, whose family were among the first American arrivals in the 1950s, these steep-roofed chalets have large bedrooms with white stucco walls, wooden floors, and huge windows. Some have markedly better views of the wooded grounds, so specify when booking. Local and international recipes, prepared with flair, are served in the dining room or on the veranda. ✉ *Apdo. 70060–1000, San José (1.5km/1mi northwest of entrance to Monteverde),* ☎ *645–5125,* 🗚 *645–5119. 28 rooms with bath. Restaurant, bar, horseback riding. AE, DC, MC, V.*

$$–$$$ ✕🗔 **Hotel Belmar.** Built into the hillside, Hotel Belmar resembles two tall Swiss chalets and commands extensive views of the Gulf of Nicoya and the hilly peninsula. The amiable Chilean owners have designed both elegant and rustic rooms, paneled with polished wood; duvets cover

the beds and most rooms have balconies. In the dining room, you can count on adventurous and delicious *platos del día* (daily specials). ⊠ *Monteverde, Puntarenas (4km/2.5mi north of Monteverde),* ☎ 645–5201, ℻ 645–5135. *34 rooms with bath. Restaurant, bar, basketball. No credit cards.*

$ ✕🗔 **El Bosque.** Convenient to the Bajo Tigre nature trail and Meg's riding stable, El Bosque is a popular shady diner with a veranda; the paneled dining room has a tile floor and wood tables. A bridge from the veranda crosses a stream, and a track from there leads to the hotel. *Casados* (rice, beans, salad, and meat or fish) are good but the service can be rather offhand. ⊠ *Apdo. 5655, Santa Elena,* ☎ 645–5221, ℻ 645–5129. *21 rooms with bath. Restaurant. No credit cards. Closed Oct.*

$ ✕🗔 **Pensión Monteverde Inn.** The cheapest inn in Monteverde is quite far—about 5 kilometers (3 miles)—from the park entrance. The bedrooms are basic, but they have stunning views of the Gulf of Nicoya and contain hardwood floors, firm beds, and powerful, hot showers. Home cooking is served by the chatty David Savage and family. Their dog, Bambi, warms up to guests soon enough. ⊠ *Monteverde, Puntarenas (next to Butterfly Farm),* ☎ 645–5156, ℻ 645–5068. *10 rooms, 8 with bath. Dining room. No credit cards.*

Nightlife

There are **dance floors** at El Sapo Dorado hotel and at La Cascada restaurant.

Outdoor Activities and Sports

HORSEBACK RIDING

Next door to Stella's Bakery, **Meg's Stables** (☎ 645–5052) offers horseback riding for everyone from toddlers to seasoned experts. Guided rides through the Monteverde area cost around $10 an hour, with prices dropping for longer rides. Reservations are a good idea in high season.

Shopping

In Monteverde, the **Cooperative de Artesanas Santa Elena y Monteverde** (CASEM, ☎ 645–5190; ⊙ Mon.–Sat. 8–5, Sun. 10–4), an artisans' cooperative, is next door to the El Bosque hotel/restaurant and sells locally made handicrafts. The **Hummingbird Gallery** (🗔 Free; ⊙ Mon.–Sat. 8:30–4:30, Sun. 10–2), near the reserve entrance, sells prints, slides, books, gifts, T-shirts, and great Costa Rican coffee. Farther down on the right is the **Cheese Factory** (☎ 645–5029; 🗔 Free; ⊙ ☎ Mon.–Sat. 7:30–4, Sun. 7:30–12:30), established by the Quakers in the 1950s, and now one of the largest dairy producers in Costa Rica. Watch the art of cheese making through a window in the sales room—you'll surely be lured into buying some.

INLAND: TILARÁN, ARENAL, AND LA FORTUNA DE SAN CARLOS

Numbers in the margin correspond to points of interest on the Northwest map.

If your bones can take it, a very rough track leads from Santa Elena, near Monteverde, to Tilarán via Cabeceras, doing away with the need to return to the Inter-American Highway. You may well need four-wheel drive—inquire as to the present condition of the road—but the views of Nicoya Peninsula and Lake Arenal and Arenal Volcano reward those willing to bump around a bit. Consider also the fact that you don't really save much time—it takes about 2½ hours as opposed to the three required via Lagarto and Cañas on the highway.

Arenal Volcano

2 *128 km (80 mi) northwest of San José; 2½–3 hrs north of Santa Elena.*

The quiet whitewashed town of **Tilarán,** on the west side of **Lake Arenal,** is used as a base by bronzed windsurfers. If you took away the volcanoes, you might mistake the surrounding countryside of green, rolling hills for the English Lake District. The lake has two distinct personalities: the northwest end is windsurf central, whereas the more sheltered southeast end, closer to the dam, is popular for other water sports, especially fishing for *guapote* (rainbow bass). The southeast is also a marvelous place from which to view the volcano.

For those who have never seen an active volcano, Arenal makes a spectacular first—its perfect conical profile dominates the southern end of Lake Arenal. To get to the base of the volcano, head northwest from Tilarán around the top end of the lake and then southeast along the northern lakeshore. You'll pass a couple of small villages and several charming hotels ranging from the Cretan-inspired fantasy Hotel Tilawa to the rustic Rock River Lodge (☞ Dining and Lodging, *below*). If you're staying overnight in the area make sure you find a hotel with a view of the volcano. Just south of the town of Nuevo Arenal there is one short stretch of road still unpaved, adding a bone-jarring hour to an otherwise lovely drive with spectacular lake and volcano views all the way. Shortly before the dam at the southern end of the lake is the turn to Arenal Lodge (☞ Dining and Lodging, *below*). Next you come to the right turn to the **Smithsonian Institution's Observatory.** The track provides access to the base of the volcano, but you should attempt exploration only with a guide, either from the observatory or from the town of **Fortuna de San Carlos,** 17 kilometers (11 miles) beyond the dam.

Arenal lay dormant until 1968; on July 29 of that year an earthquake shook the area, and 12 hours later Arenal blew. The town of Pueblo Nuevo to the west bore the brunt of the shock waves, poisonous gases, and falling rocks; 80 people died in all. Since then, Arenal has been in a constant state of activity—eruptions, accompanied by thunderous sounds, are sometimes as frequent as one per hour. Night is the best time for observing it, when you can clearly see rocks spewing skyward and red-hot molten lava enveloping the top of the cone. Phases of inactivity do occur, however, so it is wise to check just before you go to judge whether your trip will be worthwhile. Hiking is possible on the volcano's lower slopes, but definitely not higher up; in 1988 two people were killed when they attempted to climb it. Ask at the observatory or the Burío Inn in Fortuna (☞ La Fortuna Dining and Lodging, *below*).

NEED A BREAK?	Kick back at the **Tabacón Resort** (☎ 222–1072), 12 kilometers (7 miles) northwest of La Fortuna on the highway from Nuevo Arenal. There is a restaurant and spa with bubbling thermal waters, waterfalls, a Jacuzzi, and a poolside bar with great views of the volcano.

Dining and Lodging

$$$$ ✕⛺ **Hotel Joya Surena.** In the midst of a working coffee plantation about 1½ kilometers (1 mile) outside of the town of Nuevo Arenal, this property's variously sized suites occupy a hacienda-style building; some have balconies, and the property is surrounded by tropical gardens. The style is fairly luxurious for upcountry Costa Rica. There are extensive trails in and around the property, with a rich diversity of plant, animal, and bird life to view. ⊠ *Nuevo Arenal de Tilarán, Guanacaste,* ☎ *694–4057,* FAX *694–4059. 28 rooms with bath. Restaurant, pool, hot tub, massage, sauna, health club, horseback riding, boating, fishing. AE, MC, V.*

$$$ ✕⌷ **Hotel Tilawa.** Eight kilometers (5 miles) beyond Tilarán, this unique-looking hotel on a bluff overlooking the windy western end of Lake Arenal is devoted primarily to servicing the needs of the wind-surfing set. The hotel is designed to resemble the Palace of Knossos on Crete in the Greek Islands—not exactly what one would expect on the shores of a lake in Central America, but the designers have managed to pull it off! It's a multicolored, multicultural original, with neoclassical murals, columns, and arches draped with flowering plants as well as spectacular views of the lake and volcano. Owned and operated by serious windsurfers, the hotel runs a windsurf school and shop on the shore of the lake below and offers packages that include use of windsurfing gear. For the water-loving nonwindsurfer, the hotel now provides sailing tours in a 36-foot catamaran to the east end of the lake for volcano viewing. ⊠ *Apdo. 92–5710, Tilarán,* ☎ *695–5050,* FAX *695–5766. 28 rooms with bath. Restaurant, bar, pool, hiking, horseback riding, boating, windsurfing. AE, MC, V.*

$$–$$$ ✕⌷ **Arenal Lodge.** This modern white bungalow is surrounded by
★ macadamia trees and rain forest, high above Lake Arenal Dam and midway between Arenal and Fortuna. Four-wheel drive is needed to negotiate the steep 2-kilometer (1¼-mile) drive, but the hotel will ferry you from the bottom for a small fee. The bedroom suites, some in a newer annex, are all pleasantly furnished, and there are also cheaper, smaller, and darker rooms that don't look out at the volcano. The lodge's perks include an extensive library, a small snooker table, and manicured gardens. ⊠ *Apdo. 1139–1250, Escazú, reservations office in San José:* ☎ *289–6588,* FAX *289–6798. 6 rooms with bath, 9 suites. Dining room, library, hiking, fishing. AE, MC, V.*

$$–$$$ ✕⌷ **Rock River Lodge.** This handsome little hotel is on a grassy hill above the road leading from Tilarán to Nuevo Arenal. A long building houses half a dozen rustic wooden cabinas sharing a shaded front porch offering a wonderful view of the lake and volcano, with eight new Santa Fe–style freestanding cabinas recently completed farther up the hill. The restaurant, bar, and lobby occupy another charmingly rustic wooden building a bit closer to the road, with plenty of porch space and lounging sofas, an open kitchen, a welcoming fireplace (the evenings can be cool around the lake), and cafeteria-style dining tables. The owner is a dedicated windsurfer and rents gear; he will organize tours for inner tubing on the Sarapiquí and bird-watching as well. One bookish complaint: the original cabina rooms are quite dark, and the wall-mounted bedside lamps are nice to look at but worthless for reading. The restaurant serves well-made food at reasonable prices. ⊠ *Apdo. 95, Tilarán,* ☎ FAX *695–5644. 14 rooms with bath. Restaurant, bar, horseback riding, mountain biking, fishing. No credit cards.*

Outdoor Activities and Sports

BICYCLING

For those days when the windsurfers get "skunked" (the wind fails to blow), the **Hotel Tilawa** (☞ Dining and Lodging, *above*) rents mountain bikes for riding a network of roads and trails in the area at the north end of Lake Arenal. You can rent mountain bikes from **Desafío** (☎ 479–9464) in La Fortuna for strenuous guided and unguided excursions in the proximity of the Arenal Volcano. Run by Indo-Californian Suresh and his Swedish partner Jessica, Desafío also offers white-water rafting on the nearby Sarapiquí River.

FISHING

Lake Arenal has the best **freshwater fishing** in Costa Rica, with guapote (rainbow bass) aplenty, although it is difficult to fish from the shore. Arenal Lodge (☞ Dining and Lodging, *above*) has boats and guides.

HORSEBACK RIDING

The **Hotel Tilawa** (☞ Dining and Lodging, *above*) is but one of many area hotels offering guided and unguided horseback rentals. There are a number of good trails for horses and/or bikes in the area. **Desafío** (☞ *above*) runs 4½-hour horseback rides from La Fortuna to Monteverde.

WINDSURFING

Experts are promoting Lake Arenal as a world-class windsurfing site due to the consistently strong winds during the dry season, between December and April. The lake is somewhat choppy due to its narrow shape, but strong winds, fresh water, and quality, hassle-free rigging and launch sites on both shores make it worthwhile. Several hotels, including the **Rock River Lodge** (☞ Dining and Lodging, *above*) have equipment for rent, but the best selection can be found at **Tilawa Viento Surf** (☎ 695–5008), the lakefront shop associated with the Hotel Tilawa (☞ Dining and Lodging, *above*).

Shopping

Along the road between Nuevo Arenal and La Fortuna, **Toad Hall** (☎ 470–9178), an eclectic store-café, is open daily from 8:30 to 5 and sells everything from indigenous art to maps to recycled paper. The store is also a terrific information center—the owners can give you the low-down on every tour and tour operator in the area. There's also a deli café with tables on a veranda featuring stunning views of the lake and volcano.

La Fortuna de San Carlos

❸ *40 km (27 mi) east of Arenal Volcano.*

At the foot of teeming Arenal Volcano, the small farming community of La Fortuna de San Carlos attracts volcano watchers from around the world. The town overflows with restaurants, hotels, and tour operators. La Fortuna is also the number-one place to arrange tours to the Caño Negro refuge (☞ *below*). The $35 tour is much easier, faster, and cheaper than busing up north to Los Chiles and hiring a boat on your own to take you down through the rain forest on Río Frío.

OFF THE
BEATEN PATH

CAÑO NEGRO WILDLIFE REFUGE – This 24,600-acre refuge (☎ 460–1301), in the far northern reaches of the province, is miles off most people's itineraries, but the vast Lake Caño Negro makes this an excellent place for watching waterfowl like the roseate spoonbill, jabiru stork, and anhinga, as well as for observing a host of resident exotic animals (☞ Chapter 2). In the dry season you can rent horses; in the rainy season you are better off renting a boat for exploration of the area. Camp or stay in basic lodging for around $8, including meals. Approach via Upala—a bus from there takes 45 minutes—or take **Esteban Cruz's** (☎ 471–1032) popular tour down the Río Frío. The tour starts in Los Chiles, about a 90-minute drive from La Fortuna (100 km/62 mi), near Arenal Volcano. **Sunset Tours** (☎ 479–9099) in La Fortuna also runs daylong tours down the Río Frío to Caño Negro.

Dining and Lodging

$–$$ ✕ **La Vaca Muca.** It isn't a posh place, but the food is good (the cook, Emilce Vargas, used to be chef at the Arenal Lodge) and you get more than you pay for. Just 1 kilometer (½ mile) west of town, this restaurant is draped with foliage outside and, inside, has turquoise paneling and bamboo aplenty. ☎ 479–9186. *Reservations not accepted. MC, V.*

$ ✕ **El Jardín.** Opposite the gas station, this friendly diner serves respectable fish dishes. Try guapote if it's on the menu, but it's very bony, so ask if they'll fillet it. The extensive menu also includes chicken legs, pork chops, liver, tongue, and more. The *refrescos naturales* (fruit juices) are especially good. ☎ 479–9072. *Reservations not accepted. MC, V.*

$$$ ✕🏠 **Las Cabañitas Resort.** One of the few resorts in the area with a swimming pool, this group of red-roof cabinas set on landscaped grounds several blocks outside of town has terraces that face the volcano and rocking chairs from which to enjoy the view. The wood-panel cabins have solid wood furnishings and quilted bedspreads. The hotel can arrange tours and car rentals. ☒ *Apdo. 5–4417, La Fortuna, San Carlos (1 km/½ mi east of La Fortuna),* ☎ 479–9343, 📠 479–9408. *30 cabins with bath. Restaurant, bar, room service, pool, car rental. AE, MC, V.*

$$ ✕🏠 **Arenal Observatory Lodge.** On your way to the observatory, the closest lodge to Arenal's base, you cross three large rivers whose bridges are regularly washed away, restricting access to those with four-wheel drive. Built in 1987 for researchers, the lodge is rustic but comfortable; some bedrooms are dorms, and some are doubles. The dining room has great views in both directions and serves hearty food that is included in the price of the room. ☒ *c/o John Aspinall, Arenal Observatory Lodge, Box 025216–1660, Miami, FL 33102–5216 (3 km/2 mi east of dam on Lake Arenal, you'll come to an intersection; turn right and continue on 9km/5½ mi),* ☎ 📠 695–5033. *(Reservations office in San José:* ☎ 257–9489, 📠 257–4220.) 23 rooms with bath, 1 cabin with 5 rooms shares 2 baths. Dining room. AE, MC, V.*

$$–$$$ 🏠 **Hotel San Bosco.** The owners have added a two-story hotel covered
★   in blue-tile mosaics to complement the string of small, inexpensive cabinas. Two kitchen-equipped cabinas (which sleep 8 or 12) are a good deal for families. The spotlessly clean, white rooms have polished wood furniture and firm beds and are linked by a long veranda lined with benches and potted plants. ☒ *La Fortuna de San Carlos (220 yds. north of La Fortuna's gas station),* ☎ 479–9050, 📠 479–9109. *18 rooms, 11 cabinas with bath. MC, V.*

$–$$ 🏠 **Burio Inn.** Bedrooms here have firm beds, sloping polished wood ceilings, framed textiles, and modern bathrooms with (sporadically) hot showers. Continental breakfast is served in the common room, surrounded by fishing rods and natural-history books. Available activities include nocturnal trips to the lower slopes of the volcano, tours to Caño Negro, horseback riding, and fishing. ☒ *La Fortuna de San Carlos, Alajuela (town center across from gas station),* ☎ 📠 479–9076. *8 rooms with bath, dormitory with bath. Breakfast room. AE, MC, V.*

Outdoor Activities and Sports

HIKING

A pleasant day hike from Fortuna takes you to the 50-meter (164-foot) high **Fortuna waterfall.** The 6-kilometer (3½-mile walk begins off the main road toward the volcano; look for the yellow sign marking the entrance. After walking 1.6 kilometers (1 mile) and passing two bridges, turn right and continue hiking straight until you reach the river turnoff. Swimming under the waterfall is fairly safe, but watch out for the current in the first part of the river. Call Desafío for information (☞ Arenal Volcano Outdoor Activities and Sports, *above*).

En Route   The journey from La Fortuna to San José takes roughly three hours by car, via Ciudad Quesada and Zarcero. The road initially runs through flat fertile farmland before climbing to the lively, if not particularly picturesque, mountain market town of Ciudad Quesada. Looking back, you'll take in excellent views of Arenal rising from the surrounding plain.

Ciudad Quesada

❹   *115 km (71 mi) northwest of San José.*

The new national park of Juan Castro Blanco (☞ Chapter 2) can be found near Ciudad Quesada; also close by are the soothing thermal waters of El Tucano Resort.

Dining and Lodging

$$$$ ✕⊞ **Hotel El Tucano Resort and Spa.** You come to El Tucano for the
★   waters. Hot, healing natural springs, the waters of El Tucano are marvelously refreshing and invigorating. With 90 rooms and suites, the hotel itself is somewhat overscale, and its public interior spaces—lobby, restaurant, card room—are possessed to a slight degree by the impersonality that affects any hotel subject to a plethora of tour group bookings, but the complex is surrounded by primary-growth forest, and the guest-room buildings are well-designed, intimately scaled, and embrace the pool and patios in a kind of tropical chalet mode. The interiors of the guest rooms are a study in understated luxury: simple, elegant, and comfortable. Most important, the hotel's two large, outdoor hot tubs, Olympic-size swimming pool, freestanding natural steam room, cool plunge, and in-room shower/tubs are all fed by the aptly named Río Aguas Caliente, the rocky, cascading river that flows through the property close to the swimming pool and hot tubs. The hotel sits atop rocks laced with hot springs bubbling forth out of fissures, and the hot tubs contain different blends of cool river and hot spring water, creating a choice of temperatures. If you are anywhere in the area, don't miss this place. But don't be fooled by advertisements for a casino: it's been turned into a game room and lounge, and there are no slot machines to be seen. The hotel has tennis courts, and the proprietors can arrange bicycling, horseback riding, and tours of Arenal and other nearby destinations. ⊠ *Apdo. 114–1017, San José, (8km/5mi east of Ciudad Quesada),* ☎ *460–3141 or 460–3142,* ℻ *460–1692. (Reservations office in San José:* ☎ *233–8936,* ℻ *221–9095.) 90 rooms and suites with bath. Restaurant, bar, pool, spas, shop. AE, MC, V.*

En Route   Between Ciudad Quesada and San José: Climbing a cliffhanger of a road with splendid views and a couple of nail-biting switchbacks, you traverse the Cordillera to arrive at Zarcero, set below a steep ridge.

Zarcero

❺   *70 km (43 mi) west of San José.*

Ninety minutes from San José, the small town of Zarcero looks like it was designed by Dr. Seuss. For a fan of **topiaries**, this place is a must: Cypress shrubs in bizarre animal shapes—motorcycle riding monkeys, for example—decorate the park in front of the church. The church interior is covered with elaborate pastel stencils and detailed religious paintings by Misael Solis, a local old-timer. Zarcero is renowned also for its **peach preserves** and **white cheese,** both of which are sold in stores around town and on the highway.

Stop at **El Tiesto Souvenir Shop** (☎ 463–3196) across from the park and talk politics with owner Rafael, a native Tico who lived in New Jersey for a while. He knows everything about the area and can arrange day trips to nearby waterfalls.

NEED A   **Super Dos,** on the main road opposite the church in Zarcero, is a tiny
BREAK?   café-store where you can get a coffee and empanada *de piña* (of
           pineapple) while you mull over buying some of the excellent local peach
           preserves.

THE NICOYA PENINSULA: PUNTARENAS TO CABO BLANCO

Numbers in the margin correspond to points of interest on the Northwest map.

Catch a ferry from Puntarenas to the southern Nicoya Peninsula, home to spectacular beaches like Montezuma and Tambor. The peninsula also offers well-preserved and undervisited national parks; come here to explore caves, waterfalls, and pristine forests, or travel by boat to remote islands for snorkeling, diving, or soaking in the sun. Not too remote, and thus at times somewhat overcrowded, is Isla Tortuga, accessible by day boat from Puntarenas, Montezuma, and other beach towns. Tortuga offers some of the most beautiful, palm-lined beaches in all of Costa Rica for snorkeling, swimming, or just lounging about on the sand. Near Puntarenas itself is the spectacularly long surfing wave of Boca Barranca—surfers have reported single rides up to 15 minutes in length! For those who like to mix nightlife with their outdoor experiences, the little town of Montezuma and its nearby beaches are frequently jammed with an international cast of hippies, mystics, musicians, and misfits of all sorts, from German boys in leather pants to Swedish girls in nothing at all. (One wise guy has called it a gathering place for the "toxic youth of Europe.") Hang out in a bar there and you'll surely get into an adventure of some sort. The beaches east of Montezuma, including Cocal, Cocalito, and Quizales, are gorgeous, with waterfalls and tide pools galore. The Cabo Blanco Strict Nature Preserve at the tip of the Nicoya Peninsula is one of the more undervisited parks in Costa Rica; also worth noting: when founded in 1963 it was the first protected nature area in the country.

Puntarenas

❻ *95 km (59 mi) west of San José.*

Five kilometers (3 miles) beyond Esparza, a popular truck stop about 90 kilometers (56 miles) northwest of San José on the Inter-American Highway, is the turn to Puntarenas. As its name implies, this erstwhile coffee-shipping port is on a narrow spit of sand protruding into the Gulf of Nicoya, with splendid views across to the peninsula. Most tourists stop here only on the way to the **Nicoya Peninsula** (by ferry). The boardwalk is pleasant in a honky-tonk kind of way, but this downtrodden town suffers from rising crime and polluted water and is not worth a special trip. Its grid-plan streets abound in restaurants and markets, and the southern palm-lined promenade is popular with day-trippers from San José, although the Ministry of Health warns against swimming here. On Saturday nights the massive influx of weekenders from

San José presents a golden opportunity to watch Costa Rica's middle class at play. In summer the series of theater, music, and dance shows at the **Casa de la Cultura** can be fun. The murky estuary to the north is fringed with mangroves; at its western end pelicans cast a watchful eye from the treetops over the Nicoya ferries, whose departures provide the only sound reason to stay overnight. A modern harbor has been built at **Caldera,** 10 kilometers (6 miles) south.

The Puntarenas ferries connect with **Playa Naranjo, Paquera,** and, more informally, with **Montezuma** (☞ Getting Around by Boat *in* Northwest A to Z, *below*). If you're driving, be prepared to spend some hours at the wheel: the road to the southern tip of the peninsula is partly paved, partly gravel, and it winds up and down and around various bays. Much of the countryside is still wild and wooded, although some has been turned into fruit farms or cattle pasture. Paquera, 45 minutes away, is the next place with shops and bars, also linked to Puntarenas by ferry.

Dining and Lodging

$$–$$$ ✕ **La Caravelle.** The red-pattern tablecloths and dark-blue walls adorned with antique musical instruments create a chic ambience in this unexpectedly classy French restaurant opposite the sea. The cooking concentrates on sauces: Try the corvina *al gratin con hongos* (with a white wine sauce and mushrooms) or filet *con salsa Oporto y hongos* (with port and mushroom sauce). If you want to accompany this with claret, prepare to dig deep into your pocket. ⊠ *Paseo de los Turistas,* ☎ 661–2262. MC, V. Closed Mon.–Tues.

$$–$$$ ✕⊞ **Hotel Las Brisas.** A white, two-story, motel-style building wraps around the swimming pool of this hotel out near the west end of town, where the views of the sun setting over the Nicoya Peninsula are terrific. The beach is across the street; it's not far from the ferry docks, and the restaurant serves fine Greek-influenced seafood and meats. The fluorescent lighting in the open-air dining room could be improved. ⊠ *Puntarenas (Paseo de Los Turistas),* ☎ 661–4040, ⻑ 661–2120. *19 rooms with bath. Restaurant, pool. MC, V.*

$$ ✕⊞ **Hotel Porto Bello.** Porto Bello's main asset is its thickly planted garden next to the wide estuary. Bedrooms are housed in white stucco bungalow units with tile floors, zanily patterned bedspreads, air-conditioning, TVs, and verandas. ⊠ *Apdo. 108, Puntarenas (2 km/1½ mi from downtown, 1 block north of main road),* ☎ 661–1322, ⻑ 661–0036. *35 rooms with bath. Restaurant, bar, pool. AE, MC, V.*

$$ ⊞ **Hotel Tioga.** The blue-and-white courtyard in this central hotel has
★ the look of an ocean liner. Bedrooms, the best of which are upstairs overlooking the gulf, have air-conditioning, tile floors, quilted pink bedspreads, floral pastel curtains, and functional 1970s furniture. There is a tiny pool in the courtyard with a palm tree growing from the islet in its center. ⊠ *Apdo. 96, Puntarenas (Paseo de los Turistas),* ☎ 661–0271, ⻑ 661–0127. *46 rooms with bath. Bar, cafeteria, pool. AE, MC, V.*

Curú Wildlife Refuge

➐ *7 km (4 mi) south of Paquera.*

South of the ferry dock at Paquera is the private Curú Wildlife Refuge, where you'll find hordes of phantom crabs on the beach, howler and white-faced monkeys readily visible in the banana trees, and plenty of bird-watching opportunities. Some very basic accommodations, originally designed for students and researchers, are available by the beach; call ahead if you're interested. ☎ 661–2392. ✑ *$10; lodging $25 per person, including 3 meals per day and admission.*

The next village that you reach after Curú is **Tambor,** nestled in the back of the large half-moon Ballena Bay. Thanks to the massive and controversy-plagued Hotel Playa Tambor, this area is undergoing a land-sale frenzy similar to that at Tamarindo. You can hike from here around the Piedra Amarilla point to Tango Mar resort; it's about an 8-kilometer (5-mile) trek. The trees nearby resound with the throaty utterings of male howler monkeys, and a new marina is being built at the southern end of the beach. Tambor can also be reached by plane from San José.

Dining and Lodging

$$$$ ✕⊡ **Tambor Tropical.** This collection of 5 cabinas surrounding a pool
  ★   in the palm trees off Playa Tambor in Bahía Ballena is remarkable for the buildings themselves. Utilizing local hardwoods, the builders have outdone themselves: The details are exquisitely wrought. Each comfortable and spacious 1,000-square-foot cabina contains a living room, a bedroom, a hot-water bathroom, and a fully equipped kitchen. ⊠ *Tambor Tropical, c/o Public Affairs Counsel, 867 Liberty St. NE, Salem, OR 97301 (follow main street of Tambor toward water; hotel fronts beach),* ☎ *381–0491, 503/363–7084 in the U.S.,* ℻ *503/371– 2471. 5 cabinas (10 rooms) with bath. Restaurant, bar, kitchenettes, pool, hot tub. AE, MC, V.*

$$$$ ✕⊡ **Tango Mar.** At this fine resort choose between rustic palm-thatch
  ★   cabins on stilts or rooms in the main hotel. The former are much more interesting; some have fully equipped kitchens and all are paneled and come with clock radios, fans, and hot showers. Those in the main hotel are luxurious by conventional standards but largely uninspired, and all have balconies and excellent sea views. The restaurant serves international cuisine. On the grounds are a small spring-fed pool that is sculpted from rock and an immaculate nine-hole golf course. There is a good surfing wave in front of the hotel. ⊠ *Box 3877–1000, San José (2 km/1½ mi west of Tambor),* ☎ *661–2798,* ℻ *683–0003. (Reservations office in San José:* ☎ *222–3503.) 6 villas with bath, 18 rooms with bath, 12 suites. Restaurant, bar, pool, golf course, boating, waterskiing, fishing, motorbikes. AE, DC, MC, V.*

En Route   As you continue past the turn to Tango Mar resort, Cobano is the next real village, a motley collection of wooden bungalows straddling a dusty crossroads. Turn left to Montezuma and Cabo Blanco, and mind that the final hill down to Montezuma is extremely steep and shouldn't be attempted in an ordinary car if the hill is wet.

Montezuma

⑧ *7 km (4 mi) southeast of Cobano.*

Montezuma is beautifully positioned next to a sandy bay, hemmed in by a precipitous wooded bank. Young foreigners in sandals and ethnic clothing seem to make this their first destination after touching down in San José, and if you don't mind entering the odd conversation on such *Mother Jones*–related subjects as yogurt and cheap deals, it is an entertaining place to be. But Montezuma is on the international vagabond circuit these days, and its hippie aura has taken on a distinctly seedy quality, although the beaches remain gorgeous. In 1995, hotel owners in Montezuma banded together to form the **Cámara de Turismo de Montezuma (CATUMA),** an organization dedicated to cleaning up the area, clearing out the drug abusers and dealers, and otherwise improving the area with a new bridge, water purification, and, in time, a paved road. No doubt the results will soon be evident; meanwhile, the atmosphere feels ripe for intrigue, and the bars are full and

In case you want
to see the world.

At American Express, we're here to make your journey a
smooth one. So we have over 1,700 travel service locations
in over 120 countries ready to help. What else would you
expect from the world's largest travel agency?

do more

http://www.americanexpress.com/travel

AMERICAN EXPRESS

Travel

In case you want to be welcomed there.

We're here to see that you're always welcomed at establishments everywhere. That's why millions of people carry the American Express® Card – for peace of mind, confidence, and security, around the world or just around the corner.

do more®

In case you're running low.

We're here to help with more than 118,000 Express Cash locations around the world. In order to enroll, just call American Express before you start your vacation.

do more

AMERICAN
EXPRESS

Express
Cash

And just in case.

We're here with American Express® Travelers Cheques
and Cheques *for Two.*® They're the safest way to carry
money on your vacation and the surest way to get a
refund, practically anywhere, anytime.
Another way we help you...

do more.

AMERICAN
EXPRESS

Travelers
Cheques

resound with endearing out-of-date music from the 1960s to the early 1980s. Just over a bridge 900 feet south, a path leads upstream to a 100-foot waterfall, a good swimming spot but overcrowded at times.

Dining and Lodging

$$$ ✕🖫 **Cabinas El Sano Banano.** This unpretentious vegetarian restau-
★ rant and bungalow colony serves creative dishes and is a good place to acquaint yourself with the town's vaguely hippie atmosphere. Try the eggplant Parmesan with mashed potatoes. The owners have built several cabins and some funky new domed bungalows (sleep four) in the woods near the beach, about a 10-minute walk from town. Some bungalows have kitchen facilities. ✉ *Montezuma (on right of road into Montezuma),* ☎ *642–0272,* 🖷 *642–0068. Reservations not accepted. 3 rooms with bath, 8 bungalows. Restaurant. AE, MC, V.*

$$ ✕🖫 **Cabinas Mar y Cielo.** The advantage of this property is its quiet location—still on the beach, but far from the boisterous bars. Decor and prices are much like those in the Hotel Moctezuma. Book ahead. ✉ *Puntarenas, Montezuma (43 yds. from center of town),* ☎ 🖷 *642–0036. 6 rooms with bath. Restaurant, bar. AE, MC, V.*

$ ✕🖫 **Hotel Moctezuma.** The large rooms in this beachside hotel have
★ varnished paneling, firm beds, large fans, and clean bathrooms. The best ones open onto a wide veranda over the beach. ✉ *Montezuma, Cobano de Puntarenas (center of Montezuma),* ☎ *642–0258. 21 rooms, 15 with bath. Restaurant, bar. V.*

En Route Fording two streams en route, the rough track leads from Montezuma to Cabo Blanco (about a 40- to 60-minute drive), named by conquistadors on account of the white earth and cliffs.

The Cabo Blanco Strict Nature Reserve

❾ *10 km (6 mi) southwest of Montezuma.*

The Cabo Blanco Strict Nature Reserve, 2,895 acres in all, was created by the pioneering efforts of the Wessbergs. Nils Olof Wessberg and his wife Karen were Swedish immigrants who arrived during the 1950s to live in the southern Nicoya Peninsula near Montezuma. Appalled by the first clear-cut in the Cabo Blanco area in 1960, they launched an international appeal to save the forest. In time their efforts and the efforts of their supporters not only led to the creation of the Cabo Blanco Strict Nature Reserve in 1963, but also to the founding of Costa Rica's national parks service. Olof Wessberg was murdered in the Osa Peninsula in 1975 while researching that area's potential as a national park. As a strict reserve, no tourist facilities exist in Cabo Blanco, although rangers will act as guides to visitors who turn up. A 4-kilometer (2-mile) trail leads from the entrance to Playa Cabo Blanco. It's a fairly strenuous two-hour hike in each direction. The reserve receives more rainfall than other parts of the peninsula, and hence the vegetation is properly described as tropical moist forest; there are more evergreen species here than in Santa Rosa, and it is generally lusher. The most abundant trees are strawberry, *apamate,* brazilwood, cow tree, *capulen, pochote,* and sapodilla. Sapodillas produce a white latex used to make gum; you will often see V-shape scars where they have been cut to allow the latex to run into containers placed at the base. The wildlife is quite diverse, notwithstanding the comparatively diminutive size of the reserve. Olof Wessberg cataloged a full array of animals here: porcupine, hog-nosed skunk, spotted skunk, gray fox, anteater, cougar, and jaguar. Resident bird species include coastal pelicans, white-throated magpies, toucans, cattle egrets, green herons, parrots, and turquoise-browed motmots. **Playa Cabo Blanco,** the beach at the end of the hike, is magnificent, with hundreds of pelicans flying in formation, dive-bombing for fish, and paddling in the calm waters right offshore. You can wade right in and join them. Trickling down a small cliff behind the beach is a small stream of potable water. Off the tip of the cape is the 7,511-square-foot Isla Cabo Blanco, with pelicans, frigate birds, brown boobies, and an abandoned lighthouse. 🖭 $6. ⊘ Daily 8–4.

THE TEMPISQUE RIVER DELTA REGION

Numbers in the margin correspond to points of interest on the Northwest map.

This area encompasses the parks in and around the Tempisque River basin and Nicoya, the commercial and political hub of the northern Nicoya Peninsula. There are two ways to reach the parks near the Río Tempisque: by car and boat via the Tempisque River ferry or by car from farther north. Heading north from San José on the Inter-American Highway, you turn left about 48 kilometers (30 miles) north of the Puntarenas turnoff, and drive 25 kilometers (16 miles) to the ferry, which takes you across to the riverside hamlet of Puerto Moreno; from here it is possible to leave your car and hire a boat to take you north up the river into the Palo Verde National Park. Remember, the ferry gets extremely crowded during high season and a wait of several hours is possible. The second option is to continue north another 42 kilometers (26 miles) on the Inter-American Highway and make a left at the gas station in Bagaces, 15 kilometers (9 miles) north of Cañas, which will lead you after 15 kilometers to the Lomas Barbudal Reserve and after 35 kilometers (22 miles) to the adjacent Palo Verde National Park, refuges for migratory waterfowl (☞ Chapter 2). Whew!

Palo Verde National Park/ Lomas Barbudal Biological Reserve

⑩ *28 km (17 mi) from Bagaces to Palo Verde; 20 km (12 mi) from Bagaces to Lomas Barbudal via Inter-American Highway.*

Bordered in the west by the meandering Río Tempisque, the territories in Palo Verde and Lomas Barbudal extend over 23,381 acres of mainly flat terrain. Migrant herons, egrets, ducks, and grebes pause here to rest up on the Tempisque's abandoned oxbow lakes and lagoons. You can camp in the park, and sometimes lodging and meals are available on request. Lodging is also available at the **Organization for Tropical Research station** (Reservations office in San José: ☎ 240–6696). ☎ 671–1062 (both parks). 🖭 Palo Verde: $6, Lomas Barbudal: $6. ⊘ Daily 8–4.

Barra Honda National Park

⑪ *6 km (4 mi) west of Puerto Moreno and the Tempisque River Ferry.*

Barra Honda National Park covers 5,681 acres north of the road that runs between the Nicoya–Carmona highway and Tempisque ferry (☞ Chapter 2). The limestone ridge that rises from the surrounding savanna was once thought to be a volcano but was later found to contain an intricate network of caves, formed as a result of erosion once the ridge had emerged from beneath the sea. Some remain unexplored, and surprisingly abundant animal life exists in the caves, including bats, birds, blind fish and salamanders, snails, and rats. In the dry season, with a week's notice rangers will take you down a 60-foot steel ladder to the Terciopelo cave, which shelters unusual formations shaped like fried eggs, popcorn, shark's teeth, and sonorous columns collectively known as the organ. Travel companies no longer take tourists or speleologists deeper underground, but local groups reportedly have organized tours into the caves. Check with park guards to verify safety standards before taking a trip, and don't attempt to visit the caves on your own unless accompanied by a park guard. Those with vertigo, asthma, or claustrophobia are advised not to attempt these explorations. **Barra Honda peak** (1,082 feet) can be climbed from the northwest; follow in sequence the Ojoche, Trampa, and Terciopelo trails (the southern wall is almost vertical). From the summit plateau there are fantastic views over the islet-studded **Gulf of Nicoya;** the plateau surface is dotted with small orifices and whimsically eroded white rocks, and some of the ground feels dangerously hollow. Surface wildlife includes howler monkeys, skunks, coatis, parakeets, and iguanas. The relatively open, deciduous-forest vegetation makes viewing the fauna easy. The park has camping facilities. ☎ 671–1062. ▨ $6. ⊘ Daily 8–4.

Nicoya

⑫ *30 km (19 mi) west of Puerto Moreno and the Tempisque River Ferry (via paved road).*

Nicoya, although often referred to as Guanacaste's colonial capital, is a typical small town, not really worth visiting unless you want a taste of everyday life. Its only colonial landmark is the whitewashed San Blas church in the central square. It was built in the 16th century and contains a museum of silver, bronze, and copper objects dating from pre-Columbian times. The Chorotegan chief Nicoya greeted the Spanish conquistadors upon their arrival here in 1523, and many of his people were converted to Catholicism. Great emphasis is currently being placed on reviving the culture and traditions of the Chorotegans.

A small Chinese population, descendants of 19th-century railroad workers, gives the place a certain cosmopolitan feel, as evidenced by the numerous Chinese restaurants in town.

Lodging

$ ⊞ **Hotel Jenny.** If you do need to stay in Nicoya, choose this hotel—it's a bit sterile, but adequate. The rooms have white walls, wooden beds, tile floors, and reasonable rates. ⊠ *South of main square,* ☎ *668–5050,* ℻ *668–6471. 24 rooms with bath. Air-conditioning. No credit cards.*

En Route Follow the road that leads southwest from Nicoya via Curime to Sámara, Nosara, Carrillo, Guiones, Punta Islita, and Ostional. (Nicoya is also linked by road to Santa Cruz and the northern Guanacaste towns, and by way of Carmona to Playa Naranjo and the southern Nicoya Peninsula.) Only part of the 35-kilometer (21-mile) road from Nicoya to the beaches is paved, and the unpaved section is slow. The roads that do exist between these beach towns are also subject to washouts, and are often passable only by four-wheel drive. There are air strips at Carrillo, Punta Islita, and Nosara, so flying in from San José is worth considering.

CENTRAL NICOYA BEACHES: PUNTA ISLITA TO NOSARA

Numbers in the margin correspond with points of interest on the Northwest map.

Strung along the coast of the Nicoya Peninsula are sparkling sand beaches lined with laid-back fishing communities. Bus service connects the larger cities to each other and to the more popular beaches, but forget about catching a bus from beach to beach; you'll have to backtrack it to the inland hubs of Nicoya, Carmona, or Santa Cruz. Consider renting a Jeep, especially for Nosara. Don't be in a rush to get anywhere; take life one day at a time, and you'll soon be as mellow as the locals. In this section you'll find several beach communities listed— we've given you dining and lodging options up and down the coast, so take your pick.

Punta Islita

⑬   *8 km (5 mi) south of Carrillo.*

Hidden in a small cove, Islita beach is rather rocky, but there is good snorkeling around the point, and the only hotel in the area, the small, luxurious Hotel Punta Islita, has a private dry forest nature preserve laced with well-made trails.

Dining and Lodging

$$$$ ✕⊡ **Hotel Punta Islita.** This secluded inn overlooking the Pacific south
★   of Carrillo and Sámara may be Guanacaste's best. Adobe-style bungalows with barrel tiles and clay-colored walls surround the main building, where a massive thatched dome rises over the open-air restaurant. The hotel's French chef turns fresh seafood into inventive daily specials, and both bar and restaurant open onto a blue-tiled pool that pours over an invisible wall, giving the illusion that it flows into the ocean far below. Rooms have private porches and are complete with hammock, big windows, red tile floors, and rough-hewn wooden bedposts, which lend a rustic air that is belied by such amenities as satellite TV and hair dryers. Suites have private hot tubs and interior gardens behind the bathtubs. Boat tours to nearby beaches are available. ⊠ *SJO 2505, Box 025 5216, Miami, FL 33131-5216. (Reservations office in San José:* ☎ *296–5787,* ⒻⒶⓍ *296–5773.) 22 rooms with bath, 2 suites. Restaurant, bar, air-conditioning, fans, minibars, pool, driving range, tennis court, exercise room, horseback riding, boating, fishing, mountain bikes, laundry service, private airstrip. AE, DC, MC, V.*

Carrillo

⑭   *6 km (4 mi) south of Sámara.*

A long, reef-protected beach backed by an elegant line of swaying palms and sheltering cliffs, Carrillo is good for swimming, snorkeling, walking, and lounging. Camping is allowed here, too. This is one of the most beautiful and undeveloped beaches in Costa Rica—fly in and land at its own airstrip.

Dining and Lodging

$$$$ ✕⊡ **Hotel La Guanamar.** Beautifully positioned above the southern end
★   of Playa Carrillo, this used to be a private fishing club, and as a hotel it continues its tradition as a sportfishing mecca. It occupies several levels, connected by wooden terraces and steps, thus bringing to mind a luxury cruiser. The white bedrooms have elaborate headboards, patterned bed covers, olive-green carpets, and amazing views. ⊠ *Costa Sol International, 2490 Coral Way, Suite 301, Miami, FL 33145,* ☎ *680–0054, 800/245–8420 in the U.S.,* ⒻⒶⓍ *686–6501. 41 rooms with bath. Restaurant, bar, pool, casino, private airstrip. AE, MC, V.*

Sámara

⑮ *29 km (18 mi) south of Nicoya.*

When you reach Sámara, you'll see a sign proclaiming it the "best beach in America." Maybe this is a slight overstatement, but not much. Two forest-covered hills jut out on either side of a clean, white sand beach, forming one giant cove ideal for swimming (the coral reef a mile from shore is a snorkeler's utopia). A few hotels have sprung up around town, but Tico spirit, not tourist spirit, still dominates.

Dining and Lodging

$$$$ ✕🏨 **Hotel Villas Playa Sámara.** This lovely and secluded beachfront hotel on peaceful Playa Sámara has rooms set up in 57 freestanding, Spanish-style white bungalows with red-tile roofs. The architect has done a fine job of putting a lot of buildings in place without creating any sense of crowding. Designed with several different floor plans, the bungalows range in size from one bedroom to three, and they are nicely dispersed among gardens, a pool, and the beachfront. Each unit has a kitchen along with living, bed, and bathrooms, so guests are able to cook their own meals if desired. The hotel runs tours to most destinations, and equipment for every water sport from snorkeling (there's a little reef-surrounded island a few hundred yards offshore) to waterskiing can be rented or booked through the recreation department. The windsurfing equipment is free of charge. *Reservations office in San José:* ☎ *233–0223, 223–7587, FAX 221–7222. 88 rooms with bath. Restaurant, bar, kitchenettes, pool, hot tub, 2 tennis courts, horseback riding. AE, MC, V.*

Garza

⑯ *16 km (10 mi) north of Sámara.*

Playa Garza occupies a small, horseshoe-shaped bay at the north end of Playa Sámara. The sand is white, although somewhat pebbly. The water is excellent for swimming here and at nearby Guiones, just to the north around the point. Guiones sometimes has large waves so be careful.

Dining and Lodging

$$$$ ✕🏨 **Hotel Villagio La Guaria Morada.** Don't be confused by the rustic thatch: This is a luxury complex whose elegant white bedrooms form an arc around a landscaped tropical garden. Activities include deep-sea fishing, waterskiing, horseback riding, scuba diving (bring your own gear), croquet, and volleyball. ✉ *Apdo. 860–1007, Centro Colón, San José,* ☎ *680–0784. (Reservations office in San José:* ☎ *233–2476, FAX 222–4073.) 30 rooms with bath. Restaurant, bar, pool, casino, dance club. MC, V.*

Nosara

⑰ *10 km (6 mi) northeast of Garza.*

Set a bit inland, the small and not very exciting town of Nosara is a good base from which to explore neighboring beaches. This whole area of Guanacaste is currently being subdivided and settled by Europeans and Americans at a fairly rapid pace. If you're looking to buy a little piece of Costa Rica and you want the security of other expatriates nearby, try Nosara.

Dining and Lodging

$$ ✕ **Bambú Bar.** Swiss expatriates Rolando and Ruth Weber run this downtown bar and pizzeria. Three nights a week they serve the only wood fire–cooked pizza in the area, and it's great, as are the fish and meat dishes dished up on nonpizza nights. Dine al fresco under an enormous, high-ceiling *palapa* (thatched hut) built by the owner. The bar, up front, draws a local crowd as well as tourists. ✉ *Across from soccer field, no phone. No credit cards.*

$$$ ✕🏨 **Lagarta Lodge.** Named for the alligators that live in the river delta (where the Rivers Nosara and Montana meet and enter the sea), which is visible from the hotel's bird- and beach-watching lobby area, this low-key little hotel, its street-side hidden behind a high stone wall, belongs to a Frenchman, Roland Lelin. The hotel's promontory setting is magnificent, and the rooms are in a separate building with hot showers and private balconies. Follow the signs with alligator jaws to find it, and don't be scared by the "art" in the lobby: The owner has a penchant for dressing up mannequins in what appears to be castoff 1970s disco clothes. Tours of the estuaries and the Ostional Turtle Refuge can be arranged, and a 10-minute walk through a monkey-filled forest takes you out onto a beautiful beach. ✉ *Apdo. 18, Nosara,* ☎ 🖷 *680–0763. 7 rooms with bath. Restaurant (dinner reservations essential), pool. V.*

$$$ ✕🏨 **Hotel Playas de Nosara.** This bungalow hotel is perched high on a promontory overlooking rain forest and palm-fringed crescents. Bedrooms have balconies, terra-cotta floors, white walls, and tapestry wall hangings, but they're actually rather plain and uninspired compared with the magnificent setting and the building, which includes the hotel's lobby, restaurant, and pool. This white, wave-covered work-in-progress falls somewhere between Greece and Morocco in its architectural style and is surely one of the odder buildings you'll see in Costa Rica. However, it is taking years to complete, and at press time (mid-1996) the pool was almost, but not quite, finished—and still empty. ✉ *Apdo. 4, Bocas de Nosara, Nicoya (look for hotel's sign 2 km/1½ mi south of Nosara),* ☎ 🖷 *480–0495. 16 rooms with bath. Restaurant, bar. No credit cards.*

Ostional Wildlife Refuge

⑱ *7 km (4 mi) north of Nosara.*

Apart from sun and sand (☞ Pleasures and Pastimes, *above*), the main reason for this trip is to visit the Ostional Wildlife Refuge, with its wonderful opportunities for turtle-watching. During the rainy season you will probably need four-wheel drive to ford the river just north of Nosara. A track then leads through shrubs to the reserve, which protects one of Costa Rica's major breeding grounds for olive ridley turtles. Local people run the reserve on a cooperative basis. During the first 36 hours of the arribadas they harvest the eggs—eggs laid during this time would as likely as not be destroyed by subsequent waves of mother turtles. These eggs, believed by some to be powerful aphrodisiacs, are sold to be eaten raw in bars! Thereafter members of the cooperative take turns to guard the beach from poachers, but they are happy to let visitors view the turtles.

Turtle arrivals at this and most other nesting sites are dependent on the moon and tides as well as the time of year. Wherever you go to watch the turtles, be sure to consult with local people to get a feel for the conditions and a sense of when, if ever, the turtles will arrive. (For further information on the turtles consult the section devoted to Nancite in Santa Rosa National Park, below.)

THE PLAINS AND MOUNTAINS OF NORTHERN GUANACASTE

Numbers in the margin correspond to points of interest on the Northwest map.

This area encompasses the mountains and plains north of Palo Verde and Lake Arenal up to the border of Nicaragua. Here you'll find Liberia, the capital of Guanacaste and the region's largest city—most people pass through here on their way up north to Rincón de la Vieja National Park. Rincón, an active volcano that last erupted in 1991, has strange volcano-related wonders such as boiling creeks, bubbling mud pools, and vaporing streams—look, but don't touch! West of Rincón de la Vieja, on the coast, is the Parque Nacional Santa Rosa, a former cattle ranch, where Costa Ricans defeated the invading mercenary army of American William Walker. Santa Rosa is also home to Playas Naranjo and Nancite, where hundreds of thousands of olive ridley turtles lay their eggs between June and November. And, closer still to the Nicaraguan border, are Guanacaste National Park and the town of La Cruz.

Liberia

⑲ *234 km (145 mi) north of San José.*

North of San José on the Inter-American Highway, Liberia is a low-rise, grid-plan, cattle-market town, with a huge central square dominated by a hideous modern church. It is the capital of Guanacaste province, and acts as the gateway to a northern route that encompasses Rincón de la Vieja Volcano, several spectacular and biologically important national parks, and a turtle-nesting site on the Pacific coast. The Liberia Airport's jet runway is near completion, and when it opens, the city's proximity to the beaches of Guanacaste will make it the arrival point of choice for even more travelers. There isn't a lot to see or do in Liberia, but if you do have the time, visit the museum and obtain tourist information at the **Casa de Cultura** (☎ 666–1606; ☉ Mon.–Sat. 8–4), three blocks south of Central Park.

Dining and Lodging

$$ ✕ **Pókopí.** In Costa Rica's cattle capital, Pókopí eclipses rival steak houses. Try the delicious Chateaubriand with salsa *Barnesa* (béarnaise sauce, fresh vegetables, and a stuffed tomato). And it isn't all beef: Dig into the dorado in white sauce with mushrooms, onions, green pepper, and white wine. ⊠ *500 yds. down road to Nicoya—on the right, 75 yds. west of gas station;* ☎ *666–1036. AE, MC, V.*

$$$ ✕🖬 **Hotel El Sitio.** El Sitio is worth considering, if you're overnighting in Liberia, for the spacious, modern rooms as well as the on-premises restaurant, two swimming pools, and walking trails. ⊠ *Liberia (80 yds. west of fire station on road to Santa Cruz),* ☎ *666–1211,* ᖴᐯX *666–2059. 52 rooms with bath. Restaurant, TVs, 2 pools, spa, horseback riding, mountain bikes, meeting rooms. AE, MC, V.*

$$ 🖬 **Hotel La Siesta.** The advantage of this modern hotel, though slightly pricier than the Bramadero, is its quiet location three blocks south of the central plaza. The rooms surround a landscaped patio with a small pool. Narrow, firm beds; white walls; and functional bathrooms beginning to show signs of age characterize the pickings. The upstairs rooms are slightly larger and quieter. ⊠ *Apdo. 15–5000, Liberia,* ☎ *666–0678,* ᖴᐯX *666–2532. 24 rooms with bath. Restaurant, bar, air-conditioning, pool. AE, MC, V.*

Nightlife

The **Fiestas Bravas** at the Hacienda la Cueva Liberia (☎ 666–0450) will appeal to the John Wayne in you. Hollering, whooping cowboys accompany visitors on the last stretch as they arrive at the working ranch and 1824 adobe farmhouse. Music, lasso shows, bull-riding, dancing, and a Guanacaste specialty dinner all follow.

Rincón de la Vieja

⑳ *27 km (17 mi) east of Liberia.*

The composite mass of Rincón de la Vieja, often enveloped in a mixture of sulfurous gases and cloud, dominates the scenery to the right of the Inter-American Highway as you head north (☞ Chapter 2). Some compare this national park's geysers, mud pots, and hot springs to those of Yellowstone National Park in the United States. Access to the park— 34,787 protected acres in all, much of it dry forest that has been regenerated since the park's inception in 1973—is via 26 kilometers (16 miles) of unpaved road. The road begins 6 kilometers (4 miles) north of Liberia off the Inter-American Highway (for Albergue Guachipelín) or 25 kilometers (15 miles) along the Colonia Blanca route northeast from Liberia, which follows the course of the Río Liberia to the Santa María park headquarters. Both tracks are veritable bone shakers. Nonetheless, the wildlife here is tremendously diverse: 200 species of birds, including keel-billed toucans and blue-crowned motmots, plus mammals such as brocket deer, tapirs, coatis, jaguars, sloths, armadillos, and raccoons. Needless to say, hiking here is fantastic, but it's wise to do some planning to know where to head. Some information is available at the park headquarters by the entrance gate, but you are advised to head to **Rincón de la Vieja Mountain Lodge** (☞ Dining and Lodging, *below*), which has guides for foot or horseback hiking available. ☞ *$6.* ☉ *Daily 8–4.*

The volcano complex has two peaks: **Santa María** (6,284 feet) and **Rincón de la Vieja** (6,225 feet) to the northeast. The latter is vegetationless and has two craters. Rincón de la Vieja is thought unlikely to erupt violently due to the profusion of fumaroles through which it can constantly let off steam. The last violent eruptions were between 1966 and 1970. If you want to explore the slopes of the volcano, it is advisable to go with a guide; the abundant hot springs and geysers have given unsuspecting visitors some very nasty burns in the past. **Las Hornillas** ("the kitchen stoves"), to the south of the volcano, is a 124-acre medley of mud cones, hot-water pools, bubbling mud pots, and vent holes, most active during the rainy season. To the east, **Los Azufrales** are hot sulfur springs in which you can bathe; be careful not to get sulfur in your eyes, though. The Rincón de la Vieja Mountain Lodge (☞ Dining and Lodging, *below*) has guides, but phone ahead to check availability.

Dining and Lodging

$$ ✕🖾 **Rincón de la Vieja Mountain Lodge.** Resting on the slopes of
★ Rincón de la Vieja, this is an ideal base for exploring the volcano. The lodge and cabins are paneled, and beds are in small, comfy bunk dormitories; if you come midweek in low season you probably will get a room to yourself. The sitting room has a terra-cotta floor, varnished paneling, maps of the surroundings, and cases of butterflies and some fairly hairy, hair-raising insects. A large upstairs veranda has sofas and chairs. The food is good: meat, fish, and vegetarian entrées, with much of the produce being homegrown. The owner Alvaro's affable staff can

take you to explore the volcano on foot or on horseback through the woods. One trail leads to a hot-water, sulphur bathing pool. ⊠ *Apdo. 114–5000, Liberia,* ☎ *695–5535. (Reservations office in San José:* ☎ *225–1073,* FAX *234–1676.) 22 dormitories with bath, 3 with shared bath. Dining room, pool. AE, MC, V.*

Santa Rosa National Park

㉑ *48 km (30 mi) south of the Nicaraguan border.*

Campers enjoy the Santa Rosas's rugged terrain and isolated feel. The sparseness of vegetation in this arid zone makes it easier to see animals. From the entrance gate 7 kilometers (4½ miles) of paved road leads to the park headquarters. A campsite, overhung by giant strangler figs, is located here and provides washing facilities and picnic tables. Be careful of snakes.

Santa Rosa was established in 1971 to protect **La Casona hacienda,** scene of the famous 1856 battle in which a ragged force of ill-equipped Costa Ricans routed the superior army of William Walker. A U.S. filibuster from Tennessee, Walker had established himself as chief of staff of the Nicaraguan army as part of his Manifest Destiny–influenced scheme to create a slave empire in the region. In 1857, the hostilities having continued onto Nicaraguan soil, Juan Santamaría, a drummer boy from Alajuela, threw burning wood into the building where Walker and his henchmen were gathered, so ending the war, and thereby winning undying national fame for himself (Walker was later turned over to Honduras and shot by a firing squad). The rambling colonial-style farmstead of La Casona stands as a monument to this national triumph and contains an interesting museum (◷ Daily 8–4:30) with maps, weapons, uniforms, and furniture. The start of a short explanatory nature trail is visible just out front.

For ecologists, Santa Rosa has a more important role—protecting and regenerating 122,300 acres of moist, basal belt transition, and deciduous tropical dry forests. The central administrative area is a hive of scientific activity. Much of the research here has been into forest propagation, the fruits of which are evident in former cattle pastures where windblown seeds have been allowed to establish themselves. Bush fires are a constant hazard in the dry season, making firebreaks a necessity. Typical dry forest vegetation includes oak, wild cherry, mahogany, calabash, bull-horn acacia, hibiscus, and gumbo limbo, with its distinctive reddish-brown bark. Because of its less luxuriant foliage, the park is a good one for viewing wildlife, especially if you station yourself next to water holes during the dry season. Inhabitants include spider, white-faced, and howler monkeys, deer, armadillos, coyotes, tapirs, coatis, and ocelots. Ocelots, commonly known as *manigordos* (fat paws) on account of their large feet, are striped wildcats that have been brought back from the brink of extinction by the park's conservation methods. These wildlands also define the southernmost distribution of many North American species such as the Virginia opossum and the *cantil* moccasin.

Thirteen kilometers (8 miles) west of the administrative area—a two- to three-hour hike or one hour by four-wheel drive—is the white-sand **Playa Naranjo,** popular for beachcombing due to its pretty shells and for surfing because of its near-perfect break. The campsite here has washing facilities, but bring your own water. Make sure to catch the lookout at the northern tip of the beach with views over the entire park. Turtle arribadas—the phenomenon of turtles arriving on a beach to nest—do take place on Naranjo, but the big ones occur at a point reached via a two-hour walk north to **Playa Nancite** (also accessible by four-wheel drive).

It is estimated that 200,000 of the 500,000 turtles that nest each year in Costa Rica choose Nancite. Backed by dense hibiscus and button mangroves, the gray-sand beach is penned in by steep, tawny, brush-covered hills. Previously a difficult point to get to, it is now the only totally protected olive ridley turtle arribada in the world. The busy time is August to December, peaking September and October. Olive ridleys are the smallest of the sea turtles (average carapace, or hardback shell, is 21–29 inches) and the least shy. The majority arrive at night, plowing the sand as they move up the beach and sniffing for the high-tide line, beyond which they use their hind flippers to dig holes in which they will lay their eggs. They spend an average of one hour on the beach before scurrying back to the sea. Hatching also takes place at night. The phototropic baby turtles magically know to head for the sea, which is vital for their continued survival, since the brightest part of any beach is over the ocean. Many of the nests are churned up during subsequent arribadas, and predators such as *pizotes* (coatis), ghost crabs, raccoons, and coyotes lie in wait; hence just 0.2% of eggs reach the sea as young turtles. Between Naranjo and Nancite, another campground at Estero Real is available with tables only. Permits are needed to stay at Nancite; ask at the headquarters. Throughout the park it is wise to carry your own water since water holes are none too clean. ✉ *Park: $6.* ☉ *Daily 7–5.*

Cuajiniquil

㉒ *10 km (6 mi) north of Santa Rosa.*

North from Santa Rosa on the Inter-American is the left turn to Cuajiniquil, famous for its waterfalls. If you have time and a four-wheel-drive vehicle, Cuajiniquil has lovely views. The **Bay of Santa Elena** is renowned for its calm waters, which is why it is now threatened by tourist development. **Playa Blanca** in the extreme west has smooth white sand, as its name implies. The rough track there passes through a valley of uneven width, caused, according to geologists, by the diverse granulation of the sediments formerly deposited here. To the south rise the rocky **Santa Elena hills** (2,332 feet), bare except for a few *chigua* and nancite shrubs.

Guanacaste National Park

㉓ *32 km (20 mi) north of Liberia.*

To the east of the Inter-American Highway is Guanacaste National Park (☎ 695–5598 at Santa Rosa for information and/or reservations), created in 1989 to preserve rain forests around **Cacao and Orosí volcanoes**, which are seasonally inhabited by migrants from Santa Rosa. Much of the park's territory is cattle pasture, which it is hoped will regenerate into forest. Three biological stations within the park have places for visitors to stay. **Mengo Biological Station** lies on the slopes of Cacao Volcano at an altitude of 3,609 feet; accommodation is in rustic wooden dormitories with bedding provided, but bring a towel. From here a trail leads up Cacao Volcano (5,443 feet), another north to the modern **Maritza Station**, a three-hour hike away at the base of Orosí (4,877 feet), with more lodging available. You can also reach Maritza by four-wheel drive. From here you can trek two hours to **Llano de los Indios**, a cattle pasture dotted with volcanic petroglyphs. Farther north and a little east is rustic **Pitilla Station** and, despite its lower elevation, it has views of the coast and Lake Nicaragua.

La Cruz

㉔ *56 km (35 mi) north of Liberia; 20 km (12 mi) south of the Nicaraguan border.*

Farther north from Guanacaste National Park on the west side of the highway is a turnoff to the town of La Cruz. The town is noteworthy for the views of **Bahía Salinas** from the restaurants and hotels along the bluff, and it also serves as a gateway to **Puerto Soley,** and the beaches of the **Gulf of Santa Elena.**

LIBERIA TO HERMOSA AND SOUTH TO TAMARINDO

Numbers in the margin correspond to points of interest on the Northwest map.

Highway 21, from Liberia south toward Nicoya, starts opposite Liberia's Hotel Bramadero on the Inter-American Highway. It runs in straight sweeps through cattle country sporadically shaded by *guanacaste* and *tabebuia* trees. Just past the village of Comunidad is the turn to Hermosa, Playa del Coco, and Ocotal. Continue on toward Belén and 5 kilometers (3 miles) past the town of Filadelfia you'll hit the turn to the surfing hot spot of Tamarindo and ritzy Flamingo, paved as far as Huacas junction. At this crossroads, branch right for Flamingo, left for Tamarindo and Playa Grande. Surrounding these towns and beaches are numerous other playas like Pan de Azúcar, Portrero, and Langosta, all of which have hotels and restaurants scattered behind them. Take your pick, one beach runs into another; the more artistically inclined, however, can continue on toward Nicoya to explore the artisan communities of Santa Cruz and Guaitil.

Santa Cruz

㉕ *16 km (10 mi) south of the Belén junction.*

If you head toward Nicoya, south of the Belén junction you'll find the National Folklore City of Santa Cruz, dedicated to preserving Guanacaste's rich traditions and customs. Music and dance programs are still held in town despite a recent fire, which destroyed much of the town's center and the popular Casa de la Cultura.

NEED A BREAK? **Coope-Tortillas** has enjoyed resounding success as a country restaurant and tortilla bakery founded to help create jobs for local women. Watch tortillas bake the old-fashioned way—on thick, round plates on an open fire—and have a hearty, family-style meal at a picnic table in this former electricity-generating plant. ☉ *Daily 5 AM–7 PM.*

Guaitil

㉖ *Between Santa Cruz and Nicoya.*

Near the town of Santa Bárbara is the village of Guaitil. Artists here have rescued a vanishing tradition by producing clay pottery in the manner of pre-Columbian Chorotegans. You can visit the workshop (☉ 6 AM–9 PM) and select designs of your choice. The hand-wrought pots, jars, dishes, and urns are painted with natural earth-based pigments before being fired in a stone kiln and polished with a natural glaze. You'll also see pots for sale outside private houses, often slightly cheaper.

Hermosa

㉗ *13 km (8 mi) east of Playa del Coco.*

Hermosa has a relaxed village atmosphere, although several large hotels have recently opened here. This crescent of grayish sand—many of the beaches in northern Guanacaste feature gray rather than white sand—fronts a line of trees that provide a welcome respite from the heat of the sun. At the north end of Hermosa, low tide reveals great rock-lined tide pools for exploring.

Dining and Lodging

$$$$ ✗⊞ **Malinche Real.** One of the first completed in the wave of new, large-scale projects around Playas Hermosa and Panama, the Malinche Real is unique, for the moment anyway, in that it is an all-inclusive, with meals (there are several restaurants and a swim-up bar on the property) and use of all facilities included in the per-couple price. The hotel consists of 49 freestanding villas, each housing a pair of guest rooms complete with private baths, marble floors, and daily maid and valet service. More appealing are the wonderful views of sea, forest, and mountains. All water sports and tours can be arranged through the concierge desk. ⊠ *Apdo. 1216–1007, Centro Colón, San José,* ☎ *670–0033,* FAX *670–0300. (Reservations office in San José:* ☎ *233–8566, 221–0739.) 100 rooms with bath. Restaurants, bars, air-conditioning, minibars, TVs, pools, hot tub, health club, tennis court, meeting rooms. AE, MC, V.*

$$$ ✗⊞ **El Velero Hotel.** This elegant, two-story beachfront hotel has large, white rooms with arched doorways. Instead of giving the rooms ocean views, the Canadian owners built the restaurant, pool, and bar on the beach side for a delightful dining experience. Sample the jumbo shrimp with rice and vegetables. ⊠ *Playa Hermosa, Guanacaste,* ☎ FAX *670–0310. 13 rooms with bath. Restaurant, bar, pool. AE, MC, V.*

$$ ✗⊞ **Hotel Cabinas Playa Hermosa.** Monkeys, coatis, and birds frolic outside these peaceful white cabinas (sleep five) on the far end of one of Costa Rica's (until recently) relatively undeveloped beaches. The restaurant serves pasta, steak, and seafood; try the lobster or the hearty surf and turf. A fishing boat is available for rent. ⊠ *Apdo. 112, Liberia, Guanacaste,* ☎ FAX *670–0136. 22 cabinas with bath. Restaurant. No credit cards.*

$–$$ ✗⊞ **Aqua Sport.** This beachfront complex has a gift shop and watersports equipment rentals, but the main draw is a casual open-air restaurant decorated with tree trunks. The seafood platter of lobster, shrimp, calamari, and oysters is highly recommended. ⊠ *Apdo. 100–5019, Playa del Coco,* ☎ FAX *670–0450. 6 rooms with bath, 1 suite. Restaurant. AE, MC, V.*

Outdoor Activities and Sports

BOATING AND WATER SPORTS

Condovac Hotel (☎ 670–0283) on Playa Hermosa rents canoes, kayaks, and catamarans for 3,500–9,000 colones.

Playa del Coco

㉘ *35 km (22 mi) west of Liberia.*

Playa del Coco is the perfect place for those who want noise, discos, and bustle. This is a hopping, beachfront town! As perhaps the most accessible beach in Guanacaste, Playa del Coco is crowded and dusty, and serves as a playground for Costa Rica's college kids, who are unfortunately not all possessed of a high level of environmental awareness. The beaches can get quite trashy, and the holiday season is impossibly crowded. This is a party town. If you don't want to live it up, stay away.

Dining and Lodging

$–$$ ✕ **Mariscos La Guajira.** Try *ceviche* (raw seafood salad, marinated in lime juice and chilis) for starters at this open-sided, orange-painted restaurant. As main courses, dorado served with salad and fried bananas, *camarones* (shrimp in garlic and butter served with fries and salad), and *langosta al ajillo* (lobster in garlic) are all recommended. The informal, beachy decor consists of wooden tables, cement floor, and potted plants. ✉ *West along beach, fronted by round, palm-thatch shades,* ☎ *670–0107. Reservations not accepted. AE, MC, V.*

$$ 🏨 **Cabinas Chale.** Turn right 500 yards down a dirt road just as you come into town. Families from San José invade these modern cabinas on weekends; if you can't stand the sight of children, steer clear. The bedrooms are bright and large, containing up to five beds, a fridge, table and chairs, tile floor, and overhead fans. They are spotlessly clean and have modern bathrooms. The location is remote and quiet: Take a 50-yard stroll to the beach straight ahead, and walk west another 500 yards to Coco proper. ✉ *Playa del Coco, Guanacaste,* ☎ *670–0036,* 🖷 *670–0303. 16 rooms with bath, 5 bungalows with bath. Pool, badminton, basketball. V.*

$ 🏨 **Hotel Anexo Luna Tica.** This new two-story wooden structure is on
★ the street that runs parallel to the beach, west of the soccer pitch. Don't confuse it with the dingy cabins of the same name on the opposite side of the street, closest to the sea. The bedrooms—all connected by a single veranda—have red wood floors, polished paneling, firm beds, overhead fans, and decorative photos. Those upstairs have more light, although none look out on the sea. ✉ *Apdo. 67, Liberia,* ☎ *670–0279,* 🖷 *670–0392. 18 rooms with bath. V.*

Ocotal

㉙ *3 km (2 mi) west of Playa del Coco.*

Ocotal is isolated in spite of its proximity to Coco and very small in size. At the entrance to the Gulf of Papagayo, it's a good spot for sportfishing enthusiasts to hole up between excursions. There is good diving at Las Corridas, just 1 kilometer (½ mile) away.

Dining and Lodging

$$$–$$$$ ✕🏨 **El Ocotal Beach Resort.** Three kilometers (2 miles) west of Playa
★ del Coco down a paved road, this luxury hotel is situated above secluded Ocotal Bay. Apart from the sportfishing fleet, exceptional views are its main asset. From the upper rooms you look north to the Santa Elena Peninsula and northwest to Rincón de la Vieja. These rooms have blue carpets, patterned bedspreads, white walls, watercolors, overhead fans, TVs, and huge French windows. Units down the hill are bigger and triangular in shape with polished wood floors, but they afford less expansive views. The pool is large and attractively landscaped into the hillside; the dining room and other public areas have a captain's bridge position, and huge windows allow you to take full advantage of the panorama. ✉ *Apdo. 1, Playa del Coco, Guanacaste,* ☎ *670–0321,* 🖷 *670–0083. 40 rooms with bath, 3 suites, 6 bungalows. Restaurant, bar, pool, tennis court, horseback riding, dive shop. AE, DC, MC, V.*

Playa Pan de Azúcar

㉚ *8 km (5 mi) north of Flamingo.*

Pan de Azúcar's lovely beach, at the end of a hilly dirt road, lends its only hotel one quality that is no longer easy to come by in this booming area—privacy. There are good islands for snorkeling just offshore.

Dining and Lodging

$$$–$$$$ ✕🏨 **Hotel Sugar Beach.** Reached via a dirt track 8 kilometers (5 miles)
★   north of Flamingo, this hotel overlooks a small, curving white-sand beach. Four small but well-furnished bedrooms occupy sections of a raised circular hut; they have hardwood floors, fans, and oil paintings. The six posher rooms—set slightly farther back—all face the sea and have air-conditioning. Behind these, the owners have built 16 rooms with similar amenities. You'll find the islet-scattered bay very pretty; in the rainy season, however, much of the "sugar" is washed away to expose a rocky shoreline, but sandy spots remain for swimming. The islets, in fact, are cunningly positioned to blot the Flamingo condos from view. Wildlife abounds, most noticeably howler monkeys and iguanas, and excellent snorkeling is to be had at either edge of the bay. The hotel charges extra for use of snorkeling and other gear, but given its isolated location, guests have no choice but to rent, at rather high rates, from here. These charges can add up fast. The open-sided rotunda restaurant should not disappoint, especially if you choose seafood. ✉ *Apdo. 90, Santa Cruz, Guanacaste,* ☎ *654–4242,* 🖷 *670–4239. 26 rooms with bath. Restaurant, bar. AE, MC, V.*

Playa Portrero

③① *1 km (½ mi) north of Flamingo.*

Although lovely Portrero previously has been known mostly for its views of nearby Flamingo, it is possessed of its own charm, primarily due to the presence of a wide, white sand beach. There's excellent swimming to a small offshore island, and the bird refuge **Isla Santa Catalina** is 10 kilometers (6.2 miles) offshore. Several major hotel projects are in the works here, so the relatively bucolic atmosphere of the place may soon be history.

Dining and Lodging

$$$$ ✕🏨 **Bahía Portrero Beach and Fishing Resort.** At this squat, white bungalow fishing and water sports are the major activities. The beach is ideal for young children because the sea is shallow and safe, and the long, practically deserted strand is relaxing for all. ✉ *Apdo. 45, Santa Cruz, Guanacaste,* ☎ 🖷 *654–4183. 14 rooms with bath. Restaurant, bar, pool. MC, V.*

Flamingo

③② *39 km (24 mi) west of Filadelfia.*

With the mega–Hotel Flamingo Beach dominating the landscape, Flamingo is one of the first of the northern Guanacaste beaches to experience the wonders of overscale resort development. The beach is still lovely, however. If you like large, characterless hotels—and some do, strictly for their impersonality—with your beach, this is a good place for you.

Dining and Lodging

$$ ✕ **Marie's Restaurant.** Sadly, the pool and garden attached to this restau-
★   rant have been filled in, but the friendly owner and fresh food make it worth a visit. Shortly after the road bends to the north end of Flamingo, look for Marie's small veranda furnished with sliced tree-trunk tables and settle back for a rewarding meal of generous helpings of fresh seafood at very reasonable rates. The house specialty is plato de mariscos (shrimp, lobster, and oysters served with garlic butter, pota-

toes, and salad), but be sure to save room for pudding—the *tres leches,* topped with the cream of three different milks, is superb. ☎ *654–4136. Reservations not accepted. V.*

$$ ✕ **Tio's Sports Bar and Restaurant.** This thatched-roof hangout is a favorite among locals, who gather on weekends to eat Mexican food, tee off from the driving range, watch cable TV, use the tennis court, or play baseball. The rustic dining room with plastic lawn furniture and floral-print tablecloths is a fun, relaxed place. ⊠ *Playa Flamingo,* ☎ *654–4236. Reservations not accepted. No credit cards. Closed Oct., Dec.–Apr., and weekdays May–Nov.*

$$$$ ✕🏨 **Flamingo Beach Hotel.** Holiday Inn purchased this luxury resort and has completed major renovations aimed at turning it into a five-star hotel. Reality check: Stay here and you could easily forget that you are in Costa Rica; you might, instead, think yourself to be in Miami, Cancún, or Palm Springs. ⊠ *Apdo. 692–4050, Alajuela,* ☎ *654–4010,* FAX *654–4060. 136 rooms with bath, 36 condominiums. 2 restaurants, 2 bars, 3 pools, tennis court, dive and surf shop. AE, DC, MC, V.*

$$$ ✕🏨 **Mariner Inn.** Near the marina, this white, two-story building is the most inexpensive hotel in Flamingo. Rooms are tiny, but they have ceiling fans and firm beds. ⊠ *Apdo. 65, Santa Cruz,* ☎ *654–4081,* FAX *654–4024. 11 rooms with bath, 1 suite. Restaurant, bar, air-conditioning, pool. AE, MC, V.*

Brasilito

㉝ *35 km (22 mi) west of Filadelfia.*

Brasilito is a pretty little fishing village with boats lined up just offshore of a white sand beach that is the equal of Flamingo, but without the mega-hotels. This little town still has some charming local color and character in spite of the nearby boom.

Dining and Lodging

$ ✕ **El Camerón Dorado.** This bar-restaurant derives much of its appeal from the shady setting on Brasilito's beautiful beach, and no less from the small-vessel fishing fleet anchored offshore that assures you of the freshness of seafood available. Due to the spectacular sunsets, it's a popular place for an early evening drink. ⊠ *656 ft. north of Brasilito Plaza,* ☎ *654–4252. Reservations not accepted. AE, DC, MC, V.*

$$ ✕🏨 **Hotel Brasilito.** This German-run establishment has a high-ceilinged dining room just off the beach. Two rooms feature great sea views. ⊠ *Next to square and soccer field, no phone. 17 rooms with bath. Restaurant. No credit cards.*

Las Baulas

㉞ *37 km (23 mi) west of Filadelfia.*

Just north of Tamarindo, the Las Baulas Marine National Park protects the long, virtually deserted **Playa Grande,** an important nesting site of the leatherback sea turtle (☞ Chapter 2). It's a great surf spot as well.

Dining and Lodging

$$$ ✕🏨 **Hotel Las Tortugas.** This hotel stands at the edge of Las Baulas National Park right on the edge of the beach. The restaurant—with surprisingly healthy, high-quality food—has an impressive ocean vista (which is rapidly disappearing as the owners intend to bury the hotel behind a screen of trees to better serve the turtles) and although the rooms don't have great views, they are comfortable, with good beds and air conditioning, as well as stone floors and stucco walls. Las Tortugas stands in front of the surf break and sometimes has dangerous rip currents, but most people who stay there come to see the turtles nesting. There's a turtle-shaped swimming pool, and local guides escort visitors along the beach at night. The hotel also offers ecologically educational canoe trips in the wildlife refuge during the day. ⊠ *Apdo. 164, Santa Cruz de Guanacaste,* ☎ 𝔽𝔸𝕏 *680–0765. 11 rooms with bath. Restaurant, pool. No credit cards.*

$$$ ✕🔟 **Villa Baulas.** Like the Hotel Las Tortugas, the Villa Baula is hidden in the mangrove swamps and trees directly behind the Las Baulas National Park, where the turtles come to nest. The hotel is just a few hundred yards north of the river separating Tamarindo from Playa Grande—they'll pick you up on the Tamarindo side of the river, or you can ford it yourself at low tide—and its 20 rooms and five villas are lovely, palm thatch-roofed cabinas with elegantly rustic interiors, ceiling fans, and balconies. Playa Grande is a 3-kilometer (2-mile) stretch of virtually deserted beach, with great surfing by day and turtle watching by night. Nearby Tamarindo has a number of high-quality restaurants if you get bored with the hotel's offerings. The hotel offers guided turtle tours (the egg-laying areas are very close by) as well as estuary tours, sea kayaking, snorkeling, biking, and surfing. ⊠ *Apdo. 111– 6151, Santa Ana 2000,* ☎ 𝔽𝔸𝕏 *680–0869. (Reservations office in San José:* ☎ *257–7676,* 𝔽𝔸𝕏 *257–1096.) 22 rooms, 5 villas, all with bath. Restaurant, pool, horseback riding, surfing, fishing, bicycles. AE, MC, V.*

Tamarindo

㉟ *37 km (23 mi) west of Filadelfia.*

Tamarindo is a lively little town with a great variety of restaurants, cabins, bars, and hotels at all price levels. In spite of the developmental hustle, everywhere evident in the presence of condo projects, mini–strip malls, and other resort town evils, Tamarindo remains one of the most appealing places in Guanacaste. Its wonderful array of beaches are great for snorkeling, boating, kayaking, diving, surfing, and just plain swimming; there are estuaries north and south of town for bird and animal watching, and the proximity of two turtle-nesting beaches—**Langosta** to the south and **Grande** to the north—make Tamarindo a virtually complete self-contained Costa Rican destination. With an **air strip** just outside town, Tamarindo's a great base from which to explore all of Guanacaste. There's something here for everyone.

Dining and Lodging

$$$$ ✕🔟 **Hotel Tamarindo Diriá.** A shady tropical garden next to the beach does away with the need to stray far from the bounds of Tamarindo's poshest hotel. The modern three-story building has new owners who have remodeled and filled the previously dark rooms with striking white-painted furnishings with aqua trim and matching ceilings. It's a bit much, but each has a spacious balcony looking onto treetops. The thatched rotunda bar and restaurant overlook a large rectangular pool. ⊠ *Apdo. 676–1000, San José,* ☎ *654–4030. (Reservations office in San José:* ☎ *289–8616,* 𝔽𝔸𝕏 *289–8727.) 70 rooms with bath. Restaurant, bar, pool, tennis. AE, DC, MC, V.*

$$$–$$$$ ✕🔟 **Hotel Capitán Suiz.** The "Swiss Captain" is Ruedi Schmid, and he's created a charming collection of 8 bungalows and 16 rooms at the south end of Tamarindo, near a lineup of high-priced beachfront houses. The bungalows surround a swimming pool, and a relatively quiet stretch of Tamarindo's gorgeous beach is just a few steps away.

The restaurant serves international cuisine. ☎ 680–0853. *24 rooms with bath. Restaurant, pool. AE, MC, V.*

$$$ ✕🏨 **El Jardín del Eden.** This resort is smaller and a better value than
★ the Diría, the only disadvantage being that it's not directly on the beach.
The three-tiered, mauve hotel, set among lush gardens (hence the name
Garden of Eden) on a hill, has rooms with green interiors and elegantly
styled bathrooms. All rooms have ocean views, air-conditioning, re-
frigerators, and fans. Two pools, a hot tub, and a thatched-roof restau-
rant that prepares French and Italian food are set amid the landscaped
grounds. The hotel restaurant now serves outstanding steaks. Fishing
packages are available. ✉ *Apdo. 1094–2050, San Pedro,* ☎ FAX *654–
4111. 18 rooms with bath, 2 apartments. Restaurant, 2 bars, 2 pools,
hot tub. AE, MC, V.*

$$–$$$ ✕🏨 **El Milagro.** One of Tamarindo's more innovative hotels started
★ off as a restaurant run by a young English-speaking Dutch couple. Robert
Boasson, the chef, mastered his art in Switzerland and Amsterdam be-
fore coming to Costa Rica. The couple recently built individual tile-
roof cabins with wood ceilings, firm beds, large fans, and terraces. Views
of the small pool can be enjoyed with candlelight dinners in the open-
air restaurant. The menu is short but refined; if you feel like a very worth-
while splurge, order the platter of three fish with four sauces. ✉ *Playa
Tamarindo, Guanacaste (across road from beach),* ☎ *654–4042. 32
rooms with bath. Restaurant, bar, pool. AE, V.*

$–$$ ✕🏨 **Cabinas Zullymar.** At the southern end of Tamarindo, these clean
★ and varied cabins are a good bargain. Bedrooms have white walls, slop-
ing wood ceilings, and large modern bathrooms; air-conditioning and
a fridge come for a price. Pre-Columbian–style statues adorn the garden. Across the road on the beach, the restaurant serves inexpensive
maritime food in a colorful setting marked by white wooden chairs,
pink and green tablecloths, and abundant potted plants. ✉ *Apdo. 68,
Santa Cruz, Guanacaste,* ☎ *226–4732,* FAX *286–0191. 27 rooms with
bath. Restaurant, bar. AE, MC, V.*

$$$ 🏨 **Bella Vista Village Resort.** Just off the beach and up a hill behind
Tamarindo, the Bella Vista is a secluded, quiet, and dust-free retreat—
this last feature being a real plus in the height of the dry season, when
Tamarindo can disappear in a dust bowl. The resort is also graced with
magnificent views—Bella Vistas, as it were—of the coastline and the
sea. With in-room kitchenettes, it's a convenient place to hole up for
a few days and forgo the at-times wearying task of eating every meal
in a restaurant. Gabe and Judy Bettinsoll, the American couple who
own and operate the resort, can set up any or all of the usual activi-
ties, from fishing to windsurfing to horseback riding. There's a pool
on the premises. Each bungalow sleeps up to four in private sleeping
areas. The bungalows have fans, two double beds (one a fold-out
futon sofa), and one single bed. The hotel also possesses one of
Tamarindo's few private phone lines. ✉ *Apdo. 143–5150, Santa Cruz,
Guanacaste,* ☎ FAX *653–0036. 5 bungalows with bath. Kitchenettes,
pool. V.*

Outdoor Activities and Sports

BOATING

Iguana Surf (☎ 654–4019) has a catamaran for rent on the beach,
with the very able Frenchman Jean Baptiste at the helm. He also guides
kayakers into the bird-watching paradise of the nearby San Francisco
River estuary.

Playa Langosta

③⑥ *2 km (1.2 mi) south of Tamarindo.*

Playa Langosta is a leatherback-turtle nesting beach that is less protected than the beach at Tamarindo. Informal viewings with private guides are a lot cheaper than the more organized Playa Grande turtle tours, but eggs are being stolen in huge quantities, and the whole arrangement will most likely be formalized in the near future.

Dining and Lodging

$$$–$$$$ ✕🏠 **Sueño del Mar.** This is the only hotel on Playa Langosta. Langosta has great surf, turtle nesting at night, the isolated and quite fantastic bird-watching estuary of the San Francisco River behind it; and now it has American Susan Money's gorgeous little dream of a hotel. The adobe-style buildings house 3 double rooms with overhead fans and Balinese-style showers that are open to the sky. Also available is a *casita* (small cottage) that sleeps four, and has its own kitchen and veranda. The complex is decorated with frescoes and colorful tile from an old building in Nicaragua and sources in Mexico, and includes a courtyard with hammocks and a "community" room where Ms. Money serves gourmet breakfasts everyday, and three-course dinners a couple of times a week. Playa Langosta is lovely and very private. ✉ *Playa Tamarindo, Santa Cruz, Guanacaste,* ☎ *653–0284* ℻ *653–0001. 3 rooms with bath, 1 casita with 2 rooms. Restaurant, kitchenettes. No credit cards.*

THE NORTHWEST A TO Z

Arriving and Departing

By Bus

There is bus service from San José to the following northwest destinations: **Ciudad Quesada** (daily, every hour 5 AM–7:30 PM; 3-hr trip; leaves from C. 16, Avdas. 1 and 3; ☎ 255–4318); **Monteverde** (Mon.–Fri. at 6:30 AM and 2:30 PM; 3 hrs; from C. 14 between Avdas. 9 and 11; ☎ 222–3854); **Tilarán** (daily 7:30 AM, 9:30 AM, 12:45 PM, 3:45 PM, and 6:30 PM; 4 hrs; from C. 14, Avda. 9/11; ☎ 222–3854); **Puntarenas** (daily, every 30 mins 5 AM–7 PM; 2 hrs; from C. 12 between Avdas. 7 and 9; ☎ 222–0064); **Liberia** (7 buses daily, 7 AM–8 PM; 4 hrs; from C. 14 between Avdas. 1 and 3; ☎ 222–1650); **Nicoya** (daily 6:30 AM, 8 AM, 10 AM, 11:30 AM, 3 PM, and 5 PM; from C. 14, Avdas. 3 and 5; ☎ 222–2750); **Arenal Volcano** (daily, 6:15 AM, 8:40 AM, and 11:30 AM, returning at 2:45 PM; 4½ hrs; from C. 16 between Avdas. 1 and 3; ☎ 232–5660); **Tamarindo** (daily at 4 PM; 5½ hrs; from C. 14 between Avdas. 3 and 5; ☎ 222–2750); **Coco Beach** (daily 10 AM; 5 hrs; from C. 14, Avdas. 1 and 3); **Brasilito-Flamingo-Potrero** (daily 8 AM and 10:30 AM; 6 hrs; from C. 20, Avdas. 3 and 5; ☎ 221–7202); **Hermosa and Panama** (daily 3:20 PM; 5 hrs; from C. 12, Avdas. 5 and 7; ☎ 666–1249); **Nosara** (daily 6:15 AM; 6 hrs; from C. 14, Avdas. 3 and 5; ☎ 222–2750; and **Sámara** (daily 12:30 PM; from C. 14, Avdas. 3 and 5, ☎ 222–2750).

By Car

Road access to the northwest is by way of the paved two-lane Inter-American Highway, which starts from the top of Paseo Colón in San José.

By Plane
Sansa and **Travelair** fly to Liberia, Tamarindo, Carrillo, Nosara, Punta Islita, and Tambor. **Lacsa** also flies to Liberia once a week from Miami (☞ Air Travel *in* Smart Travel Tips A to Z).

Getting Around

By Boat
The **Puntarenas–Playa Naranjo car ferry** takes 1½ hours and departs daily at 3:15, 7, 10:30 AM, 2:50 and 7 PM. The 1½-hour **Puntarenas–Paquera ferry** departs daily at 6 and 11 AM and 3 PM, returning at 6 and 10:30 AM and 2:30 and 7:15 PM. The **Tambor ferry** departs from Puntarenas daily at 4:15 and 8:45 AM, 12:30 and 5:30 PM. Bus links and cabs are available at the Nicoya ends of the ferry lines. Private ferry service from Montezuma to Paquera and Puntarenas is also available; just ask around in town. The **Tempisque car ferry** crosses continuously and takes 20 minutes; lines can get very long in the dry season.

By Bus
Bus service within the area includes the following: to Arenal and Tilarán from Ciudad Quesada daily 6 AM, noon, 3 PM, via La Fortuna; to La Fortuna from Ciudad Quesada daily 7, 11 AM, 6 PM; to Garza, Guiones, and Nosara from Nicoya bus station daily at 1 PM; to Sámara and Carrillo from Nicoya weekdays at 4:20 PM and weekends at 8 AM; to Tilarán from Monteverde daily at 7 AM (three-hour trip); to Flamingo and Brasilito from Santa Cruz daily at 6:30 AM and 3 PM; to Tamarindo from Santa Cruz daily at 8 PM, returning at 6:45 AM; to Montezuma from Paquera daily at 8 AM and 5 PM, returning at 5:30 AM and 2 PM. There may be schedule changes and added routes since press time: the best place to check for the latest routes and times is the tourist office in San José.

By Car
Paved roads run to the Nicaraguan border, to Fortuna from San José, and down the spine of the Nicoya Peninsula as far as Carmona. Once you get off the main highway, the pavement holds out only so far, and then dirt, dust, mud, potholes, and other factors come into play. If you're headed down to the coast or through the mountains via unpaved roads, be sure to get as much information as possible, in advance, regarding the condition of the roads you plan to travel. Go with four-wheel drive if possible.

Contacts and Resources

Emergencies
Police (☎ 117 in towns or 127 in rural areas). **Traffic Police** (☎ 227–8030). **Fire** (☎ 118). **Ambulance** (☎ 221–5818).

Guided Tours
DAY TRIPS
Day trips to the idyllic Tortuga Island in the Gulf of Nicoya are very popular, and **Calypso Tours** (☎ 233–3617) has been doing them the longest. Monteverde can be included in the package. The **Burío Inn** (☞ Dining and Lodging, *above*) in Fortuna offers a wide range of excursions, including visits to Caño Negro National Wildlife Refuge, Venado Caverns, Fortuna River waterfall by horseback, and the lower slopes of Arenal Volcano. **Guanacaste Tours** (☎ 666–0306) is recommended for day trips from within the northwest to Santa Rosa, Rincón de la Vieja, Palo Verde, Playa Ostional and Playa Grande by night (to see

turtles), and Arenal; it picks up tour participants from large hotels in the area.

Swiss Travel (☎ 231–4055) has tours to Arenal out of San José, as well as to Monteverde. **Costa Rica Sun Tours** (☎ 255–3518) will take you to the Arenal Observatory, perhaps combined with a trip to Monteverde. **Costa Rica Expeditions** (☎ 222–0333) offers 8- to 14-day tours around the whole country, including the northwest.

Tikal Ecoadventures (☎ 223–2811) runs highly informative week-long tours that take in Carara, Manuel Antonio, the Lomas Barbudal Reserve, Playa Grande, Santa Rosa, and Arenal. **Geotur** (☎ 234–1867) operates a three-day horseback exploratory tour of the dry forests around Los Inocentes Lodge, where participants stay. The excellent **Horizontes** (☎ 222–2022) specializes in more independent tours with as few as eight people, including transport by four-wheel drive, naturalist guides, and guest lectures.

Visitor Information

The **tourist office** (☞ Chapter 3) in San José has information covering the northwest. In Liberia, the **Casa de la Cultura** (3 blocks from Central Plaza, ☎ 666–1606) has local tourist information. It is open Monday–Saturday 8–4.

7 The Southwest

*The landscape of the Southwest, one of
Costa Rica's most diverse and wild
regions, ranges from the cloud forests
of the Talamanca Mountains to the
isolated beaches of the Osa Peninsula.
Among the area's many attractions are
two of the country's most popular
beach resorts, one of the finest
botanical gardens in Latin America,
and many of its best hotels and nature
lodges. Moreover, the Southwest, with
its excellent surfing, fishing, hiking,
bird-watching, skin diving, and white-
water rafting, is seventh heaven for
outdoor aficionados.*

Updated by
David
Dudenhoefer

TRAVELERS TO THE SOUTHWEST—a lush, tropical coastal plain overlooked by the highest mountain chain in the country, the Cordillera de Talamanca—should thank the national park system for preserving some of the most breathtaking natural areas in the country. The Carara Biological Reserve, for example, is a transition zone between the dry north and humid south where massive, buttressed trees and scarlet macaws vie for attention with a waterfowl- and crocodile-inhabited lagoon. Manuel Antonio, synonymous for many people with tropical paradise, protects an indented stretch of coastal rain forest that serves as a backdrop for a series of idyllic white sand beaches. Visitors to Chirripó National Park can climb Costa Rica's highest mountain and explore remote wilderness ranging from rugged forest to glacial lakes. On the Osa Peninsula, the creation of Corcovado National Park put something of a halt to the furious logging and gold mining that was destroying the rain forest. Corcovado contains a wide range of habitats, including large areas of swamp, deserted beaches, cloud forest, and luxuriant lowland rain forest, which provide habitat for most of the country's endangered species.

The Southwest has the most dramatic and diverse scenery and wildlife in Costa Rica as well as some of its best beaches. The region also has excellent conditions for practicing a variety of outdoor sports. Some of Costa Rica's best surfing breaks, for example, as well as its second best skin diving area can be found here. Anglers can fish the renowned Pacific waters, rafters can take on the rambunctious General River or the less threatening Savegre, trekkers can climb Chirripó, and bird-watchers who head to the right spots are almost guaranteed glimpses of the country's two most spectacular birds: the brilliantly colored quetzal and the scarlet macaw. Botany lovers, too, will go gaga here, especially at the Wilson Botanical Garden near San Vito, with its spectacular displays of the local plant life.

Bordering the southwestern region of Costa Rica is the Chiriquí province of Panama, home to lush rain forests and teeming rivers. If you have more than a few days to explore the Southwest, you may want to consider venturing over the border for two or three days (☞ Chiriquí Province *in* Chapter 8).

Pleasures and Pastimes

Dining
The Southwest may not be renowned for its gourmet cooking, but it does have a remarkable number of spots where you can enjoy excellent meals. Both Manuel Antonio and Jacó have good restaurants, and some of the region's best hotels and nature lodges have kitchens to match their accommodations. Given the world-class fishing of the area, it's no surprise that seafood is the forté of the area's best chefs. Pineapples and *mamones chinos,* whose red spiky shells contain a succulent white fruit that resembles a cross between a litchi and a grape, are also both widely eaten.

Lodging
The Southwest's accommodations are as varied as its scenery. There are simple oceanside *cabinas* (cottages), tranquil mountain retreats, and luxury hotels set amidst the greenery of the rain forest. Some of the country's premier hotels and nature lodges are found here, but there

are also enough low-budget options to make the region accessible to all travelers. Be aware that nature lodges may appear to be more expensive than they are in reality, since the price of rooms includes three hearty meals a day. Budget travelers visiting Manuel Antonio should note that it is less costly to stay in Quepos and then take the bus to the park.

Outdoor Excitement

There is no shortage of outdoor diversions to choose from in this corner of the country. Several white-water rivers flow out of its mountains: the Savegre, Naranjo, and the longer General. Horseback riding is available just about everywhere, and possible hikes range from one-day jaunts through private reserves in Dominical, Matapalo, and San Gerardo de Dota to more demanding treks up Chirripó or into the jungles of Corcovado. The snorkeling is good in Manuel Antonio and Ballena National Parks, whereas the ocean around Caño Island has some of Costa Rica's best skin diving. The sportfishing is also excellent up and down the southern Pacific coast, with charter boats operating out of half a dozen ports. The region also has at least a dozen popular surf breaks, and several operators that offer sea kayaking excursions.

Private Preserves

In addition to the Southwest's selection of national parks and biological reserves, there are a growing number of private nature preserves, some of which have their own lodges. Dominical's Hacienda Barú, a 700-acre reserve, offers a number of ways to experience the rain forest, as does Lapa Rios, on the southern tip of the Osa Peninsula, with its extensive protected rain forest. Other private rain forest reserves include the one surrounding the Costa Rica Expeditions' tent camp near Corcovado, the Tiskita Jungle Lodge, Wilson Botanical Garden's primary forest, and the waterfall reserve next to Carara. Cabinas Chacón, in San Gerardo de Dota, has a large cloud forest reserve crisscrossed by footpaths.

Exploring the Southwest

The Southwest can be divided into two parts: the coast near San José, which has some of the country's most accessible beaches, and the Southern Zone, which comprises the Pacific slope of the Talamanca Mountains, the General Valley, and the Osa Peninsula. The coast near San José is easily reached by driving west on the Inter-American Highway to the road to Atenas and Orotina, where the coastal highway heads south to Carara, Jacó, and Quepos. Although a dirt road connects Quepos and Dominical, the Southern Zone is best reached by taking the Inter-American Highway south over the Talamanca Mountains. Since much of the Southern Zone lies far from San José, it may be worthwhile to fly there. Each of the Great Itineraries begins in San José.

Great Itineraries

IF YOU HAVE 3 DAYS

Numbers in the text correspond to numbers in the margin and on the Southwest map.

Leave San José early to spend the morning at ⚏ **Carara National Park** ① and, in the afternoon, check into a hotel either in the ⚏ **Tárcoles** ② area or in ⚏ **Jacó** ③. Spend the next morning on the beach or visit the waterfall near Tárcoles then head south to ⚏ **Quepos** ⑤. The next morning, visit Manuel Antonio National Park then head back to San José. Those who prefer a mellower vacation may choose to fly to Manuel Antonio or the Osa Peninsula.

IF YOU HAVE 5 DAYS
Start the day off with the cool mountain air of **San Gerardo de Dota** ⑥, the perfect place for hiking and bird watching. After a morning in the highlands, head down to the coast of ▨ **Dominical** ⑨, which has waterfalls, nature reserves, and great beaches. After either one or two nights there, follow the coast north to ▨ **Manuel Antonio,** where, in addition to the national park, you can enjoy white-water rafting, horseback riding, sportfishing, and other marine diversions. Those who prefer to escape the crowd, however, may want to head further north to one of the lodges near ▨ **Parrita** ④ or ▨ **Tárcoles** ② for the last night.

IF YOU HAVE 8 DAYS
Drive south on the Inter-American Highway, spending the first night in ▨ **San Gerardo de Dota** ⑥. On day two, head to ▨ **Dominical** ⑨, which deserves two nights. If you have four-wheel drive, you can take the coastal highway south from Dominical, visiting Ballena on the way, and ending near **Golfito** ⑫ or ▨ **Wilson Botanical Gardens** for the fourth night. If you are so inclined, you can slip across the border into Panama for two or three days to explore Chiriquí Province (☞ Chapter 8). Otherwise, head back to ▨ **San Isidro** ⑦ and take the Inter-American Highway southwest to **San Vito** ⑩ and the garden. Between ▨ **Golfito** ⑫ and San Vito, which are separated by a one-hour drive, you could easily spend two nights. Then head out to the Osa Peninsula, one of the wildest and most beautiful areas in the country, by either driving to **Cabo Matapalo** ⑰ or parking in Sierpe and boating it to **Drake Bay** ⑱. The Osa deserves a minimum of two nights but could easily be given three or more. On day seven, it's time to head back toward San José, spending a night in either ▨ **San Isidro** ⑦, ▨ **Dominical** ⑨, or ▨ **San Gerardo de Dota** ⑥.

When to Tour the Southwest

The Southwest follows the same wet season/dry season scenario as the rest of the Pacific, but it rains considerably more here than in the Northwest during the rainy months. During the dry months, especially during July and August, you may catch a week without any serious precipitation. The Osa Peninsula and Talamanca highlands are especially susceptible to downpours, and the region is probably the last place you want to visit during the September/October deluge season, unless you have ambitions of becoming a duck. You can do a lot of exploring without getting drenched during the rest of the year, especially if you observe the basic active-morning/sheltered-evening tropical climate etiquette during the rainy months. The beach resorts of Jacó and Manuel Antonio are not only popular among tourists, but they are also the preferred destinations of Ticos on weekends or holidays, which means hotels often book up ahead of time, especially for the week between Christmas and New Year's and Holy Week.

THE COAST NEAR SAN JOSÉ

Carara, Jacó, and Manuel Antonio

Numbers in the margin correspond to points of interest on the Southwest map.

This short stretch of Pacific coast holds some of Costa Rica's most accessible beaches and popular protected areas. Since its attractions lie just a few hours' drive from San José, it is a region where travelers who

The Southwest

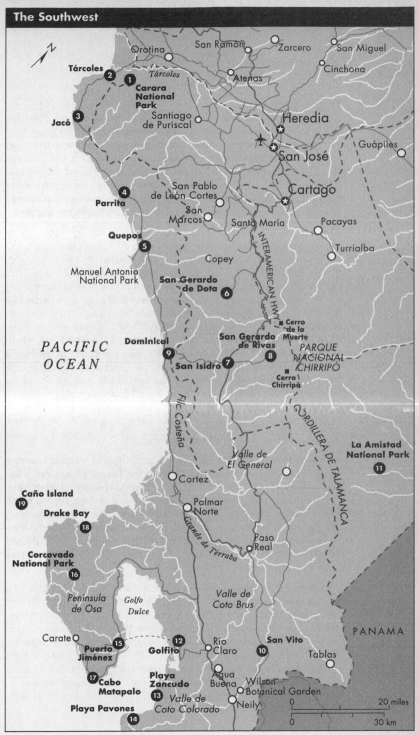

San Ramón • Zarcero • San Miguel

Orotina • Cinchona •

Tárcoles 2 **1** Tárcoles Atenas

Carara National Park

Jacó 3 Santiago de Puriscal Heredia ✈ Guápiles

San José

Parrita 4 San Pablo de León Cortes Cartago

San Marcos Pacayas

Santa María Turrialba

Quepos 5 Copey INTERAMERICAN HWY

Manuel Antonio National Park **San Gerardo de Dota 6**

Cerro de la Muerte

Dominical 9 **San Gerardo de Rivas** PARQUE NACIONAL CHIRRIPÓ

PACIFIC OCEAN **San Isidro 7** **8** Cerro Chirripó

Río Costeña

Valle de El General

Cortez CORDILLERA DE TALAMANCA

Caño Island 19 Palmar Norte **La Amistad National Park 11**

Drake Bay 18 Paso Real

Grande de Térraba

Corcovado National Park 16

Península de Osa Golfo Dulce Valle de Coto Brus

PANAMA

Carate **Puerto Jiménez 15** **Golfito 12** Río Claro **San Vito 10** Tablas

Cabo Matapalo 17 **Playa Zancudo** Agua Buena Wilson Botanical Garden

13 Valle de Coto Colorado Neily 0 20 miles

Playa Pavones 14 0 30 km

are short on time can get a quick overview of what the country has to offer. The scenery ranges from steep slopes draped with lush foliage that stretch down to the sea to protected rain forests.

Carara National Park

❶ *83 km (51 mi) southwest of San José.*

Situated between Costa Rica's drier Northwest and more humid South, Carara National Park (☞ Chapter 2) makes for a nice day trip from San José. The reserve also provides an enjoyable hike for those who start out early in the morning to see the animals. You'll find the ranger station on the left shortly after the bridge that spans the Tárcoles River. A horseshoe lagoon, which was abandoned as an oxbow lake by the meandering Tárcoles, is now almost entirely covered with water hyacinths and is home to exotic birds such as the jacana as well as large crocodiles. Waterfowl, amphibians, and reptiles live in the marshes.

Much of the 11,614-acre reserve is covered in primary forest, growing on quite steep slopes. The trees, laden with vines and epiphytes, are immense—the smooth-bark cow tree reaches 150 feet in height. Carara makes a worthwhile stop because the relatively less-dense undergrowth means that wildlife is easier to see here than in many other places. You might see spectacled owls, boat-billed herons, blue-crowned motmots, scarlet macaws, roseate spoonbills, crocodiles, iguanas, sloths, coatis, and white-faced monkeys. Deep in the forest artificial nests have been built to protect the endangered scarlet macaw, which is under constant threat from poachers who sell chicks in the illegal international pet trade. Important archaeological discoveries have also been made at Carara, in particular the Lomas Carara pre-Columbian cemetery, which covers 15 acres. ▨ *$6.* ✆ *Daily 8–4.*

Tárcoles

❷ *2 hours south of San José by car.*

Although the town of Tárcoles itself has nothing to warrant a stop, it is the departure point for a boat tour up the Tárcoles River and it lies near two excellent hotels, as well as a spectacular waterfall set in a private nature reserve. Tárcoles is on the west side of the road, just south of the Carara Biological Reserve—across from the entrance to town is a dirt road that leads to the Hotel Villa Lapas and the waterfall reserve. Boat trips up the **Tárcoles River** depart daily at high tide and are arranged out of the La Guaria Restaurant (☎ 661–0455), across from the soccer field.

The **Manatial de Agua Viva** is a 600-foot waterfall in the heart of a private reserve across from Tárcoles. The waterfall flows into 10 natural pools, perfect for a refreshing dip after the hike into the reserve. The forest surrounding the waterfall is home to parrots, monkeys, scarlet macaws, and most of the other animals found in the adjacent Carara National Park. A 2.5-kilometer (1.6-mile) trail makes a loop through the woods, passing the waterfall and pools; it can take from 40 minutes to two hours to hike, depending on how much bird watching you do. The entrance is 5 kilometers (3 miles) from the coastal highway, up the same dirt road that leads to Villa Lapas. ▨ *1,500 colones.* ☉ *Daily 8–5.*

Dining and Lodging

$$$$ ✕▥ **Villa Caletas.** Set amidst the rain forest atop a promontory, this
★ elegant collection of villas may seem remote, but it is only minutes from
Jacó and Carara. Although the architecture is reminiscent of southeast
Asia, guest rooms are decorated in the French style, with fine antiques
and art, black furniture, and sweeping draperies. The villas are built
along slopes covered with lush foliage, and all of them have astounding views of both rolling mountains and the ocean far below. French
is also the predominant influence in the cuisine, which is served in an
attractive open-air restaurant. The cleverly designed pool appears to
blend into the horizon. You'll find the Villa Caletas on the west side
of the road, several kilometers south of Tárcoles. ✉ *Apdo. 12358–
1000, San José,* ☎ *257–3653,* ℻ *222–2059. 8 rooms with bath, 17
villas, 3 suites. Restaurant, bar, pool. AE, MC, V.*

$$$ ✕▥ **Hotel Villa Lapas.** The grounds of this hotel are shaded by tall trees,
with a stream flowing by, making it a great spot for bird watching. A
trail heads up the valley into the hotel's patch of protected forest, and
it lies just a short drive from Carara and the waterfall reserve. White
bungalows with barrel tile roofs and small porches hold two rooms
each; those closest to the restaurant overlook the stream. Rooms have
tile floors, wood ceilings, desks, and ceiling fans. The open-air restau-
rant overlooks the stream and forest and serves international cuisine.
✉ *Apdo. 419–4005, Heredia (across from entrance to Tárcoles),* ☎
293–4265, ℻ *293–4104. 46 rooms with bath. Restaurant, bar, pool.
AE, MC, V.*

Jacó

❸ *108 km (67 mi) southwest of San José, 70 km (43 mi) north of Que-
pos.*

The relative proximity to San José, coupled with the attractiveness of
its wide sandy bay, hemmed in by rocky forested outcrops, has con-
tributed to Jacó's popularity as a resort. Around 40 well-dispersed ho-
tels line the beach here, but they are largely hidden behind palms. In
the low season, you'll still have the impression that the place is rela-
tively quiet and undeveloped. High season, however, is bustling. If you
do want fun in the sun and something vaguely resembling nightlife,
this is the closest beach resort to the capital.

� Jacó's beach has dark gray, dirty-looking sand that can burn the soles
of your feet on a sunny afternoon. The surfing is good, but riptides
make the sea hazardous for swimmers when the waves are big. The
water is also often a bit murky, thanks to sediment from the Tárcoles
and other nearby rivers, which means it isn't a great area for snorkel-
ing. Aside from sun bathing and surfing, you can rent bicycles and motor
scooters to explore the surrounding countryside, go horseback riding,
or take a tour to Carara, the Tárcoles River, or a deserted beach
nearby. Those traveling with children should visit the **petting zoo**,
across from the gas station on the town's southern entrance, which has
a number of friendly animals and asks visitors for donations. There is
also a **miniature golf course** on the town's main drag.

Dining and Lodging

$$–$$$ ✕ **Flamboyant.** On the west side of the main street, in the heart of town, ★ this is the best seafood place around. The front of the restaurant opens onto a small porch with a few tables and surrounding gardens. Inside, the decor is simple: tile floor, green tablecloths, and ceiling fans. The daily specials are usually the best bet, with either shrimp or lobster and a few types of fish prepared a variety of ways. ✉ *West side of main street, downtown Jacó,* ☎ *643–3023. Reservations not accepted. AE, MC, V.*

$$$ ✕⌂ **Hotel Club del Mar.** It's easy to forget you're in busy Jacó when ★ you stay at this secluded spot on the southern extreme of the beach. Bungalows are shaded by giant trees, and iguanas lounge on the lawn of this oceanfront hotel. Handsome superior rooms have green tile floors, high ceilings, and wooden shutters that open onto balconies, many of which overlook the ocean. Most of the superior rooms have air-conditioning. Smaller standard rooms in back have small kitchens, sitting areas, and balconies. Budget rooms are a bit cramped but have porches. ✉ *Apdo. 107–4023, Jacó (follow main road to Quepos, turn right at first street past service station),* ☎ FAX *643–3194. 18 rooms with bath. Restaurant, bar, pool. MC, V.*

$$$ ✕⌂ **Tangeri Chalets.** If there are several of you, Tangeri's eccentrically designed bungalows, which sleep six, offer good value. No longer in the first flush of youth, they are nonetheless clean enough and comfortable. The best part is the veranda dining patio; bedrooms are rather dark but perfectly okay. Relax in the beachside garden with its shady palms and two pools. Posh, new, air-conditioned and comfortable bedrooms, without kitchens, go for the same price as whole bungalows. ✉ *Apdo. 622–4050, Alajuela,* ☎ FAX *643–3636. 10 bungalows, 14 rooms with bath. Restaurant, pool, basketball. AE, MC, V.*

$$ ⌂ **Villas Miramar.** Six colonial-style white bungalows surround Jacó's ★ most attractive garden and pool. Each contains two double bedrooms, a bathroom, and a fully equipped kitchen. Decor is minimal and seaside-ish: white walls, tile floors, and wooden beds. The owners are friendly but unobtrusive. ✉ *Apdo. 124, Playa de Jacó (center of town, 17 yds. north of Supermercado Rayo Azul),* ☎ *643–3003,* FAX *643–3617. 12 rooms with bath. Pool. MC, V.*

Nightlife and the Arts

During the high season, Jacó gets lively when the sun goes down. Cut loose at popular disco **La Central** (☎ 643–3076), on the beach opposite Tienda La Flor, and **Los Tucanes** (☎ 643–3226), next door. Those who prefer a seat and a view of a game should hit the **sports bar** by the Copacabana Hotel's pool.

Outdoor Activities and Sports

SURFING

Jacó has an excellent beach break, but it is only good around high tide. The town's reputation as a surfer's paradise has spread far and wide, and there are consequently dozens of surfboard-toting tourists in Jacó at any given point in time, in addition to the dozens of locals who surf. A more consistent break can be found at **Playa Hermosa,** about 5 kilometers (3 miles) south of Jacó. Surfboards can be rented at **Chuck's** (no phone), a block west of the main street near the Hacienda Restaurant.

Parrita

❹ *150 km (93 mi) southwest of San José, 46 km (28.5 mi) south of Jacó, 24 km (15 mi) north of Quepos.*

Set in the heart of an African palm plantation, Parrita is a dusty town of painted wooden bungalows. First planted in 1945 by a banana company, after their banana plantations were decimated by Panama disease, the palms are cultivated for their fruit, from which oil is extracted for margarine, cooking oil, scent, and soap. To the south of town is a right turn to **Playa Palo Seco**, an endless beach backed by palms and mangrove swamps.

Lodging

$$–$$$ ▥ **Apartotel La Isla.** Situated between the sea and a mangrove-filled river, this hotel has rooms in its main building as well as in modern white cabinas that sleep six but are still a good value for four. The cabins are set well apart from one another, and since no other hotels exist in the vicinity, the beach is virtually deserted. Each cabina has tile floors, fans, a kitchen, two bedrooms, and rustic wooden furniture; you can cook either in your own kitchen or on the central barbecue. Activities include surfing, canoeing, and horseback riding. ✉ *Playa Palo Seco, Parrita,* ☎ *222–6561,* ℻ *233–5384. 16 rooms with bath, 16 bungalows. Restaurant, bar, pool, hot tub, tennis. AE, MC, V.*

Quepos

❺ *174 km (108 mi) southwest of San José, 70 km (43 mi) south of Jacó.*

Quepos is the largest town in this area with around 12,000 inhabitants. Juan Vásquez de Coronado, the first Spanish conquistador to arrive here, in 1563, encountered the Quepos Indians, an offshoot tribe of the Borucas, who lived by a combination of farming and fishing. Clashes, displacement, and intermarriage served to drastically deplete the indigenous population, for whom colonies were only established at the end of the 19th century. Like Golfito, Quepos was once a major banana port but saw its fortunes dwindle along with those of the United Fruit Company. Only recently has revenue from tourism, fishing, and African palms begun to remove the shabbiness that had set in. The town has some good budget hotels, but for beaches you'll have to head to nearby Manuel Antonio.

Manuel Antonio National Park begins 5 kilometers (3 miles) south of Quepos (☞ Chapter 2). This park, although touted as a paradise, is lovely but can get overcrowded; for peace, quiet, and animal life, stick to the less-traveled parks. The road between Quepos and the park is growing increasingly crowded by hotels, none of which are very cheap and some of which fit into the super deluxe category. Environmentalists are pushing to halt the unbridled development on Costa Rica's most beautiful stretch of coast, which was terribly battered by tropical storm Gert in September 1993. You'll find the cheapest accommodations near the end of the road at the park entrance or in Quepos. To enter the park, you'll need to wade through a narrow estuary, waist-deep at high tide, ankle-deep at low tide.

The park is small, only 1,685 acres. It protects a remarkable stretch of coast comprising three idyllic white-sand horseshoe beaches, divided by some primary forest, although many of the biggest trees were knocked down by the storm. Bully, black locust, cow, and silk cotton trees all grow in the area; mangrove swamps, marshland, and open-water lagoons contribute further to the park's biodiversity. The park is home to squirrel monkeys, which live only here and on the Osa Peninsula; the monkeys are thought to be in danger of extinction. From the beach and trails you might glimpse two- and three-toed sloths, iguanas, agoutis, and white-faced monkeys. Be careful of the *manzanillo* tree (indicated by warning signs), whose leaves, bark, and fruit—which resemble apples but aren't—secrete a toxic gooey substance that irritates the skin. Also, do not feed or try to touch the monkeys, which have seen so many tourists that they sometimes walk right up to them, and have bitten several overfriendly visitors.

Plan for sunbathing, swimming, snorkeling, hiking, and a respite at the picnic area; a full day is advisable. The first beach after the ranger station, **South Espadilla,** is the longest and least crowded, since rip currents make it treacherous for swimmers. At its southern end is a tombolo (isthmus formed from sedimentation and accumulated debris) leading to a steep forested path to **Cathedral Point.** Visible east of here is the precipitous vegetation-crowned **Mogote Island,** one of the park's 12 islands and site of pre-Columbian Quepos Indian burials. East of the tombolo is **Playa Manuel Antonio,** a small, sandy, and relatively safe beach. At low tide you can see an obsolete Quepos Indian turtle trap near the rocks on the right—turtles would become stranded as the tide receded in a pool formed by a semicircular rock. This deep bay is a good snorkeling area. Walking even farther east you arrive at the slightly rockier **Playa Puerto Escondido,** with its dramatic blowhole, and the nude gay beach called **Playitas.** ☒ *$6.* ☉ *Daily 8–4.*

The long beach before Manuel Antonio park is also quite nice, and it's free. It's a popular area with sunbathers, surfers, volleyball players, and families on holiday. There are several inexpensive restaurants right on the beach, where you can enjoy a cool drink or a meal while watching the surfers. Unfortunately, it also has some deadly rip currents whenever the waves are big, which is much of the time. A series of open-air stands that line the road just before the park sell souvenirs and rent belly boards and snorkeling gear. It's a lively area, especially on weekends, when those seeking solitude will want to walk toward the north end of the beach. You can also rent horses at a nearby stable for riding on the beach, but the best horseback trips head into the rain forests behind town.

If you're traveling with children, or have a keen interest in wildlife, you may want to visit the **Jardín Gaia,** a small zoo that rehabilitates captured and injured animals and releases them back into the wild. The zoo holds mostly monkeys and birds—about a dozen species of parrots and macaws. Most of the birds were confiscated by officials from the Wildlife Department, whereas many of the monkeys were found after being electrocuted while playing on power lines. Guided tours are given in the afternoon. ☒ *On left side of road to Manuel Antonio, 2.7 km (1.6 mi) from Quepos.* ☒ *$5.* ☉ *Thurs.–Tues. 2–5* PM.

Dining and Lodging

$$–$$$ ✕ **Barba Roja.** With a reputation as lofty as its setting, Barba Roja's
★ chief draws are its sweeping view over the Manuel Antonio shoreline and its chic clientele. The partly open dining room is furnished with dark hardwoods; local landscapes hang on the walls. Food takes a very

close second to atmosphere; opt for one of the daily specials on the board. Excellent sandwiches are served at lunchtime. Breakfasting here is also popular because of the delicious whole-wheat toast. ⊠ *On hill between Quepos and Manuel Antonio,* ☎ 777–0331. *Reservations not accepted. Mon. dinner only.* V.

$$$$ ✕⊞ **Hotel La Mariposa.** High on a promontory, Manuel Antonio's classi-
★ est hotel has even better views than its neighbor, Barba Roja: Here you can admire the inland hills as well as the shoreline. The main building is a white Spanish-style villa with an open dining room and pink and purple wicker furniture. The split-level units cling to the steep garden and have sitting rooms, balcony bedrooms, and conservatory bathrooms alive with plants. There are also a couple of rooms above the restaurant, and five rooms behind the parking lot, which are inferior in quality and price to the others. ⊠ *Puerto Quepos, Manuel Antonio (on hill between Quepos and Manuel Antonio),* ☎ 777–0355, ℻ 777–0050. *10 villas with bath. Restaurant, bar, pool. No credit cards.*

$$$–$$$$ ✕⊞ **Costa Verde.** The builders of this place, near the end of the road
★ to Manuel Antonio, were careful to damage the forest as little as possible. The result is a hotel surrounded by lush foliage, where you might spot squirrel monkeys, iguanas, parrots, and a variety of other birds in the branches outside your room. There are two types of rooms spread through five buildings, smaller efficiencies, which are short on privacy, and spacious studios, with tile floors, larger beds, tables, and chairs. All of them have ceiling fans, lots of screened windows, basic cooking facilities, and large balconies that are shared between two rooms. Ask for a room with an ocean view. An open-air restaurant serves good seafood and killer tropical drinks. ⊠ *Apdo. 106, Quepos,* ☎ 777–0584, ℻ 777–0560. *46 rooms with bath. Restaurant, bar, 2 pools. AE, MC,* V.

$$$–$$$$ ✕⊞ **Hotel Plinio.** This large wooden cabin, draped with jungle foliage, lies to the north of the Quepos–Manuel Antonio road, just outside Quepos. The bedrooms are set beneath a high, cool, thatched roof and have firm beds, wood floors, and varnished paneling. They're linked by a wide, covered balcony, with armchairs and large maps of the country. The jungle cabin with kitchen is more secluded and cheaper, if there are four or more of you (sleeps six). All prices include breakfast, which is served in the popular restaurant, renowned for its home-baked German bread and spinach lasagna. The private nature reserve has an extensive trail system and observation tower. ⊠ *Apdo. 71, Quepos,* ☎ 777–0055, ℻ 777–0558. *12 rooms with bath, 1 cabin with bath. Restaurant, bar, pool. AE, MC,* V.

$$$ ✕⊞ **Villas El Parque.** The more elevated of these tiered, whitewashed
★ apartments have wonderful views over the Pacific. Those at the bottom look out at the jungle. Half the units have well-equipped kitchens; all have terra-cotta floors, modern printed textile furnishings, and seaward balconies. Some of the rooms interconnect to form larger units. Waterfalls joined together separate two- and three-tier pools that are surrounded by lush greenery. The restaurant, The Mambo Grill, has a distinct Tex-Mex slant and specializes in fresh seafood and grilled meats. It's a tasteful, chic, and friendly place. ⊠ *Apdo. 111, Quepos (halfway between Quepos and Manuel Antonio on ocean side),* ☎ 777–0096, ℻ 777–0538. *34 rooms with bath. Restaurant, pool. AE, MC,* V.

$–$$ ✕⊞ **Hotel Vela Bar.** A hundred yards back from the first Manuel Antonio beach—left after the Bar del Mar—the bedrooms here have white stucco walls, terra-cotta floors, wooden beds, fans, and framed tapestries. The apartments (sleep four) are a good value for groups. No views to speak of here—the hotel is neatly tucked away in the trees. A rustic rotunda restaurant remains popular as a vegetarian hangout but also serves entrées such as *pollo en salsa blanca* (chicken in white sauce) and fresh seafood served in a variety of ways. ⊠ *Apdo. 13, Quepos,* ☎ *777–0413,* FAX *777–1071. 7 rooms with bath, 2 bungalows. Restaurant, bar. AE, DC, MC, V.*

$–$$ 🛱 **Hotel Malinche.** A block west of the bus terminal in Quepos, this
★   hotel has older rooms that are a bargain. They are simple but clean, with tile floors, bare white walls, small beds, fans, and white tile baths. The refurbished rooms have carpeting, air-conditioning, and hot water, but they cost more than twice as much. ⊠ *Center of Quepos,* ☎ FAX *777–0093. 29 rooms with bath. MC, V.*

$ 🛱 **Hotel Quepos.** This simple lodge across the street from the Quepos soccer field has basic rooms with hardwood floors and small beds. The ones on the second floor in front have decent views. There are also cheaper rooms that share baths. ⊠ *Apdo. 79, Quepos,* ☎ *777–0274. 25 rooms, 14 with bath. No credit cards.*

Outdoor Activities and Sports

HORSEBACK RIDING

Horses can be rented in Manuel Antonio from **Equus** (☎ 777–0001) and **Malboro Stables** (☎ 777–1108), and Equus can provide a guide to lead you through the forest. The most exciting horseback riding experiences, however, are tours offered by agencies in Quepos. **Lynch Travel** (☎ 777–1170) has two horseback tours, a three-hour ride along the Savegre River to a scenic overlook, and an all-day trip to the Catarata de Nara, a waterfall that pours into a natural swimming pool.

SEA KAYAKING

Iguana Tours (☎ 777–1262) runs sea kayaking adventures to the islands of Manuel Antonio National Park, which requires a bit of experience when seas are high, and a mellower paddle to the mangrove estuary of Isla Damas, where you might see monkeys, crocodiles, and plenty of birds.

SPORTFISHING

The Southwest waters have some of the country's best deep-sea fishing, and Quepos is one of the best ports from which to head out. There are fewer boats trolling those waters, and plenty of sailfish, marlin, wahoo, rooster fish, yellowfin tuna, and snapper. Charters are available out of Quepos with **Costa Rican Dreams** (☎ 777–0593) and **Sportsfishing Costa Rica** (☎ 257–3553 or 800/862–1003).

SWIMMING

Manuel Antonio's only truly safe swimming area is the second beach in the park, which also has some of the best snorkeling. Rip currents are a big problem on the popular main beach before the park whenever the surf gets big. Riptides are characterized by a strong current running perpendicular to the shore at about waist depth and then out to sea for a hundred yards or so. The important thing to remember is that if you feel yourself being caught don't struggle against it, but let it take you out to where its power dissipates beyond the breakers. Having conserved your strength, you should then be able to swim diagonally back to shore away from where the current has just brought you—i.e., still farther away from your original starting position.

WHITE-WATER RAFTING

There are two white-water rivers near Quepos: the **Savegre** (class II–III), which is perfect for a first rafting trip, and the **Naranjo** (class III–IV), which requires some experience. The Savegre's emerald waters wind down a narrow valley, past steep, forested hillsides, and plenty of birds. It can be run in rafts from May till January, when it drops so low that it is only navigable in two-person inflatable "duckies." The Naranjo can only be descended from June to December. Local rafting companies include **Iguana Tours** (☞ *above*), **Outward Bound** (☎ 777–0052), and **Ríos Locos** (☎ 777–1170).

Shopping

There is certainly no shortage of shopping opportunities in this town, from the T-shirt vendors that line the road near the national park to the boutiques in the big hotels. There is little in the way of local handicrafts, so you'll find much the same things you would in San José, at slightly elevated prices. **La Buena Nota** (☎ 777–0345) is one of the oldest souvenir shops in town, with two locations: on the left as you enter Quepos, and on the right just past the top of the hill, between Quepos and Manuel Antonio.

THE SOUTHERN ZONE

Talamanca Mountains, El General Valley, and Osa Peninsula

Numbers in the margin correspond to points of interest on the Southwest map.

The El General Valley is bounded to the north by the massive Talamanca Mountains and to the south by the Osa Peninsula. Together those areas comprise some of Costa Rica's largest expanses of wilderness: isolated beaches, marine attractions, and highland ecosystems. One of the last parts of Costa Rica to be settled, it is a spectacular region, with such varied environments as the high-altitude *páramo* (tableland) of Chirripó to the lowland rain forest of Corcovado. It is also the region that receives the least tourists, with many of its most impressive spots lying far from the beaten track. Some of the country's best nature lodges are found here, and they specialize in getting people to these hard-to-reach spots.

San Gerardo de Dota

❻ *80 km (50 mi) southeast of San José, 54 km (34 mi) north of San Isidro.*

Cloud forests, cool mountain air, pastoral scenes, and excellent bird-watching make San Gerardo de Dota one of Costa Rica's great overlooked destinations. You'll find San Gerardo in a narrow valley of the Savegre River, 9 kilometers (6 miles) down a twisting track that descends abruptly to the west from the Inter-American Highway. This tranquil and beautiful spot more closely resembles the Rocky Mountains than something you would see in Central America; hike down the waterfall trail, however, and the vegetation quickly becomes tropical again. The trail is steep and isn't for every traveler, but is well worth the effort for those up to it. Other activities include horseback tours and trout fishing, but most people are content to wander around the pastures and forests marveling at the valley's varied avian inhabitants.

The damp, epiphyte-laden forest of giant oak trees, now broken up by bare, stump-strewn patches, is renowned for its high count of quetzals, for many the most beautiful bird in the New World. Males are the more spectacular, with metallic green feathers, bright crimson stomachs, helmetlike crests, and long tail streamers that are especially dramatic in flight. Quetzals commonly feed on *aguacatillos*, similar to the avocado tree, which grow along the roadside. The people who run your hotel can usually point you in the direction of where the quetzals have been hanging out. Morning and evening are the best times to spot them.

Dining and Lodging

$$$ ✕🏠 **Trogon Lodge.** A collection of green cabins nestled in a secluded part of an enchanting valley, the Trogon Lodge overlooks the cloud forest and boulder-strewn Savegre River. Each cabin contains two rooms, with hardwood floors, colorful quilts, big windows, white tile baths with hot showers, and small electric heaters for those chilly mountain nights. Meals are served in a small dining hall and can be purchased separately or as part of a package. ✉ *Apdo. 10980–1000, San José,* ☎ *222–5463,* 𝖥𝖠𝖷 *255–4039. 10 rooms with bath. Restaurant, bar. AE, MC, V.*

$$ ✕🏠 **Cabinas Chacón.** Nearly 30 years ago, Efrain Chacón and his brother
★ bushwhacked their way through the mountains to homestead in San Gerardo. With hard work and business acumen, they built a successful dairy farm. Now a hotelier and staunch conservationist, Efrain aids researchers and takes visitors on tours of his extensive farm. The tours provide a wealth of information on natural and political history and nearly always include quetzal-spotting. The cabins are comfortable and clean, and the main house has a bar with a fireplace and a veranda. Meals are included. Efrain will pick up guests from anywhere in the country for a fee. ✉ *Apdo. 482, Cartago,* ☎ 𝖥𝖠𝖷 *771–1732. 18 cabins with bath. Restaurant, bar. V.*

Outdoor Activities and Sports

HIKING

There are enough trails and country roads around San Gerardo de Dota to keep you hiking for days. A short trail heads through the forest above the Trogon Lodge, ending in a pasture, whereas Cabinas Chacón has miles of trails winding through their forest reserve. The best trail in the valley, however, is the one that follows the **Savegre River down to a waterfall.** Follow the main road past Cabinas Chacón to a fork, where you veer left, cross a bridge, and head over the hill to a pasture, where it narrows to a footpath. The path becomes steep near the bottom and takes about three hours both ways. A longer, guided hike is offered by Cabinas Chacón: they'll drive you up to the páramo near **Cerro de la Muerte,** from where you hike back down into the valley.

San Isidro

❼ *134 km (83 miles) southeast of San José, 205 km (127 mi) northwest of Golfito.*

The second-largest town in the province of San José, San Isidro has a bustling market and colorful, grid-plan streets. The large central square is the town's hub, with a large, modern church towering to the east. A couple of blocks south is the market, where buses depart for San Gerardo de Rivas and Dominical. For those on their way to **Chirripó National Park** (☞ Chapter 2), the market is a good place to stock up on provisions. The regional office of the **National Parks Service** (☎ 771–3155) can provide information about Chirripó and reserve space in the park's cabin. San Isidro has no attractions of its own, but it's not a bad place to get stuck spending a night, since it has friendly inhabitants and a fairly agreeable climate.

Dining and Lodging

$$$ ✕⌧ **Hotel del Sur.** This white, motel-style building with a red barrel-tile roof is 6 kilometers (4 miles) south of town. It is the most comfortable option here, with tile floors, wood furniture, and pastel walls, bedspreads, and cushions. Bedrooms have plain carpets, white walls, black wood furniture, patterned bedspreads, and springy beds; those overlooking the courtyard with its bubbling fountain are nicest. Bungalows farther back offer escape from the drone of the highway. ⌧ *Apdo. 4–8000, San Isidro, P.Z.,* ☎ *771–3033,* 🆇 *771–0527. 48 rooms with bath, 12 bungalows. Restaurant, bar, pool, tennis, basketball, Ping-Pong. DC, MC, V.*

$ ⌧ **Hotel Iguazú.** A couple of blocks north of the main square, opposite the Banco Nacional, the Iguazú has spotless bright bedrooms with tile floors, firm beds, tables, and TVs. Ask for a west-facing window overlooking Chirripó. ⌧ *San Isidro, P.Z.,* ☎ *771–2571. 21 rooms, 16 with bath. V.*

Outdoor Activities and Sports

WHITE-WATER RAFTING

Boasting the country's longest white-water run, the **General River** makes for a fun rafting or kayaking trip. The white water begins to the south of San Isidro, flowing through predominantly agricultural land before winding its way through a rocky canyon. A class III–IV river, it can only be run during the rainiest months (September–November), and is offered by the major rafting companies in San José as a three-day camping expedition. A new company based in San Isidro, **Brunca Tours** (☎ 🆇 771–2150), has begun offering one-day rafting trips on the river.

San Gerardo de Rivas

❽ *20 km (12 mi) northeast of San Isidro.*

Even if you aren't up for the hike into Chirripó National Park, San Gerardo de Rivas is a great place to spend a day. It's a quiet agricultural community with lovely views and an agreeable climate, where the outdoor options include hiking—on the trail up to Chirripó and others—and horseback riding. There are also small hot springs and a waterfall nearby. You can easily visit the area on a day trip from San Isidro or Dominical.

Dominical

❾ *22 km (14 mi) southwest of San Isidro.*

Fifty minutes to the southwest of San Isidro, Dominical, once a sleepy fishing village, is slowly being discovered, but it still has a mere fraction of the tourists found at Jacó or Manuel Antonio. It is certainly no less beautiful than Manuel Antonio—the steep hillsides are covered with lush foliage, palm-lined beaches, waterfalls, and the green **Barú River** flowing into the Pacific. The beaches are long and practically empty, perfect for strolling and shell collecting, with several excellent surf breaks offshore.

Dominical's magic lies in its combination of terrestrial and marine wonders. The rain forest grows right up to the beach at some points; the sea offers world-class sportfishing, surfing, and skin diving. There are several good surf breaks in and around Dominical, which is why there are surfers always hanging around, but the ocean can be dangerous for swimmers when the waves are big. For deep-sea fishing fans: During the dry season, Tropical Waters can arrange sportfishing charters out of their office in the center of town. **Ballena National Park,** 20 kilometers (12 miles) to the southeast of Dominical, protects a long beach, sandy point, and a collection of offshore islets. They weren't charging an entrance fee in mid-1996, since there are so many ways to enter the park. Boat tours are available to the park as well as to more distant **Caño Island.**

There is also plenty to see and do on land at Dominical. Several private nature reserves are trying to finance preservation of the rain forest through ecotourism by offering hiking and horseback tours. **Hacienda Barú** is definitely the best organized, leading such unusual tours as a trip into the rain-forest canopy, which entails being hoisted up to a platform in the crown of a giant tree, and a night spent in a shelter in the woods. Another private reserve 12 kilometers (8 miles) north of town offers horseback trips to the **Nauyaca Waterfalls,** where several cascades pour into a natural swimming pool; visits can be arranged through hotels in Dominical or by calling the reserve's owner, Don Lulo (☎ 771–3187). The **Pozo Azul** is a waterfall in the jungle about 5 kilometers (3 miles) south of town, which is accessible by foot or on horseback. Another popular excursion is the inner-tube trip down the **Barú River,** which can be arranged through your hotel or Tropical Waters.

Dining and Lodging

$$ ✕ **Manigordo.** Occupying the second floor of Dominical's only shop-
★ ping center, this restaurant relies on pink stuccoed walls, a red tile floor, and original paintings for ambience. Italian chef Roberto Bearch prepares such authentic Old World dishes as penne *arrabbiata* (in a spicy red sauce), while taking advantage of the local supply of fresh seafood with spaghetti *frutti di mare* (with seafood) and *pesce al cartoccio* (fish stuffed with tomatoes in a white wine sauce). ✉ *Plaza Pacífica, no phone. No credit cards. Closed Wed.*

$–$$ ✕ **San Clemente.** Since this place is the local surfer hangout, it is most crowded whenever it is too dark or too flat to catch a wave. Dozens of broken surfboards hang between the rafters and the corrugated metal roof; Foosball and pool table occupy most of the floor space. Seating is in wooden booths, inside and out in the garden, and satellite TV keeps customers in touch with the U.S. goings-on. They serve good seafood dishes, Tex-Mex delicacies such as burritos and nachos, veggie food, and, of course, your basic burger. ☎ *787–0026. No credit cards.*

$$$ ✕▥ **Villas Río Mar.** Upriver from the beach, this is Dominical's most
★ luxurious hotel. The adobe-style bungalows have thatched roofs, white tile floors, and cane ceilings. Though the rooms and baths are on the small side, each has a large porch with several chairs, a hammock, a dining area, a wet bar with fridge, and mosquito-net curtains that make it insect-proof at night. The bungalows are set amid nicely landscaped grounds, surrounding a large pool with a bar and fountain. The restaurant sits beneath a giant thatched roof, with lots of plants and bamboo, colorful cushions, and elegant table settings. The menu ranges from

such Costa Rican standards as *gallos* (black beans and rice) to freshly caught shrimps served Newburg style. ✉ *Apdo. 1746–2050, San José,* ☎ *283–5013,* FAX *224–2053. 40 rooms with bath. Restaurant, bar, pool, exercise room, tennis court. AE, DC, MC, V.*

$$–$$$ ✕🏨 **Escaleras Inn.** Tucked away in the jungle overlooking the Pacific, the tiny Escaleras opened in the spring of 1995 and is a welcome addition to the area. The spacious guest rooms, decorated with colorful natural fabrics and plants, have hardwood floors, tile baths, pressurized hot water, and queen-size orthopedic mattresses. The restaurant, where meals are served both indoors and out, has a spiffy international menu specializing in seafood and fresh vegetables. After dinner relax in the hotel's library or watch the stars from the large terrace. ✉ *Suite 2277 SJO, Box 025216, Miami, FL 33102 (turnoff for inn is 3.5 km/2 mi south of Dominical on coast highway),* ☎ FAX *771–5247. 3 rooms (expansion was under way in mid-1996). Restaurant, bar, pool, snorkeling, boating. AE, MC, V.*

$$ ✕🏨 **Cabinas Punta Dominical.** Perched on a point in the jungle over-
★ looking rocky Dominicalito Beach, at the southern end of Dominical Beach, these simple cabins were designed to take advantage of the fantastic views. Built of local hardwoods, the cabins have plenty of windows, large balconies, and ceiling fans. Each unit sleeps four people. ✉ *Apdo. 196, San Isidro de El General (5 km/3 mi south of bridge),* ☎ FAX *771–0283. 4 cabins with bath. Restaurant, bar. AE, MC, V.*

$$–$$$ 🏨 **Hacienda Barú.** These bungalows are part of a large private reserve, which makes it a great spot for anyone who wants to explore the rain forest. Each bungalow has a small kitchen, sitting room, and either two or three bedrooms. Although the decor is basic—red cement floors and bare white walls—you'll probably spend most of your time in the forest or on the beach. Outdoor activities include horseback riding, a variety of guided hikes, an hour on a platform in the rain-forest canopy, and an overnight at a shelter in the heart of the forest. The bungalows are a good deal for three or four people. ✉ *Selva Mar c/o AAA Express Mail, 1641 N.W. 79th Ave., Miami, FL 33126–1105 (from center of Dominical, the hotel is 1,000 yds. along carretera [highway] to Quepos),* ☎ FAX *771–1903. 6 bungalows. Kitchenettes. AE, MC, V.*

$ 🏨 **Cabinas San Clemente.** Just across the road from the beach and south of the Barú River, this small lodge is a real bargain, with a variety of rooms and several small houses for rent. Rooms are well-ventilated and have screens, fans, hardwood floors, and small tile baths. ✉ *Dominical,* ☎ FAX *771–1972. 18 rooms with bath, 5 houses. Restaurant, bar, laundry service. No credit cards.*

San Vito

⑩ *267 km (166 mi) southwest of San José, 93 km (58 km) northeast of Golfito.*

San Vito is a charming little town that lies at an altitude of 3,150 feet, close to the Panama border. It owes its foundation in 1952 to a government scheme whereby 200 Italian families were given grants to convert the rain forest into coffee, fruit, and cattle farms. After much initial hardship and wrangling over the size of the agreed grant, a relatively large modern town with some 40,000 inhabitants quickly sprang up. Since it lies near the **Coto Brus Indian Reservation,** San Vito is one of the few towns in Costa Rica where you might see **Guaymí Indians,** who are easy to spot, thanks to the colorful dresses worn by the women.

It's also a good place to enjoy some Italian food, but the real reason folks head to this corner of Costa Rica is to explore the nearby botanical garden.

Six kilometers (4 miles) south of San Vito is the fantastic **Wilson Botanical Garden.** These 25 hillside acres were converted from a coffee plantation in 1961 by U.S. landscapers Robert and Catherine Wilson, who planted a huge collection of tropical species (today the gardens hold around 3,000 native species and 4,000 exotic species), including palms (an amazing 700 species!), orchids, aroids, ferns, bromeliads, heliconias, and marantas, all linked by a series of neat grass paths. The property was transferred to the Organization for Tropical Studies (OTS) in 1973 and in 1983 became part of the **Amistad Biosphere Reserve.** Destroyed by fire in 1994, the facilities, including the main building, have been completely rebuilt. The garden functions mainly as a research and educational center, but visitors are welcome (☞ *Also* Dining and Lodging, *below*). Helpful booklets provide you with a self-guided tour. ⊠ *Apdo. 73–8257, San Vito,* ☎ ℻ *773–3278.* ☞ *$16 (including lunch).* ⊙ *Daily 7:30–5.*

OFF THE **CIUDAD NEILY** – The 33 kilometers (21 miles) that separate San Vito from
BEATEN PATH Ciudad Neily are twisty and spectacular, with views over the Coto Colorado plain to the Golfo Dulce and Osa Peninsula beyond. Much of this steep terrain is covered with tropical forest, which makes it an ideal route for bird-watching and photography.

Dining and Lodging

$ ✕ **Pizzeria Liliana.** A simple, small-town restaurant near San Vito's cen-
★ tral square, the Liliana serves large portions of good food at remarkably low prices. The decor is basic, with wooden tables and a bar at one end, but the pastas and pizzas are tasty. Go for the baked chicken or the steak with mushroom sauce if you aren't up for Italian. ⊠ *1½ blocks west of central square,* ☎ *773–3080. Reservations not accepted. No credit cards.*

$$$$ ✕⌸ **Wilson Botanical Garden.** A row of 12 cabins line a ridge in the
★ heart of the garden, with hardwood floors, high ceilings, and large balconies that overlook the forest and distant mountains. Bird watchers can spot rare species from their rooms, while botanical enthusiasts need merely walk down the hill. Four guest cabins that survived the 1994 fire have small sitting rooms and large windows. Two cabins are equipped for travelers using wheelchairs. Rates are high, but remember that you get three hearty meals a day with the room, and, besides, you are also helping to maintain the garden. Staying overnight is the easiest way to see the garden at dusk and dawn, a highly recommended experience. ⊠ *OTS Apdo. 676-2050, San Pedro,* ☎ *240–6696,* ℻ *240–6783. 30 beds in halls with shared bath, 16 cabins with private bath. Restaurant.* V.

$ ✕⌸ **Hotel El Ceibo.** El Ceibo's owner, Antonio, arrived here from Italy at age two, and he'll readily chat about early San Vito life at the bar. His modern bedrooms are pleasant and clean—foam rubber mattresses are their only drawback—and the bathrooms have powerful, hot showers. Those in the back of the two-story buildings overlook a forested ravine. The airy restaurant, with its sloping wood ceiling, arched windows, and wine trolley, serves solidly good fare. After dinner, relax at the bar with its comfortable sofas and TV. ⊠ *San Vito (center of San Vito behind the Municipalidad),* ☎ ℻ *773–3025. 40 rooms with bath. Restaurant, bar.* MC, V.

$ 🏚 **Cabinas Las Mirlas.** These wooden cabins are set on stilts overlooking a creek and a wooded park and have hardwood and tile floors, white walls, and showers. More basic than those at El Ceibo, the rooms are also around half the price. Take the road to Coto Brus and, after passing the Parque Educativo Aprenabrus, look for the sign on the left after 400 yards. ✉ *San Vito,* ☎ *773–3054. 8 cabins with bath. No credit cards.*

Shopping

An old farm house on the east side of the road between San Vito and the botanical garden houses a shop called **Cántaros** (☎ 773–3760), which features handicrafts by the local Guaymí and Buruca Indians, as well as ceramics from San José artists. Profits from sales help support the adjacent children's library.

La Amistad National Park

⓫ *40 km (25 mi) northwest of San Vito.*

La Amistad National Park, at 490,000 acres, is by far the largest park in the country, but it is actually a mere portion of the vast Amistad Biosphere Reserve—a collection of protected areas that stretches from southern Costa Rica into western Panama (☞ Chapter 8). The park itself covers altitudes ranging from 700 to 11,600 feet, with an array of ecosystems that hold two-thirds of the country's vertebrate species. Unfortunately, the national park is practically inaccessible, but the wilderness it protects can be experienced in the nearby **Las Tablas Protected Zone**, where La Amistad Lodge is located (☞ Dining and Lodging, *below*).

Dining and Lodging

$$–$$$ ✕🏚 **La Amistad Lodge.** This remote, Swiss-style lodge in the tiny border town of Las Mellizas, where blue mountains run crookedly into Panama, was once a private family home. On a 3,000-acre farm in the Las Tablas Protected Zone, contiguous with the forests of La Amistad National Park, it is a good base for venturing off into Costa Rica's least-explored territory. Walk the trails with a guide or relax beside a huge fieldstone fireplace in a second-floor salon. Rooms are sparsely but comfortably furnished, with firm beds. Only 90 minutes from San Vito by four-wheel-drive Jeep, the lodge has packages that include meals, tours, and round-trip land transportation from San José. ✉ *Apdo. 774–1000, San José; reservations c/o Tropical Rainbow Tours,* ☎ *233–8228,* 🖷 *255–4636. Restaurant, bar. AE, MC, V.*

Golfito

⓬ *339 km (211 mi) southeast of San José, 58 km (36 mi) northwest of Paso Canoas: the Panamanian border.*

Once thriving, the Golfito area was devastated when United Fruit pulled out in 1985 due to labor disputes, rising export taxes, and a diminishing Pacific banana market. The company had arrived in 1938 to supplement its diseased plantations in Limón, and Golfito became the center of activity, with a dock that could handle 4,000 bananas per hour and elegant housing for its plantation managers. In order to inject new life into Golfito, the government declared the town a duty-free port in 1990. The **Depósito Libre** (Duty-free Zone) does much of its business during the month preceding Christmas, when it can be very difficult to find a room in Golfito, especially on weekends.

Golfito is beautifully situated overlooking a small gulf (hence its name) and is hemmed in by a steep bank of forest, all of which lies within protected areas. At the northwestern end is the so-called **American zone,** full of elegant stilted wooden houses where the expatriate managers lived, courtesy of United Fruit. With a golf course nearby, life here must have been just about bearable. The hills behind Golfito are covered with the lush forest of the **Golfito Wildlife Refuge** and the adjacent **Piedras Blancas National Park,** which makes it a good area for bird-watching. Follow the main road northwest through the old American zone, past the air strip, and a new housing project, where a dirt road heads into the rain forest—this is the best area to see birds. If you have four-wheel drive, you can follow that dirt track through the heart of Piedras Blancas National Park to the community of **La Gamba,** the **Esquinas Rain Forest Lodge,** and **Villa Briceño,** on the Inter-American Highway. This back route can cut miles off a trip to or from the north, and it passes through a gorgeous patch of wilderness.

Although Golfito doesn't have a beach itself, **Playa Cacao** lies just across the bay from town—just a five-minute boat ride. The beach has several restaurants and lodges, which make it a convenient option when the hotels in Golfito fill up. The old banana port can also serve as a base for trips into the Golfo Dulce, to Zancudo, or Pavones—two remote and beautiful spots that are reached by boat or by four-wheel-drive vehicle.

Outdoor Activities and Sports

SPORTFISHING

There is some great fishing to be had out of Golfito, either in the Golfo Dulce or out in the open ocean. This area has plenty of sailfish, marlin, and roosterfish during the dry months, with dolphin and wahoo during the rainy season, and excellent bottom fishing any time of year. **Golfito Sportfishing** (☎ 288–5083) can arrange charters, as can **Roy Ventura** (☎ 775–0515, ℻ 775–0631) in nearby Zancudo.

Shopping

Bargains on such imported items as TV sets, stereos, linens, and tires are what draw most visitors to Golfito. Tourists can shop in the **Depósito Libre,** but you won't find things much cheaper than they are at home. To purchase things in the Depósito you have to spend the night, which means you register in the afternoon, with your passport, and shop the next morning. Shopping here is sheer madness during December.

Playa Zancudo

⑬ *32 km (20 mi) south of Golfito.*

Playa Zancudo is a long, palm-lined beach with a tiny fishing village behind it, which can be reached either by road or by hiring a boat at the municipal dock. Zancudo has a good surf break, but it is nothing compared with Pavones. There are also some good swimming areas, and if you get tired of playing in the surf and sand, you can arrange a boat trip to the nearby mangrove estuary to see birds and crocodiles. Zancudo is also home to the area's best sportfishing operation.

Dining and Lodging

$$ ✕ **Cabinas Sol y Mar.** A 20-minute walk south of where the boat ★ from Golfito drops you, these beachside cabins are easily the nicest place to stay in Zancudo. The owners have designed and built structures that look like polyhedral space modules, furnished Asian style with elegant charcoal clay tiles, wooden beds, and white canvas sofas. Transportation can be arranged from the dock if you call ahead. ✉ *Apdo. 87, Golfito,* ☎ FAX *775–0353. 4 cabins with bath. Restaurant. V.*

Outdoor Activities and Sports

SPORTFISHING

If you've got your own gear, you can do some good shore fishing from the beach or the mouth of the mangrove estuary, or hire one of the local boats to take you out into the gulf. **Roy Ventura** (☞ *above*) runs the best charter operation in the area, picking up customers in Golfito and Puerto Jiménez as well.

Playa Pavones

⑭ *45 km (28 mi) south of Golfito.*

On the southern edge of the Golfo Dulce's mouth stands Pavones, a wind-swept spot at the end of a dirt road. Famous among surfers for having one of the longest waves in the world, the area also boasts pristine beaches and virgin rain forest. It's far from everything—with neither phones nor electricity—but there are ample attractions for adventurous travelers willing to make the trip.

Dining and Lodging

$$–$$$ ✕🏠 **Tiskita Jungle Lodge.** South of Golfito, 2½ hours by car (15 min-
★ utes by plane), Peter Aspinall has planted 100 different fruit trees from all over the world as a kind of research exercise into alternative exports for Costa Rica. For his guests he has built wooden cabins on stilts, surrounded by screens and lush vegetation and equipped with rustic furniture and open bathrooms from which you can observe wildlife. Trails allow you to safely explore the jungle and the wide variety of wildlife lured by the fruit trees' fine pickings. Other activities include horseback riding, snorkeling (equipment available), swimming, and beachcombing. ✉ *c/o Costa Rica Sun Tours, Apdo. 1195–1250, Escazú,* ☎ *255–2011,* FAX *255–3529. 12 cabins with bath. Dining room. AE, DC, MC, V. Closed Sept.–Oct.*

Puerto Jiménez

⑮ *364 km (226 mi) southeast of San José.*

There isn't much to write home about in Puerto Jiménez, a one-horse town surrounded by pastures and rice fields. Its claim to fame is that it's the biggest town on the Osa Peninsula, which holds one of the largest expanses of wilderness left in the country. There aren't any pigeons in this urban center, but you are likely to see scarlet macaws flying noisily over the rooftops or perched in the Indian almond trees. The headquarters of the **National Parks Service** (☎ 735–5036) are at the southern end of town, opposite the Texaco gas station. This is where you obtain permission to enter **Corcovado National Park,** ask about hiking routes and present conditions, and arrange meals and lodging at the **Sirena ranger station.** During the dry season, you'll want to reserve park admission, meals, and accommodations well ahead of time.

Most people spend a night here either before or after visiting Corcovado. A truck that carries hikers to Carate leaves from the Mini Mercado El Tigre every morning, and taxis cruising town can be hired to take you to the **Rincón River,** near Los Patos. If you have a four-wheel-drive vehicle, it's just a 30-minute drive to Dos Brazos, and the Tigre sector of the park, which few hikers explore. It also lies just 40 minutes from spectacular **Cabo Matapalo,** where virgin rain forest meets the sea at a rocky point. Puerto Jiménez is also a good base for boat or sea kayaking trips on the **Golfo Dulce,** or to one of the nearby mangrove estuaries and rivers.

Dining and Lodging

$$ ✕🏠 **Cabinas Manglares.** Although fairly basic, this white, quasicolonial group of cabinas is the most comfortable accommodation in Puerto Jiménez itself. The cabins have tile floors, white walls decorated with *artesanía* (arts and crafts), fans, tables, and comfy wooden beds. Five of them stand by the parking lot, and five are scattered around a lawn on the other side of the mangroves, which are crossed by a catwalk. A thatched roof covers the restaurant, which serves fresh seafood and pizza. Located across from the airport, a 10-minute walk will get you here from where the *lancha* (ferry) drops you. ✉ *Apdo. 55–8203, Puerto Jiménez,* ☎ *735–5002,* 🆑 *735–5121. 10 rooms with bath. Restaurant, bar. MC, V.*

$ ✕🏠 **Restaurante Carolina.** This popular restaurant in the heart of town has simple rooms in back, making it a good spot for backpackers on their way in or out of Corcovado. Rooms are your basic cement boxes, with private bathrooms and cold running water, but at least they are clean and convenient. The daily truck to Carate leaves from in front of the restaurant, which has the typical Tico menu, plus some fresh seafood. ☎ *735–5007. 5 rooms with bath. Restaurant. No credit cards.*

Shopping

On the north side of the road to Puerto Jiménez, near the community of La Palma, is a thatch-roofed building that is the seat of a local women's association: **ASOFEP.** The building includes a simple shop that sells locally produced handicrafts. The profits help support the town library and ASOFEP activities.

Corcovado National Park

🔟 *There are three entrances to Corcovado: San Pedrillo to the north, Los Patos to the east, and La Leona to the south.*

Comprising 108,000 acres, Corcovado National Park is one of the largest and wildest protected areas in the country. Much of the park is covered with virgin rain forest, where massive *espavel* and *nazareno* trees tower over the trails, thick lianas hang from their branches, and animals such as toucans, spider monkeys, scarlet macaws, and poison dart frogs abound. There are no roads in the park, and the ones that approach it are dirt tracks that require four-wheel-drive vehicles most of the year. Visitors to Corcovado often arrive by boat from Drake Bay or Carate, but the best way to explore the park is to sling on a backpack and hike into the wilderness.

There are three hiking routes into Corcovado (☞ Chapter 2), two of which begin near Puerto Jiménez, the other in Drake Bay, which follows the coast down to San Pedrillo. You can hire a taxi in Puerto Jiménez to go to the Los Patos trailhead, or at least to the first crossing of the Río Rincón (from where you have to hike a few kilometers upriver to the trailhead). The beach route, via La Leona, starts in Carate, about 16 kilometers (10 miles) southwest of Puerto Jiménez. A four-wheel-drive truck carries hikers to Carate every day, departing Puerto Jiménez at 6 AM and returning at 7:30 PM; for information call the Mini Mercado El Tigre (☎ 735–5075).

Dining and Lodging

$$$$ ✕🏠 **Corcovado Lodge.** It isn't easy to get here—the lodge is accessi-
★ ble only by air—but the effort is certainly worth it. Costa Rica Expeditions runs this beachfront property, 20 tents pitched on wooden platforms with single beds, adjacent to the southern border of Corcovado. There are communal bathrooms and a bar/restaurant that serves family-style meals. Explore the forest canopy from a platform 100 feet off the forest floor with a naturalist guide, hike the many nature trails, or relax on the quiet beach. Bring a flashlight—there's electricity only a few hours each day—you'll need it to get around at night. Planes depart from San José via Carate every Wednesday and Friday. ✉ *Apdo. 6941–1000, San José,* ☎ *257–0766,* 🅵🅰🆇 *257–1665. 20 tents. Restaurant, bar. AE, MC, V.*

Cabo Matapalo

⑰ *16 km (10 mi) south of Puerto Jiménez.*

The southern tip of the Osa Peninsula possesses the kind of natural beauty that people are happy to travel halfway across the country to experience. Its ridges afford views of the blue Pacific, where schools of dolphin and whales may sometimes be spotted in the distance. The forest is tall and dense, its giant trees draped with thick lianas, branches covered with aerial gardens of bromeliads and orchids. The translation of Cabo Matapalo is "Strangler Fig Cape," a reference to the fig trees that germinate in the branches of other trees and eventually grow to smother them with their roots and branches. Strangler figs are common to the area, as they are nearly everywhere in the country, but Matapalo's greatest attractions are its rarer species, like the brilliant scarlet macaw and the *gallinazo* tree, which bursts into yellow blossom as the rainy season draws to an end.

A forested ridge extends east from Corcovado, where the foliage clings to almost vertical slopes and waves crash against the black rocks below. This continuous forest corridor is protected within a series of private preserves, which means that Cabo Matapalo has most of the same wildlife as the national park—even the big cats. Most of the point itself lies within the private reserves of the area's two main hotels, and that forest is crisscrossed by footpaths, some of which head to tranquil beaches, or to waterfalls that pour into small pools. On the eastern side of the point, the waves break over a platform that creates a perfect right that draws surfers from far away. The area also has excellent sea kayaking, and both the big hotels can arrange horseback excursions, guided tours to Corcovado, or deep-sea fishing.

Dining and Lodging

$$$$ ✕🏠 **Bosque del Cabo.** The tip of the point lies within the 200-acre grounds of this nature lodge, more than half of which is primary forest. Rustic, wooden bungalows are scattered along the edge of a wide lawn—from here, guests can enjoy breathtaking views of the ocean. Each bungalow is slightly different, but they all have wood floors, private baths, solar energy, and porches with hammocks. Meals are served in a simple, open-air restaurant, with a cement floor and thatched roof. Trails wind down through the forest to two secluded beaches and a waterfall with a natural swimming pool. Activities include horseback riding, sportfishing, surfing, sea kayaking, and bird-watching. ✉

Puerto Jiménez (55 yds. to the north of gas station), ☎ *735–5206,* FAX
735–5206. 6 rooms with bath. Restaurant, horseback riding. AE,
MC.

$$$$ ✕🏨 **Lapa Rios.** More than one of Costa Rica's finest hotels, Lapa Rios
★   is part of an innovative conservation project. Owners Karen and John
Lewis built the hotel as part of an effort to preserve a patch of endangered
wildlife, and the money guests spend there helps them pay off the mort-
gage on the hotel's 1,000-acre nature reserve. Guests can explore the
pristine wilderness on foot or horseback, accompanied by naturalist
guides, but the wildlife that can be spotted from the rooms and restaurant is simply amazing. The hotel is spread along a ridge, surrounded
by the jungle, with views of the nearby ocean. Spacious bungalows feature thatched roofs, hardwood floors, large balconies, and screened walls,
which make the best of the ocean breezes and views. The bar and restaurant sit beneath a giant thatched roof, with a spiral staircase leading
up to a lookout platform at the peak, and a long porch that is a great
bird-watching spot. The kitchen prepares some of the best food in the
country, specializing in fresh seafood, fruit, and vegetables. ✉ *Box
025216, SJO 706, Miami, FL 33102–5216,* ☎ *735–5130,* FAX *735–5179.
14 bungalows with bath. Restaurant, bar, pool, horseback riding. AE,
MC, V.*

Drake Bay

⑱   *40 km (25 mi) southwest of Palmar Sur, 10 km (6 mi) north of Corcovado.*

Drake Bay, to the north of Corcovado, was named after Sir Francis
Drake, the British explorer who, legend has it, anchored there some
400 years ago. The only road into this isolated area is a muddy track
that could swallow a Jeep, and apart from those who come on the occasional sea plane, the only arrivals are by boat via the Sierpe River,
or by hiking north out of Corcovado. Thanks to its inaccessibility, Drake
Bay remains a wild and scenic spot, where the forest rises up behind
the beaches and rocky points, and monkeys, ospreys, toucans, and
macaws are common sights. The town of Drake is scattered along the
bay, and its inhabitants earn their living by fishing, farming the hin-
terlands, or from tourism.

Several nature lodges stand at the southern end of the bay, near the
Agujitas River. They offer access to the area's luxuriant forests and rich
marine resources. The forests around Drake hold plenty of wildlife and
can be explored on foot or horseback. Another popular diversion is
to paddle up the **Agujitas River** at high tide. Most of the lodges run
guided tours to the **San Pedrillo** sector of Corcovado, where you can
see even more wildlife, and an ancient trail runs along the coast between Drake Bay and San Pedrillo—it's about a three-hour hike. The
ocean here is just as big an attraction as the rain forest, and the big
lodges offer snorkeling and scuba trips to nearby **Caño Island,** and deep-
sea fishing.

Dining and Lodging

$$$$ ✕🏨 **Aguila de Osa Inn.** The philosophy behind this place is that just
★   because you're out in the woods doesn't mean you have to rough it.
Rooms are perched along a ridge, with views of the bay below and the
surrounding greenery. Each has a unique hand-carved door, ceiling fans,
colorful bedspreads, original art, and spacious tile baths with brass fix-
tures. The restaurant and bar sit under a thatched roof and have an

impressive hardwood floor and ocean view. Meals are served family style, but the quality is comparable with that of San José's finest restaurants, and the fish has usually been caught that day by a guest. The inn specializes in sportfishing and has a fleet of four boats and an extensive tackle room, but it also runs scuba and snorkeling excursions to Caño Island, natural history tours to Corcovado, and horseback trips through the nearby forest. All meals are included. Transportation can be arranged in San José. ✉ *Apdo. 10486–1000, San José,* ☎ *296–2190,* ℻ *232–7722. 14 rooms with bath. Restaurant, bar, horseback riding, boating. AE, MC, V.*

$$$$ ✕🖫 **Drake Bay Wilderness Camp.** One of the area's oldest lodges, the Wilderness Camp is just across the Agujitas River from Aguila de Osa. Most of the people who stay here come to see the rain forest, but scuba diving and sportfishing are also offered. Cabins scattered around the manicured grounds have cement floors, ceiling fans, and hot-water showers. The small, open-air bar has an ocean view; the dining hall is more enclosed. Unfortunately, most rooms don't have great views. Tent cabins with shared baths are less expensive. All meals and laundry service are included in the price. Horseback tours and canoeing on the Agujitas River are offered, but the most popular excursions are to Corcovado and Caño Island. The camp can arrange transportation from Palmar Norte or San José. ✉ *Apdo. 98–8150, Palmar Norte,* ☎ ℻ *771–2436 or 285–4367. 20 cabins with bath, 5 tent cabins with shared bath. Restaurant, bar, horseback riding, boating, dive center. MC, V.*

$$$$ ✕🖫 **Marenco.** Covering about 500 hectares of rain forest along the
★   coast between Drake Bay and Corcovado National Park, the Marenco Biological Reserve was one of the country's first ecotourism enterprises. Simple rooms and an open-air dining hall overlook the beach from a high ridge. All rooms have hardwood floors, thatched roofs, small bathrooms, and porches facing the ocean. ✉ *Apdo. 4025–1000, San José (11 km/7 mi north of Drake Bay),* ☎ *221–1594,* ℻ *255–1346. 25 rooms with bath. Dining room. AE, MC, V.*

Caño Island

⑲ *19 km (12 mi) off the Osa Peninsula, due west of Drake Bay.*

Most of the 740 acres of this uninhabited island are covered in evergreen forest containing fig, locust, and rubber trees. Coastal Indians used it as a burial ground, and the numerous bits and pieces unearthed here have prompted archaeologists to speculate about pre-Columbian long-distance maritime trade. The island's big attraction is the ocean, which offers superb conditions for scuba diving and snorkeling. Lodges listed under Drake Bay offer day trips to Caño, as does Selva Mar (☎ 771–1903) in Dominical.

THE SOUTHWEST A TO Z

Arriving and Departing

By Bus

Buses from San José to **Jacó** leave C. 16 between Avdas. 1 and 3 (Coca-Cola Bus Station, ☎ 223–1109) daily at 7:15 and 10:30 AM and 3:30 PM, returning at 5 AM and 3 PM, with more frequent direct buses on weekends, (2½-hour trip); to **Manuel Antonio/Quepos** from the Coca-Cola Station (☎ 223–5567) daily at 6 AM, noon, and 6 PM (3½-hour trip), returning at 6 AM, noon, and 5 PM; to **San Isidro** daily from Musoc, next to the Coca-Cola Station (☎ 222–2422), hourly between 5:30 AM and 5 PM (three-hour trip, returning at the same times); to **Dominical** via Quepos from the Coca-Cola Station (☎ 223–5567) daily at 3 PM (six-hour trip), returning at 5:30 AM; to **Golfito** from Avda. 18 between C. 2 and 4 (☎ 221–4214) daily at 7 AM, 11 AM, and 3 PM (eight-hour trip), returning at 5 AM and 1 PM; to **Puerto Jiménez** from C. 12 between Avdas. 7 and 9 (☎ 771–2550) at 6 AM and noon (eight-hour trip), returning at 5 and 11 AM; to **San Vito** from C. 14 between Avdas. 3 and 5 (☎ 222–2750) daily at 5:45, 8:15, and 11:30 AM and 2:45 PM (seven-hour trip).

By Plane

Sansa (☎ 221–9414) flies to Quepos, Golfito, Palmar Sur, and Coto 47. **Travelair** (☎ 220–3054) flies to Quepos, Golfito, Palmar Sur, and Puerto Jiménez.

By Car

The quickest way to reach the coastal route that leads to Tárcoles, Jacó, and Quepos is to take the Inter-American Highway west past the airport to the turnoff for Atenas, turning left and driving through Atenas to Orotina, where you head south on the coastal highway. The rest of the Southwest is best reached by taking the Inter-American Highway south, past Cartago and over the Cerro de la Muerte to San Isidro, El General Valley, and the Osa Peninsula. Foggy conditions atop Cerro de la Muerte make it best to travel that route as early in the day as possible.

Getting Around

By Boat

A small ferry crosses the Golfo Dulce, leaving Puerto Jiménez at 6 AM and returning from Golfito at 11:30 AM. You can negotiate with the boat owners at the **Muelle Público,** a pier north of the gas station, for rides to Zancudo or the more distant Pavones; it is cheaper, however, to locate someone who is already headed that way. Drake Bay is usually reached by boat from Sierpe, south of Palmar Norte.

By Bus

Buses leave Puntarenas for Quepos daily at 5 AM and 2:30 PM (three hours) and leave Quepos for Dominical daily at 3 PM (3½ hours). From San Isidro, buses leave for Dominical at 5:30 AM, 1:30 and 3 PM (one-hour trip); for San Gerardo de Rivas, the trailhead for Chirripó, at 5 AM and 2 PM; for Puerto Jiménez at 9 AM and 3 PM (five-hour trip). A truck for hikers leaves Puerto Jiménez daily at 6 AM for Carate, returning at 7:30 AM.

By Car

To reach Carara, Jacó, Quepos/Manuel Antonio, and Tárcoles take the Inter-American Highway west past the airport to the exit for Atenas, where you turn left, and drive through Atenas to Orotina, where the coastal highway heads south to Jacó and Quepos. A dirt road heads south from Quepos to Dominical, but the easiest way to reach the rest of the Southwest is to take the Inter-American Highway south, via Cartago, over the Talamanca Mountains to San Isidro, where paved roads head northeast to San Gerardo de Rivas and west to Dominical. A dirt track follows the coast south from Dominical, passing Ballena

National Park, to Cortez and the Inter-American Highway, but it requires four-wheel drive. The Inter-American Highway continues southeast from San Isidro to the turnoffs for San Vito, Puerto Jiménez, and Golfito, before reaching Paso Canoas and the border of Panama. The dirt road to Puerto Jiménez and Cabo Matapalo was in bad shape at press time. The turnoff for the back road to Golfito (four-wheel drive only) is on the right at Villa Briceño; look for signs to La Gamba and the Esquinas lodge.

By Plane
Aeronaves (☎ 775–0278), in Golfito, and **Aerotaxi Alfa Romeo** (☎ 735–5178) offer charter flights to Carate, Drake Bay, Puerto Jiménez, Sirena, Tiskita, and anywhere else you want to go. You have to charter the whole plane, which is expensive, so it's best to fill it with the maximum capacity of five.

Contacts and Resources

Emergencies
Police (☎ 911, or 117 in towns, 127 in rural areas). **Traffic Police** (☎ 227–8030). **Fire** (☎ 118). **Ambulance** (☎ 221–5818).

Guided Tours
An array of tours are offered out of Jacó by **Fantasy Tours** (☎ 643–3032), which has an office in the Hotel Jacó Beach; the most popular being hiking in Carara, a boat trip to a secluded beach nearby, and crocodile watching on the Tárcoles River. In Quepos, **Lynch Travel** (☎ 777–1170) offers several boat trips, horseback tours, sea kayaking, and white-water river rafting. The **Outward Bound School** (☎ 777–0052) offers a variety of outdoor trips, ranging from rock climbing to river rafting. In Manuel Antonio, **Iguana Tours** (☎ 777–1262) specializes in sea kayaking and white-water rafting. **Brunca Tours** (☎ 771–2150), in San Isidro, offers hiking and nature tours to Chirripó and other areas, as well as white-water rafting on the General River. In Dominical, **Tropical Waters** (☎ 771–2264) runs snorkeling tours to Ballena National Park and Caño Island, and can arrange inner tubing on the Barú River and horseback riding tours; **Hacienda Barú** (☎ 771–1903) has a number of guided hikes through the rain forest. In Puerto Jiménez, **Escondido Trex** (☎ 735–5210) guides sea kayaking tours that range from a sunset paddle to a one-week trip that explores the entire Golfo Dulce.

There are also a number of tours to the Southwest that can be arranged out of San José: **Jungle Trails** (☎ 255–3486) has a day tour to Carara that allows visitors to plant an endangered tree to expand the buffer zone, a four-day hiking trip to climb Chirripó, and a five-day camping trip to Corcovado. **Costa Rica Expeditions** (☎ 222–0333) offers guided hikes out of its Corcovado Tent Camp, near Carate, on the southern edge of Corcovado National Park. **Costa Rica Sun Tours** (☎ 255–2011) arranges visits to the remote Tiskita Jungle Lodge (☞ Dining and Lodging, *above*) in the far Southwest at around $400 for four days and three nights.

CRUISES
Cruceros del Sur (☎ 232–6672) runs three- and six-day natural-history cruises along the southern Pacific coast that visit Manuel Antonio and Corcovado National Parks and Caño Island Biological Reserve. It also offers 10-day skin-diving expeditions to distant Cocos Island.

The **Undersea Hunter** (☎ 224–2555) is a smaller vessel that runs similar expeditions to Cocos Island.

Visitor Information

The tourist office in San José has information on the Southwest (☞ Chapter 3). **La Buena Nota** (☎ 777–0345), on the left just after the bridge entering Quepos, is a crafts-shop-cum-informal local information center. **Tropical Waters** (☎ 771–2264) in the center of Dominical has plenty of information on local sights and diversions and can also set up tours.

8 Excursions to Panama

After exploring Costa Rica's Southwest or Atlantic Lowlands, you may wish to head farther south—either to the green hills and mountains of Chiriquí Province or to the islands of the Bocas del Toro Archipelago in the Caribbean Sea. In Chiriquí, you can explore lush rain forests, run raging rivers, or climb Barú Volcano. In the Bocas del Toro you'll find stunning coral reefs and a tumbledown provincial capital.

THE AMERICAN VISION OF PANAMA BEGINS, and seemingly ends, with Teddy Roosevelt, the Panama Canal, and General Manuel Noriega. Throw in an argument, now irrelevant, about who should "own" the canal in the next century, and you've pretty much covered what Americans know about the country. Which is to say very little. Look at Panama on a map. Although it connects the North and South American continents, it lies east to west. And the famous canal, that engineering marvel of the late, great American Imperium, is oriented from the northwest to the southeast. Not at all what one pictures imagining Panama.

Beyond the Canal Zone the country offers many other destinations worthy of a visit. Isolated Chiriquí Province, for example, across the border from Costa Rica, with its agricultural communities surrounded by lush valleys and cloud forests. Or the equally isolated islands of the Bocas del Toro Archipelago, most easily reached from the Atlantic Lowlands region of southeastern Costa Rica, that is just beginning to be "discovered" by travelers.

This chapter begins with an excursion to Chiriquí Province in western Panama (☞ Chapter 7); the second half of the chapter covers the Bocas del Toro Archipelago (☞ Chapter 5).

CHIRIQUÍ PROVINCE

The province of Chiriquí is a land of rolling plains, green mountain valleys, raging rivers, and luxuriant forests. The lowlands were deforested long ago and are now dedicated to pasture and sugar and banana plantations, but the upper slopes of the Talamanca Mountain range remain covered with thick, wildlife-rich cloud forests. Much of the province is home to cowboys and Indians—vast haciendas cover the better part of the lowlands while Guaymí Indian villages pepper the eastern highlands—whereas such agricultural communities as Boquete and Cerro Punta are populated by the descendants of European immigrants. Consequently the province reflects Panama's varied cultural spectrum, which includes half a dozen indigenous ethnicities, a mestizo majority, and the descendants of immigrants from all corners of the world.

Although exposure to the local culture enriches any visit, people are drawn to Chiriquí because of its natural assets. There are several islands and deserted beaches in and along the Gulf of Chiriquí, but the region's greatest attractions lie to the north in the high country of the Talamanca mountain range. The mountain valleys of Cerro Punta and Boquete are blessed with regular precipitation and some of Panama's most fertile soil, which has led to their development as vegetable and coffee farming centers. These tranquil agricultural communities have cool air, splendid views, plenty of outdoor diversions, and good accommodations for every budget.

The mountains above the agricultural communities retain much of their forest cover, which makes them excellent areas for bird watchers or for anyone who enjoys nature. The highland forests are luxuriant year-round thanks to the clouds that are regularly pushed over the continental divide by the trade winds. The abundant mist combines with the afternoon sun to make rainbows, such a common sight in the area that the locals ignore them. It is possible to drive up long-extinct Barú

Volcano, the country's highest peak, in a four-wheel-drive vehicle, but there are dozens of trails through the area's forests that are accessible only to hikers and horses. Two of the rivers that wind down those mountain valleys are currently "run" by professional rafting outfitters.

As you go south from southwestern Costa Rica, with the Inter-American Highway descending into the El General Valley, squat, silvery-green pineapple plants blanket the gentle contours. The road is fast and the scenery spectacular, with the jagged gray-blue profile of the 11,000-foot Cordillera de Talamanca forming a lofty backdrop to the east while the 3,000-foot Fila Costeña attempts a vague symmetry to the west. After Paso Real you can continue on the Inter-American or turn left across the river to San Vito and Wilson Botanical Garden. If you stay with the Inter-American, you'll follow the snaking Río Grande de Térraba through an impressive canyon to Palmar Norte, and Puerto Jiménez, or Golfito.

The San Vito road climbs along a spur ridge south of the Coto Brus Valley. North of the Coto Brus is the vast mountainous Parque Internacional de La Amistad, which, contiguous with the Chirripó Park, forms the largest and most diverse protected area in Costa Rica. Nearly all travelers first head to the provincial capital of David, but since that town has few attractions, you'll want to quickly move on to the nearby highland towns. Boquete is the closest of these, just a short trip due north, whereas Volcán, Bambito, and Cerro Punta all lie near each other, to the northwest of David.

Pleasures and Pastimes

Dining

Western Panama is unlikely to ever become an epicurean mecca, but the region does have a few excellent restaurants and many inexpensive eateries. Panamanian food tends to be a bit greasy, but the kitchens of the mountains of Chiriquí adhere to a more northern—but still fried—style of cooking. There are also a few restaurants that specialize in food from other parts of the world. Unlike Costa Rica, there is no service charge included in the bill at a Panamanian restaurant, so a 10%–15% gratuity is expected.

RATINGS

CATEGORY	COST*
$$$$	over $20
$$$	$10–$20
$$	$5–$10
$	under $5

Per person including a first course, entrée, and dessert; drinks, taxes, and gratuities not included.

Festivals

The annual Feria Internacional in David is a commercial exposition that takes place in late March, which is a good time to avoid this town. Boquete's extensive fair grounds on the east bank of the river are the site of the annual Flower Festival. Held in mid-January, it is a colorful but noisy affair that includes performances of folk music and dancing but lots of loud disco music as well.

Lodging

Since tourism has yet to take off in Panama, there is a relatively small selection of accommodations available in the western provinces. Nevertheless, Chiriquí has several of Panama's nicest hotels. The region's most charming inns are in its stunning mountain valleys, and one of them is set in the middle of the forest. Although you can usually show up and find a room, reservations are necessary during Panamanian holidays (☞ When to Tour Chiriquí, *below*).

RATINGS

CATEGORY	COST*
$$$$	over $90
$$$	$50–$90
$$	$25–$50
$	under $25

For a double room, excluding service and 10% tax.

National Parks

Chiriquí's two national parks, Barú Volcano and La Amistad, both lie within the binational Amistad Biosphere Reserve: a collection of protected areas that together cover the better part of the Talamanca Mountain range. Although most of La Amistad National Park—contiguous with the Costa Rican park of the same name—lies within the province of Bocas del Toro, Chiriquí offers the best access to that protected area. The two sectors of the park accessible from Cerro Punta consist of cloud forest, which is home to the quetzal, the three-wattled bellbird, and the long-tailed silky flycatcher. Barú Volcano National Park covers the northern slope and upper reaches of Panama's only volcano, the peak of which affords views of two oceans, on those rare clear days. That park is home to most of the same wildlife found in La Amistad, which it borders, as well as the rare volcano junco, a bird that lives near the summit. A four-wheel-drive-only road winds its way up to the volcano's summit from Boquete, and a footpath heads up the other side, beginning near Bambito and Volcán. There is also a footpath through the cloud forest on the volcano's northern side, which connects the tiny agricultural outposts of Respingo and Alto Chiquero, above Cerro Punta and Boquete respectively.

Rafting

Two white-water rivers flow out of the Chiriquí highlands with enough water to make them navigable, and two rafting companies currently offer trips down them. The Chiriquí, which pours down from the Fortuna Reservoir, to the northeast of David, is a class-III river during the wet season, which means it can be run by people with no rafting experience. During the rainiest months, October–December, the water level rises and the river gets wilder, with some of the rapids becoming class IV. The Chiriquí Viejo, which begins in the mountains above Cerro Punta and flows through the western end of the province, provides an invigorating class-IV white-water trip that is really only appropriate for people with some rafting experience—the Viejo is only safe to descend during the dry season.

Exploring Chiriquí Province

Great Itineraries

IF YOU HAVE 3 DAYS

Numbers in the text correspond to numbers in the margin and on the Chiriquí Province and the Bocas del Toro Archipelago map.

If you have three days in Chiriquí, you won't want to spend too much time in **David** ①. Head straight for the mountain air of 🏨 **Boquete** ②, which has a good selection of accommodations. You'll want to

Caribbean Sea

Las Tablas

Guabito

Changuinola

Isla
Colón

Bocas del Toro

Almirante

*PARQUE NACIONAL
MARINO ISLA BASTIMENTO*

*PARQUE
INTERNACIONAL
LA AMISTAD*

Chiriquí
Grande

*Golfo de
los Mosquitos*

COSTA
RICA

Cerro
Punta

Volcán
Barú

BOCAS DEL TORO

Volcán

Bambito

Boquete

Caldera

Paso Canoa
Internacional

Concepción

CHIRIQUÍ

David

San Félix

Puerto
Armuelles

*Playa
las Lajas*

Golfo de Chiriquí

get up early the next morning, either for bird watching or the pre-dawn drive up Barú Volcano to catch the sunrise from the summit. You can stay the second night in Boquete, or make the trip to ☷ **Cerro Punta** ⑤, which is higher and thus cooler. Whether you spend one or two nights in Cerro Punta, you'll definitely want to explore the forests of La Amistad National Park. White-water rafting trips are available out of both towns; other diversions include horseback riding, hiking, and mountain biking.

When to Tour Chiriquí

Since Panama's history has differed considerably from Costa Rica's, each country has its own political holidays, whereas they share religious holidays. You'll want to make reservations well ahead of time for travel during most holidays, especially Holy Week (the week leading to Easter Sunday) and Carnival Week, which takes place approximately six weeks before Holy Week. The massive Talamanca Mountain Range divides western Panama into Atlantic and Pacific slopes, and the weather can differ considerably between its two provinces. Chiriquí experiences its nicest weather during the December–May dry season and gets some sunny days in July and August.

David

❶ *37 km (23 mi) east of the border with Costa Rica.*

This provincial capital has little to offer travelers, but it is practically unavoidable, since it is the local transportation hub. The town is the political and economic center for a vast agricultural area, which means it houses banks, rent-a-car companies, and an airport. Not only do the province's scattered inhabitants head here to take care of business, Costa Ricans sometimes travel to David on shopping trips, since most imported items are considerably cheaper in Panama than in Costa Rica. The busy boulevards near the center of town are consequently lined with a variety of modern shops and other businesses. If you wander past some of the clothing and department stores, you may notice the peculiar habit Panamanian salesmen have of clapping, shouting about the merchandise, and walking along next to passersby telling them to come into the store and buy something.

David is a fairly modern, grid-plan city, centered around the shady **Parque Cervantes** and skirted by the Inter-American Highway. It is not a terribly pretty town, and its lowland location means that it is usually very hot. Mountain communities to the north feature more pleasant climates and scenery, but David can be a convenient base for such **day trips** as white-water rafting, a boat tour of the mangroves and islands of the Golfo de Chiriquí, or a day hike on Los Quetzales Trail, which heads through the forest on the northern slope of Barú Volcano.

If you have some extra time in David, you should visit the **Museo José de Obaldía,** on Avenida 8 Este and Calle A Norte (☎ 507/775–7839; ⊙ Tues.–Sat. 8:30–4:30; ⌑ 25¢), which has exhibits about the region's pre-Columbian cultures and colonial history.

A good way to escape the heat is to head to one of the *balnearios* (spas) north of town, on the road to Boquete. These swimming holes in the Río David have open-air bars next to them; although packed on weekends and holidays, they are usually quiet the rest of the time.

Dining and Lodging

$$–$$$ ✕ **Mar del Sur.** The best seafood in David is served at this Peruvian
★ restaurant, which is owned by the same people who run San José's popular Machu Pichu. It is on the north end of town, a few blocks from
the bus station, in a former home. The dining area has tile floors, wooden
ceilings, arched doorways, and a few posters and paintings of Peru hanging on the walls. Appetizers include *ceviche* (raw fish marinated in lemon
with spices), *chicharón de calamar* (deep fried squid), and *papas a la
huancaina* (boiled potatoes in a peanut cream sauce). Entrées, like the
picante de langostinos (prawns in a spicy cream sauce) and the corvina prepared six different ways, are delicious. ☒ *Behind Fe de Dole-
guita supermarket,* ☎ *507/775–0856. AE, MC, V. Closed 3 PM–6 PM.*

$–$$ ✕ **Churrascos Place.** This open-air restaurant, one block from Parque
Cervantes, serves a good selection of inexpensive food and is open 24
hours a day. Plants line two sides of the restaurant, which has a red-
tile floor, a high sloping roof, and a bar on one end. The menu is pretty
basic, with several cuts of beef, fish filets, rice with chicken, soups, and
sandwiches. Main dishes come with a simple salad. ☒ *Avda. 2 Este
and C. Central,* ☎ *507/774–0412. AE, MC, V.*

$$ ✕▥ **Hotel Fiesta.** Just east of town, the Fiesta is David's best hotel. A
one-story affair, with rooms surrounding a large swimming pool, the
Fiesta is slightly run down, but clean and quiet. Rooms are on the small
side, with colorful bedspreads, thin carpeting, tiled baths, air condi-
tioning, and satellite TV. The hotel's large, air-conditioned restaurant
serves an ample selection of international dishes. ☒ *North side of Inter-
American Hwy., 1 km/½ mi east of town,* ☎ *507/775–5454,* FAX
*507/774–4584. 55 rooms with bath. [df]Restaurant, pool. AE, MC,
V.*

$ ▥ **Hotel Iris.** This centrally located hotel offers basic, clean accom-
modations at good rates. The rooms all have tile floors, telephones,
fans, decent beds, and hot-water baths; those with air conditioning and
TV cost a few dollars more. A small restaurant off the lobby serves
the basic Panamanian fare. Ask for a room facing the street or all the
way in back, since these rooms have large windows that make them
cooler and brighter. ☒ *C. A Norte, across from Parque Cervantes,* ☎
FAX *507/775–7233. 62 rooms with bath. [df]Restaurant. MC, V.*

Boquete

② *38 km (24 mi) north of David.*

Boquete is a pleasant little town of wooden houses and colorful gar-
dens that sits 1,175 meters (3,878 feet) above sea level, in the verdant
valley of the Caldera River. For much of the year the trade winds blow
over the mountains and down through that valley, often bringing a mist
that keeps the area green year-round and makes rainbows a common
sight. The mountains above town still have plenty of trees on them,
which makes it a great place for bird watching, and the roads and trails
that head into those hills can be explored on foot, mountain bike, horse-
back, or on four wheels.

Thanks to its rich soil, Boquete has become an important agricultural
center, famous for its coffee, flowers, strawberries, and apples. The com-
bination of good farming conditions and a pleasant climate have led
many Europeans and North Americans to settle here, which is why you'll
see plenty of fair-skinned people and architecture that differs signifi-
cantly from that of the lowlands. From November to February, you

may also see **Guaymí Indians,** who migrate there from the eastern half of Chiriquí to work the coffee harvest. Tidy homes and abundant blossoms make Boquete a nice place for a stroll; a short loop can be made by crossing the **Caldera River** twice on two large suspension bridges.

The real attraction of this area lies a bit higher than town, where several roads and footpaths wind past the farms and forest. The main road forks above town, running into two hilly loops through the mountains that can be driven in any vehicle, hiked, or ridden. Both roads pass some breathtaking views, and patches of forest that hold plenty of birds. The loop reached by veering left is considerably longer, but it passes a small waterfall and much more forest. A dirt road that heads west from that loop leads to Alto Chiquero and the footpath to Cerro Punta. The road to the top of **Barú Volcano** begins in town, heading west from the main road, two blocks north of the blue and white church. A large sign marks the route one block north of the main road; it is paved for the first 7 kilometers (4 miles), after which it becomes a dirt track requiring four-wheel drive for the 14 kilometers (9 miles) to the summit. Mauricio Tour (☎ 507/720–1153) and Río Monte Tours (☎ 507/720–1327) both offer trips to Barú's summit. Other possible day tours include white-water rafting or a visit to the hot springs and pre-Columbian petroglyphs of Caldera.

Dining and Lodging

$ ✗ **Tato's Cafe.** From the outside it doesn't look much different from
★ the rest of Boquete's inexpensive restaurants, but you need only step through the door to realize that Tato has a different view of dining than do most Panamanians. Watercolors hang on the simple white walls, and tables are nicely set with white tablecloths and vases holding dried flowers. Only two or three daily specials are served: hearty meat and fish dishes that are low-fat by Panamanian standards. There's no alcohol, and the restaurant closes at 7:30, but it's a good place for a quick lunch or early dinner. ⊠ *Avda. Central and C. Central, no phone. No credit cards. Closed Thurs.*

$$$ ✗⊞ **Panamonte.** This charming country inn on a quiet street near the
★ Caldera River seems oddly out of place: you would expect to find it in rural New England but not in Central America. The Collins family, of North American origin, has been pleasantly surprising guests since they opened the hotel in 1946. A two-story wooden building painted baby blue holds a lobby adorned with a small collection of colonial art, an elegant restaurant, and several guest rooms; a yellow house across the street has a few more rooms. The restaurant is known for serving the best food in the region, and a large bar in back has a fireplace and views of the garden. The hotel rents horses and mountain bikes, and the in-house tour company, Río Monte, offers bird watching on the family farm, sunrise on Barú's summit, and a coffee tour. ⊠ *Avda. 11 de Abril (right at fork after town),* ☎ *507/720–1327,* 𝖥𝖠𝖷 *507/720–1324. 19 rooms with bath. Restaurant, bar, horseback riding, bicycles. AE, MC, V.*

$ ✗⊞ **Hotel Fundadores.** On the main road near the center of town, this older hotel has a stream running right through the middle of it. Rooms are in back, on both sides of the tiny waterway, which is traversed by several footbridges and has tables and chairs around it. Most rooms have several soft beds, thin carpeting, fans, and tiled baths; furniture and decorations vary from room to room. Each room has one price no matter how many use it, and if several people share a room it can be quite a bargain. A large restaurant faces the street, and below it is a windowless bar complete with a sunken dance floor and disco lights. ✉ *Avda. Central,* ☎ *507/720–1298,* FAX *507/720–1034. 35 rooms with bath. Restaurant, bar, meeting room. AE, MC, V.*

$$ ⌂ **Hotel Rebequet.** This small hotel on a quiet corner two blocks east
★ of the main road is an excellent option for people who like to cook, since it has a kitchen and dining area for the use of guests. Rooms surround a small courtyard and are relatively large, with parquet floors, windows, wood ceilings, blue-tile baths, TVs, and small fridges. ✉ *C. 6 Sur,* ☎ *507/720–1365. 9 rooms with bath. No credit cards.*

$ ⌂ **Pensión Marilos.** The small, clean rooms in this family-run lodge
★ are the best deal in Boquete and perhaps the entire country. They all have tile floors and windows, and all but two have private baths. The pensión is on the corner of two quiet side streets, a few blocks south of the central park. ✉ *C. 6 Sur,* ☎ *507/720–1380. 7 rooms, 5 with bath. No credit cards.*

Outdoor Activities and Sports

BIRD-WATCHING

The forested hills that surround Boquete are the perching grounds for abundant and varied avian life, which includes such colorful critters as collared redstarts, emerald toucanets, and about a dozen species of hummingbirds and their relatives. The area is also one of the best places in the world to see the legendary quetzal. Cattle pastures and coffee farms actually facilitate birding, since birds are easier to see when they leave the forest and enter wide open areas. The Hotel Panamonte has tours to **Finca Lérida,** the family farm, where you're practically guaranteed to see a quetzal during the dry season. The trip to the top of **Barú Volcano** takes you to higher life zones that have bird species you won't see around Boquete.

HIKING

There are plenty of hiking routes near Boquete, some of which can also be explored on horseback or mountain bike. The two paved loops above town can be hiked, but be aware that the loop reached by veering left at the fork is considerably longer and steeper. The **Sendero los Quetzales,** the footpath to Cerro Punta, is reached by following the road to Alto Chiquero. The trail heads through the forest along Caldera River, crossing it several times, and then over a ridge to El Respingo, in the hills above Cerro Punta. The 6-kilometer (4-mile) hike is easier if you start in Cerro Punta, and a guided trip offered by Mauricio Tour (☎ 507/720–1153) includes transportation to El Respingo and pickup at Alto Chiquero. The hike to the summit of **Barú Volcano** is considerably more demanding, more than twice as long and much steeper. You'll want to leave a car, or arrange to be dropped off and picked up, at the entrance to the national park, which is 14 kilometers (9 miles) from the summit. Bring lots of water and warm, waterproof clothing for any hike, but especially for the trek up Barú.

Volcán

❸ *60 km (36 mi) northwest of David, 16 km (10 mi) south of Cerro Punta.*

A windy little town at a crossroads, Volcán's greatest asset is its view of Barú Volcano. The town is spread along the road on a plain to the south of Barú, in an area that lost its forests long ago. The highland towns of Boquete, Bambito, and Cerro Punta are all so close to the volcano that you can't see it in its entirety from any of them. From Volcán, however, you can often admire that massive peak and the mountains beyond it, weather permitting. Like Bambito and Cerro Punta, Volcán was largely settled by immigrants from Switzerland and Yugoslavia during the early part of this century. Volcán is a good place to stay if you intend to hike up the volcano's southern side—you'll want to get up before dawn if you're attempting that grueling ascent. There are some lakes to the south of Volcán that have been stocked with bass, but you'll need a car to reach them. The area also tends to be warmer than either nearby Bambito or Cerro Punta, which can get very chilly at night, so it's a good place to stay if you didn't pack warm clothes. If you don't hike up the volcano, you'll want to use Volcán as a base for day trips to the Cerro Punta area, which has much more to see and do.

Dining and Lodging

$$ ⨉▣ **Hotel Dos Ríos.** Some of the rooms in this two-story wooden build-
★ ing west of town face the volcano, and all of them open onto porches that overlook a small garden. It is definitely Volcán's nicest hotel: large rooms have wood floors, walls, and ceilings, with windows on the volcano side and small tile baths in back. Two larger suites on the far end of the building have sitting areas and lots of windows and are well worth the extra $6; the one upstairs has the best view of Barú. A large restaurant in front serves the basic selection of meat and seafood dishes, and the bar next door is a bit on the ugly side, but a large window lets you gaze at the volcano while you sip your martini. The hotel can arrange early morning transport to the foot of the volcano and a guide to the summit. ⊠ *2 km (1.2 mi) west of Volcán,* ☎ *507/771– 4271. 14 rooms with bath, 2 suites. Restaurant, bar. AE, MC, V.*

$ ⨉▣ **Motel California.** The California has a central location and some of Volcán's lowest rates. Rooms are in duplexes spread around the grounds, each with a covered parking spot. They have gray tile floors, soft beds, windows, and small baths. A large restaurant and bar will prepare whatever you want, as long as they know how to make it. The motel is down a dirt road on the left, after the turn to Cerro Punta. ⊠ *Apdo. 317, Volcán,* ☎ *507/771–4272. 25 rooms with bath. Restaurant, bar. No credit cards.*

Bambito

4 *6 km (4 mi) north of Volcán, 10 km (6 mi) south of Cerro Punta.*

Not really a town to speak of, Bambito consists of a series of farms, homes, and lodges scattered along the narrow valley on the western side of Barú Volcano that the Chiriquí Viejo River winds its way down. The scenery is quite impressive, with sheer rock walls, trees clinging to steep hillsides, and suspension bridges spanning the boulder-strewn river. The trade winds whip down through the valley for much of the dry season, which keeps it fairly cool, but it gets more sun than the Cerro Punta area. Small coffee and vegetable farms line much of the road, and several roadside stands sell local vegetables and fruit preserves. It's a lovely spot, and is an excellent base for exploration of the mountains around Cerro Punta, or rafting on the Chiriquí Viejo River, since it has one of the country's best hotels.

Dining and Lodging

$$$$ ⨉▣ **Hotel Bambito.** This full-service, luxury resort has a great loca-
★ tion at the entrance to the Bambito Valley, and all its rooms overlook

a massive rock wall draped with foliage that towers over the Chiriquí Viejo River. Rooms have hardwood floors, high ceilings, picture windows, large tile baths, and satellite TV. Junior suites feature balconies, and master suites have bedroom lofts—several of them also have tubs. There is a small exhibit of pre-Columbian art and a fireplace in the lobby, next to which is a spacious, plush restaurant and cocktail lounge that share a view of a multilevel fountain and the valley beyond. The large, heated pool is enclosed in a sort of greenhouse; there is also a simple gym and two lighted tennis courts. The hotel rents bicycles and mountain bikes and has nature guides who can take guests bird watching and hiking in the nearby national parks. ⊠ *Bambito,* ☎ *507/771–4265,* 𝖥𝖠𝖷 *507/771–4207. 37 rooms with bath, 10 suites. Restaurant, bar, pool, spa, tennis courts, horseback riding. AE, MC, V.*

Cerro Punta

❺ *78 km (48 mi) northwest of David, 16 km (10 mi) north of Volcán.*

This bowl-shaped valley embraced by the Talamanca Mountain Range is the remnant of what was once the crater of a gigantic volcano, and its dark, volcanic soil is consequently some of the most fertile in the country. That soil has been a mixed blessing: it is a boon for local farmers, but it has also led them to deforest most of the valley. Nevertheless, Cerro Punta has some splendid pastoral scenery, with a patchwork of vegetable farms, some clinging to steep slopes, and an extensive ranch that raises dairy cattle and thoroughbred horses. Several foliage-clad rocky formations tower over the rolling landscape, and the upper slopes of the mountains that ring the valley still retain most of their forest. Since the trade winds regularly push clouds over the continental divide and into the valley, Cerro Punta is regularly swathed in a gray mist, which keeps everything green year round, and makes for frequent rainbow sightings.

Cerro Punta is considerably higher than Boquete and can consequently get quite cold. It sometimes drops below 40°F at night, which means you'll want to bring warm clothes and a waterproof jacket. The cool climate no doubt played a part in the decision of many Swiss and Yugoslavian families to settle here earlier this century. That European influence is reflected in some of the valley's architecture and the complexions of many of its inhabitants. You may also see full-blooded **Guaymí Indians** in Cerro Punta, some of whom are the Europeans' temporary farm laborers; others have purchased their own land and stayed on.

The pastoral landscapes, distant mountains, colorful farmhouses, and abundant flowers of Cerro Punta are enough to impress any visitor, but those interested in birds, or those who like to hike in the mountains, have even more reason to head there. The paved road that enters the valley makes a small loop; several dirt roads branch from the paved road and head into narrow valleys. These dirt roads follow small streams past farms and patches of forest, which make them ideal routes for bird watching. There are also several footpaths into the mountains around town, such as those at **La Amistad National Park.** Two trails head into the forest near the park headquarters, which are reached by turning left after the Hotel Cerro Punta, and veering left at the next intersection. Another way to explore that park's forest is to visit the private reserve of **Los Quetzales,** which lies up a four-wheel-drive road from the neighborhood of Guadelupe. Visitors must be accompanied by one of the reserve's guides, who charge each person $3 per hour, but they can take you to waterfalls and may help you spot a quetzal.

Dining and Lodging

$ ✗ **Mama Lola.** Sandwiches, milk shakes, and homemade desserts are the specialties of this tiny restaurant down the hill from Cerro Punta's main intersection. The restaurant has lots of windows, and small Formica tables and benches attached to the walls. The limited menu includes basic burgers, pies grandes (grilled sandwiches), dulce de zanahoria or plátano (carrot or banana cake), fresh yogurt, and a variety of fruit shakes. ⊠ *C. Central,* ☎ *507/771–2053. No credit cards. Closes at 7* PM.

$$–$$$ ✗▥ **Los Quetzales.** This exemplary ecotourism project includes two ★ private reserves that cover more than 600 acres of cloud forest in the area where La Amistad and Barú Volcano National Parks meet. Two spacious wooden cabins stand on a ridge in the midst of the forest, where they afford a gorgeous view of the valley through the trees. A cement building at the edge of the forest holds six rooms that share two kitchens and baths. Trails wind through the forest past waterfalls and abundant birds. One birder spotted 45 species from the balcony of the big cabin during a four-day stay and noted that quetzals abound in the area. There's no electricity, but there are gas heaters for the showers and kerosine lanterns; guides, rubber boats, and rain gear are also provided. Smoking and loud music are prohibited. The cabins each have two stories, several beds, wood stoves, countless windows, balconies, and fully equipped kitchens, and are a good deal if you have four or more people, but are expensive for one couple. Rooms in the cement house, on the other hand, cost slightly more than the Hotel Cerro Punta, in town. You have to bring your own food and carry out your nonorganic garbage. Four-wheel drive is needed to enter the reserve, but the hotel can provide transportation from Guadelupe. At press time, the owners were also building a small hotel and restaurant in Guadelupe, where large rooms have hardwood floors and ceilings, windows, and small tiled baths. ⊠ *Altos de Guadelupe,* ☎ *507/771–2182,* FAX *507/771–2226. 2 cabins and 6 rooms with shared bath in reserve, 10 rooms with bath in town. Restaurant, hiking. MC, V.*

$–$$ ✗▥ **Hotel Cerro Punta.** This small lodge across from the old gas station features great views of the surrounding farms and distant peaks, simple rooms, and hearty food. Rooms are on the small side, with worn wooden floors, picture windows, and tiled baths. The restaurant also has a nice view and serves a basic menu—daily specials are the best bet. There's a tiny bar out front facing the street. The grounds are planted with flowers, which attract a steady stream of hummingbirds. ⊠ *C. Principal,* ☎ FAX *507/771–2020. 9 rooms with bath. Restaurant, bar. MC, V.*

$ ▥ **Pensión la Primavera.** The cheapest rooms in Cerro Punta can be had at this family-run pension. The two-story wooden house, painted several shades of brown, is down the hill from the main intersection. A small garden in front of the house is popular with the local hummingbirds. Guest rooms are small and musty, with peeling wallpaper, but most of them have private baths with hot water. The wide entranceway has several couches and an old TV in it. This places occasionally shuts down when the owner has to leave town. ⊠ *C. Central* *(turn left after Hotel Cerro Punta), P 507/775–3955. 3 rooms with bath, 2 share bath. No credit cards.*

Outdoor Activities and Sports

BIRD-WATCHING

Although the valley's floor and lower slopes have been almost completely deforested, Cerro Punta is surrounded by mountain forests, and that high-altitude wilderness is home to a large and diverse avian population. The region's varied feathered inhabitants can be spotted all around the bowl-shaped valley, especially near the streams and rivers that flow in and out of it, thanks to the trees that grow along their banks. Several roads head off the main loop around the valley's floor, and all of them lead to prime birding territory. The trails into the national parks offer access to the vast expanses of wilderness that border the valley, but the best birding area in Cerro Punta is probably the forest that surrounds the cabins in the private Los Quetzales nature reserve.

HIKING

There's a decent selection of trails that head into the mountains around Cerro Punta, ranging from short paths through the woods to the six-hour trek around the back of Barú Volcano to Boquete. There are several trails through the cloud forests of **La Amistad National Park,** both near the ranger station and within the private reserve of Los Quetzales. The most challenging, and rewarding, hike out of Cerro Punta is the six-kilometer (4-mile) trek over the northern slope of **Barú Volcano,** from El Respingo to Alto Chiquero, high in the hills above Boquete. The most challenging aspect of that expedition, however, may be getting back to Cerro Punta, which lies about four hours by bus from Boquete. The last buses from Boquete and David leave at 6 PM, which means it's safer to make that hike while based in David, since it gives you a couple more hours to get back to your hotel.

Chiriquí A to Z

Arriving and Departing

BY BUS

Several buses make the trip between San José and Chiriquí every day, but be warned that it is a nine-hour trip between the Costa Rican capital and David. **Tracopa** (☎ 506/221–4214) has two buses daily from San José to David, departing San José daily from Avda. 18 between C. 2 and 4 at 7:30 AM and noon; and departing David daily from Avda. 5 Este and C. A Sur (Tracopa in David, Panama: ☎ 507/775–0585) at 8:30 AM and 12:30 PM. **Tico Bus** (☎ 506/221–8954) has daily service between San José and Panama City, departing San José from next to the Iglesia de la Soledad at 10 PM and passing David around 9:30 AM the next day. Buses from Panama usually pick up extra passengers at the border, from where they depart at around 8 PM.

BY CAR

Since you can't cross an international border with a car rented in Costa Rica, the only way to drive to Panama is with a private car. The Inter-American Highway enters Panama about 15 kilometers (9 miles) before the turnoff to Volcán and Cerro Punta, and about 37 kilometers (23 miles) before David.

BY PLANE

More than half a dozen international airlines have daily flights between San José and Panama City, but the attractions of Chiriquí lie almost equidistant from both of those two capital cities. The Panamanian airline **Aeroperlas** (☎ 507/269–4555) has several flights daily between Panama City and David, and at least one flight daily between David and Changuinola, in Bocas del Toro. The quickest way to get to Chiriquí from San José is to take a **Sansa** (☎ 506/233–5330) flight to Coto 47, an airstrip in the banana fields a short drive from the border. If you fly to Coto 47, you'll want to call and arrange to have a border taxi (☎ 507/732–2355) meet you at the air strip. Another option is to fly either **Sansa** or **Travelair** (☎ 506/220–3054) to Golfito, where taxis and buses abound.

Getting Around

BY BUS

Buses travel regularly between David and the following destinations: **Paso Canoas** (Costa Rican border) every 20 minutes from 5 AM to 7 PM (a one-hour trip); Cerro **Punta, Bambito,** and **Volcán,** every 30 minutes from 5 AM to 6 PM (a two-hour trip); **Boquete,** every 30–60 minutes from 5 AM to 6 PM (a 90-minute trip).

BY CAR

Renting a car is an excellent way to explore Chiriquí, since there are several rent-a-car companies in David (☞ Contacts and Resources, *below*), and most roads are in good repair. The road to Boquete heads straight north out of David, no turns required. To reach Volcán, drive west on the Inter-American Highway to the town of Concepción—a collection of modern buildings 24 kilometers (15 miles) west of David—where you turn right. The road to Bambito and Cerro Punta, on the right in Volcán, is well marked.

Contacts and Resources

CAR RENTALS

Several international car rental companies have offices in David, among them **Hertz** (☎ 507/775–6828), **Budget** (☎ 507/775–1667), and **Dollar** (☎ 507/774–3385), all of which offer four-wheel-drive vehicles.

EMERGENCIES

Panama's health care standards are quite high for such a poor country, and David has a large hospital (☎ 507/775–4221). The following are important numbers: police (☎ 104), fire department (☎ 103), and ambulance (☎ 507/775–2161). **International calls** can be made at the INTEL office (✉ C. C Norte and Avda. Cincuentenaria).

GUIDED TOURS

Chiriquí Island Tours (☎ 507/774–3117; when they answer, dial 1212) in David runs a full-day boat tour that begins in the mangroves and continues to Gamez Island, in the Gulf of Chiriquí, where a hot lunch is served on a white sand beach. **Mauricio Tour** (☎ 507/720–1153) and **Río Monte Tours** (☎ 507/720–1327), in Boquete, offer a variety of day trips in that area, including bird watching, jeep trips up Barú Volcano, and visits to nearby hot springs. **Panama Expedition** (☎ 507/771–4265, ext. 119), across from the lobby of the Hotel Bambito, offers a variety of cultural and ecological one-day excursions. **Panama Rafting** (☎ 507/774–5743) and **Chiriquí River Rafting** (☎ 507/774–0204) run trips down the province's white-water rivers.

VISITOR INFORMATION

The regional tourist office, which is across from Parque Cervantes (✉ Avda. 3 de Noviembre and C. A Norte, ☎ 507/775–5120), is open weekdays 8:30–4:30.

THE BOCAS DEL TORO ARCHIPELAGO

By Justin
Henderson

Near the top of Panama is an isolated little cluster of islands, the archipelago of Bocas del Toro, part of the province of the same name. The province includes a large piece of the mainland as well, but this part of mainland Panama is nothing special—it's the Chiquita Republic, an area virtually blanketed with banana plantations. The real interest for travelers here lies offshore, on the islands where the capital city, also called Bocas del Toro, is located. The islands' original inhabitants were Guaymí Indians, and they're still around in isolated island villages and intermingled with Afro-Caribbeans and Hispanics in the larger towns. The language, too, is an interesting mix, called Guari-Guari, which combines English and Indian dialects. The islands were "discovered," or at least visited, by Christopher Columbus in 1502. After the first Europeans appeared, several of the islands in the chain evolved into supply and repair stations for the shipping industry, which explains the names of at least two of them: *Bastimentos* translates as "supplies," which is why the ships landed there. And *carenero* refers to "careening"—heeling a ship over on one side to effect repairs on the other side. The capital island, **Isla Colón** (after Cristóbal Colón, or Christopher Columbus), and the little city upon it, **Bocas del Toro**, founded in 1826, along with the other nearby islands in the chain, comprised a thriving community for many decades. At one point Bocas del Toro (the source of its own odd name, which translates as "mouths of the bull," is lost in legend) was the third largest city in Panama, and there was talk of making it the capital. It was the hub of the banana business in the early days of that industry, and elegant wooden houses belonging to the banana kings lined the town's waterfronts and main streets.

With the advent of the Panama Canal, everything in Bocas del Toro changed. Although the nearby mainland town of Almirante is today a shipping port for the banana plantations that cover much of the Panamanian mainland in this area, the islands of Bocas del Toro and their once-thriving capital town lost importance, and in time the banana kings left town. According to local lore, when they did so, their former slaves moved in and took over the town (resulting in a very confused situation regarding deeded property ownership, which may eventually play havoc with those looking to exploit the area for tourism). The town's slow fade into disrepair and obscurity was hastened by the disastrous earthquake of 1991, which wrecked many of the buildings in town and left many others teetering precariously. There are dozens of buildings in Bocas that would be condemned and torn down anywhere in the United States. In Bocas, there's no money to repair or rebuild, and so occasionally, as you ascend a staircase to a dilapidated second-story restaurant or hotel room, you have the feeling that you're entering an amusement park fun house.

Everything seems to be cockeyed, askew. Another strange element: a couple of hundred yards offshore of the town, directly offshore of the Hotel Las Brisas, there's a little island that sank a couple of feet in the 1991 earthquake. The entire island is underwater, but parts of it lie in water less than a foot deep. You can paddle a kayak or swim out there and walk around; there's even an underwater tennis court.

A look at a map of the archipelago shows what an odd piece of geography Isla Colón is. The town of Bocas del Toro sits on a little head of land, connected to the main body of the island by a narrow neck, or isthmus, that is at most a hundred yards wide. During certain fiestas Panamanians crowd into Bocas by the thousands (there's a car ferry service from Chiriquí Grande, down the coast) and along both sides of the isthmus road that connects Bocas with the rest of Isla Colón are dozens of seafood, beer, and soda shacks, all of which stand empty most of the time. Behind these shacks are beaches on both sides. A road follows the island's perimeter to the other side, where there's a little village called **Bocas del Drago** (no hotels there just yet, although rumor has it that an Italian consortium is making big plans for the area), and between the two Bocas, **Isla Colón** is mostly undeveloped jungle, bordered at several points by stretches of pristine beach, good for swimming, snorkeling, and surfing, too, at certain times of the year.

Many of the colonial era buildings in Bocas del Toro are lovely if dilapidated, with carved porch rails, fretwork, and trim, and the town is worth wandering through—check out the classic, beautifully kept circa 1926 fire engine in the fire department garage—before taking off by boat to reach the real draw of these islands: the diving in and around **Bastimentos Island National Marine Park.** There are dozens of great diving and snorkeling spots, especially around the two **Zapatilla Cays (major and minor)**, and the richness and variety of sea life—over two dozen type of coral, for starters—is amazing. Several islands lie within the park's boundaries as well, so it's possible to combine a little jungle hiking with your snorkeling—and possibly a peaceful encounter with indigenous peoples as well. There are leatherback turtle nesting beaches like those at Tortuguero in Costa Rica, and the animals roaming the islands include armadillos, pacas, several types of frogs, boa constrictors, two- and three-toed sloths, raccoons, coatis, and monkeys. Unlike Costa Rica, the islands of Bocas harbor no poisonous snakes. To visit the national park you'll need a permit, which can be obtained from the **Institute of Renewable Natural Resources (INRENARE)** office on First Street in Bocas del Toro.

Rumor has it there are good surfing waves at a couple of reefs in the area, and there's no doubt that several of the islands, including Isla Colón, have long, deserted, world-class beaches. Although less than a dozen Americans and Europeans lived there in mid-1996, either hiding out from the world or nudging into place the beginnings of a tourist industry framework, the place was a hotbed of developer fantasies on our last visit at that time. It seems that Europeans living in Costa Rica are required to spend 72 hours out of the country every 90 days, and many of the Europeans living or hanging out around Cahuita and Puerto Viejo began by going to Guabito, Changuinola, and Almirante to pass the required time. Eventually they went further, to Bocas, and the word started getting around: this is a very cool place, offbeat, out of the way, with great beaches, cheap rooms and food, excellent diving, and mellow local people. Now the word is very much out. We recommend a tour soon if you want to experience this place before it gets seriously "discovered."

You might want to visit the little village of **Bastimentos,** whose Guari-Guari speaking residents are very friendly. There are a couple of bodegas there, so you can stock up on stuff for a hike or a snorkeling day in the national park, of which the island is a part. A dollar will get you on the water taxi from Bocas to Bastimentos.

It would appear that the real downside of being undiscovered is the lack of infrastructure, illustrated most appallingly in Bocas del Toro by the trash service. Two or three guys atop an unmuffled, painfully loud wooden vehicle that appears to be a reject from the Australian futuristic action film "The Road Warrior" cruise around town, gathering the bags of garbage. They drive out of town and dump the bags off the side of the road, where they spill down, split open, and fall onto the beach and into the sea—not more than a mile from town. With some luck, the town leaders or the people who start making money off the expected tourist influx will see fit to divert some of their dollars into landfill construction. The sight of that garbage settling into the sea is enough to scare some visitors right off the island.

Pleasures and Pastimes

Dining and Lodging

There is excellent seafood to be had at the restaurants in Bocas del Toro. Remember that there is no service charge included in the bill at a Panamanian restaurant, so a 10%–15% gratuity is expected.

Being undiscovered means there isn't a whole lot of choice in restaurants or hotel rooms—around 50 or so rooms were available in mid-1996, and they ranged from low budget to moderately low budget. For the most part the hotels have been installed in former banana company houses, so they are nice buildings if somewhat ramshackle—and yet what charm! For example: the high end, best in the house, $20 rooms at the Las Brisas rest on stilts over the Caribbean Sea, which laps beneath your bed quite soothingly through the night (there's a deck right there, too, from which you can dive into the water); and the uninterrupted views across the sea aren't bad, either. These old hotels are special places, albeit a little shabby.

RATINGS

CATEGORY	COST*
$$$$	over $20
$$$	$10–$20
$$	$5–$10
$	under $5

Per person including a first course, entrée, and dessert; drinks, taxes, and gratuities not included.

RATINGS

CATEGORY	COST*
$$$$	Over $90
$$$	$50–$90
$$	$25–$50
$	under $25

For a double room, excluding service and 10% tax.

Great Itineraries

To reach Bastimentos Island National Marine Park in Panama takes roughly 6 hours from Puerto Viejo de Limón, Costa Rica, via a sequence of buses, taxis, and water taxis. At the end of that 6-hour haul you might want to spend at least a couple of days in the Bocas del Toro before heading back.

IF YOU HAVE 2 DAYS

Spend your first day wandering through the town of Bocas del Toro and visit the tourist office to obtain a permit for Bastimentos Island National Marine Park. On day two, wake up early and head for the national park—en route explore the village of Bastimentos.

When to Tour the Bocas del Toro

Bocas del Toro experiences mini dry seasons in September–October and March–April, but since most of that region's rain falls at night, it's a pleasant place to visit any time of year.

Dining and Lodging

$–$$ ✕ Las Delicias. Downstairs from the Pensión of the same name—also on 3rd—Las Delicias serves good, reasonably priced fare, and there is a man barbecuing beef and chicken on an open-air grill on the sidewalk in front of the restaurant a couple of nights a week. You'll have to ask to find out when he'll be at it next. ⊠ *C. 3 (close to pier)*, ☎ *507/757–9318. No credit cards.*

$–$$ ✕ Pomodoro. Also on 3rd, Pomodoro is an Italian restaurant on the second story above the Mangrove Roots Shop. The food is good if not memorable, and the dishes with seafood, like lobster linguine, are generously laden with fresh-caught fish. *No phone. No credit cards.*

$–$$ ✕ Red Lobster. This place mixes seafood and Chinese food, and is associated with the Las Brisas Hotel across the street. Again, good cheap fare. A low-cost meal like fried rice with meat or chicken can go a long way. *No phone. No credit cards.*

$–$$ ✕ Todo Tropical. All of two blocks off the beaten track over on 1st Street, Todo Tropical is run by an older American man who seems to have been there long enough to know most everyone in town. In addition to renting snorkeling gear, he can get hold of fresh lobsters and cook them up on demand; plus he's got a pretty good technique behind the bar. *No phone. No credit cards.*

$ ✕ Boca Banana. This place is actually little more than a bar, but it is the main hangout for expatriate locals and for vagabonds as well—or at least it was in early 1996—and you're sure to meet some fellow travelers there who might be able to tell you what they've discovered during their trip through the area. It's where the road divides, a minute's walk down North Avenue from the Las Brisas, on the ground floor of a house. *No phone.*

$ ✕ Restaurant Don Chicho. In the middle of town on 3rd Street—almost everything's on 3rd Street—Don Chicho's is probably the cheapest place to get *típico* (typical) dishes. It's a cafeteria-style place, and a favorite with low budgeteers. ☎ *507/757–9288. No credit cards.*

$ ✕⊡ Hotel Bahía. Another grand old building that has fallen on hard times, although the arrival of a new Italian restaurant in the front courtyard, and a paint job for the whole exterior, have spruced the place up somewhat. It's right across the street as you come off the ferry dock, and some say its rooms are the nicest in town. ☎ *507/757–9629. 19 rooms with bath. No credit cards.*

$ ✕⊡ Hotel Las Brisas. Built on stilts over the water on North Avenue
★ at the end of 3rd Street—you can see it as you come off the ferry at

the other end of the street, some 10 blocks away—Las Brisas is a ramshackle, somewhat shabby old hotel, housed in a 50-year-old building. It offers basic rooms with or without private baths and/or hot water. The location is wonderful, however. At the back of the main floor is a deck with hammocks and lounge chairs and a small bar that a couple of Americans opened at the end of 1995. You can dive off the deck and swim to the sunken island, or kayak to Carenero, or have your boatman pick you up for the ride to the national marine park or other snorkeling and diving spots. The hotel rents kayaks and bicycles by the hour and the day and can arrange tours. The Red Lobster restaurant is across the street, in the building that houses the hotel's less expensive "pensión" rooms with shared baths. ☎ *507/757–9248,* ☒ *507/757–9247. 15 rooms with bath. No credit cards.*

$ ✕☷ **Pensión Delicias.** Above the restaurant of the same name, the Delicias has basic rooms ranging in price from $5.50 to $24. More money buys privacy and hot water. ☒ *C. 3,* ☎ *507/757–9318. 8 rooms with bath.*

$–$$$ ☷ **La Coralina.** This rather elegant, hacienda-like guest house is the only place, other than the Mangrove Inn, that is not in town. Instead, you'll find it on a rise on the road that leads to the other side of the island. One local wag inferred it was built with the intention of using it as a brothel, but whatever its original purpose, it's a new Panamanian building meant to have the look of an old Spanish hacienda, it would appear, and it does have a certain charm due to the beautiful woodwork inside. You can also camp on the grounds for $5. ☎ ☒ *507/757–9158.*

$ ☷ **Pensión Peck.** Although the legendary Mrs. Peck passed away in 1995, her children have kept the Pensión open, and for all its dilapidation and the sign relating to malaria on the facade of the building, it still has fantastic views from its waterfront windows and decks. ☒ *Next to public market on Avda. Norte,* ☎ *507/757–9252. 10 rooms, some with private baths. No credit cards.*

Outdoor Activities and Sports

Snorkeling and Scuba Diving

This is the main event around Bocas, so it's hard to believe that there are only two shops, and neither of them that well-equipped, according to divers visiting the area. Aside from these two, there are plenty of people willing to rent you snorkeling gear. **Bocas Dive Shop** (☎ 507/757–9541) is on 3rd Street—talk to Gustavo. He rents tanks and takes people out for guided dives for $70 per day or $18 per hour. Charter trips to the national marine park cost $45, to Bird Island or Swan Cay $35, to Hospital Point $25. The **Mangrove Roots Shop/Turtle Divers,** associated with the Mangrove Eco-Dive Resort (☎ 507/757–5954), is also on 3rd Street. They offer much the same stuff as Bocas. The shop has some interesting locally produced crafts as well.

To reach the snorkeling spots you can also negotiate a ride with any one of the dozens of freelance boatmen in and around town. Ask around, negotiate a price, and go. You do not have to go all the way to the park on and around Bastimentos Island and the Zapatilla Cays, however. Hospital Point is quite close, and there are dive spots off Carenero, the nearest island. You also have the option of biking out to one of the many dive spots off the beaches on the other side of Isla Colón. There may be dozens of reefs out there that no one has even discovered yet. The potential is fantastic, not only for diving but for surfing and windsurfing as well, although as of early 1996 there were no surf-board or sailboard rentals anywhere in Bocas. If you have any time and the sun is out, however, we do recommend a trip to the Zapatilla Cays, which takes from 45 minutes to an hour and a half to reach by boat (depending on the wind, which can force the boatman to use the slower inside passage to get there). This is the prime snorkeling spot in the area, and you will be delighted and amazed at the teeming sea life in and around the coral. For further information on the park, stop by the ANCON office (☎ 507/757–9367), which is next door to the Las Brisas Hotel. They can direct you to the best places to see wildlife as well as dive.

Bocas del Toro A to Z

Arriving and Departing

BY BOAT

Water taxi from Almirante is the most common means of transport to Bocas del Toro. Water taxis leave Almirante for Bocas on the following schedule: Monday at 6, 6:30, and 7:30 AM and 3 and 4:30 PM; Tuesday and Thursday at 7:30 AM, noon, and 3 PM; Wednesday at 8 AM and 3 PM; Friday at 6:30 AM and 5 PM; Saturday at 6:30 AM and 4:30 PM. The taxis leave Bocas for Almirante Sunday at 7 AM, and 2 and 4 PM; Monday at 5, 6, and 7 AM, and 2 and 4 PM; Tuesday and Thursday at 7 and 8 AM and 2 PM; Wednesday at 7:30 AM and 2 PM; Friday at 5:30 AM and 4 PM; Saturday at 5:30 AM and 4 PM. That duly noted, it appears that there is a lot of leeway in this schedule. Expect a certain level of unpredictability and improvisation. And if you're staying at the Las Brisas, you can have the front desk call the water taxi to come pick you up on the hotel deck. The free **"workingman's ferry"** leaves Bocas every day early in the morning and returns in the evening (hours are variable). You'll find it down on the Almirante docks. There is a **car ferry** that comes up the coast from Chiriquí Grande twice a week. It leaves Bocas for Chiriquí Grande every Friday and Sunday at 9 AM, and travels between Almirante and Chiriquí Grande at 5 PM on the same days. There's a **direct ferry** from Almirante to Chiriquí Grande every day at 8 AM and 2 PM except Monday when it only runs at 2 PM, and Tuesday when it only runs at 8 AM.

BY BUS

If you're traveling to the Bocas through the Costa Rican Atlantic Lowlands here's our suggested itinerary: from Puerto Viejo there's a bus that runs to the border at Sixaola with a 15-minute break at BriBri where you can grab a cup of coffee. If you get bored, try to translate the BriBri writing on the wall of the coffee shop. From BriBri to Sixaola is an hour by bus. At Sixaola you hike across the railroad bridge (converted, with planks, into a narrow road) from Costa Rica into the Panamanian town of Guabito. Immigration paperwork takes a little time, depending on the number of people in line, at each end of the bridge. From Guabito a $1 ride in a cab—Panama's currency is the American dollar—will get you to the rather hectic market town of Changuinola and the bus to Almirante and the bay of the same name. (There is also a direct bus from San José to Changuinola that leaves daily at 10 AM from Calle 14, Avenidas 5/7—it's an eight-hour trip.) Almirante is a slightly seedy port town, dominated by the banana biz, but some of the do-it-yourself housing on stilts over the water is pretty amazing to see. There's not much going on here, and the only reason to stay, really, is if you miss the last boat to Bocas or the last bus to the border.

There's no need to go out of your way to view the stilt housing, either—it's all very evident from the water taxi that will take you from Almirante to Bocas del Toro. The water taxis are about $3 each way, but there's a free "workingman's ferry" every night from Almirante to Bocas, and every morning from Bocas to Almirante. If you're traveling in a group you can taxi all the way from Guabito to Almirante for $20. Just remember, if you don't have a visa—they are not required, but you can get one at the Panamanian embassy in San José—you need to spend $10 for an exit stamp in order to get out of Panama. You can also take an express bus from San José to Changuinola, then taxi or bus from there to the water taxi docks in Almirante. That bus trip takes about eight hours, but it is a big, comfortable bus, and it stops for lunch en route.

BY PLANE

At press time (mid-1996) the airport had recently reopened on Bocas, and planes were flying in from Changuinola, David, and Panama City. Call **Aeroperlas** (☎ 507/757–9341) for flight information.

Getting Around
BY BIKE

There are several bicycle rental shops in town—**Hotel Las Brisas** (☞ Dining and Lodging, *above*) and **Farmacia Chen** both have bikes for rent—and it's a good way to see the town. You can also ride a rented bike to the beach. It's about an hour's ride to Paunch, one of the several beautiful, deserted beaches that lie between the Bocas.

BY BOAT

This is the main mode of transportation in the area. Water taxis bring you out to Bocas from Almirante and can also deliver you to Bastimentos Island. Individually chartered, motorized dugouts are the usual means of interisland travel, although there are a few people running larger, American-style motor boats in the area, and there's at least one catamaran for charter in town. Ask around the docks and town to find the kind of boat you're interested in chartering.

BY CAR

You won't see much in the way of auto traffic here, although there is a daily 8 AM van-sized taxi that will take you to Bocas del Drago at the other end of the island. You can also hire cabs to drive you out to the beaches, such as Paunch, that lie between the two Bocas.

Contacts and Resources
BANKS

A branch of the **National Bank of Panama** is across the street from the government office buildings by Simón Bolívar Park. The currency is the American dollar, also called the balboa, with some variations from American money in the silver currency. Remember, you need to buy an exit stamp at the bank and go to Immigration, in the Government House off the Simón Bolívar Square, to have it stamped into your passport before you can leave the country.

EMERGENCIES

The **fire department** (☎ 0+103) is on the corner of 1st Street and North Avenue; the **hospital** (☎ 507/757–8201); information (☎ 507/757–9257); **international operator** (☎ 0+106); the **police** (☎ 0+104) station is next to the ferry arrival dock on 3rd Street.

To visit Bastimentos Island National Marine Park you need a permit, which can be obtained from the **INRENARE office** (☎ 507/757–9244) on First Street. The **Immigration Office** is in Government House. This and other government offices are in a row of buildings on one side of the town square, called Simón Bolívar Park. The **Panamanian Tourist Board (PAT)** has an office a few doors down 3rd Street from the ferry dock. There is a **public telephone** in Simón Bolívar Park; there are also public phones in the Bahía Hotel and by the Fire Department on 1st Street.

INDEX

NOTES

Your
Window
To The
World
While You're
On The
Road

Keep in touch when you're traveling. Before you take off, tune in to CNN Airport Network. Now available in major airports across America, CNN Airport Network provides nonstop news, sports, business, weather and lifestyle programming. Both domestic and international. All piloted by the top-flight global resources of CNN. All up-to-the minute reporting. And just for travelers, CNN Airport Network features two daily Fodor's specials. "Travel Fact" provides enlightening, useful travel trivia, while "What's Happening" covers upcoming events in major cities worldwide. So why be bored waiting to board? TIME FLIES WHEN YOU'RE WATCHING THE WORLD THROUGH THE WINDOW OF CNN AIRPORT NETWORK!

Fodor's Travel Publications

Available at bookstores everywhere, or call 1–800–533–6478, 24 hours a day.

Gold Guides

U.S.

Alaska	Florida	New Orleans	Santa Fe, Taos, Albuquerque
Arizona	Hawai'i	New York City	
Boston	Las Vegas, Reno, Tahoe	Pacific North Coast	Seattle & Vancouver
California		Philadelphia & the Pennsylvania Dutch Country	The South
Cape Cod, Martha's Vineyard, Nantucket	Los Angeles		U.S. & British Virgin Islands
	Maine, Vermont, New Hampshire	The Rockies	
The Carolinas & the Georgia Coast	Maui & Lāna'i	San Diego	USA
Chicago	Miami & the Keys	San Francisco	Virginia & Maryland
Colorado	New England		Washington, D.C.

Foreign

Australia	Europe	Montréal & Québec City	Scotland
Austria	Florence, Tuscany & Umbria		Singapore
The Bahamas		Moscow, St. Petersburg, Kiev	South Africa
Belize & Guatemala	France		South America
Bermuda	Germany	The Netherlands, Belgium & Luxembourg	Southeast Asia
Canada	Great Britain		Spain
Cancún, Cozumel, Yucatán Peninsula	Greece	New Zealand	Sweden
	Hong Kong	Norway	Switzerland
Caribbean	India	Nova Scotia, New Brunswick, Prince Edward Island	Thailand
China	Ireland		Tokyo
Costa Rica	Israel	Paris	Toronto
Cuba	Italy	Portugal	Turkey
The Czech Republic & Slovakia	Japan	Provence & the Riviera	Vienna & the Danube
Eastern & Central Europe	London	Scandinavia	
	Madrid & Barcelona		
	Mexico		

Fodor's Special-Interest Guides

Caribbean Ports of Call	Halliday's New Orleans Food Explorer	Sunday in New York	Where Should We Take the Kids? Northeast
The Complete Guide to America's National Parks	Healthy Escapes	Sunday in San Francisco	
		Walt Disney World, Universal Studios and Orlando	Worldwide Cruises and Ports of Call
Family Adventures	Kodak Guide to Shooting Great Travel Pictures		
Gay Guide to the USA		Walt Disney World for Adults	
	Net Travel		
Halliday's New England Food Explorer	Nights to Imagine	Where Should We Take the Kids? California	
	Rock & Roll Traveler USA		

Fodor's
Special Series

Affordables

Caribbean

Europe

Florida

France

Germany

Great Britain

Italy

London

Paris

Fodor's Bed & Breakfasts and Country Inns

America

California

The Mid-Atlantic

New England

The Pacific Northwest

The South

The Southwest

The Upper Great Lakes

The Berkeley Guides

California

Central America

Eastern Europe

Europe

France

Germany & Austria

Great Britain & Ireland

Italy

London

Mexico

New York City

Pacific Northwest & Alaska

Paris

San Francisco

Compass American Guides

Arizona

Canada

Chicago

Colorado

Hawaii

Idaho

Hollywood

Las Vegas

Maine

Manhattan

Montana

New Mexico

New Orleans

Oregon

San Francisco

Santa Fe

South Carolina

South Dakota

Southwest

Texas

Utah

Virginia

Washington

Wine Country

Wisconsin

Wyoming

Fodor's Citypacks

Atlanta

Hong Kong

London

New York City

Paris

Rome

San Francisco

Washington, D.C.

Fodor's Español

California

Caribe Occidental

Caribe Oriental

Gran Bretaña

Londres

Mexico

Nueva York

Paris

Fodor's Exploring Guides

Australia

Boston & New England

Britain

California

Caribbean

China

Egypt

Florence & Tuscany

Florida

France

Germany

Ireland

Israel

Italy

Japan

London

Mexico

Moscow & St. Petersburg

New York City

Paris

Prague

Provence

Rome

San Francisco

Scotland

Singapore & Malaysia

Spain

Thailand

Turkey

Venice

Fodor's Flashmaps

Boston

New York

San Francisco

Washington, D.C.

Fodor's Pocket Guides

Acapulco

Atlanta

Barbados

Jamaica

London

New York City

Paris

Prague

Puerto Rico

Rome

San Francisco

Washington, D.C.

Mobil Travel Guides

America's Best Hotels & Restaurants

California & the West

Frequent Traveler's Guide to Major Cities

Great Lakes

Mid-Atlantic

Northeast

Northwest & Great Plains

Southeast

Southwest & South Central

Rivages Guides

Bed and Breakfasts of Character and Charm in France

Hotels and Country Inns of Character and Charm in France

Hotels and Country Inns of Character and Charm in Italy

Hotels and Country Inns of Character and Charm in Paris

Hotels and Country Inns of Character and Charm in Portugal

Hotels and Country Inns of Character and Charm in Spain

Short Escapes

Britain

France

New England

Near New York City

Fodor's Sports

Golf Digest's Best Places to Play

Skiing USA

USA Today The Complete Four Sport Stadium Guide

Fodor's Vacation Planners

Great American Learning Vacations

Great American Sports & Adventure Vacations

Great American Vacations

Great American Vacations for Travelers with Disabilities

National Parks and Seashores of the East

National Parks of the West

WHEREVER YOU TRAVEL, *H*ELP IS NEVER FAR AWAY.

From planning your trip to providing travel assistance along the way, American Express® Travel Service Offices are always there to help.

Costa Rica

Agencia Super Viajes (R)
Oficentro Ejecutivo La Sabana
Edificio #1, Sabana Sur
Costa Rica
506/220-0400

Banco de San Jose (R)
Between 3rd and 5th Avenues
Central Street
Costa Rica
506/223-3644

Banco Del Cafe, S.A. (R)
Avenida Reforma 9-30, Zona 9
1er Nivel-Torre Del Pais
Guatemala City
502-2/613-680

Clark Tours (R)
Torre 11, 1er Nivel-107
Diagonal 6, 10-65, Zona 10
Guatemala City
502-2/392-877

Belize Global Travel Services Ltd. (R)
41 Albert Street
Belize City
501-2/77185

Travel

http://www.americanexpress.com/travel